SAGE was founded in 1965 by Sara Miller McCune to support the dissemination of usable knowledge by publishing innovative and high-quality research and teaching content. Today, we publish more than 750 journals, including those of more than 300 learned societies, more than 800 new books per year, and a growing range of library products including archives, data, case studies, reports, conference highlights, and video. SAGE remains majority-owned by our founder, and on her passing will become owned by a charitable trust that secures our continued independence.

Los Angeles | London | Washington DC | New Delhi | Singapore

Armed Conflict, Peace Audit and Early Warning 2014

Thank you for choosing a SAGE product! If you have any comment, observation or feedback, I would like to personally hear from you. Please write to me at contactceo@sagepub.in

—Vivek Mehra, Managing Director and CEO,
SAGE Publications India Pvt Ltd, New Delhi

Bulk Sales

SAGE India offers special discounts for purchase of books in bulk. We also make available special imprints and excerpts from our books on demand.

For orders and enquiries, write to us at

Marketing Department
SAGE Publications India Pvt Ltd
B1/I-1, Mohan Cooperative Industrial Area
Mathura Road, Post Bag 7
New Delhi 110044, India
E-mail us at marketing@sagepub.in

Get to know more about SAGE, be invited to SAGE events, get on our mailing list. Write today to marketing@sagepub.in

This book is also available as an e-book.

Armed Conflict, Peace Audit and Early Warning 2014

Stability and Instability in South Asia

Edited by
D. Suba Chandran
P.R. Chari

www.sagepublications.com
Los Angeles • London • New Delhi • Singapore • Washington DC

Copyright © D. Suba Chandran and P.R. Chari, 2015

All rights reserved. No part of this book may be reproduced or utilized in any form or by any means, electronic or mechanical, including photocopying, recording or by any information storage or retrieval system, without permission in writing from the publisher.

First published in 2015 by

SAGE Publications India Pvt Ltd
B1/I-1 Mohan Cooperative Industrial Area
Mathura Road, New Delhi 110 044, India
www.sagepub.in

SAGE Publications Inc
2455 Teller Road
Thousand Oaks, California 91320, USA

SAGE Publications Ltd
1 Oliver's Yard, 55 City Road
London EC1Y 1SP, United Kingdom

SAGE Publications Asia-Pacific Pte Ltd
3 Church Street
#10-04 Samsung Hub
Singapore 049483

Published by Vivek Mehra for SAGE Publications India Pvt Ltd, typeset in 10/12 pts Book Antiqua by Diligent Typesetter, Delhi and printed at Chaman Enterprises, New Delhi.

Library of Congress Cataloging-in-Publication Data Available

ISBN: 978-93-515-0076-6 (HB)

The SAGE Team: N. Unni Nair, Isha Sachdeva, Nand Kumar Jha and Dally Verghese

Contents

List of Tables ix
List of Figures xi
Preface xiii

PART I
Armed Conflict

CHAPTER 1
Overview 3
P.R. Chari

CHAPTER 2
Security Transition and Peace Process in Afghanistan:
Trends in 2013 26
Mariam Safi

CHAPTER 3
Armed Conflicts in Pakistan 2013: Continuing Violence
despite Changes in Leadership 53
D. Suba Chandran and Ayesha Khanyari

CHAPTER 4
Myanmar: Tentative Consolidation of Peace 73
Bibhu Prasad Routray

CHAPTER 5
Northeast India: Bordering on Renewed Conflict or
Building on the Peace? 102
Mirza Zulfiqur Rahman

CHAPTER 6
Left-wing Extremism in 2013: A Mixed Bag 126
N. Manoharan

PART II
Peace Audit

CHAPTER 7
Peace Process in Jammu and Kashmir 2013: Hope to
Simmering Discontent? 155
Ashok Bhan

CHAPTER 8
Peace Process in Manipur: A Perspective 188
Chitra Ahanthem

CHAPTER 9
Auditing Peace and Conflict in India's Northeast:
Do We Need a 'Peace Policy'? 201
Nani Gopal Mahanta

CHAPTER 10
Elections 2013 and Peace Process in Nepal 228
Nishchal Nath Pandey

CHAPTER 11
Maoist Insurgency and Peace Process in Nepal:
Integration (of the Maoist Combatants) and the Divide
within the Maoist Party 247
Uddhab Prasad Pyakurel

CHAPTER 12
Sri Lanka: Positive Peace at a Distance 271
N. Manoharan

CHAPTER 13
State, Society and Talks with Taliban: Everywhere
and Nowhere   290
D. Suba Chandran

PART III
Early Warning

CHAPTER 14
Communal Divide in Jammu and Kashmir   309
Kavita Suri

CHAPTER 15
Maoists in Northeast India: The Spread of a Rebellion   328
Wasbir Hussain

CHAPTER 16
Convergence and Divergence of Madhes Politics in
Nepal and Its Implication   352
Sohan Prasad Sha

CHAPTER 17
The Political Direction of the Maoist Party in Nepal:
Possibilities, Recommendations and Incentives   374
Sisir Devkota

CHAPTER 18
Sinhala Buddhist Radicalization in Post-war Sri Lanka:
2013 and Ahead   395
Thiranjala Weerasinghe

About the Editors and Contributors   415
Index   419

List of Tables

7.1	Terrorist Violence in Jammu and Kashmir (1996–2013)	158
7.2	*Hartal* Calls by Separatists, Ceasefire Violations by Pakistan, Infiltration and Terrorists Killed (2006–2013)	159
7.3	Votes Polled in the Elections to the Jammu and Kashmir Assembly	179
7.4	Low Voter Turnout Constituencies during Assembly Polls in J&K	180
10.1	The Result of Constituent Assembly 2013 of Nepal	232
10.2	Summary of Tourism Scenario, 2011–2012	243
16.1	Representation of Different Groups in Constituent Assembly of Nepal	366
16.2	The Possible Trajectory of Self-determination Movements in Nepal	372

List of Figures

2.1	Civilians Deaths and Injuries from January to June: 2009–2013	35
2.2	Civilian Deaths by Parties to the Conflict from January to December: 2009–2013	36
3.1	Violence Profile—Pakistan 2013: Fatalities (region-wise)	57
3.2	Suicide Attacks in Pakistan (2002–2013)	58
3.3	Drone Attacks in Pakistan: 2005–2013	61
3.4	Sectarian Violence in Pakistan	63

Preface

Armed Conflict, Peace Audit and Early Warning is the latest and the eighth annual review of armed conflicts in South Asia (ACSA) conducted by the Institute of Peace and Conflict Studies (IPCS), New Delhi. Each of the earlier volumes had a unique focus highlighting the issues relevant to the national security that arose during the past year which found reflection in their subtitle.

Unlike its predecessors, the present volume—published by SAGE Publications—surveys armed conflicts along with two additional aspects concerning security issues, namely peace audit and early warning. While a comprehensive survey of the armed conflicts is essential, as a part of expanding the focus on the subject, it was decided to include the above two issues: peace audit and early warning. Thus, the new edition not only provides a detailed survey of the trends in conflict, but also analyses the multiple peace processes which were in varying stages in South Asia in the recent past. In certain theatres of conflict, armed violence has come to an end, but the peace is yet to prevail; in others, the dominant armed group has been either neutralized or joined the mainstream; yet the society is witnessing the fruits of this transformation. The study on early warning is an innovative and bold attempt to forecast the process of transformation in the conflict and peace process as well. It is based on the premise that both conflicts and peace processes emit signals.

All 18 chapters are grouped under the above three broad sections dealing with three interrelated aspects of peace and conflict: armed conflicts, peace audit and early warning. While the first two sections make a diagnosis of the current state of peace and conflict in South Asia, the third one seeks to project the future based on the assessment of the current developments.

Thematically structured, this volume provides sound theoretical underpinnings to armed conflicts by undertaking peace audits—using the conflict-related data supplemented by field surveys—assessing whether the state of affairs in any armed conflict situation has improved, deteriorated or remained unchanged. Its spans the entire range of armed conflict, including both inter-state and intra-state conflicts. Being a unique venture, it comprehensively covers almost all of South Asia including Afghanistan, Pakistan, India (Jammu and Kashmir, and the Northeast), Nepal, Sri Lanka and Myanmar.

The SAARC regional office of the Konrad Adenauer Stiftung (KAS) has been supportive of this process. The encouragement and participation of Dr Beatrice Gorawantschy and Mr Tomislav Delinic in particular from the KAS have ensured that this process would be continued since it was launched in 2006. The editors are grateful to all the efforts made by the respective contributors; without their unstinting cooperation, it would not have been possible to meet the schedules for publication. Finally, a special thanks to the SAGE team, in particular Mr N. Unni Nair; they have enthusiastically agreed to publish this annual review and also to enlarge the scope of the project. The timely publication of this project would not have been possible without their active involvement.

D. Suba Chandran
P.R. Chari

PART I
Armed Conflict

1

Overview

P.R. Chari

Prelude

The instant volume is the eighth in a series of annual reviews of the armed conflicts in South Asia that has been undertaken by the Institute of Peace and Conflict Studies (IPCS). Each of the earlier volumes had a unique focus highlighting the issues relevant to national security that arose during the past year which found reflection in their subtitle. Thus, the last and seventh volume (2013) underlined *Transitions*. The sixth volume (2012) was subtitled *Uneasy Stasis and Fragile Peace*; it concerned itself with the causes underlying armed conflicts in the region and the peace processes that were being pursued. The fifth volume (2010) examined the transformative changes occurring in the region relevant to armed conflicts therein, while the fourth highlighted the expanding Left-wing extremism and religious violence in South Asia. Earlier volumes had emphasized the growing violence, continuing violence and the failing peace processes in South Asia. It is proposed to emphasize the role of *Internal and Electoral Politics*, with particular attention being accorded to *Peace Audit* and *Early Warning* in this 2014 edition of the ACSA Annual.

This chapter is organized in two parts. The first part concerns the discussion about the several terms used to delineate the contours and scope of armed conflicts, and to recognize their limitations. The second part seeks to highlight some conceptual issues underlying armed conflicts in South Asia and recognizing some of those that excoriated the region during 2013 and likely to extend themselves into 2014.

The Definitional Issues

The term *armed conflicts* might initially be considered, which has been discussed in earlier volumes of this series. They are generally recognized in terms of the total number of deaths that resulted from any organized violence. The statistics in this regard have been collated by the Uppsala Conflict Data Program (UCDP), which have gained wide global acceptance, and is generally relied upon in such analyses. Organized violence around the world has been clustered by the UCDP[1] into 'three categories of violent action: state-based conflict, non-state-based conflict and one-sided violence'. And the threshold for recognizing incidents of organized violence has been pegged at those leading to the deaths of 25 persons or more in a particular year. The UCDP had in earlier years recognized a category of organized violence to constitute *major armed conflicts*, defined as those responsible for occasioning over 1,000 deaths over the entire period of the conflict. This definition, first applied in 1988–1989, was made more restrictive thereafter by redefining *major armed conflicts* to include only those clashes that had resulted in 'at least 1,000 battle-related deaths in a calendar year'.[2]

Proceeding further, the phrase *Internal and Electoral Politics* gained special traction in 2013. General elections were held in Nepal, Bhutan, Pakistan and the Maldives. Sri Lanka also held its provincial elections that included the recently pacified Northern Province. The underlying domestic compulsions that influenced these elections and the violence that accompanied some of them will, no doubt, be noticed in the individual country chapters in this

---

[1] This definition has been evolved by the Uppsala Conflict Data Program (UCDP). Cf. *SIPRI Yearbook 2013: Armament, Disarmament and International Security* (Oxford: Oxford University Press, 2013), p. 2.

[2] *SIPRI Yearbook 2007: Armament, Disarmament and International Security* (Oxford: Oxford University Press, 2005), p. 91, F.N. 2.

volume. Bangladesh held its highly controversial elections in the first week of 2014, but the violence and disorder that preceded them will have serious long-term implications. Afghanistan and India are scheduled to hold their general elections in the first half of 2014. South Asia would thus have witnessed elections being held in all the countries in the region over 2013–2014, which is calculated to strengthen democratic impulses in the region and worldwide.[3]

Going into greater specifics, the elections in Nepal held in November 2013 yielded a wholly unexpected result with the United Communist Party of Nepal (Prachanda group) and the Madhesi parties suffering a defeat followed by their not unexpected accusations of the polls having been rigged by the victorious Nepali Congress Party. These elections were marked by violence with the Communist Party of Nepal-Maoists (Baidya group) claiming to have set off bombs across the country, including a bomb exploded near a voting station on the day of the elections. By year end, Nepal's political parties had yet to find a modus vivendi to establish a government and proceed ahead with framing a Constitution for the country.

In regard to Bangladesh, the violence preceding and during its general elections held on 5 January 2014 had attracted worldwide attention. The issues between Sheikh Hasina (Awami National Party) and Khaleda Zia (Bangladesh National Party) are both personal and political. Briefly, Khaleda Zia's coalition (now in Opposition) had demanded that Sheikh Hasina should step down and establish a caretaker government to oversee the elections and ensure their impartiality. This was not accepted by Sheikh Hasina who had, in fact, arrested the previous caretaker government in 2007; it had been established earlier by Khaleda Zia, then in the office, and packed with her allies, notably the communal Jamaat-e-Islami party. By year end, over 100 lives had been lost in senseless violence.[4] The long-term implications of this impasse will be discussed later in this chapter. The issues listed in the subtitle can now be debated and have been discussed below.

[3] Frederic Grare, Milan Vaishnav, 'The Year of the Voter in South Asia', *Carnegie Endowment for International Peace*, 16 December 2013, available online at http://carnegieendowment.org/2013/12/16/year-of-voter-in-south-asia (accessed 2 January 2014).

[4] Julfikar Ali Manik and Gardiner Harris, 'Political Clashes Grow in Bangladesh's Capital', *New York Times*, 29 December 2013.

Peace Audit

It might initially be underlined that *peace audit* has not been defined in the strategic literature. A Google search reveals the recognition secured by IPCS for its work in this field. Peace audit in the context of armed conflicts would be designed to explore questions such as the following. Why peace does not prevail despite the end of conflict? Why do beliefs persist that the conflict continues beneath the surface despite a civil war overtly concluding? How can it be ensured that new fault lines do not develop in the post-conflict situation? How can positive peace which implies proceeding beyond the negative concept of an absence of conflict be sustained?[5]

Furthermore, the thesaurus informs us that *audit* means *check*, inspect or *overlook*, and that this term connotes *examination*. In the South Asian context, the term 'audit' has a strong nexus of financial administration, more especially of examining and checking accounts. Increasingly, however, greater stress is being placed now on *higher audit* which is concerned with appraising administrative processes and suggesting reforms to avoid the lapses that are generally observed. Reams, of course, have been written about the scope and contours of *peace*. There is fair unanimity that the concept of *peace* goes beyond the absence of conflict, although it would be difficult to argue how *peace* could realistically be expected to prevail alongside a state of war. Increasingly, *peace* is being linked in the present state of the international system with *reconciliation* to be sought after the armed conflict phase. Indeed, *peace audit* is the new mantra animating global society. But it is not an easy concept.

For instance, conflating peace with territorial and political integrity could militate against democratic urges for autonomy and independence. The peace of the grave is not the peace that one seeks, especially if a people-centric and not state-centric approach to national security is being sought. Hence, the wise admonition needs to be heeded: 'Security should not be viewed simply as protecting existing political and territorial forms at all cost. Rather security should be defined to accept non-violent change that is

---

[5] IPCS-KAS Peace Audit Series: 'Peace Audit Nepal', IPCS Special Report, November 2013, p. 3.

supported by respective populations'.[6] Before discussing how a *peace audit* might be conducted, two related terms need to be discussed, viz. *peace dividend* and *peace process*.

1. *Peace dividend.* George H.W. Bush and Margaret Thatcher had publicized the phrase *peace dividend* to promote the belief that economic benefits would accrue from a reduction in defence expenditure. Indeed, scholarly attention has also been paid on the opportunity costs underlying defence spending, which makes the case for seeking peace. No doubt, the end of the Cold War heralded a decrease in defence spending in Europe, Russia and the United States. But American military spending began rising sharply after 9/11 to fund its intervention and conflicts in Afghanistan and Iraq, which has occasioned its present financial woes. The costs of these conflicts in monetary and human terms can easily be computed.

A similar phenomenon has manifested itself in South Asia. The promise of the Simla Agreement (1972) has been wasted. Besides, the belief that establishing nuclear deterrence would lead to a reduction in spending on conventional arms has also been belied as evident from the rapid increase in defence expenditure on both nuclear and conventional weapon systems in India and Pakistan. A review of their defence expenditure after 1972 and 1998 would inform that no peace dividend has accrued in South Asia after the Simla Agreement was signed, or the nuclear tests were conducted.

Furthermore, the Kashmir Valley has passed through difficult times during its two-decade long proxy war starting in 1989, influenced by other events in the region like the Afghan conflict. The resulting increase in outlays on deploying the armed forces, paramilitary forces and strengthening the police forces can be estimated from the budget figures. However, the excellent tourist season in the Kashmir Valley over the past few years manifests the quantifiable peace dividend that has accrued for its residents due to the joint efforts of the State administration, local trade and business interests.

[6] Muthiah Alagappa, 'Building Peace and Security in the Asia-Pacific', PacNet #85, 2 December 2013.

But cross-border incidents, promoted by Pakistan, could vitiate this atmosphere after the American and European forces withdraw from Afghanistan in 2014. The consequent loss in tourist traffic could also be quantified to estimate the peace dividend.

2. *Peace processes*. It is a common ground that peace requires the removal of differences and the resolution of conflicts. Therefore, peace processes include both peace building and conflict resolution. Since the end of the Cold War, several agreements have been reached to establish peace in regional settings; some have collapsed resulting in the resumption of conflict, others have survived. The reasons underlying these varying outcomes are worth investigating to guide the pursuit of peace processes. Here, it might be added that avoiding grasping the nettle by shifting disputes to the back-burner leaving it to future generations to resolve them is an irresponsible way of evading responsibility. Another assumption often made is that resolving non-traditional security issues before addressing traditional security problems amounts to an over-statement. It is not true beyond a point, since there are no water-tight compartments into which these threats to national security can be neatly confined.

Proceeding further, *peace processes* can include dialog at different levels—official (Track One), quasi-official (Track One and a Half), or non-official (Track Two). According to Nicole Ball,[7] peace processes fall into two stages, each having two phases. The first stage is the cessation of violent conflict, which she divides into two phases: negotiations and cessation of hostilities. The second stage is peace building, which moves from a transition to a consolidation phase. The popular belief exists that the longer a conflict proceeds, the longer the peace agreement will take to be implemented. But this assertion is not always true. The empirical evidence reveals that disparate long-duration events such as the Cold War's demise and the removal of apartheid in South Africa led to early agreements to consolidate peace and achieve reconciliation between the former contending parties.

---

[7] Nicole Ball. 'The Challenge of Rebuilding War-Torn Societies', in *Turbulent Peace*, eds Chester A. Crocker, Fen Osler Hampson and Pamela Aall (Washington, D.C.: U.S. Institute of Peace, 2001), pp. 721–722.

Shifting the focus now to South Asia, we might examine the theoretical proposition that communal violence acquires an international remit by 'stretching structural conflicts over several societies, constructing "imagined communities" that reflect patterns of extensive migration and diasporas'.[8] The obvious examples here are India getting involved in the Sri Lankan ethnic conflict due to the influence of its own Tamil community in southern India. The communal-religious links that India and Pakistan have with Kashmir—also premised on their *imagined communities*—has fuelled tensions and conflicts since the two countries became independent in 1947. Given the primordial roots of these conflicts, peace processes between the contending parties are notoriously fragile. Indeed,

> It is very difficult for peace settlements to be agreed when the negotiations are proceeded with amidst ongoing violence—which is why most peace accords begin with ceasefires—but those opposed to the agreement can easily break the ceasefire, making negotiations or final settlements difficult to stabilize.[9]

These observations illustrate the need for patience and persistence in seeking to ameliorate armed conflicts and establish peace in zones of conflict like South Asia.

Undertaking Peace Audit

Reverting to the manner of discussion on *peace audit*, it is apparent that public perceptions are of the essence. Hence, public surveys to ascertain popular beliefs in regard to the peace process are to be commended. The art lies in persuading target groups to opine on specific parameters relevant to the peace dividend such as the state of law and order, degree of assurance about personal security, confidence in the police and justice system and so on. Also, to ascertain the level of assurance or scepticism regarding the progress of the peace process and current state of the peace,

---

[8] John D. Brewer, *Peace Processes: A Sociological Approach* (Cambridge, U.K.: Polity Press, 2010), p. 13.
[9] Ibid. p. 31.

the direction(s) in which it is proceeding, relevance of the parties involved and so on. Each armed conflict has its unique aspects; hence, the criteria for estimating the state of the peace process would need to suit the situation. This is an area of inquiry which needs greater research, using the available data to test the models developed. A more orthodox modality would be to evaluate the statistics on the number of violent incidents that have occurred over a period of time, the casualties suffered by the security forces, the militants and the bystander public collated and published by official and non-official organizations.

There are obvious flaws in both these approaches. The public surveys modality will suffer from the usual limitations associated with identifying target groups and individuals, apart from ensuring their geographical and cultural diversity, but also interviewing adequate numbers in the interests of evening out statistical analysis. Relying on conflict-related statistics suffers from the liability of being altogether too mechanistic, without being able to distinguish nuances. Thus, making comparisons over time intervals of the number of *incidents* that have occurred does not enable their seriousness to be distinguished, neither do these statistics take into consideration the value of property destroyed—public and private—which is a relevant consideration for ascertaining the seriousness of an *incident*. Wisdom, therefore, dictates that both these basic approaches be utilized to undertake more meaningful *peace audits*, which could be refined over time in the light of experience gained.

Early Warning

Finally, the *early warning* modality requires notice, which is of special relevance for peace processes and peace dividend and, consequently, for peace audits. No doubt, surprise attacks are part of accepted strategic doctrine and find approval by strategists since they confer an advantage on the aggressor during an armed conflict. Early warning systems, apropos, have a close nexus with nuclear crises; the availability of advance warning could ensure that appropriate counter measures are taken in a timely fashion to avert catastrophic loss of lives. Fortunately, technological advances in surveillance and communications technology have made it progressively more difficult for states to initiate offensive military actions, since hostile preparations and cross-border intrusions can be detected with greater celerity. Early warning has also become critical to meet natural disasters that could be most destructive such as floods, typhoons and earthquakes. For instance, timely intimation of a cyclone and its likely *landfall* would enable the population at risk to be evacuated, fishing vessels to be called back to harbour, adequate arrangements made for food, shelter and emergency medical services and so on. Ultimately, these early warnings of man-made or natural disasters are designed to reduce casualties and avoidable damage to property.

Atypically, early warning systems comprise detection and communication systems, and include assessments and predictions that need to be disseminated to populations that might get adversely affected. Early warning systems are majorly concerned with the mitigation of natural disasters like the devastating tsunamis that occur with some frequency in the Indian and Pacific Oceans. The armed forces have a role to play here in pursuance of their aid-to-civil duties that involves providing military assistance to the civil administration during calamities. The relevance of early warning systems arises from perceptions regarding the immediacy of threats and the crises they would engender. Thus, anticipation and early warning of the civil unrest that marked the Arab Spring in the Maghreb and Gulf regions, or the anti-Rohingya violence that flared up in Myanmar, or the panic that gripped migrants from Northeast India to flee home from other parts of India were of the essence to take remedial action. Long-term threats as, for instance, from unemployment due to the adverse impact of the demographic dividend have little immediacy and may not have the same relevance for early warning systems.

On the other hand, the emerging Naxalite threat in the northeastern states of India, growing sectarian divide in Sri Lanka, Bangladesh and Pakistan, and violent Maoism in Nepal fall in the genre of problems requiring early warning systems to be emplaced for taking ameliorative action. A looming aspect of this Naxalite threat is the spread of Left-wing extremism to urban centres. Unplanned urbanization in South Asia, apropos, has resulted in the growth of megacities (population in excess of 10 million) that have now become 'a witch's brew of conflicting religious and ethnic identities, traditional cultures and western modernity, leading to increasing turmoil and violence'.[10] Unless the early warnings of this dangerous trend are recognized and remedial steps are taken, the large urban centres in the region could become the new loci of armed conflicts. Incidentally, several of the world's megacities are situated in South Asia; they include Delhi, Dhaka, Karachi, Lahore, Kolkata and Mumbai.

A special problem linking the issues of urban violence and the vital need for early warning of armed conflicts is represented by the *flash mobs* phenomenon. It was defined in last year's Annual Report as 'mindless violence being triggered by a minor incident, which then spreads like wildfire. Such unpredictable violence derives from dormant and unresolved grievances such as demands for greater autonomy, communal, sectarian and communal-religious tensions and so on'.[11] It is conventional in these cases to estimate the violence by *flash mobs* in terms of lives lost. But this is inadequate, since it does not give adequate weight to the number and value of property lost, usually to arson. The challenge of the *flash mobs* phenomenon for early warning systems and internal security cannot be over-emphasized, especially since riots can be triggered by trivial incidents and develop without much warning.

Standard operating procedures for checking communal and other types of violence in South Asia require that lists of bad characters be maintained in police stations with the more desperate among them being placed under surveillance that can be undertaken with different levels of severity. On anticipation of a breach of the peace, preventive arrests are made of these bad characters and potential troublemakers. What is being urged here is that early warning and ameliorative steps to meet threats to law and order, internal and external security may be difficult to segregate, nor does it seem necessary on pragmatic considerations.

---

[10] P.H. Lotta and James F. Miskel, 'The Leviathan Returns: The Rise of the Megacity and Its Threat to Global Security', available online at www.fpri.org (accessed 8 February 2010).

[11] P.R. Chari, 'Introduction: Review of Armed Conflicts in 2011', in *Armed Conflicts in South Asia 2012: Uneasy Stasis and Fragile Peace*, eds D. Suba Chandran and P.R. Chari (New Delhi: Routledge, 2013), p. 5.

Parsing the South Asian Scene

The above are global considerations. It is proposed now to focus on the conceptual issues underlying armed conflicts in South Asia. They fall into recognizable genres such as armed conflicts between states and within states, between state and non-state actors and between non-state actors. They could arise from traditional causes such as territorial disputes, support to subversion or militancy by neighbouring states, attempts to bring about regime change, and so on. Or they could have their roots in non-traditional causes such as internal or cross-border migration, environmental decay, food or water insecurity and pandemics. Over the years, the belief has strengthened that the focus of armed conflicts worldwide, as also in South Asia, has decisively shifted from the external to the internal sphere. It would be argued below that this assertion greatly overstates the case. But domestic conflicts, exacerbated by the electoral process, have increasingly become a hallmark of armed conflicts in South Asia. Some of these armed conflicts had excoriated the region during 2013 and seem likely continue into 2014.

The incipient violence in the Maldives before its Presidential elections is of recent provenance. Similarly, Nepal witnessed great violence before its Constituent Assembly elections were finally held in November 2013 that led to the surprise sidelining of its Maoist and Madhesi parties, and the ascendancy of the Nepali Congress. Bangladesh remained in the throes of resolving the crisis following its flawed general elections, which has stoked tensions and conflicts in the country. These issues will, no doubt, be discussed at greater length in subsequent chapters of this volume. But the nexus between domestic and electoral violence in South Asia is marked.

Peering ahead, the several elections slated for 2014 will have discrete implications for regional peace and security in South Asia. The Afghan presidential elections (April 2014) have the distinct potential to catalyze violence across the border with Pakistan, which could spread to Kashmir and impinge on India–Pakistan relations. The run-up to the general elections in India—slated for mid-2014—has already begun, and there is speculation that the *aam admi* (common man) movement will spread throughout the country and seminally influence the electoral prospects of the major political parties. No doubt, Indian democracy has acquired an inherent stability, and there is little possibility of minor incidents that could occur as the electoral process unfolds, triggering any larger unrest. A close watch needs to be kept; however, on Left-wing extremists, Right-wing fundamentalists and ethno-national elements in the country that have a vested interest in disrupting the electoral process. How the crisis in Bangladesh evolves and some form of stability accrues in the country will, of course, be of immense significance for the region.

Not all armed conflicts, however, would qualify for inclusion in this study. Civil riots, for instance, might flare up suddenly, being an aspect of the *flash mobs* phenomenon, but they would reflect long-subsisting, dormant resentments that are of little significance for armed conflicts in South Asia. Instead, some generic factors could be reviewed that are significant in this regard. They include the following.

1. *Civil–military relations' problematique.* A major development in 2013 was the hiatus that developed between its political and military leaderships. Quite obviously, the armed forces are no threat to India's civilian leadership. Indeed, the tradition of civilian control over the military that is part of the British heritage is firmly established in India, unlike in Pakistan, despite the latter's armed forces also tracing their origins to the British Indian Army. The trajectory followed since Independence by the Indian and Pakistani armed forces have been remarkably different, but its details need not detain us here. The most controversial incidents in India involved an individual—General V.P. Singh, the former Army Chief—who made an issue of his date of birth close to his date of retirement. His petitioning the Supreme Court in this regard against the ruling of the Ministry of Defence (MoD) accentuated this civil–military hiatus. And his further actions such as using a military intelligence unit to watch over the MoD, encourage a Public Interest Litigation against his successor and allege that the army had paid bribes to ministers in Jammu and Kashmir (J&K) constituted new depths being plumbed

in civil–military relations.[12] But the unwillingness of the MoD to discipline the former Army Chief and its deference to the army's views on political issues like resolving the Siachen dispute, or alleviating the provisions of the draconian Armed Forces Special Powers Act (AFSPA), or establishing a permanent head of the Chiefs of Staff Committee revealed a certain lack of confidence within the Indian political leadership in dealing with the military.

Apropos, Prime Minister Nawaz Sharif's pyrrhic struggle to bring Pakistan's armed forces under civilian control is noteworthy. He had requested the Supreme Court to bring the former President Pervez Musharraf to trial for treason, which creates a dilemma for the Pakistan Army. Will it accept the rule of law and defer to the hallowed tradition of civilian and judicial control over the military? The retirement of the Army Chief, General Kayani, in November 2013, and the elevation of General Raheel Sharif, Prime Minister Nawaz Sharif's personal choice, reveals yet another attempt by him to assert civilian control over the military. It shall soon become evident whether the civilians or the military will set Pakistan's future national security agenda on issues like India and Afghanistan, and policy towards Kashmir.

The differences in civil–military relations between India and Pakistan became significant for armed conflicts in South Asia in 2013 on two counts.

- First, persisting ceasefire violations along the Line of Control (LoC) and cross-border attacks excoriated India–Pakistan relations and remained unresolved till year end. On the historical note, it bears mention that a ceasefire had been negotiated by the two countries in November 2003, later extended to the Siachen sector, which continued without incident for almost a decade. Why was this peace initiative disrupted? Mutual allegations levelled by both countries have indicted each other's acts of commission and omission. High-level talks between military officials have not resolved this imbroglio. The Indian authorities

[12] Dinesh Kumar, 'Lack of Cohesion Hurting India's Defense', *Tribune*, 30 September 2013.

hold that these ceasefire violations are expressions of the Pakistan Army's desperate attempts to infiltrate insurgents and terrorists into J&K, where the ground situation has been steadily normalizing. Militant activities, too, are steadily declining; hence, cross-border firings and attacks are designed to distract the Indian army's attention and facilitate infiltration by the militants across the border.

Despite Prime Ministers Manmohan Singh and Nawaz Sharif agreeing in New York during their September 2013 meeting that the two Directors General of Military Operations (DGMOs) would negotiate an end to these incidents, the latter had not met till the end of 2013. However, it was planned that they would meet in Wagah. Meanwhile, cross-border firings and attacks continued with rising casualties on both sides. Symbolism is important in such matters, especially in South Asia; hence, the decision that the DGMOs would meet at a crossing point along the LoC suggests that their meeting would be little more than a higher level flag meeting to relieve the immediate situation. A more structured meeting in their national capitals could imbue this exercise with the imprimatur of a policy-oriented dialogue to address the larger political-military issues involved. For instance, the decision to proceed ahead with positioning offensively oriented forces along the border by India (identified as its Cold Start strategy) and Pakistan's plans to deploy its *Nasr* Hatf IX short-range nuclear missiles could have been reviewed by the two countries. India's concerns with cross-border militancy and terrorism could also have been addressed by them.

It seems the lack of a synchronization of views between the civilian and military leaderships in India and Pakistan is responsible for this parlous situation. Islamabad might also have come to believe that no serious peace negotiations with India are possible until after the Indian elections in mid-2014; hence, a dialogue between the two militaries on technical issues is all that is currently possible. For its part, the Indian political leadership feels that Pakistan's strategic perceptions derive from its Army's basic opposition to the normalization of India–Pakistan

relations, since this would reduce the Pakistan Army's centrality in the national polity, which is against their institutional interests.
- Second, the hiatus in civil–military relations in 2013 has manifested in India–Pakistan nuclear deterrent relations established after 1998 weakening, while the likelihood of another India–Pakistan clash became real. Apropos, the India Army's Cold Start, a military doctrine, was specifically designed to cater for a possible crisis with Pakistan and involves the various arms of India's military conducting offensive operations through unified battle groups, while the bulk of its conventional forces would perform a holding role to prevent retaliation.

The rationale for this Cold Start Doctrine was the slow mobilization by Indian forces after the attack on its Parliament in December 2001 that allowed international pressure to be mounted which inhibited India from conducting a retaliatory strike. In operational terms, Cold Start envisages undertaking rapid cross-border offensives as a punitive measure to counter Rawalpindi's mounting another Mumbai-style terrorist attack. The Pakistan Army's response has been to threaten the deployment of its short-range nuclear-armed *Nasr* Hatf IX short-range missile, which has serious implications for bilateral security.[13] The general belief obtains that deploying short-range nuclear missiles is ipso facto dangerous since they could be easily attacked or captured by the adversary; hence, a mentality accrues that they might as well be used early in a conflict rather than lost, which would greatly aggravate the crisis.

A qualitative nuclear arms race is proceeding between India and Pakistan, which has manifested itself in the testing and deployment of missiles with increasing ranges to target larger tracts of adversary territory. These developments might be framed against the backdrop of persisting India–Pakistan hostility, punctuated by armed

---

[13] P.R. Chari, 'South Asia: The Most Dangerous Place on Earth', 7 November 2013, available online at http://www.claws.in/1104/south-asia-the-most-dangerous-place-on-earth-pr-chari.html

conflicts, border clashes and recurrent crises. Hence, another armed conflict between India and Pakistan that could acquire nuclear overtones cannot be ignored.

Proceeding further, the received wisdom informs that the focus of national and regional security has shifted from interstate to intrastate conflicts. No South Asian nation remains unaffected by internal security threats. They continue to consume the attention of their political leaderships and the resources of their armed forces. A further shift has now occurred, with 'an increase in the number of intrastate conflicts that are internationalized—that have another state supporting one side or another. Such involvement often has the effect of increasing casualty rates and prolonging conflicts'.[14] This new verity is increasingly visible in South Asia. The Pakistan Army, for instance, has been diligently providing moral and material assistance to insurgents and terrorists like the Lashkar-e-Taiba, Jaish-e-Mohammed and al Qaeda to operate in India, Afghanistan and elsewhere.

Islamabad, however, believes that Afghanistan has not been remiss in supporting elements of the Taliban operating in Pakistan; it has also convinced itself that India is using its consulates in Jalalabad, Herat and so on to stir up revolt in Balochistan. Moreover, non-state actors like the Harkat-ul-Jihad al-Islami (HuJI) profess a Taliban-influenced brand of Islamic fundamentalism, which is rabidly anti-communist, but also pan-Islamic. Founded in Pakistan, the HuJI has been active in Afghanistan and Kashmir, and has currently become a political force in Bangladesh.

2. *India–Pakistan Relations.* This bilateral relationship, critical for armed conflicts in South Asia, can be parsed in terms of domestic and electoral politics. It is egregious that India's Prime Minister Manmohan Singh has lowered his profile to near invisibility while determinedly, pursuing his do-nothing policy. Governance has been at a total premium, ostensibly because he was forced to make compromises on

---

[14] *SIPRI Yearbook 2013: Armaments, Disarmament and International Security* (Oxford: Oxford University Press), p. 2.

norms and principles due to the compulsions of coalition government. This insouciance has precluded taking meaningful steps to check widespread corruption, generating an ambience favouring the *aam admi* (common man) civil society movement, which had formed the government in the city state of Delhi after the five-state elections in the end of 2013. India's lack of direction in the spheres of foreign policy and national security also reflected in a sharp decline in its relations with Pakistan. Following his return to power in June, Prime Minister Nawaz Sharif had pledged to improve relations with India; instead, there were frequent violations of the Ceasefire Agreement on the LoC reached by the two countries in 2003, leading to a steady loss of lives. It is, however, apparent that, despite his victory in the elections, Nawaz Sharif needs to defer on security-related issues to the dictates and interests of Pakistan's Army.

Will the elevation of General Raheel Sharif in 2013 as the Army Chief—Prime Minister Nawaz Sharif's personal choice following General Kayani's retirement—bring about a change in India–Pakistan and Pakistan–Afghanistan relations?

Some peripheral questions need to be addressed first and recent history rehearsed. Nawaz Sharif fought the elections in Pakistan in June 2013 promising to accord the highest priority to peace with India, and to promote confidence-building measures such as buying electricity from India, granting India most-favoured nation status, apart from resolving the long-pending disputes over Siachen and Sir Creek. Nawaz Sharif's inclination may have been to improve Indo–Pak relations by broadening trade, improving people-to-people relations and lowering border tensions. The question remains: Can he establish greater control over General Headquarters (Pakistan Army), Rawalpindi, and Islamabad's foreign and defence policy?[15]

In truth, an escalation in ceasefire violations and cross-border attacks had started in J&K, with Hafiz Mohammed

---

[15] P.R. Chari, 'Ten Years of Ceasefire along the LoC: An Evaluation', Article No. 4201, 30 November 2013, available online at http://www.ipcs.org/article/peace-audit-and-ceasefire-monitor/ten-years-of-ceasefire-along-the-loc-an-evaluation-4201.html

Saeed, the leader of the rabid Jama'at-ul-Dawah, located in Lahore, inflaming anti-India animosities. Incidentally, the back-channel negotiations being conducted between the two countries had reportedly envisaged maximum autonomy being accorded to all parts of the former princely state, with the LoC being made irrelevant by freeing trade and movement in Kashmir. Joint resource development would be undertaken, with phased demilitarization starting with non-state actors, to be supervised by India and Pakistan undertaking joint monitoring.[16] These laudable goals need to be diligently pursued if tensions and instabilities in South Asia are to be mitigated. But it seemed that by year end Nawaz Sharif had decided that no dialogue with India was possible until after its General Elections in mid-2014.

Incidentally, the India–Pakistan dialogue on J&K is supported by the Mirwaiz-led Hurriyat and Yasin Malik's Jammu Kashmir Liberation Front, and they should be supported by New Delhi; unfortunately, India has no access to dissidents in Pakistan-held Kashmir. The unfortunate fact remains, however, that the India–Pakistan dialogue remains hostage to the electoral calculations of their political parties. Violence in Pakistan has shown an upward trend with 2,113 people being killed between 4 June — when Prime Minister Nawaz Sharif came to power — and the end of 2013. The new government's focus remained on talks with the Pakistani Taliban, but little progress was possible due to its obduracy. Thereafter, the killing of Tehreek-e-Taliban (TTP) leader, Hakimullah Mehsud, in a US drone strike ended this peace process. The security establishment appears to have lost its patience and has decided to take pro-active steps against the TTP, which will further shrink the space available for peace talks.

The other pressing security concern in Pakistan is the spread of sectarian violence and tensions with several incidents during the year suggesting a widening sectarian divide in the country. With the North Atlantic Treaty Organization forces' withdrawing from Afghanistan in 2014, threats to

[16] Radha Kumar, 'Renewing an India-Pakistan Peace Process?', *Hindu*, 16 November 2013.

physical security seem likely to increase in Pakistan but ideological polarization also appears set to escalate. Islamabad, however, will find it difficult to prosecute these terrorists due to its indigenous support base in the population and its bureaucracy. New Delhi is also in a state of denial regarding the indigenous roots of Islamic terror in India and witness the rising profile of the Indian Mujahideen. A concerted strategy has, therefore, to be evolved by Islamabad and New Delhi to deal with cross-border tensions, instabilities and domestic terrorism.

3. *Afghanistan post-2014.* The other significant development slated for the end of 2014 that rapidly evolved over 2013 — the year under review — is the planned withdrawal of American and European forces from Afghanistan. How this will develop has serious implications for the entire region. Three possible post-2014 scenarios are foreseeable. First, Afghanistan descends into chaos with Kabul exercising minimal control over the warlords dominating different tracts of territory. Second, civil war breaks out between the Pashtun-majority eastern and southern provinces pitted against the non-Pashtun Northern Province that could result in a geo-political partition, as anticipated several decades back by Selig Harrison. Third, Pakistan, in collaboration with Taliban factions supported by its Inter-services Intelligence, dominates Afghanistan. The US and its European allies may not be averse to this arrangement to ensure their hold over Afghanistan. All these developments are evolving against the backdrop of the Afghan presidential elections scheduled for April 2014.

However, these scenarios beg the question whether US–International Security Assistance Force (US–ISAF) forces would truly leave Afghanistan after 2014. Will the Americans–ISAF leave behind a vacuum to be filled by Russia and China? The continued US presence in Afghanistan would also ensure their ability to target the al Qaeda and Taliban in their hideouts along the Pak–Afghan border. However, a change in mission seems on the cards, premised on continuing drone attacks from secure American/ISAF bases in Afghanistan, ignoring the problem of *collateral* civilian deaths occurring alongside the targeted killings of militants.

A *New York Times* report details how 'residents paint a portrait of extended terror and strain within a tribal society caught between vicious militants and the American drones hunting them'.[17] The number of troops that would remain behind in Afghanistan after 2014 if a deal is finalized has not been quantified by the Obama administration, but guesstimates are that their numbers would be around 10,000.

In the end of 2013, however, a glitch appeared in implementing these arrangements following the US insistence that Afghanistan must sign an agreement allowing the US troops to remain after 2014 in Afghanistan. President Karzai has said that he would only sign this agreement after the 2014 Presidential elections. The US counter argued that eight months is too short a period for an orderly withdrawal to be effected.[18] A parallel issue raised by Karzai is that the Americans stop raiding Afghan homes to search for militants, which is greatly resented by local residents. Unstated by Karzai, however, is his angst that the Americans might support their own preferred candidate in the Presidential elections to the detriment of his (Karzai's) political interests.

Apropos, the US Special Representative for Afghanistan and Pakistan, James Dobbins, had informed the Senate Foreign Relations Committee that the Administration wished to continue its troop presence in Afghanistan, despite Karzai laying out new conditions for signing a bilateral security agreement. However, if no deal is signed, it would lead to a cutback, if not total stoppage, of military and civilian assistance to Kabul.[19] The worst case scenario suggests that the Afghan government would collapse thereafter, with the Taliban and other militants regaining strength, and civil war afflicting Afghanistan once again.

A residual problem facing the American/ISAF forces is disposing off some $7 billion worth of equipment that is no

---

[17] Declan Walsh, Ihsanullah, Tipu Mehsud, 'Civilian Deaths in Drone Strikes Cited in Report', *New York Times*, 22 October 2013.

[18] US Wants Afghanistan to Sign Pact This Year, *Dawn* (Karachi), 23 November 2013.

[19] 'US "Nowhere Near" Decision to Pull All Troops Out of Afghanistan,' *NewsmaxWorld*, 11 December 2013.

longer required and is too costly to ship back. Most of this equipment includes vehicles and old munitions that may not be useful for regular forces, but it would become highly problematical if militants were to gain access to them. Therein lies a new danger for security and armed conflicts in South Asia. A related issue is how other countries in the region should respond to Kabul's fervent plea for economic and financial aid, but more particularly for military assistance to upgrade the operational worth of the Afghan National Army (ANA) and the Afghan National Police (ANP). India, for instance, has provided facilities for training the ANA and ANP, apart from granting some $2 billion in economic aid, and deploying teachers, doctors and other professionals in the country. India is still weighing Kabul's request for the supply of weapon systems such as attack helicopters, apart from small arms and ammunition. Unsurprisingly, Pakistan views askance all Indian assistance to Afghanistan as being designed against Islamabad's national interests.

4. *The imbroglio in Bangladesh*. The potential for serious internal dissensions and violence in Bangladesh, deriving from its electoral process, however, is immense. Their contours, briefly noticed above, are tethered in an ideological conflict between the Awami League-led government and the Bangladesh Nationalist Party–Jamaat-e-Islami (BNP–Jamaat) opposition alliance. What does early warning about the prevailing events portend for the future of Bangladesh? This critical question has been dramatically posed: 'It's an election centered around the very idea of Bangladesh — should it be a secular democracy or a theocratic state? A Bengali republic or an Islamic nation?'[20] The elections since held on 5 January 2014 were boycotted by the opposition parties, with a third of the Awami League legislators getting elected unopposed; hence, these elections have been fairly castigated as being undemocratic, even farcical. Therefore, it is possible that fresh elections would be held if — improbable as it may seem — a modus

---

[20] Shubajit Roy, 'Fight for Bangladesh: Country Seeks to Retain Its Identity Amid Growing Islamic Influence', *Indian Express*, 5 January 2014.

vivendi is discovered between the two warring Begums in Dhaka. Apart from the presentiments of greater violence and chaos, the early warning signals emanating from Dhaka inform that the radicalization of its polity and its Islamizing might be anticipated.

The roots of the present crisis in Bangladesh can be traced to the establishment of an International Crimes Tribunal in 2010 to prosecute the collaborators with the Pakistan army who had committed atrocities on civilians in 1971 before the India–Pakistan War that created Bangladesh. In February 2013, the Jamaat-e-Islami leader Abdul Qader Molla was convicted of killing 344 persons and sentenced to imprisonment for life. On the Supreme Court's orders, the sentence was enhanced and Molla was awarded the death penalty. He was executed in December 2013, leading to widespread protests and violence. Incidentally, the Jamaat has traditionally been close to Khaleda Zia's BNP, but also the Bangladesh Army that had ruled the country for several years after Mujib's assassination, and remains a potent force in the country's politics. The Jamaat, incidentally, is known to sponsor the HuJI that has targeted India on several occasions. As in the case of Pakistan, the linkage between religious fanaticism and the military is also strong in Bangladesh.

Conclusions

The preceding four major issues pertaining to armed conflict in South Asia had relevance to the region in 2013 and are likely to shape these issues in 2014. They span the entire range of armed conflicts, and include both interstate and intrastate conflicts. Besides, they include conflicts involving state and non-state actors, including the sectarian and religious forces that are becoming increasingly significant in South Asia.

It is important to provide a theoretical underpinning to armed conflicts in South Asia by undertaking peace audits using the conflict-related data published by official and non-official sources, supplemented by field surveys to evaluate public opinion whether any armed conflict situation is improving or deteriorating or remains unchanged. Furthermore, early warning of impending armed conflicts would obviously not only permit the placement of ameliorative measures, but also for dealing with the situation from a law-and-order perspective. The role of internal and electoral politics is of special significance here.

2

Security Transition and Peace Process in Afghanistan: Trends in 2013

Mariam Safi

Given the magnitude of problems, Afghanistan has had to confront and overcome in the last 12 years, we can conclude that it has either been on the verge of collapse all this time or that it has been shockingly stable. In 2001, the international community sought to restore peace and stability in Afghanistan after it removed the Taliban regime from power. Having learnt the consequences of abandoning Afghanistan once before, the US, its European allies and under the umbrella of the UN agreed to pursue a state-building strategy that would prevent Afghanistan from once again becoming a safe haven for terrorists. Thus, with the development and military assistance of the international community, Afghanistan has been able to build good governance and improve its education, health and economic indicators. However, despite the gains made, the country continues to grapple with challenges from a weak government, declining economy, rampant corruption, warlordism and insecurity. In 2010, the Afghan government along with its international partners launched a comprehensive security transition framework and peace process to develop local security forces, enable foreign troops to withdraw by 2014 and negotiate a political settlement with the insurgency. Nonetheless, by 2013, both initiatives had yet to show substantial progress leaving Afghans unprepared to tackle the challenges that lied ahead.

Background Context in 2013

In 2013, the Human Development Index (HDI) report rated Afghanistan along with 14 other countries as showing 'impressive HDI gains of more than 2 per cent annually since 2000'.[1] This mirrored a sharp increase in the life expectancy ratio of Afghans which rose to 62 years for men and 61 years for women.[2] Additionally, other significant health indicators include under-five mortality rates that dropped to one death per 10 live births,[3] infant mortality dropped to 71 per 1,000 live births[4] and maternal mortality ratio reduced to 97 per 1,000 live births.[5] Moreover, 60 per cent of women have access to health care facilities, with 2,170 clinics country wide and 30 per cent serving specifically women.[6] In terms of education, major improvements can be highlighted compared to the period before 2001. Today, there are 10.5 million registered students of which 42 per cent are girls; there are 2,10,000 teachers of which 32 per cent are female teachers; 159 districts have schools from grades 1 to 10.[7] Additionally, out of 1,000 schools that have been closed or destroyed as a result of insurgency, 250 were reopened in 2013 and in provinces that continue to see high levels of insecurity such as Zabul, Kandahar, Paktika, Ghazni, Helmand and Nooristan.[8] In terms of the Afghan economy, the GDP has increased to 22 billion and GDP per capita has increased from US$200 to US$680.[9]

[1] Human Development Report Office. Human Development Index in 2013: Report Shows Major Gains Since 2000 in Most Countries of South, 14 March 2013, available online at http://www.undp.org/content/undp/en/home/presscenter/pressreleases/2013/03/14/human-development-index-in-2013-report-shows-major-gains-since-2000-in-most-countries-of-south/

[2] Ministry of Public Health, Islamic Republic of Afghanistan (2011). [Personnel Interview]. Unpublished raw data.

[3] Ibid.

[4] The World Bank. Mortality Rate, Infant (per 1,000 Live Births), available online at http://data.worldbank.org/indicator/SP.DYN.IMRT.IN.

[5] Ministry of Education, Islamic Republic of Afghanistan (2013). [Personnel Interview]. Unpublished raw data.

[6] See note 3.

[7] See note 5.

[8] See note 5.

[9] Ministry of Finance, Islamic Republic of Afghanistan (2013). [Personnel Interview]. Unpublished raw data.

While the enormity of such achievements looks impressive, when they are compared to the exceeding low base they started from back in 2001, they end up seemingly minor and inadequate to tackle the magnitude of challenges Afghanistan is currently facing. Thus, upon a closer examination, these indicators reveal that the said progress has been largely unequal, sporadic and superficial. Rising insecurity levels have consistently made it difficult for reconstruction and development priorities to take root and as such the struggle for space and resources has predominantly been dominated by the security agenda. Thus, with past achievements laid on shaky grounds and a future security climate embroiled in ambiguity, the situation in Afghanistan will inevitably deteriorate if partial security is transformed into durable security by the time foreign troops withdraw in 2014.

Actors Involved

The conflict in Afghanistan is driven by a multitude of actors at various levels including the subnational, national, regional and international. This has created a highly complex environment where different actors have pursued diverse and at times opposing agendas that have protracted the conflict in Afghanistan. In the security and transition processes, the following actors have played the greatest role so far in their facilitation. At the subnational level, the main actors include provincial governors, Provincial Council (PC) members, different line ministries including the Directorate of the Ministry of Interior and Defence; Afghan Local Police (ALP) forces, tribal elders and religious figures, *Shura* members (traditional dispute resolution mechanisms) and ethno-tribal powers at play; illicit networks and narcotics traffickers; power brokers and their militias; and the insurgency which is comprised of the Taliban, Haqqani network, and Hizb-e-Islami and regional commanders and foot soldiers.

In recent years, the top tiers of the Taliban led by Mullah Muhammad Omar have reportedly lost some of their top aides and commanders to the US-led military attacks or during arrests in Afghanistan and Pakistan. Nevertheless, analysts have also argued that despite these instances, the inner circle of the Taliban has remained intact or have, in fact, been reinforced through the release of top Taliban figures on part of the Afghan and Pakistani governments. Other insurgent groups like Hizb-e-Islami led by Gulbudin Hekmatyar have also remained active in Afghanistan as they continue to control most territories in the eastern regions. In February 2013, the US government formally labelled Hekmatyar as a 'Specially Designated Global Terrorist', but the group itself has yet to be designated as a 'Foreign Terrorist Organization' which means that reconciliation with Hizb can still be pursued despite Hekmatyar's global terrorist designation. The Haqqani network, a third insurgent group founded by Jalaluddin Haqqani, is also very active in eastern Afghanistan and is considered as the most brutal and potent threat to security in the country. The network has become increasingly active with reportedly 3,000 fighters.[10] Moreover, though all of the insurgent groups operating in Afghanistan are thought to be receiving some sort of support from Pakistan, the Haqqani network in particularly has been singled out as a tool of Pakistani interest. The most widely cited critics of the network came from the former Joint Chiefs of Staff Chairman Mullen, who testified before the Senate Armed Services Committee, claiming that the Haqqani network 'acts as a veritable arm of the ISI'.[11] The group is also thought to be behind most targets against Indian interests in Afghanistan with a recent attack on the Indian Consulate in Nangarhar province on 4 August 2013. A number of Haqqani leaders have also been designated as Specially Designated Global Terrorists; however, unlike Hizb-e-Islami, the Haqqani network has also been designated as a Foreign Terrorist Organization by the US. This has created a tricky situation for the Afghan government's peace efforts because, on the one hand, they can no longer negotiate with the Haqqani network, and, on the other hand, the Taliban continue to cooperate and consider them as part of their group.

At the national level, the main actors include the Afghanistan National Army and the Afghanistan National Police, and these entities comprise the Afghan National Security Forces (ANSF), which constitute the countries military force fighting against the insurgency. At the regional level, Afghanistan's immediate neighbours, Pakistan and Iran, play less of a supporting role

---

[10] K. Katzman, 'Afghanistan: Post-Taliban Governance, Security, and US Policy'. *Congressional Research Service*, 23 October 2013, available online from http://fas.org/sgp/crs/row/RL30588.pdf

[11] Ibid., p. 16.

and more that of spoilers in Afghanistan. Historically, relations between Afghanistan and Pakistan have been strained, but in the last decade, it has only worsened. Though, Pakistan has articulated its determination to fight terrorism both internally and regionally, its ISI continues to harbour and support the Afghan Taliban, giving them spaces of operation in cities such as Quetta, Peshawar, Miranshah and Karachi. Moreover, the continued artillery shelling of eastern areas of Kunar provinces, which have been ongoing for over two years, has been another bone of contention between the two nations. In one instance in May 2013, the Governor of Kunar reported attacks from more than 170 rockets in just 24 hours,[12] resulting in many civilian casualties and even at one point readiness for a civilian uprising against Pakistan.

Another regional player that has a critical role in Afghanistan is its western neighbour, Iran. Highly critical of the US role in Afghanistan, Iran's strategy in Afghanistan has remained focused on limiting western presence and influence, and preventing a Taliban return while keeping friendly relations with the Afghan government. According to Afghanistan's former Intelligence Chief, Amrullah Saleh, there are three principle Iranian entities tasked with furthering Iran's hard and soft power in Afghanistan; they include the clerical establishment in Qom, the Ministry of Intelligence, and Iran's Revolutionary Guards Corps-Quds Force (IRGC-QF).[13] There are many claims illustrating Iranian support for the Afghan Taliban as a tactic to counter the US efforts in Afghanistan. A recent US Department of Defence report suggests that the IRGC-QF 'provides calibrated lethal aid to the Taliban to attrite ISAF and expedite force withdrawal'.[14] Iran has also contributed greatly to expanding its influence in Afghanistan through a 'soft-power campaign'[15] that involves a one billion dollar aid programme to 'upgrade infrastructure, provide humanitarian, cultural/religious support and economic assistance'.[16] For instance,

---

[12] Tolonews, 'No "Magic Wand" to Satisfy Conditions Overnight: Rice'. *TOLO News*, 26 November 2013, available online at http://www.tolonews.com/en/afghanistan/12869-us-has-no-magic-wand-to-deliver-on-karzais-conditions-overnight-rice

[13] Ibid.

[14] U.S. Department of Defence, 'Report on Progress towards Security and Stability in Afghanistan,' *Report to Congress*, April 2014, pp. 1–123.

[15] Ibid.

[16] Ibid.

Iran distributes these funds to Shia mosques, for Shia clerics to attain a higher education, hold public ceremonies for Ashura and ensure religious unity among influential Shia figures.[17] The aim of its soft-power campaign is to 'promote Iranian and pro-Shia sentiment' in Afghanistan.[18]

At the international level, US troops under 'Operations Enduring Freedom' and contributing countries under North Atlantic Treaty Organization (NATO)-led ISAF constitute the international military force operating in Afghanistan. The aim of US forces and NATO-led ISAF has been to assist Afghans in 'exercising and extending its authority and influence across the country, and paving the way for reconstruction and effective governance'.[19] In December 2013, there were approximately 60,000 US and 24,271 NATO-led ISAF troops representing 48 contributing countries, this brought the total troop numbers to 84,271 at the end of 2013.[20] The objective of the US and its allies, as mentioned previously, has been to develop effective national forces that would be capable enough to secure the country so that it does not become a safe haven for terrorists again. However, with only a year left until the scheduled pullout of international troops, most experts doubt whether the Afghan state is actually ready and capable of taking over full responsibility of its precarious security environment not to mention its weak government and declining economy.

Conflict in 2013: Major Trends

7 October 2013 marked the 12th anniversary of the US intervention in Afghanistan. On this occasion, Afghan President Hamid Karzai told the BBC that NATO's mission failed to bring security and

---

[17] Majidyar, A., 'Iran Wields Soft Power in Afghanistan', *American Enterprise Institute*, 2013, available online at http://www.aei-ideas.org/2013/01/iran-wields-soft-power-in-afghanistan.

[18] See note 14.

[19] S. Hess, 'Coming to Terms with Neopatrimonialism: Soviet and American Nation-building Projects in Afghanistan', *Central Asian Survey*, 29, No. 2 (2010): 171–187.

[20] North Atlantic Treaty Organization, 'International Security Assistance Force (ISAF): Key Facts and Figures', 2013, http://www.nato.int/nato_static/assets/pdf/pdf_2013_12/20131129_131201-isaf-placemat.pdf

a clear agenda on fighting terrorism. 'On the security front, the entire NATO exercise was one that caused Afghanistan a lot of suffering, a lot of loss of life, and no gains because the country is not secure', lamented Karzai.[21] These claims were sharply rejected by NATO Secretary General, Anders Fogh Rasmussen, who asserted that 'remarkable'[22] changes had been made in Afghanistan which 'no one can deny'.[23] However, there remains a greater deal of truth in Karzai's assertion than that of Rasmussen. 'Partial security', as Karzai describes the current security climate in 2013, is closer ground reality than Rasmussen's optimistic synopsis. This is reflected in local perceptions, as the annual report of the Asia Foundation accounted that 59 per cent of Afghans either 'always, often or sometimes fearing for their own safety or security, or for that of their families'.[24] This is because security indicators unlike social indicators have hardly improved over the years. This is a reality that local and international non-government organizations in Afghanistan have been echoing for a very long time, and now, foreign officials are also starting to acknowledge this reality.

US Counter-insurgency Efforts in Afghanistan

The international communities' objectives in Afghanistan have not been so much about state-building as has been about countering terrorism and then counter-insurgency (COIN) through predominantly militaristic approaches. Preventing Afghanistan from becoming a hub of terrorism that could potentially threaten American

---

[21] Yalda Hakim, 'Afghanistan's Hamid Karzai Says NATO Caused "Great Suffering"', BBC Newsnight, 7 October 2013, available online at http://www.bbc.com/news/world-24433433

[22] Deutsche Welle, 'Bomb Blast Hits Afghanistan on Security Handover Day', *Deutsche Welle*, 6 July 2013, available online at http://www.dw.de/bomb-blast-hits-afghanistan-on-security-handover-day/a-16888374.

[23] Ibid.

[24] The Asia Foundation, 'A Survey of the Afghan People,' 2013, p. 30, available online at http://asiafoundation.org/resources/pdfs/2013AfghanSurvey.pdf

citizens, their interests and allies[25] has been the primary objective. Thus, a counter-terrorism framework has marked the force behind much of thinking on state-building and its approaches. This has consequently led to a *de jure* sovereignty in Afghanistan where a highly centralized Afghan government has been established, but its ability to administer military and administrative control remains very weak causing the state to once again rely on old patronage networks for its legitimacy, resources and control.

The former US ambassador to Afghanistan General Karl Eikenberry offered harsh criticism for the US's COIN strategy in Afghanistan arguing that it 'unwittingly tried to achieve revolutionary aims through semi-colonial means'.[26] In a recently published article, Eikenberry argued that the modern COIN doctrine stressed the need for protecting civilians, eliminating insurgent leaders and helping to create legitimate and accountable governments that are able to deliver basic services to its people.[27]

The first true application of this was observed in Afghanistan in 2009 when Obama's administration deployed an additional 30,000 troops into Afghanistan after a comprehensive war strategy review. This move was deemed necessary to reverse the momentum of the insurgency and to 'secure the Afghan people by employing the method of clear, hold, and build'.[28] The overall expectations from the troop surge were that it would lead to a steady growth in the Afghan government, a reduction in the US and NATO assistance, and the eventual defeat of the insurgency.[29] According to Eikenberry and some top US officials, COIN was a complete failure in Afghanistan, largely because it was premised on inaccurate assumptions and difficult strategies that only perpetuated

---

[25] James Dobbins, 'State's Dobbins on Transition in Afghanistan' (Brussels, Belgium: Embassy of the United States), 11 December 2013, available online at http://www.uspolicy.be/headline/states-dobbins-transition-afghanistan (accessed December 2013).

[26] K. Eikenberry, 'The Limits of Counterinsurgency Doctrine in Afghanistan: The Other Side of the COIN'. *Council on Foreign Affairs*, 2013, September–October Issue, available online at http://www.foreignaffairs.com/articles/139645/karl-w-eikenberry/the-limits-of-counterinsurgency-doctrine-in-afghanistan (accessed December 2013).

[27] Ibid.
[28] Ibid.
[29] Ibid.

the conflict. Moreover, Robert Gates, Obama's former Defence Secretary, revelations in his recent book show how acutely uncommitted the US has become towards Afghanistan in the recent years as their strategies were not producing the outputs intended. Gates writes that Obama himself had no faith in the troop surge strategy and was highly mistrustful of his military commanders. Gates writes that 'the president [Obama] doesn't trust his commander, can't stand Karzai, doesn't believe in his own strategy, and doesn't consider the war to be his. For him, it's all about getting out'.[30] The impact, or thereof, of the troop surge set a thorny foundation for the launch of the security transition process which has not been able to create a sound basis for the withdrawal of NATO troops in 2014.

Rise in Civilian Casualties

The UN's Annual Report on Afghanistan's civilian casualties notes that 'armed conflict in Afghanistan took an unrelenting toll on Afghan civilian in 2013'[31] shown in the 14 per cent increase in total casualties compared to 2012. In 2013, the UN recorded 8,615 civilian casualties, with 2,959 deaths and 5,656 injured.[32] In the first six months of 2013 alone, civilian deaths and injuries rose to an alarming 23 per cent increase compared to the same period in 2012.[33] According to the UN, 1,319 civilian deaths and 2,533 injuries had

---

[30] B. Woodword, 'Robert Gates, Former Defense Secretary, Offers Harsh Critique of Obama's Leadership in Duty'. *The Washington Post*, 8 January 2013, available online at http://www.washingtonpost.com/world/national-security/robert-gates-former-defense-secretary-offers-harsh-critique-of-obamas-leadership-in-duty/2014/01/07/6a6915b2-77cb-11e3-b1c5-739e63e9c9a7_story.html (accessed January 2014).

[31] United Nations Assistance Mission in Afghanistan (UNAMA), Afghanistan Annual Report 2013: Protection of Civilians in Armed Conflict (Executive Summary, p. 1), February 2014, available online at http://unama.unmissions.org/Portals/UNAMA/human%20rights/Feb_8_2014_PoC-report_2013-Full-report-ENG.pdf (accessed March 2014).

[32] Ibid.

[33] United Nations Assistance Mission in Afghanistan (UNAMA). Afghanistan Mid-Year Report 2013: Protection of Civilians in Armed Conflict, July 2013, available online at http://unama.unmissions.org/LinkClick.aspx?fileticket=EZoxNuqDtps%3d&tabid=12254&language=en-US (accessed December 2013).

Figure 2.1:
Civilians deaths and injuries from January to June: 2009-2013

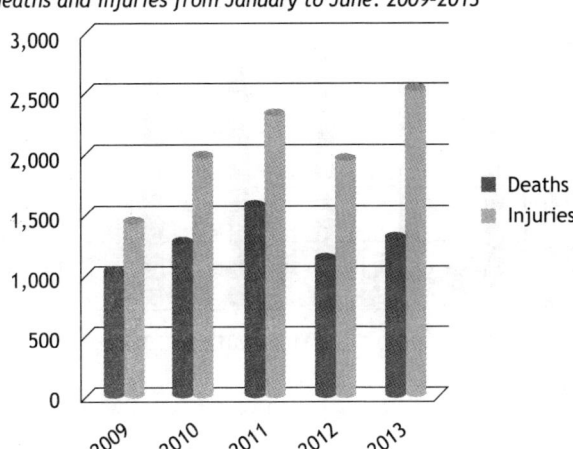

Source: UNAMA, 2013.

taken place between January and June of 2013 (see Figure 2.1).[34] The rise in civilian casualties 'reverses the decline recorded in 2012'[35] and is 'consistent with record high numbers of civilian causalities documented in 2011'.[36] From 2009 to 2013, there have been 14,064 Afghan civilians.

Afghan civilians, particularly women and children, continue to be the main victims of the conflict. Civilians are often killed by crossfire, improvised explosive devices (IEDs), assassinations, bombings, night raids, unexploded ordnances and US cluster bombs that kill even in the absence of fighting.[37] The main actors responsible for these civilian casualties in Afghanistan are 'anti-government elements' (AGEs), namely armed groups involved in

---

[34] United Nations Assistance Mission in Afghanistan (UNAMA). Afghanistan Mid-Year Report 2013: Protection of Civilians in Armed Conflict, July 2013, available online at http://unama.unmissions.org/LinkClick.aspx?fileticket=EZoxNuqDtps%3d&tabid=12254&language=en-US (accessed December 2013).

[35] Ibid.

[36] See note 31.

[37] Cost of War, 'Afghanistan: At Least 21,000 Civilians Killed', February 2013, available online at http://costsofwar.org/article/afghan-civilians (accessed December 2013).

Figure 2.2:
Civilian deaths by parties to the conflict from January to December: 2009-2013

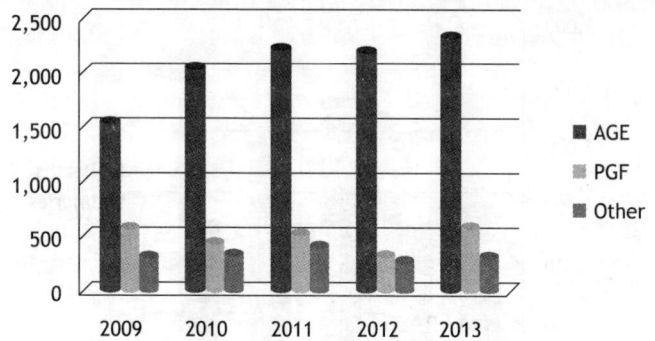

Source: UNAMA, 2014.

armed conflict with or against the government and international military forces, and 'pro-government forces' (PGFs) such as the ANSF and other groups who operate under the Afghan government in military or paramilitary COIN operations.[38]

In 2013, 74 per cent of all civilian casualties were caused by AGEs, 'a four per cent increased compared to last year' (see Figure 2.2).[39] Additionally, 11 per cent of civilian causalities were attributed to PGFs and 10 per cent to ground engagements between pro-government forces and insurgents.[40] The remaining five per cent of civilian casualties were due to explosive remnants.[41] The UNAMA report assessed that IEDs was the main cause of the spike in casualties. AGEs are thought to have planted IEDs in either frequented areas or those with a high population density.[42] Increased ground engagement between AGEs and PGFs was also noted as a key cause, and new trend, in civilian causalities. About 27 per cent of all deaths and injuries were attributed to this trend, claiming the most deaths among women, girls and boys. The UNAMA Report stipulates that 2013 witnessed the 'highest recorded number'[43] of causalities among women and children

[38] UNAMA, 2014, p. 2.
[39] Ibid., 3.
[40] See note 31.
[41] Ibid.
[42] Ibid., 2.
[43] Ibid., 2.

since 2009. For instance, compared to 2012, women casualties increased by 36 per cent and child causalities by 34 per cent.[44] The 'indiscriminate and unlawful'[45] use of IEDs, targeted killings and suicide attacks, combined with the spike in casualties, caused a serious backlash against the insurgency. Aiding this process was the constant placing of responsibility by the international community, local media channels and civil society organizations (CSOs) on AGEs. This eventually led the Taliban, who previously alleged that the casualty figures were caused by PGFs, to announce the creation of a 'special committee'[46] under the military commission of the Taliban to ensure that civilian losses are avoided.

The shocking rise in civilian casualties in 2013 reflects the 'changing dynamics of the conflict over the year'.[47] With the security transition process entering its fifth and final phase, international troops transferred virtually all security responsibilities to the ANSF, leaving 'security gaps in some areas that Afghan forces had not yet filled.'[48] As a result, certain areas became vulnerable to AGE attacks and this often led to civilian deaths and injuries.

Security Transition

On 18 June 2013, President Karzai launched the fifth and final tranche of the military transition process. Commenced in 2011, this process intended to set the required ground conditions needed for NATO-led ISAF to gradually withdrawing its forces ending the international military mission by the end of 2014. These conditions included a well-trained and equipped ANSF that could assume the lead, take the fight to the enemy and secure the population. The aim of the transition process is for Afghan forces to have the full responsibility for security across the country by the end of 2014. This target was set at the 2010 NATO Summit in Lisbon and confirmed by allied leaders at the Chicago Summit in May 2012.

[44] UNAMA, Afghanistan Annual Report 2013, 2.
[45] Ibid.
[46] Ibid., 5.
[47] Ibid., 13.
[48] Ibid., 13.

On track for full transition by the end of 2014, the ANSF assumed the responsibility of the remaining 91 districts, covering 11 provinces and 13 per cent of the population in 2013. By mid-year, they conducted 95 per cent of conventional operations and 98 per cent of special operations,[49] while NATO troops focused on 'force protection, route clearance and redeployment'.[50] International troop figures also continued to decrease in 2013, which reduced with the US pledging to reduce troop levels from nearly 70,000 to 34,000 by February 2014.[51] By next year, there will be just a little over 50,000 international troops in Afghanistan and they will be primarily responsible for advising 'the Afghan security ministries', the six army crops and the police zone headquarters'.[52] NATO-led ISAF's new role in Afghanistan will be centred on fill the 'capability gaps' that continue to exists within the ANSF.[53]

ANSF Achievements and Challenges

The ANSF have grown into a formidable force in the last 12 years showing that they can hold against the insurgency on their own, with limited ISAF support. 'ANSF capability is no longer the biggest uncertainty facing Afghanistan'[54] argues a recent US Department of Defence report. In May 2013, the Commander of ISAF General Dunford stated that he was 'optimistic'[55] that the Afghan forces would be able to take the lead security role in 2013 and assume full security responsibility by the end of 2014. In line with NATO's

[49] RT QUESTION MORE, 'Afghan Combat Deaths Nearly Double in 2013 Fighting Season, US Casualties Drop', November 2013, available online at http://rt.com/news/afghan-combat-deaths-double-2013-462/
[50] Ibid.
[51] K. Katzman, 'Afghanistan: Post-Taliban Governance, Security, and US Policy', *Congressional Research Service*, 23 October 2013, available online at http://fas.org/sgp/crs/row/RL30588.pdf
[52] U.S. Department of Defence, 'Report on Progress towards Security and Stability in Afghanistan,' p. 2.
[53] Ibid.
[54] Ibid., 5.
[55] K. Katzman, 'Afghanistan: Post-Taliban Governance, Security, and US Policy', p. 23.

decline, ANSF numbers have been gradually increasing over the years, as have been the number of operations carried out by them. There were approximately 340,632 Afghan army and police as of March 2014; this constitutes 97.4 per cent of the authorized end-strength target, 352,000.[56] Their strengths are evident in their ability to take speedy command and control of attacks and to retain their presence in tough and difficult regions transitioned to them.

In 2009, the Afghan Ministry of Interior had estimated that only 30 per cent of the country was actually under control of the government.[57] Presently, due to ANSF's growth, both in numbers and capabilities, the government retains the control of its 34 provincial capitals and major cities. This has led to pushing the insurgency away from populated areas where insurgent-initiated violence used to occur. Now, 80 per cent of the violence occurs in areas where only 25 per cent of the population live.[58] In the battle for the hearts and minds of the Afghan peoples, the ANSF have also been more successful than the insurgency. The Asia Foundation report shows that in 2013, 88 per cent of respondents said that they were confident in the ANA, and 72 per cent said that they were confident in the ANP; this marked an increase from previous years.[59] Winning over local support and sympathies, particularly in insecure regions, has helped the ANSF reverse many of the gains the insurgency had made in these areas. Local uprisings in 2012 and 2013 in Ghazni and Qandahar provinces, with the support of the ANSF, were able to dislodge the Taliban from various villages and districts in these provinces. These instances not only reflected local frustrations and sheer disapproval for the insurgency in these areas but also illustrated the level of trust and support the local populations had for the ANSF. The US Department of Defence report asserts that the ANSF have grown into a cohesive and confident forces showing 'progress in combined arms training, utilization of indirect fires systems and organic casualty evacuation'.[60] Nevertheless, despite substantial advancements, the ANSF continue to face several

[56] See note 52.
[57] Ibid.
[58] K. Katzman, 'Afghanistan: Post-Taliban Governance, Security, and US Policy', p. 22.
[59] The Asia Foundation, 'A Survey of the Afghan People,' 2013, p. 7.
[60] U.S. Department of Defence, 'Report on Progress towards Security and Stability in Afghanistan,' p. 23.

challenges such as logistical and sustainment capabilities, high attrition rates and corruption.[61]

The ANA face gaps in two critical areas, sustainment and the development of enabling capabilities. Both are considered imperative to the development of ANSF capabilities post-2014. While the majority of ANA units were field by the end of December 2013, they continue to face challenges in recruiting quality personnel and developing a logistics system. With the start of the transition process, focus was placed on meeting recruitment targets which helped boost the size of the army but did not provide it with the level of competency and skills required. Moreover, with attrition rates as high as 4.1 per cent[62] in the ANA and no 'critical mass' of ANSF recruits, many are worried about the risks this poses to the sustainability of the force in the future. The rate of desertion within the ANP was also similarly alarming. In the last three years, the attrition level in the ANP has remained at a rate of 25 per cent, increasing the need for high recruitments levels. However, the need for mass recruits to replenish losses has created a police force that suffers from an 80 per cent illiteracy level, entrenched corruption and drug use amongst personnel.[63] The lack of 'trained maintenance technicians and a logistics system'[64] has been another challenge for the ANA, preventing it from resupplying units in the field in a timely fashion. The absence of 'complex enabling support'[65] such as air support have also adversely affected the development of the ANA, impelling it to continue relying on ISAF for close air support, casualty evacuation, and logistics. Similar to the ANA, the Afghan Air Force

[61] U.S. Department of Defence, 'Report on Progress towards Security and Stability in Afghanistan,' p. 1.

[62] J. Owen, 'NATO Alarm over Afghan Army Crisis: Loss of Recruits Threatens Security as Handover Looms', *The Independent*, UK, 31 March 2013, available online at http://www.independent.co.uk/news/world/asia/nato-alarm-over-afghan-army-crisis-loss-of-recruits-threatens-security-as-handover-looms-8555238.html

[63] D. Planty and R. Perito, 'Police Transition in Afghanistan', United States Institute of Peace, *Special Report 322*, pp. 1–16, February 2013, available online at http://www.usip.org/sites/default/files/SR322.pdf.

[64] Ibid.

[65] U.S. Department of Defence, 'Report on Progress towards Security and Stability in Afghanistan,' p. 35.

(AAF) also face challenges in the maintenance and management of AAF Mi-17 fleets which hamper its ability to perform operation missions and the recruitment of qualified candidates to meet tactical requirements. The ANP too faces difficulties creating a self-sustained maintenance capacity and has to rely on a contract company for its maintenance requirements.

Although the ANSF were able to prevent the insurgency from making any territorial or kinetic gains, they were unable to break their resolve, decrease their influence in some rural areas or prevent them from carrying out attacks. Furthermore, the transfer of all security responsibilities to the ANSF in spite of its existing capacity gaps made the Afghan forces highly vulnerable to insurgent attacks in 2013. The insurgency was able to increased ANSF casualties by 79 per cent.[66] This resulted in further straining the ANSF which was already facing severe recruitment issues and high attrition levels. With both ANSF and civilian casualties on the rise, many questioned whether this was a result of ANSF's inability to secure and protect territory under their control or was it due to a rise in violence. This became even more difficult to assess when NATO stopped reporting on Taliban-initiated attacks claiming that they had 'come to realize that a simple tally of (attacks) is not the most complete measure of the campaign's progress'.[67] However, an evaluation of insurgent tactics used in 2013 could help to shed light on a few of the causes for the rise in both civilian and ANSF casualties.

Taliban Tactics

In both 2011 and 2013, the Taliban remained dependent on asymmetric warfare using the same tactics such as 'group and martyrdom seeking attacks, suicide attacks and assaults, group offensives, massed assaults; city attacks, ambushes and IED

---

[66] See note 49.
[67] Robert Burns, 'Coalition Will No Longer Publish Attack Figures.' *The Dalles Chronicle*, 5 March 2013, available online at http://www.thedalleschronicle.com/news/2013/mar/05/coalition-will-no-longer-publish-attack-figures/

attacks'.[68] Taliban targets also remained largely the same with foreign forces and their military bases, members of the government both civilian and military constituting their main targets. However, factors that differentiated in 2013 included less use of 'victim-activated pressure plate' IEDs (PP-IEDs) and more use of remote-controlled IEDs (RC-IEDs). In fact, civilian casualties resulting from RC-IEDs increased by 130 per cent in the first six months of 2013, while casualties from PP-IEDs reduced by only 24 per cent. Increased use of suicide and complex attacks including single individual wearing vests, driving vehicles charged with explosives and multiple suicide bombers that initiate complex attacks involving large numbers of fighters was also witnessed 2013. The use of insider attacks, which has posed a substantial threat in the last two years, was once again highlighted in the Taliban's 2013 'Spring Offensive', and is also a key tactic. Moreover, the use of surface-to-air missiles, turban bombs and even surgically sewn explosives also make up some of the newer tactics that the insurgency started using in 2012 and 2013.

The above comparison illustrates that the increase in civilian casualties has little to do with where the attacks are taking place and more to do with the severity and frequency of attacks. The rise in civilian casualties in 2013 demonstrates an increase in Taliban attacks and shows that the momentum of the Taliban has not been broken as often reported by the international community. Back in 2011, when NATO announced its timeline for withdrawal, experts argued that this would cause the Taliban to simply wait out foreign troops and then take over the country once they leave. However, the steady rise in conflict illustrates that the Taliban have done the opposite; moreover, many in Kabul now see the timeline as giving the Taliban a new resolve to paralyse the ANSF through persistent targeted attacks. By attacking ANSF forces, the Taliban seem to be attempting to increase the cost of war for the Afghan government. On a weekly basis, there are about 100 ANSF casualties[69] and the

---

[68] B. Roggio, 'Taliban Announce Beginning of Their "Spring Offensive"', *The Long War Journal*, 30 April 2011, available online at http://www.longwarjournal.org/archives/2011/04/taliban_announce_beg.php (accessed December 2013).

[69] M. Korosh, 'Aerial Attacks and Civilian Casualties', *Daily Outlook Afghanistan*, 8 December 2013, available online at http://outlookafghanistan.net/topics.php?post_id=8817

replenishment of each solider and their weapons system has had a substantial impact on the Afghan government's already flagging budget.

Narcotics Trade

This year also witnessed a rise in opium cultivation and trafficking, raising concerns 'that if the trend continued, opium would be the country's major economic activity after foreign military forces depart in 2014'.[70] The cultivation and trafficking of opium is one of the most serious non-traditional security threats that Afghanistan is facing today. Approximately, 90 per cent of the world's opium, most of which is processed into heroin, originate from Afghanistan. Farmer's in Afghanistan resort to poppy cultivation for a number of factors, the United Nations Office on Drugs and Crime (UNODC)'s 'Opium Risk Assessment 2013' found that the correlation 'between insecurity, lack of agricultural assistance and opium cultivation'[71] continued to exist despite years of counter measures. According to the UNODC 2013 report, 72 per cent[72] of the farmers produce opium due to its high sale price and 13 per cent of indicated poverty as the reason for their cultivation[73] The Taliban and other insurgent groups have been key contributors to the rise in opium cultivation. Reports reveal that the insurgency receives income from poppy cultivation, hashish cultivation and narcotics trafficking. Poppy cultivation and opium have provided a ready source of cash for the insurgency; the Afghan counter narcotic minister believes that in 2012 the Taliban earned approximately US$155 million from poppy production.

[70] R. Nordland,'Production of Opium by Afghans Is up Again', *New York Times*, 15 April 2013, available online at http://www.nytimes.com/2013/04/16/world/asia/afghanistan-opium-production-increases-for-3rd-year.html?_r=0.
[71] United Nations Office on Drugs and Crime (UNODC), '*Afghanistan Opuim Survey 2013, Summary Findings*, November 2013, p. 25, available online at http://www.unodc.org/documents/crop-monitoring/Afghanistan/Afghan_report_Summary_Findings_2013.pdf
[72] UNODC, '*Afghanistan Opuim Survey 2013*, p. 22.
[73] Ibid.

There is a clear correlation between the steady rise in insecurity and poppy cultivation in Afghanistan over the last 13 years. For instance in 2011, cultivation was just 8 kg hc^{-1}, but by 2004, it reached 131 kg hc^{-1}, and then by 2007, it peaked to 193 kg hc^{-1} (Basar, 2012).[74] Moreover, by 2011–2012, poppy cultivation started to increase again and not only in the Southern regions but also in the northern, north-eastern, eastern and western regions, some of which were previously declared poppy-free zones.[75] Interestingly, 70 per cent of opium production in 2013 actually came from the three provinces where the Obama troop surge had occurred in.[76] Moreover, in Afghanistan the narcotics industry has exacerbated corruption and impaired the Afghan economy. The amount of money involved in drugs and bribes is equivalent to approximately a quarter of the countries licit gross domestic product. The Afghan government and its international allies' attempts at curbing opium cultivation continue to fail as the cultivation of opium growth continues to increase in insecure areas where NATO and ANSF have been unable to penetrate.

The Bilateral Security Agreement (BSA)

'A stable, democratic, and secure Afghanistan is a US national interests' asserted Dobbins in his remarks before the Senate foreign relations committee on December 2013.[77] Though US has not so far been able to meet these objectives, they did, however, set the stage for it at the London Conference in 2010 where they laid out three prerogatives. The London Conference outlined a military transition from NATO-led ISAF to Afghan forces that ran in parallel to a two-tier peace process, facilitated by a civilian transition that would have the Afghan government extend control

---

[74] Eray Baser, 'Illicit Drugs & Afghanistan', *Counter-Narcotics in Afghanistan*. Civil-Military Fusion Centre, pp. 1–71, available online at http://reliefweb.int/sites/reliefweb.int/files/resources/CFC_Afghanistan-Counter-Narcotics-Volume_Aug2012.pdf

[75] See note 72.

[76] See note 71.

[77] See note 25.

over half of all international aid. These processes were intended to establish a strong and effective security sector, capable state institutions and an aid-independent economy. However, in 2013, the international community concluded that these objectives would not be attainable without continued international development and military assistance after 2014.

The BSA between the US and Afghan government is a decade-long security deal that is envisioned to help secure Afghanistan security sector in the post-2014 period. This agreement has been under negotiation for most of 2013, and though it was supposed to be signed in the latter part of the year, it still remains unsigned and under debate by Karzai's administration. The BSA would ensure that the US continues its contribution to the ANSF by offering approximately US$4.1 billion towards the ANSF annually. It would also mandate the size and shape of the US military presence after 2014. The initial negotiations on the BSA started in October 2012, and it was supposed to be a yearlong debate before it was to be finalized by October 2013. However, negotiations stalled at many intervals by the Afghan government who disagreed over the 'US demand for legal immunities for US troops, the authorities of US troops and Afghan demands for security guarantees against any hostile threats that may emanate from Pakistan'.[78] While the US and Afghan government eventually resolved most of these issues, what, however, remained unresolved was the issue of legal immunities for US troops and night raids.

As disagreements over these two issues flowed into the latter part of the year, some experts began to suggest that the US may eventually decide to withdraw all troops and support by 2014, foregoing the BSA. Others felt that Karzai would eventually sign the agreement once a *Loya Jirga* (Grand Council) endorses the BSA which was a mechanism suggested by the Afghan government to settle the dispute over the BSA with the US. Thus, a *Loya Jirga* was held in November and the results of the 2500-member *Jirga* led to the endorsement of the BSA and to many people's surprise called on the government to promptly sign the security pact. However, in what seemed to be an impromptu change of mind by Karzai, he

---

[78] Katzman, K., 'Afghanistan: Post-Taliban Governance, Security, and US Policy', p. 25.

refused to sign the BSA until after national elections in April 2014. Moreover, at the concluding session of the *Jirga*, he stipulated three new conditions for the US to meet in order to him to sign the BSA and they included ensuring 'transparent elections in April, no raids on Afghan homes and a breakthrough in talks with the Taliban'.[79] Karzai announced that if the US conducted one more night raid on an Afghan home, his government would step out of the BSA; he said if the US did not bring peace and reconciliation to Afghanistan, he would not sign the BSA as it was the overall objective of the agreement, and he said if the BSA did not ensure speedy elections, he would not sign the BSA.

The majority of Afghans believe that the BSA is essential to Afghanistan's future stability as it will provide much needed resources and support for the ANSF, but there are some others including the insurgency who believe it to represent a 'submission to the US which proves the Kabul government is nothing more than an American vassal'.[80] On 18 November, Dr Rangin Dadfar, Afghan National Security Advisor, revealed taped conversations between individuals in Kabul, namely the Member of Parliament, Haji Fareed, and the political analyst, Wahid Muzhda, collaborating with the Taliban to hold anti-BSA protests in Kabul. While it is not a secret that the Taliban have denounced the security pact, arguing that it would ensure close military relations between Afghanistan and the US in the years following NATO's withdrawal, it came as a surprise to many to discover collaborations between Afghan MP, member of civil society members and the insurgency. 'We can call them a spy, we can label them a traitor ... those who betray the country and hand over Afghanistan's future must be punished', asserted MP Naheed Farid[81] which echoed the majority of local sentiments concerning this revelation. However, what has proved to be more concerning has been President Karzai's lack of support the BSA which he claims the

[79] See note 12.
[80] Ibrahimkhail, S., 'Anti-BSA Quetta Shura Collaboration Sparks Outrage', *TOLO News*, 18 November 2013, available online at http://www.tolonews.com/en/afghanistan/12779-anti-bsa-quetta-shura-collaboration-sparks-outrage
[81] Ibid.

signing of represent 'an attack on Afghanistan's national pride' and one that will be out of 'desperation instead of free will'. Karzai's hesitancy in signing the BSA has garnered him much criticism and protest from political parties, members of parliament, civil society and groups alike which claim that he is acting 'irrationally, contradicting previous statements in which he has maintained the Taliban peace process and April elections must be entirely Afghan-led and managed'.[82] The future of BSA continues to remain uncertain and this has increased local fears and anxieties about what the future of their country might look like in the absence of the BSA.

The Peace and Reconciliation Process

In June 2010, a National Consultative Peace Jirga was held to determine how the government was to implement its peace and reconciliation strategy. The Peace Jirga brought together over 1,600 delegates to debate and design a plan of action for the Afghan government to start formal peace talks with the insurgency. The result of the Jirga was a plan that laid out the first steps towards a formal peace process in Afghanistan. The peace process has taken place at two levels and with two pillars: a reconciliation (national level) pillar and reintegration (subnational level) pillar. Reconciliation aimed for high-level negotiations between the Taliban leadership and the government and international community. Reintegration aimed at low-level disarmament efforts that aimed to entice foot soldiers with job programmes and other economic incentives. The peace process also set three conditions that would need to be accepted by the insurgents in order to be start talks which included renouncing violence, accepting the Afghan Constitution and severing ties with al Qaeda and all other international terrorist organizations. The entire process was led by the High Peace Council (HPC), a body of 70 appointed members. In addition to overseeing the reconciliation pillar, the HPC's subnational arm the Provincial Peace Committees were

---

[82] See note 12.

designed to oversee their integration pillar. The Jirga had also redesign reintegration efforts in the form of the Afghan Peace and Reintegration Programme (APRP), which is implemented at the subnational level to encourage to insurgents to disarm and reintegrate back into their communities.

The peace process is intended to consolidate the gains made in the security transition process. However, while there have been some gains in the reintegration pillar, the reconciliation pillar has continued to face difficulties. Contrary to the reconciliation pillar, the reintegration programme had reintegrated 6,662 foot soldiers and collected 5,442 weapons by the end of December 2013.[83] The APRP, which facilitates the reintegration pillar, has been largely responsible for this as it has implemented a framework that sees that reintegrees are provided with various incentives such as a small stipend, short-term employment opportunities, a chance to join the community police forces and prioritized reintegree communities for development projects. The reconciliation pillar, on the other hand, did witness some progress in the early part of 2013 but soon after it hit a roadblock following claims by Karzai that the US was taking hostage of a process that was supposed to be Afghan-led.

On 11 January 2013, both President Karzai and Obama announced their support for the formal opening of a Taliban office in Qatar. Though 11 months later, Karzai revealed during the BSA Jirga that he, in fact, had not been particularly happy about opening of an office in Qatar. Nonetheless, after the announcement in January, Karzai visited Qatar twice, first in March and then again in June, to discuss the opening of the office and more importantly to stress on the point that talks with the Taliban should be channelled through the HPC and not just remain a US–Taliban channel. Consequently, Karzai's led to the inauguration of the Taliban office on 18 June. At the time of opening their political office, the Taliban also issued a statement 'refusing future ties to international terrorists groups and expressing a willingness to eventually transition to Afghan government–Taliban talks'.[84]

---

[83] United Nations Development Program (UNDP). Afghanistan Peace and Reintegration Programme (APRP), available online at http://www.af.undp.org/content/afghanistan/en/home/operations/projects/crisis_prevention_and_recovery/aprp/

[84] Katzman, K., 'Afghanistan: Post-Taliban Governance, Security, and US Policy', p. 41.

However, this achievement was short lived as Taliban violated a reported understanding between them, the US and the Qatari government, by placing a plaque with the name 'Islamic Emirate' of Afghanistan written on it. This caused the Afghan government to immediately renounce the office describing the plaque to represent an intention by the Taliban of creating an entity separate from the government of Afghanistan and accused the US of having a part of this. One day after the inauguration, Karzai said that his government would 'not pursue peace talks with the Taliban unless the United States steps out of the negotiations'.[85] This issue also led Karzai to temporarily break off negotiation on the BSA which prompted the US and Qatari officials to compel the Taliban to remove the plaque promptly. The office was reportedly closed in mid-July, though Taliban officials are said to have remained in Qatar where they still hold informal discussions with foreign officials and members of the Afghan government.

There have been many reports of indirect talks taking place between the Afghan government and the Taliban in 2013. Karzai confirmed active talks were taking place between his government and the hardliners of the Taliban in as late as October.[86] Additionally, while official talks have not yet restarted, various confidence-building measures have been taken place this year to help talks move forward from the informal to the formal channel. A major measure that was taken by the Afghan government this year was the release of dozens of Taliban prisoners held in prison facilities across the country. The government justified most of these releases by claiming that most of the prisoners had either already been acquitted but were still being kept illegally or that they had no substantial evidence keeping them in prison. This was entrenched in a presidential decree passed on 16 February that stipulated that all prisoners being unlawfully held must be released immediately. Some Afghan officials, parliamentarians and CSO members believe that such efforts, particularly those that provide assurances of security for Taliban

---

[85] Ottawa Citizen, 'Karzai Won't Pursue Peace Talks With Taliban Unless the U.S. Steps Out of the Negotiations', *Ottawa Citizen*, 19 June 2013, available online at http://blogs.ottawacitizen.com/2013/06/19/karzai-wont-pursue-peace-talks-with-taliban-unless-the-u-s-steps-out-of-the-negotiations/

[86] See note 21.

leaders who are willing to reconcile, will eventually yield to a political settlement but they remain a minority. Most Afghans feel that the release of Taliban prisoners has only strengthened the insurgency, and they are worried that Karzai is starting to shift the focus of reconciliation away from the goal of reaching a political settlement to now trying to agree on a power-sharing arrangement.

Since 2012, there have been speculations that the Afghan government has been moving away from achieving a political settlement to a power-sharing arrangement with the insurgency. This was initially observed in the 'roadmap to 2015' developed by the HPC and presented to Pakistan in November of 2012. Following this, in 2013, Karzai was witnessed not only encouraging the Taliban to participate in the upcoming elections but also confirming that certain positions in the government were being offered to them. 'They [Taliban] are Afghans. Where the Afghan president, the Afghan government can appoint the Taliban to a government job they are welcome.... But where it's the Afghan people appointing people through elections to state organs then the Taliban should come and participate in elections', asserted Karzai during his interview with the BBC.[87] Though the Taliban rejected participating in the upcoming elections, they did too showed a gradual change in their attitude towards peace talks when in the summer of 2013 as part of their Eid statement they claimed to no longer seek 'a monopoly of power but rather an inclusive government, and back modern education'.[88]

Pakistan had tried to play more supportive role in the peace process in 2013. Following Karzai's visit on 26–27 August, Pakistan released seven moderate senior Taliban figures as the sign of cooperation. Following this, Pakistan also released the highest profile Taliban figure from Pakistani detention, Mullah Abdul Ghani Baradar, who was captured in 2010. The release of Baradar came after almost three years of lobbying by the Afghan government to convince Pakistani authorities to release him. Baradar, who was considered a close aid of Mullah Omar, has been described

---

[87] Hakimi. Y., 'Afghanistan's Hamid Karzai Says NATO Caused Great Suffering', *BBC News World*, 7 October 2013, available online at http://www.bbc.co.uk/news/world-24433433
[88] See note 85.

as being supportive of talks between the Afghan government and the Taliban leadership and was thought to have been arrested before he could facilitate talks. However, while Baradar was officially released on 22 September, Pakistani officials are still keeping him under house arrest. Thus far, there has only been one recorded instance of a meeting that took place between Baradar and Afghan authorities, which was only arranged three months after the date of his supposed release. Towards the end of the year, it became apparent that the Afghan and Pakistani authorities had actually made little establishing trust and cooperation. This was further reinforced when on 15 December, Pakistan's top Security Advisor Sartaj Aziz claimed that the Pakistani government's efforts to bring the Taliban to the negotiation table could do little to yield positive results when the Taliban refuse to recognize the regime in Kabul.

Some believe that there are substantial chances for a political settlement between insurgent leaders and the Afghan government and/or the reintegration of insurgent fighters into society. However, for the sake of ensuring immediate peace during the security transition process and upcoming elections in April 2014, the Afghan government and its international partners may inevitably deliberate compromises that might produce backsliding on human rights, call for the revision of the Constitution and even possibly incorporate groups such as the Haqqani network and Hizb-e-Islami into the key positions of authority. Such a scenario would not only jeopardize the achievements of the international community but also potentially give rise to an internal conflict driven by ethno-political interests.

Conclusion

The government of Afghanistan and its international partners have been trying to engage systematically to stabilize parts of the country with a mix of security, political and economic initiatives. However, security and political trends illustrate that stability in parts of the country is fragile at best. Key trends observed this year show a significant increase in Taliban attacks, civilian and ANSF casualties and opium cultivation and trafficking. Furthermore, while resources and attention have been diverted to facilitating these three processes, little or no systematic approach has been taken to quantify, understand and mitigate the impact these processes are having on people's basic human security needs. If the number of civilian casualties has any reflection of the level of violence that ensured in 2013, we could determine that it was possibly one of the worst years in the Afghan war. The outcomes of the military transition process and peace and reconciliation initiative have many in Afghanistan fearing the worst for 2014 as it marks the last year of the international peace-building mission in Afghanistan. Whereas some believe that it is the right time for Afghans to assume full ownership, most fear that government institutions and the ANSF are incapable of maintaining political stability and security after the withdrawal of the international community.

3

Armed Conflicts in Pakistan 2013: Continuing Violence despite Changes in Leadership

D. *Suba Chandran and Ayesha Khanyari*

During 2013, the violence in Pakistan led by the armed non-state actors continued unabated, as had been the case in the previous years. Though the statistics would reveal a decline in terms of numbers, the intensity of conflict remained the same. The successful elections for the National Assembly and the four provincial assemblies during the year had raised a lot of expectations within Pakistan in terms of addressing the multiple theatres of violence within the country.

As had been the case in the previous years, the violence and armed conflicts were not concentrated in a single geographic expanse within Pakistan. Though there were focussed attacks in the Federally Administered Tribal Areas (FATA), Khyber Pakhtunkhwa (KP) and Karachi, the rest of Pakistan also witnessed violence, including multiple suicide attacks.

The government at the national level led by the Pakistan Muslim League (Nawaz) (PML-N), supported by an All Parties Conference (APC) and a debate within the Parliament, decided to initiate a new round of negotiations with the Tehrik-e-Taliban Pakistan (TTP) in 2013. Though the assassination of Hakimullah Mehsud, Chief of the TTP, in a drone attack was a temporary setback to this initiative, as could be seen in the beginning of 2014, the government and political leadership appeared all set to initiate a new round of negotiations.

What was significant in 2013 was the change in leadership at every level of conflict—both in terms of those perpetrating the violence and those fighting against the same. The elections to national and provincial assemblies resulted in new governments at both the levels. The Pakistan People's Party (PPP) government was replaced by the PML-N at the federal level, while the Awami National Party (ANP) was replaced by the Pakistan Tehreek-e-Insaf (PTI) in KP. General Kayani's term ended during the year and he was replaced with General Raheel Sharif as the new Chief of Army Staff (COAS) of Pakistan.[1] There was a leadership change within the non-state actors as well; a drone attack in the second half of 2013 resulted in the assassination of Hakimullah Mehsud and his being replaced by Mullah Fazlullah.

Armed Conflict in Pakistan: Major Actors

Major actors of the armed conflict in Pakistan can be classified into three broad categories: state, non-state and external actors. Within these three actors, there are further sub-actors with specific objectives. Neither the state actors nor the non-state actors of the armed conflict in Pakistan are a monolith.

State Actors: Federal Government, Provincial Governments and the Military

The state actors can be divided into three major parts: the federal government led by the PML-N, provincial governments, especially that of KP and Sindh, and the military, along with its Interservices Intelligence (ISI).

---

[1] For an analysis of this change, see Rana Banerji, 'Pakistan: The Military Shuffle and Consolidation under the New Chief', IPCS Commentary no. 4226, 26 December 2013, available online at http://www.ipcs.org/article/pakistan/pakistan-the-military-shuffle-and-consolidation-under-the-new-chief-4226.html

In 2013, the federal government, led by its new Prime Minister Nawaz Sharif, made it clear that it would go slow on military operations vis-à-vis the Pakistani Taliban and pursue negotiations with them instead. To a large extent, there was no significant transformation in the government's approach in 2013 when compared to that of the previous government led by the PPP.

Immediately after the elections, Sharif made a statement: 'All options should be tried, and guns are not a solution to all problems.... Why shouldn't we sit and talk, engage in dialogue?',[2] which formed the basis of his government's approach in 2013. He also promised that the federal government would assist the respective provincial governments in addressing the issue of violence and conflict.[3]

The provincial governments, especially those of the KP and Sindh, have also been proactive in addressing the violence. For KP, the danger and threat was clear and present, while for Sindh, it was primarily focussed on Karachi. Though there was violence inside Balochistan as well, most of it was sectarian, led by Sunni militants against the Shia community, rather than between the non-state actors and the state. Though there were numerous blasts and related incidents within Balochistan, they were not spectacular and not in the form of armed conflicts.

The military was the third major state actor within Pakistan. Though there was a new COAS by the end of 2013,[4] there were no drastic changes in the military's approach towards violence and armed conflict within Pakistan.

Non-state Actors: Afghan Taliban, Pakistani Taliban and Al Qaeda

The non-state actors can be classified into three groups: the Afghan Taliban, the TTP and the Al Qaeda. While the Al Qaeda's presence has considerably weakened within Pakistan, the other two non-state actors are very much present within the country.

[2] 'Nawaz Sharif Calls for Taliban Talks', *Dawn*, 22 May 2013.
[3] 'No Harm in Talking to Taliban: Nawaz Sharif', *Express Tribune*, 21 May 2013.
[4] 'Lt. Gen. Raheel Sharif Chosen as New Army Chief', *Dawn*, 28 November 2011.

The Afghan Taliban is not a monolith. Broadly, there are two factions of the Afghan Taliban—Quetta Shura, led by Mullah Omar, and the Haqqani Network, led by the Haqqanis.

The Quetta Shura, perhaps the stronger of the Afghan Taliban factions, is also more independent vis-à-vis Pakistan's military and intelligence leadership. Though they do not target the Pakistani military and political leadership overtly, their support to local Taliban groups within Pakistan is significant.[5] In particular, there have been numerous reports within Pakistan that the selection of the new TTP leader—Mullah Fazlullah—was supported by Mullah Omar of the Afghan Taliban.[6]

The Haqqani Network, another faction of the Afghan Taliban, though organizing its operations in the eastern provinces of Afghanistan, is well present within Pakistan.[7] It is widely believed that the network has linkages with the Pakistani military and ISI.[8]

---

[5] For an analysis of the Quetta Shura, see the following: 'The Quetta Shura: A Tribal Analysis', available online at http://www.tribalanalysiscenter.com/PDF-TAC/Quetta%20Shura.pdf; David Clark Scott, 'What's the Quetta Shura Taliban and Why Does It Matter?' *Christian Science Monitor*, 24 February 2010.

[6] See Amir Mir, 'Fazlullah Has Mulla Omar's Backing', *News*, 9 November 2013; 'Fazlullah's Appointment Backed by Mullah Omar: Report', *Dawn*, 12 November 2013.

[7] For an analysis of the Haqqani Network, see Jeffrey Dressler, 'The Haqqani Network: From Pakistan to Afghanistan', available online at http://www.understandingwar.org/sites/default/files/Haqqani_Network_0.pdf

[8] Quoting multiple references and statements, Dressler in the above-mentioned report provides the linkages between the two. According to him, Haqqani's connection with the ISI dates back to the times of the Soviet Jihad. According to US Special Envoy and Ambassador to Afghanistan (1989-1992), Peter Tomsen, the ISI has maintained its Jihad-era ties with Haqqani. Right after the US invasion in October 2001, Haqqani was invited to Islamabad for talks about a post-Taliban government. In a transcript passed on to Mike McConnell, the Director of National Intelligence, in May 2008, Pakistan's Army Chief General Ashfaq Kayani was heard referring to Haqqani as 'a strategic asset'. A top ISI official was reported to have held talks with Sirajuddin Haqqani, one of Jalaluddin's sons who has replaced him as the leader of the movement due to his father's ill health, in Miranshah of North Waziristan in early March 2009. In a prisoner exchange with Pakistani Taliban led by Baitullah Mehsud, the Pakistani government released

The TTP is the most important non-state actor within Pakistan. There was a substantial change within the Pakistani Taliban in the second half of 2013 when a US drone attack resulted in the assassination of Hakimullah Mehsud.

Armed Conflict in 2013: Major Trends

In 2013, there was a decrease in violence and terrorist-related activities all over Pakistan in terms of the number of attacks and casualties. The total number of fatalities recorded in terrorist violence in Pakistan was 5,379 as compared to 6,211 in the previous year. As identified in earlier ACSA editions, FATA remains the most violent region in Pakistan, followed by Sindh and Balochistan (see Figure 3.1). KP was fourth on the list in terms

Figure 3.1:
Violence profile—Pakistan 2013: Fatalities (region-wise)

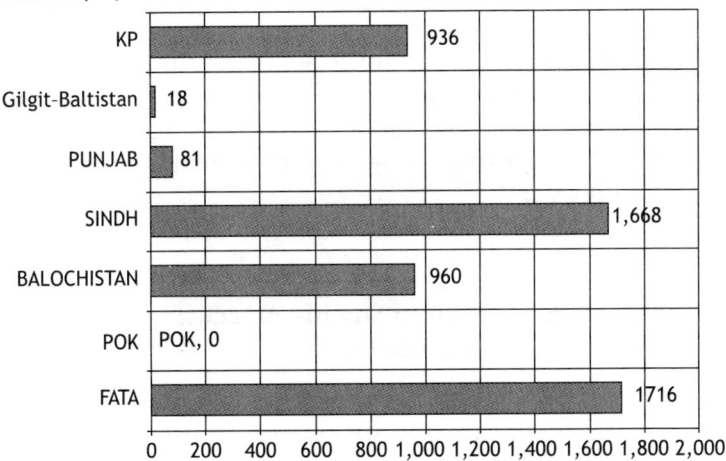

---

three family members of the Haqqani family in November 2007 – Haqqani's brother Khalil Ahmad, son Dr Fazl-i-Haqqani and brother-in-law Ghazi Khan. Haqqani is said to have mediated peace deals between the Pakistani government and Waziri and Mehsudi commanders of the Pakistani Taliban in North and South Waziristan.

Figure 3.2:
Suicide attacks in Pakistan (2002-2013)

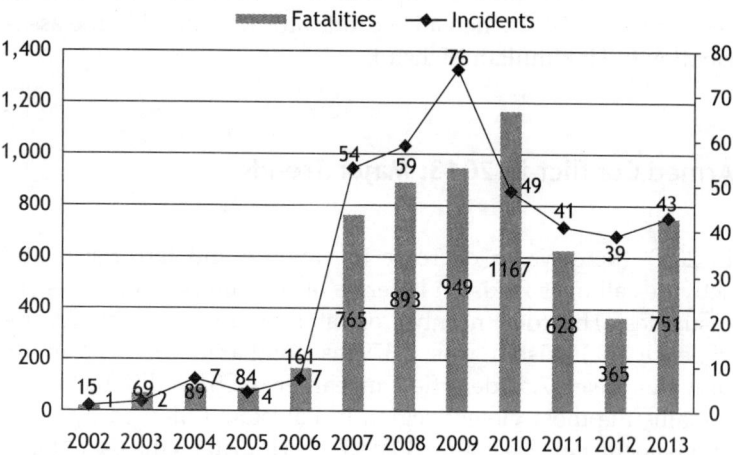

of intensity of violence. Punjab Province remained at its earlier position, the fifth, and Gilgit-Baltistan, along with Pakistan-occupied Kashmir (POK) remained the least affected.

Increase in suicide attacks in KP and Balochistan, decrease in drone attacks in FATA, spread of sectarian violence to parts of southern Punjab, targeting of minorities in Quetta and the rising graph of TTP's attacks were some of the major trends in the armed conflicts in 2013.

Considerable Escalation in Suicide Attacks: KP Continues to Be the Centre

A comparative analysis of the suicide attacks in Pakistan revealed that the highest numbers of suicide attacks were carried out in 2009. There was a rise in the number of suicide attacks from 2007 to 2009, with 76 attacks recorded in 2009 alone (see Figure 3.2). Subsequent years saw a decline in the number of attacks in 2010–2013. However, 2013 again saw a rise in the number of suicide attacks in Pakistan with KP as the prime target.

Violence Profile: KP to POK

According to figures, 48 per cent of the suicide attacks were carried out in KP where 21 out of the 43 attacks killed 350 people and injured 635. In KP, the most affected district was the capital city, Peshawar. Out of the 21 attacks on KP, nine were carried out in Peshawar. Four attacks were recorded in Hangu District, three in Bannu District, two in Mardan, two in Lakki Marwat District, one in Dera Ismail Khan and one in Swat District.

The most deadly suicide attack was carried out on 22 September 2014 at the All Saints Church in Peshawar which resulted in the death of 83 people and injured 145. There were two suicide attackers who blew themselves up after the service ended in the Church near Qissa Khawani bazaar in Peshawar, which is the provincial capital of KP. The attack was the worst that the community faced in Pakistan's history. There were huge protests and people were out on the streets in Islamabad, Lahore, Karachi and Peshawar shouting that the government had failed to protect the minorities in the state against hate attacks. In the past, Shiites have been the target of militant attacks; now the focus seems to have shifted to other religious sects.

The number of suicide attacks in KP this year were more lethal than last year. Though the number of attacks remained the same, the killings increased from 140 to 350 in 2013, which amounts to 60 per cent increase in deaths and 58 per cent increase in injuries. As identified in 2013 ACSA book, KP continues to remain the key target of suicide terrorism this year also.

The second highest number of suicide attacks in 2013 were carried out in Balochistan where 233 people were killed and 407 injured in nine such incidents. The most affected district of the province remained Quetta where six out of nine attacks were carried out.

The third highest number of suicide attacks were carried out in FATA, killing 164 people in nine such incidents. The most fatal attack was carried out in Kurram Agency of FATA where 62 people were killed and 180 others were injured in coordinated twin attacks in Parachinar. There were a total of nine incidents of suicide attacks this year, killing 256 people, mainly concentrated in the North Waziristan Agency (NWA). Out of the eight attacks in FATA, five took place in NWA and one each in Bajour, Kurram and South Waziristan, respectively.

Karachi, as in the previous year, bore the brunt of heightened terrorist activity in Sindh. On 17 January 2013, militants killed Syed Manzar Imam, the Member of Provisional Assembly (MPA) from the Muttahida Quami Movement (MQM), in Orange Town area of Karachi, the provincial capital of Sindh. Militants also attacked an MQM rally, killing four people and injuring 50 others. For the past two years, TTP cadres have been targeting MQM workers who want to *free* the people of Karachi from their *suppression*. While ANP activists in Sindh were the prime targets last year, this year, MQM earned the TTP's wrath.

Punjab and POK remained the least affected areas. Punjab recorded one such attack which was carried out in Rawalpindi on an *Imam Bargah*, killing four people and injuring several others. POK remained the least affected in terms of suicide attacks in the year 2013.

In 2013, majority of the suicide attacks were against the military and paramilitary forces. The major targets this year were prayer places and funeral gatherings—mosques and Imam Bargahs were targeted along with a church in Peshawar. Attacks on political parties continued in 2013 as well. Major political parties such as the PPP, the ANP, PTI and the National People's Party (NPP) lost activists, workers and leaders to terrorism-related violence. Hospitals, universities and courts were also targeted in Quetta and Peshawar. Senior officers, ministers and leaders of political parties were other major targets. Statistics reveal that the overall effectiveness of suicide attacks improved in 2013 in terms of target selection and execution of successful attacks.

US Drone Attacks in 2013 and Pakistan's Duplicity

There was a remarkable decline in drone strikes in Pakistan in 2013. Since 2005, drone strikes had killed 2,594 people in Pakistan in 286 such incidents, including both suspected militants and civilians. The highest numbers of drone attacks were recorded

Figure 3.3:
Drone attacks in Pakistan: 2005-2013

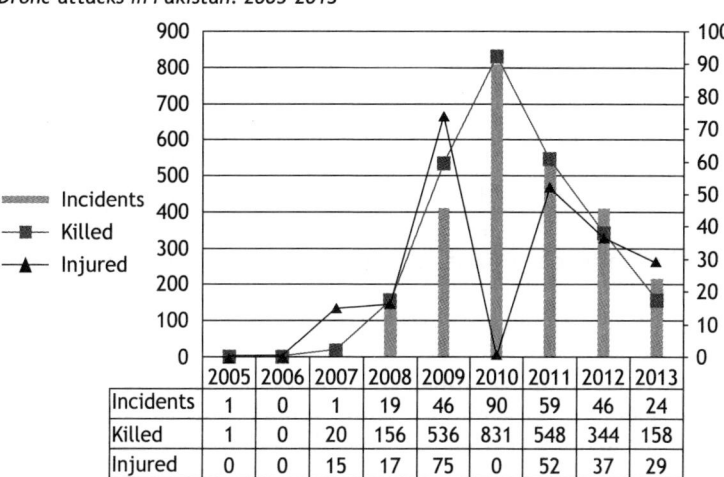

	2005	2006	2007	2008	2009	2010	2011	2012	2013
Incidents	1	0	1	19	46	90	59	46	24
Killed	1	0	20	156	536	831	548	344	158
Injured	0	0	15	17	75	0	52	37	29

in 2010 when 90 strikes killed 831 people and injured more than 85 (see Figure 3.3). Ever since, there has been a decline in the number of drone strikes. In 2013, the Central Intelligence Agency (CIA) carried out only 24 attacks, the lowest since 2008.

Drone attacks continue to be concentrated in NWA and South Waziristan Agency (SWA), especially in NWA where 16 of the 24 attacks were recorded in 2013. There were four attacks in SWA and one in Kurram Agency of FATA. The drone attacks were extended beyond FATA this year to KP, hitting a seminary in Hangu District. The spiritual leader of the Haqqani Network, Maulana Ahmed Jan, was killed amongst the eight suspected militants.

In the first quarter of 2013, the CIA intensified its drone strikes in Pakistan and carried out five attacks in the first 10 days of January in NWA and SWA. As discussed in earlier volumes, drone attacks this year also were focused on leadership neutralization. On 3 January 2013, the first drone attack of the year killed Deputy Chief of TTP Maulvi Nazir Wazir near the capital of Wana in South Waziristan. In the next quarter, the number of drone strikes was reduced to one or two strikes per month. September and November saw three strikes per month.

On 1 November 2013, US drone strikes killed Chief of TTP Hakimullah Mehsud along with five others in Dandy Parakhel area in NWA in FATA. He was TTP's Commander in Khyber, Kurram and Orakzai agencies. In 2013, after Nawaz Sharif came to power, he had raised the issue of drones at the UN General Assembly. He had made efforts to have a fresh round of peace talks with the home-grown insurgents, the TTP. However, his assassination was said to have sabotaged the peace negotiations. In October 2013, Amnesty International and Human Rights Watch produced a joint report which held the United States responsible for violating international law and accused it of committing war crimes in Pakistan.[9]

> The issue of drone strikes will always be under the scanner for legitimacy because the covert programme is carried out in the shadows of international law. The legality of the issue will always be contested. The US will be charged with human rights violation and breach of Pakistan's sovereignty, and Pakistan for its complicity.[10]

The TTP has time and again plotted against the Pakistani army and government and conducted attacks with devastating effects on the lives of innocent civilians. Ironically, the death of Mehsud was not openly welcomed by Pakistani pundits. Chaudhary Nisar Ali, Pakistan's interior minister, accused the US of disrupting peace talks with Taliban. The media further heightened anti-American sentiments. Bill Roggio, who monitors drone strikes at the Long War Journal, remarked, 'Even those of us who watch Pakistan closely don't know where they stand anymore. It's such a double game.'[11]

Pakistan's duplicity on the drone attacks continued this year as well and no coherent stand was taken.

---

[9] 'US Drone Strikes in Pakistan', report by Amnesty International, London, 2013, available online at http://www.amnesty.org/en/library/asset/ASA33/013/2013/en/041c08cb-fb54-47b3-b3fe-a72c9169e487/asa330132013en.pdf (accessed 30 December 2013).

[10] Ayesha Khanyari, 'Pakistan: Double Speak on Drones', 2013, available online at www.ipcs.org

[11] Bill Roggio, 'Drone Drama', *The Long War Journal*, 1 November 2013.

Figure 3.4:
Sectarian violence in Pakistan

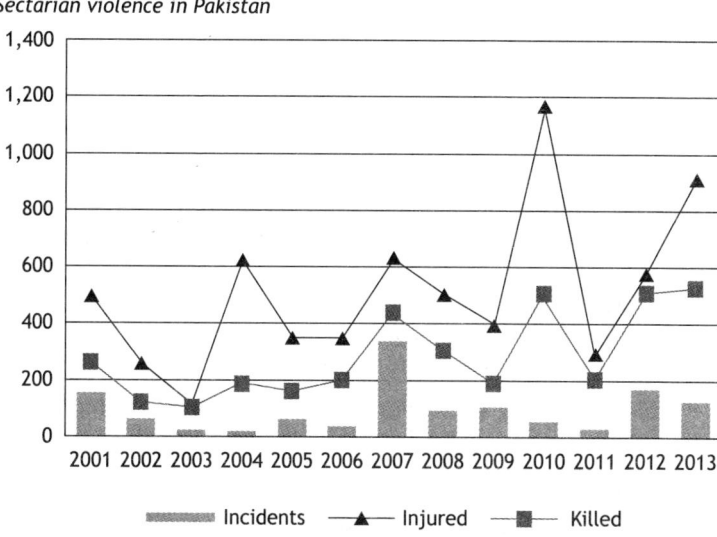

Sectarian Violence in Pakistan

A total of 128 attacks were recorded this year, causing 525 fatalities (see Figure 3.4). Although sectarian groups are active and defiant all across the country, in 2013, Karachi, Quetta and South Punjab were the most volatile regions.

Key Actors Currently Engaging in Sectarian Violence in Pakistan

> Ahle Sunnat Wal Jamaat (ASWJ): The ASWJ is the new face of the banned sectarian organization Sipah-e-Sahaba Pakistan (SSP). It is a Sunni sectarian-cum-political group, and targets mostly Shias and Barelvi groups whom it considers as infidels. Though the ASWJ has been banned since May 2012, it is somehow still very much active and operational.
> Lashkar-e-Jhangvi (LeJ): LeJ is another sectarian organization active in Karachi, Quetta and southern Punjab. Their prime target has been the Hazaras of Balochistan. It is primarily an

offshoot of SSP and shares operational and ideological ties with Al Qaeda and the TTP.

Tehrik-e-Taliban Pakistan (Pakistani Taliban): The TTP can also be credited for the current resurgence in sectarian violence as it has taken blame for many of the attacks in 2013. It is a coalition of militant groups willing to overthrow the state and impose Shariah.

Sipah-e-Muhammad Pakistan (SMP): The group has resurfaced in the recent years and is most active in Karachi and Lahore.

In addition to these four major actors, the Sunni Tehrik—working to defend the Barelvi Sunnis and many new organizations such as the Jundullah, an anti-Shia militant group—are also coming up.

Sindh continues to be home to the most violent sectarian killings. More than 75 per cent of the attacks were carried out in Sindh, followed by Balochistan, KP and FATA. In Sindh, Karachi remains the epicentre of sectarian attacks. More than 80 attacks were carried out in Karachi. Last year, 507 people were killed in 173 attacks. Though the number of incidents have decreased, more fatalities were recorded due to targeted killings, aggravating the ethnic fault lines. In 2013, political leaders, the military and police, clerics, tribal leaders and schools remained the prime targets for militant organizations. The worst hit was civilians belonging to other sects, such as doctors, students and clerics. A cycle of tit-for-tat sectarian killings, mainly between the LeJ and the ASWJ, sparked ethno-political violence with various sectarian outfits contributing to the growth. Disputes over mosques, routes for Ashura and Eid-un-Nabi processions, allotment of plots for religious purposes, etc., triggered a series of attacks.

In keeping with last year's trends, majority of sectarian violence this year has occurred between Shias and Sunnis, but violent incidents between the Barelvi and Deobandi sub-sects of Sunni Islam were also recorded; three prominent Deobandi clerics identified as Mufti Abdul Majeed Dinpuri (50), Mufti Muhammad Saleh (40) and Ehsan Ali Shah (29) were shot dead within the precincts of Tipu Sultan Police Station in Karachi. Targeted attacks were also carried out on the Bohra community in Karachi.[12]

---

[12] David Montero, 'Shiite–Sunni Conflict Rises in Pakistan', *Christian Science Monitor*, 2 February 2007.

In 2013, TTP displayed their might in Karachi, the financial hub of the country, far from their traditional home in Pakistan's Federally Administered Tribal Areas (FATA) and KP Province. In order to escape the Pakistan military's operations and drone strikes, they have moved into the country's largest city which caters to 60–70 per cent of Pakistan's revenue.[11] The various TTP factions operating in the city have been visible since 2009, but they began to escalate terror activities since 2012. Today, evidence suggests that entire Pashtun neighbourhoods in Karachi are under the influence of TTP militants. The various targets of the TTP this year remained secular political parties. In addition to this, extortion rackets and kidnapping for ransom have made the TTP factions in Karachi more brazen and violent.[12] These developments have had direct implications on Karachi's economy and security. If the law agencies fail to confront TTP's rising Karachi network, in the coming years, it can have a national impact on Pakistan's overall stability.

The Hazara Killings of Balochistan

Sectarian violence continues to be directed at disenfranchised targets such as Balochistan's Hazaras. The Hazaras are mainly Shiite Muslims who have been living in Pakistan since the 19th century when they fled from Afghanistan. The Hazara minority in Quetta, the provincial capital of Balochistan, has been the victim of persecution and violent attacks since 2001 when a vehicle was ambushed near Poodgali Chowk, killing eight Hazaras. LeJ, the Pakistani Sunni Muslim extremist militant group, is assumed to be backing all the attacks carried out against Hazaras. These killings are attributed by many as part of the sectarian divide that exists in Pakistan as a result of the widening Shia–Sunni fault line.

The annual report of the Human Rights Commission of Pakistan (HRCP) released on 4 April 2013 records 505 Hazara Shia killings

---

[11] Ur Zia Rehman, 'Taliban Bringing Their War to Streets of Karachi', *Friday Times*, 11 August 2012.
[12] Declan Walsh and Ur Zia Rehman, 'Taliban Spread Terror in Karachi as the New Gang in Town', *New York Times*, 28 March 2013.

(all in Balochistan) between 2001 and 2012. There is visibly a rising trend since 2007.[13]

In January 2013, the most lethal attack was carried out on Alamdar Road in Quetta, an area dominated by ethnic Hazara Shiites, killing at least 105 people and injuring more than 169, including senior police officials. The attack was one of the worst ever on the community. Hundreds of people belonging to the Hazara Shia community staged a sit-in on Alamdar Road and refused to bury the dead until the Provincial Government was sacked. President Asif Ali Zardari invoked Article 234 of the Constitution, imposing Governor's rule and dismissing the Provisional Assembly, soon after which the families of the bombing victims ended their protest and buried the bodies amid strict security measures. In February 2013, another huge explosion in Hazara Town of Quetta killed 73 people from the Shia community. LeJ claimed responsibility for this attack.

Majority of Hazaras are Shia Muslims, with a minority being Sunni. But common knowledge for a gunslinger is that being Hazara is equivalent to being an infidel Shia who merits death. Some economists argue that the Hazaras have a stronghold over the local markets, and this financial strength makes them a prime target. Others believe that it is all a part of the bigger game and international stakeholders are involved in these killings. Regardless of the reasons, the incompetence of the state remains the prime reason behind the plight of the Hazaras. The slackness of the authorities has cost the Hazaras their lives and kept them in a state of constant fear.

Sectarian Violence on the Rise in Punjab

Punjab was simmering with sectarian violence in 2013. The roots of violence had been extended to regions like Gujrat where sectarian violence was unheard of before. Since May 2013, sectarian organizations have intensified their activities in southern Punjab. The most violent region identified in Punjab this year was the

---

[13] 'State of Human Rights in 2012', report by HRCP, Lahore, March 2013, available online at http://www.satp.org/satporgtp/countries/pakistan/document/papers/HRCAR2012.pdf (accessed 5 January 2014).

southernmost district, Rahimyar Khan, where both Shia and Sunni organizations gave rise to incidents of violence. The reason for the scuffle was identified as being a reaction to the lethal incidents all around the country which made the people lose their calm and want to seek revenge. Sunni sectarian organizations have had an upper hand as compared to their Shia rivals. Last year, only four cases of sectarian violence were recorded in Punjab, and the number has risen to 13 cases this year with the killing of 42 people. Many of the clashes boiled to the point of deadly violence between the two sects.[14] Lahore and Rawalpindi districts were also engulfed in sectarian disharmony. At least 10 people were killed and over 78 injured after sectarian clashes erupted during the 10th Muharram procession at Fawara Chowk in Rawalpindi. ASWJ activists were shot dead in Lahore in incidences of targeted killing.

In the absence of a comprehensive state mechanism to dismantle militant groups, sectarian violence will continue to threaten Pakistan's fragile security situation.

Conflict Management

The most important aspect of conflict management in 2013 took the form of creating a political consensus within Pakistan to negotiate with the Pakistani Taliban. There were some positive responses from the TTP as well towards the government initiative, how much ever stunted they were. Towards the end of 2012, there were a few statements from the TTP signalling its intention to initiate a process of talks with the government.[15] Though there were a series of high-profile attacks just before the announcement,[16] and certain preconditions attached to the

[14] Huma Yusuf, 'Sectarian Violence: Pakistan's Greatest Security Threat?', NOREF Report submitted to Norwegian Peacebuilding Resource Centre, 2012.

[15] 'Taliban Say Yes to Talks, No to Arms Surrender', *News*, 29 December 2012.

[16] Some of these high-profile attacks would include the following: The bombing in Jamrud bazaar in Khyber agency killing 17 people, the assassination of Bashir Bilour, a member of the KP Provincial Assembly belonging to the ANP, and the kidnapping and massacre of 21 levees.

TTP's statement for talks with the government, the latter took it seriously.[17]

Perhaps, the Pakistani Taliban was willing to negotiate, as it would have seen the situation in its favour with the state forces being unwilling or incapable of fighting them militarily. Ever since the successful military operations in Swat during 2009, there were no major offensives against the TTP. In fact, it was the Taliban which was on an offensive, not only within the FATA and KP, but all over Pakistan. There were numerous high-profile attacks on the military and security installations in mainland Punjab and Sindh.

As mentioned above, the Taliban was willing to negotiate with the state on certain preconditions that included the withdrawal of Pakistan's support to the US in Afghanistan, rewriting the Constitution according to Shariah and apologizing for the war launched against them.[18]

On its part, the state agreed in principle to initiate a dialogue with the Taliban, but the process did not solidify until the elections in 2013. A major decision in the government's initiative came in the form of an APC on the subject in September 2013. The resolution, dated 9 September 2013, proposed the following:[19]

- The sovereignty and territorial integrity of Pakistan are paramount and must be safe-guarded at all costs. We reaffirm our complete trust and confidence in our valiant Armed Forces and assure them of our full solidarity and support in overcoming any challenge to our national security or threat to our national interests;

[17] The demands from the TTP included the following:

> The government will have to quit its alliance with the US and it is required to come out of its war in Afghanistan. It will have to rewrite the country's Constitution according to Shariah in place of the present secular system and also apologise for the war launched against us in the country.

See 'Taliban Say Yes to Talks, No to Arms Surrender', *News*, 29 December 2012.

[18] See 'Taliban Say Yes to Talks, No to Arms Surrender', *News*, 29 December 2012.

[19] 'Resolution of the All Parties Conference on Sept 9, 2013', *Dawn*, 10 September 2013.

- Thousands of precious lives of innocent men, women and children and defence and security personnel have been lost in the war, the illegal and immoral drone attacks and the blowback from actions of NATO/ISAF forces in Afghanistan. There have also been colossal damages to social and physical infrastructure and huge consequential financial losses and adverse effects on our economy.
- We have noted with concern the continued use of drone attacks by the United States of America in spite of clear and unambiguous protests by the democratically elected Government of Pakistan. We are unanimous that the use of drones is not only a continued violation of our territorial integrity but also detrimental to our resolve and efforts of eliminating extremism and terrorism from our country. The Federal Government should consider the possibility of taking the drone issue to the United Nation as drone attacks are a violation of International Law.
- Peace, tranquillity, stability and a tolerant and harmonious society are essential prerequisites for revival of the growth process for rapid socio-economic development. In the APC in September, 2011, it was declared that 'Give peace a chance' would be the guiding central principle henceforth and that dialogue must be initiated to negotiate peace with our own people in the tribal areas. The APCs in February 2013 reiterated that attaining peace through dialogue should be the first priority. The resolutions passed in the Joint Sittings of Parliament mentioned above contained similar recommendations, emphasizing the imperative need to review our national security strategy, in the context of an independent foreign policy, with focus on peace and reconciliation, and to attach the highest priority to dialogue.
- We, therefore, repose full confidence in efforts of the Prime Minister in this behalf and call upon the Federal Government to initiate the dialogue with all stakeholders forthwith and for this purpose, authorize it to take all necessary steps as it may deem fit, including development of an appropriate mechanism and identification of interlocutors. Needless to state, the process should be as inclusive as possible, with full participation of the Government of KP and other stakeholders. Guiding principles should include respect for local

customs and traditions, values and religious beliefs and the creation of an environment which brings peace and tranquillity to the region.

Though the political leadership had reached a consensus by mid-2013, the process could not move forward due to the assassination of Hakimullah Mehsud, the then leader of the TTP, in a drone attack carried out by the US from across the border.[20] The process got further delayed due to the selection of new leader by the TTP, and Mullah Fazlullah was finally appointed as the successor to Hakimullah Mehsud.[21]

Besides the above-mentioned efforts to initiate a process of talks with the Pakistani Taliban, another attempt at conflict management was carried out by the US, but from across the Durand Line, using the drones.

As explained in the previous section of this essay, the US continued with its drone attacks during 2013, as was the case in the previous years. Though in terms of numbers the drone attacks substantially declined, they did continue during 2013, the most spectacular being the ones responsible for the assassination of Hakimullah Mehsud.

The political leadership in Pakistan, especially the opposition, do not support the drone programme or their use by the US against any targets in Pakistan. Multiple resolutions were passed in the Parliament and numerous statements made in public against the drone attacks. However, there has been no military retaliation till date against the drone attacks. There has always been duplicity within Pakistan in terms of condemning the drone attacks.[22]

---

[20] 'Pakistani Taliban Chief Hakimullah Mehsud Killed in Drone Attack', *Dawn*, 2 November 2013.

[21] 'Leadership Change: Mullah Fazlullah Named New TTP Chief', *Express Tribune*, 9 November 2013.

[22] See Ayesha Khanyari, 'Pakistan: Double-speak on Drones', IPCS Commentary no. 4178, 14 November 2013, available online at http://www.ipcs.org/article/pakistan/pakistan-double-speak-on-drones-4178.html; D. Suba Chandran, 'Drone Attacks, a Convenient Explanation', *Hindu*, 16 November 2013.

The Road Ahead

What is Pakistan moving towards? Will there be a reduction in violence in the coming years? Will the ongoing negotiations with the Taliban yield positive results?

Given the non-monolithic nature of the actors engaged in violence in Pakistan, and the strategies adopted by the state in dealing with them, the next few years are likely to be bloody and unstable for Pakistan.

While the TTP is undoubtedly a primary non-state actor inside Pakistan, it does not hold the monopoly of violence. Outside the TTP, there are sectarian organizations which are well entrenched in Quetta and Karachi, along with select regions within the FATA and Punjab. These sectarian groups, though having links with the TTP, are not strictly a part of the Taliban hierarchy. Some of them, such as the multiple sectarian groups with their bases in Punjab and Sindh, existed much before the TTP came into existence.

A cursory look at the nature of sectarian violence and the multiple groups involved since the late 1980s would reveal the Sunni–Shia divide within Pakistan. Groups such as the SSP and LeJ have existed much before the birth of even Afghan Taliban. These groups have a sectarian agenda and have been targeting the Ahmediyas, Shias, Hindus and Christians. The sectarian fault lines within Pakistani society today are well entrenched. Recent violence against the minority communities and those who oppose the same, such as Salman Taseer, highlight the present danger.

As Pakistan moves closer to Saudi Arabia, this sectarian divide is likely to increase further. The larger Sunni assertion led by Saudi Arabia, especially through its Wahabi faith, is likely to get further entrenched in the society in Pakistan. The nature of the Pakistani workforce in Saudi Arabia and the bulk of remittances from the Gulf, along with a narrow interpretation of the religion, are likely to create further divide, even within the Sunni groups. This progress is already underway, as can be observed from the attacks against Sufi Islam in Pakistan during the last few years.

More than the ingress by non-state actors and external intervention, the nature of the state's response will play a crucial role, either in blocking the divide or further accentuating it. Unfortunately, the responses from the state so far appear weak and non-existent in terms of combating sectarian violence. Worse still, at times it appears that the state is becoming a party to the sectarian atrocities due to its indifference, or it has a hidden agenda to allow a sectarian leash to undermine any nationalistic assertions—Baloch or Pashtun.

The future of sectarian peace within Pakistan looks bleak, more because of the state's indifference to the problem. The state is certainly not incapable of dealing with the issue; if it wants to address the issue, a few legal measures and military actions would ensure a positive outcome. However, the state appears to be avoiding the issue, or worse, be in collusion with non-state actors for a political agenda.

The second major question in terms of addressing violence and maintaining peace is closely related to what the state wants to achieve in terms of the Pakistani Taliban. Though the state and the APCs during 2013 and early 2014 have been in favour of initiating a dialogue process with the Pakistani Taliban, what they want to achieve is unclear.

Much would depend on the endgame that the state wants to achieve vis-à-vis the Taliban. Is the current strategy aimed at neutralizing the Pakistani Taliban or allowing some space to them, so that they do not cross a threshold line?

Unfortunately, the current strategy of the state does not appear to be aimed at neutralizing the Pakistani Taliban. Had it been the case, the state would have pursued a military option, brought the Taliban to its knees and forced them to beg for a dialogue. Instead, the state has continually refused to use the military option, falling on its knees and begging the Taliban to consider the dialogue process. The violence led by the Pakistani Taliban and the military responses of the state during 2012–2013 have not been matching; the former is on an offensive and the latter remains inactive.

The state is likely to yield politically and militarily to the Taliban by not taking stern actions against the latter. It is likely to negotiate with the Taliban and yield to the latter's presence in the FATA and select districts of KP as well. Will the Pakistani Taliban be satisfied with having its presence and ideology limited only to the tribal belts? Or will it aim higher? The latter would pitch the Pakistani Taliban fighting for state control and not satisfied with its presence merely along the Durand Line.

4

Myanmar: Tentative Consolidation of Peace

Bibhu Prasad Routray

Introduction

In mid-December 2013, journalist Khine Khine Aye Cho, known by her pen name Ma Khine, working on a story about corruption in government, was convicted and sentenced to three months in prison by a township court in Myanmar's eastern state of Kayah.[1] This first sentencing of a local reporter to prison since the reformist government came to power in 2011, in a way, summed up the developments for 2013 in the country which has embraced a range of political and economic reforms with wide ramifications on the country's ethno-political landscape. As the country's leaders attempt to display images of openness and tolerance for freedom, the old mindset of controlling and suppressing dissent continues to guide some official actions.

A project to establish peace in the country's troubled frontiers, on the other hand, has achieved significant progress. All the major armed insurgencies have signed ceasefire agreements with the government. Barring occasional eruption of tensions, tentative

---

[1] 'Burmese Journalists Demand Release of Colleague', *Voice of America*, 2014, available online at http://www.voanews.com/content/burmese-journalists-demand-release-of-colleague/1824984.html (accessed 8 January 2014).

peace prevails at the peripheries where the ethnic minorities reside. Yet, the progress towards a comprehensive national reconciliation remains somewhat rocky, affected by a long history of mistrust between those at the centre and the periphery. Whether the country's still-powerful military is on board with the reforms process remains a matter of debate. Among the insurgencies, the emergence of a band of opportunistic leadership, out to make business with the government makes the peace processes appear somewhat sold-out affair. How Myanmar's Central Government succeeds in a delicate balancing act between the political Opposition's demand for constitutional reforms, the ethnic demand for autonomy and recognition of the rights over natural resources and the military's concern regarding a influence-less future would largely shape the country's developments in 2014.

Principal Actors

Armed Groups

Ethnic Burmans (*Bamars*), Myanmar's traditional rulers, make up about two-thirds of its estimated 52 million people.[2] A major issue since the country gained independence from Britain in 1948 has been the demand from ethnic minority groups for self-determination or autonomy under a federal system of governance. Armed insurgencies have sprung up representing the ethnicities and challenging the supremacy of the central authorities. While identity issues and domination by the Bamars were their main grievances, the wish to benefit from the lucrative border trade was another factor that sustained insurgencies.

The government in Naypyidaw[3] has spent the last six decades trying to pacify these rebellions with varying degrees of success.

---

[2] World Bank, '2012 Population Estimate', 2012, available online at http://data.worldbank.org/indicator/SP.POP.TOTL (accessed 9 January 2014).

[3] Myanmar's capital shifted from Yangon to Naypyidaw in November 2005. In rest of the chapter, Naypyidaw refers to the national capital and the central seat of power.

At least 16 armed groups are currently active in Myanmar. Twelve of these groupings are members of the umbrella organization, the United Nationalities Federal Council (UNFC) alliance. The UNFC was formed in February 2011 with the purported objective of establishing a 'genuine federal union, which guarantees full rights of national equality and self-determination within the states'.[4]

The UNFC has two levels of membership depending on the strength of the political wing, the armed wing, the control area and the number of supporters. While six groups have been given full membership, the other six are associate member groups. The groups who have full membership are: Kachin Independence Organization (KIO), Karen National Union (KNU), New Mon State Party (NMSP), Karenni National Progressive Party (KNPP), Chin National Front (CNF) and the Shan State Progress Party/Shan State Army (SSA). The associate members are: the Kachin National Organization (KNO), Palaung State Liberation Front (PSLF), Lahu Democratic Union (LDU), National United Party of Arakan (NUPA), Pa-O National Liberation Organization (PNLO) and Wa National Organization (WNO).

The UNFC is headed by the KNU. The Commander-in-Chief of the outfit's military wing Karen National Liberation Army (KNLA), General Mutu, is its Chairman. It has two Vice President posts headed by Kachin Independence Army (KIA) commander, Lt. Gen. Gauri Zau Seng, and KNPP's Khun Abel Tweed. NMSP's Nai Hongsa functions as the General Secretary.

Below are the profiles of some of the UNFC members. The section also contains profiles of other active outfits which are not a part of the UNFC.

The United Wa State Army (UWSA) is Myanmar's largest as well as best-equipped ethnic insurgent group. It was formed in May 1989 after the Communist Party of Burma (CPB) disintegrated, leading to the creation of several armed ethnic groups in the country's far north. The group seeks the establishment of an autonomous Wa state within Myanmar's national borders. Following its split from the CPB, UWSA went on to sign a ceasefire agreement with the Central Government, which recognized

---

[4] 'Reply to the Open Letter', *Burma National News*, 2011, available online at http://www.burmanationalnews.org/burma/images/Documents/unfcreplytoasskeng20110805.pdf (accessed 20 January 2013).

the group's territory in northern Shan state and its headquarters in Panghsang and Mongpawk.[5] This tactical arrangement with the military regime allowed

> UWSA commanders to profit from involvement in the narcotics trade while running an essentially autonomous state in its area of control with little interference from the junta. In return, the UWSA acts as a proxy force against other ethnic rebel groups who remain militarily opposed to the junta, such as the Shan State Army-South.[6]

UWSA's cadre strength is estimated to be anywhere between 20,000 and 30,000. Divided into five fighting divisions, the outfit has a vast array of weapons, acquired through a wide network, including those from China. Writings have indicated that China might be supplying QBZ-03/Type-03 assault rifles—a weapon that resembles the AK rifles—externally to the UWSA.[7] In the middle of 2012, UWSA reportedly received its first supply of Chinese-made PTL02 Wheeled Tank Destroyers.

UWSA's vast financial empire is built on an extensive network of drug and weapons smuggling. The outfit reportedly acts as the middleman between Chinese arms manufacturers and insurgent groups in India's northeast, with most weapons routed through China's Yunnan province. The UWSA has also been accused of investing its vast resources in a private airlines company in Myanmar.

In 2009, after 20 years of tentative peace, skirmishes broke out between the outfit and the military government over a disagreement over the creation of the Border Guard Force (BGF). The resulting fighting caused thousands of refugees to flood into

---

[5] Nang Mya Nadi, 'United Wa State Army Mark Anniversary', 2012, available online at http://www.dvb.no/news/united-wa-state-army-mark-anniversary/21541 (accessed 26 May 2012).

[6] Janes 2012, 'United Wa State Army (UWSA) (Myanmar)', available online at http://articles.janes.com/articles/Janes-World-Insurgency-and-Terrorism/United-Wa-State-Army-UWSA-Myanmar.html (accessed 25 May 2012).

[7] 'China Supplies QBZ-03 Rifle to United Wa State Army', Fire Arm Blog, 2012, available online at http://www.thefirearmblog.com/blog/2012/05/07/china-supplies-qbz-03-rifle-to-united-wa-state-army/ (accessed 12 May 2012).

China. However, after prolonged negotiations, the UWSA on 26 December 2011 signed a ceasefire agreement with the government. The KIA is the armed wing of the KIO operating in Myanmar's north, along the border with China. It was formed in February 1961 in response to attempts by the then (democratically elected) U Nu government to make Buddhism the state religion, and discontent with a 1960 Border Agreement with China. Subsequently, the KIA resisted the attempts by the military government headed by General Ne Win to consolidate Burmese control over regions on the periphery of the state which were home to various ethnic groups. KIA fought a guerrilla war against the government forces till 1994, when a ceasefire agreement was signed by both sides. The KIA has since renounced its goal of independence and seeks 'autonomy within a federal union of Burma'.[8]

Described as 'one of the best equipped and trained forces among the armed rebel groups',[9] KIA is better trained and better disciplined than other groups, although in terms of arms and heavy weapons, the UWSA, which receives steady supplies from China, is a far superior fighting force. The KIA does not get any weapons from China. The cadre strength of the outfit is described by its commanders to be in the range of 10,000 regular troops and 10,000 reservists.[10] It is impossible to verify the number. Other estimates, however, put the number of total soldiers barely at 4,000.[11] Although well equipped for jungle warfare, the KIA has a modest weaponry collection of AK-47s, artillery and at least one high-calibre anti-aircraft gun.[12]

---

[8] Patrick Bodenham, 'Burma Keeps Lid on Kachin Abuses and Humanitarian Crisis', *Guardian*, 27 June 2012, available online at http://www.guardian.co.uk/global-development/poverty-matters/2012/jun/27/burma-kachin-abuses-crisis-conflict (accessed 23 August 2012).

[9] 'Video Shows Burma Military Targeting Kachin Rebels', *BBC*, 2012, available online at http://www.bbc.co.uk/news/world-asia-20886377 (accessed 3 January 2013).

[10] Alastair Leithead, 'Burma's Kachin Army Prepares for Civil War', *BBC*, 22 February 2010, available online at http://news.bbc.co.uk/2/hi/asia-pacific/8528985.stm (accessed 11 February 2012).

[11] Thomas Fuller, 'Ethnic Groups in Myanmar Hope for Peace, but Gird for Fight', *New York Times*, 10 May 2009, available online at http://www.nytimes.com/2009/05/11/world/asia/11iht-myanmar.html (accessed 11 February 2012).

[12] See note 10.

The ceasefire with the government troops allowed the organization to control a large swathe in northern Myanmar, making them the de facto rulers in that part of the country. The KIA and the KIO 'provide power, roads and schools funded by taxes on the brisk trade from China as well as the jade and gold mines and teak'.[13] KIA's headquarters are outside the town of Laiza, near the Chinese border.

The KNU is the oldest of the armed groups in Myanmar. It describes itself as 'a democratic organization representing the Karen people of Burma' and its goal as 'peace and prosperity in a democratic federal Burma'.[14] This predominantly Christian insurgency has been fighting the Central Government since the very early days of the country's independence from Britain six decades ago. Incidentally, the Karens grew in strength as a result of support from the colonial British against the repressive treatment by the Burmese nationalist military.

The KNU has been one of the strongest of the ethnic insurgencies in Myanmar. At one time, they boasted an army of 14,000 men and controlled much territory along the eastern border.[15] However, in recent years, their operations have been reduced to relatively small-scale guerrilla attacks on army troops. Large numbers of Karen villagers have fled their homes, in one of the world's least reported refugee crises, and about 100,000 still live in rudimentary camps on the Thai side of the border.

The NMSP was formed in July 1958 under the leadership of Nai Shwe Kyin, alias Nai Ba Lwin, after the Mon People's Front (MPF) surrendered to the Central Government. The MPF launched an armed rebellion in 1948 and surrendered after the government promised an autonomous Mon state. Few MPF dissidents were not convinced and went on to form the NMSP, which carried on with its armed rebellion.[16] The Mon National Liberation Army

[13] See note 10.

[14] KNU, 'About the KNU', 2014, available online at http://karennationalunion.net./index.php/burma/freedom/about-the-knu (accessed 9 January 2014).

[15] Charles Scanlon, 'Who Are Burma's Karen Rebels?' *BBC*, 12 January 2012, available online at http://www.bbc.co.uk/news/world-south-asia-16528737 (accessed 9 January 2014).

[16] NMSP, 'NMSP History', 2014, available online at http://www.nmsp.info/nmsphis.php (accessed 9 January 2014).

(MNLA), NMSP's military wing, was formally founded as its armed wing on 29 August 1971. The MNLA is one of the smaller armed ethnic minority groups in the country with about 1,000 cadres based in the hills of southeast Myanmar. The objective of the NMSP/MNLA is to establish autonomy for the Mon-inhabited areas of southeastern Myanmar. According to the NMSP's website, the group's aim is to reclaim the traditional and historical homeland of the Mon people, which were conquered by the Burmese in 1757 and which did not receive its own rights after independence from Great Britain in 1948. More specifically, the group claims that it is fighting to 'establish an independent sovereign state unless the Burmese government is willing to permit a confederation of free nationalities exercising full right of self-determination inclusive of the right of secession'.[17]

The SSA was formed in 1964. However, within no time, the organization split into two factions—SSA-North and SSA-South. The former aligned itself with the Central Government till 2011, when fighting broke out between the SSA-North cadres and the Myanmarese troops, following the former's refusal to become a BGF. However, in late January 2012, the outfit agreed for a truce with the government. The SSA-South too signed a ceasefire agreement with the government in December 2011. The SSA-South is a member of a parallel ethnic alliance called the National Democratic Front which was formed in 1976. That was cited as the reason when the SSA-South did not opt to join the UNFC. SSA-South has strength of 10,000 cadres and has a wide repository of arms.

The CNF was formed on 20 March 1988. Its military wing, the Chin National Army (CNA), was constituted on 14 November 1988. It seeks autonomy for Chin state within Myanmar. According to a CNF statement, the group was

> founded out of a desire to defend the rights of the Chin people from the Burmese military dictatorship that seeks to annihilate the Chin cultural, religious and ethnic identities, and to build a federated

---

[17] Janes 2012, 'Mon National Liberation Army (MNLA) (Myanmar)', available online at http://articles.janes.com/articles/Janes-World-Insurgency-and-Terrorism/Mon-National-Liberation-Army-MNLA-Myanmar.html (accessed 23 January 2012).

Union of Burma based on respect for human rights, democracy and equality for all ethnic nationalities.[18]

In recent years, the group has broken up into several factions, leaving the mainstream CNF with about 200 cadres.

The Democratic Karen Buddhist Army (DKBA) pursues an autonomy demand in the Myanmar–Thailand border area. The DKBA had split from its mother organization, KNLA's political wing, the KNU, in 1995. In 2010, the DKBA itself split into two factions after its Brigade 5, with an estimated 1,500 troops, walked away from the mother group of 6,000 cadres and restarted armed conflict with government troops. The move followed the DKBA being forced by the government to join the BGF and observe a ceasefire agreement with the government in 1995. On 7 November 2010, DKBA Brigade 5 temporarily took control of several government buildings in the town of Myawaddy on the Thai border, and the fighting that followed forced over 20,000 people to flee to Thailand.[19]

The Arakan Liberation Army (ALA) is the military wing of the Arakan Liberation Party (ALP), which was established in 1967 demanding the independence of the western Rakhine state from the then Burma. The ALA was formed in the early 1970s with assistance from the KNU through an 'agreement of assistance'.[20] The ALA had a long history of skirmishes with the troops till the first week of April 2012 when it signed a ceasefire agreement with the government. According to an estimate, nine clashes between the ALA cadres and the troops took place in 2009 and seven clashes in 2008.[21]

---

[18] Janes 2012, 'Chin National Army (CNA) (Myanmar)', available online at http://articles.janes.com/articles/Janes World-Insurgency-and-Terrorism/Chin-National-Army-CNA-Myanmar.html (accessed 23 May 2012).

[19] Saw Yan Naing, 'DKBA Brigade 5 Reaches Ceasefire with Naypyidaw', 4 November 2011, available online at http://www.irrawaddy.org/article.php?art_id=22390 (accessed 22 February 2012).

[20] 'The Summary of Arakan Liberation Party (ALP)', Arakan Eagle, 2008, available online at http://arakaneagle.blogspot.sg/2008/10/summary-of-arakan-liberation-partyalp.html (accessed 23 February 2012).

[21] Nyein Chan, 'One Killed in Clash between ALA and Burmese Army', Mizzima News, 15 February 2010, available online at http://www.mizzima.com/news/inside-burma/3535-one-killed-in-clash-between-ala-and-burmese-army-.html (accessed 24 May 2012).

On 3 January 2012, the ALA attacked an army base in Paletwa in Chin state killing four soldiers. On 14 March, another clash resulted in the death of a soldier at a village in the Rakhine state. The ALA's cadres' strength, however, has been estimated at only 100 fighting men.

Tatmadaw (Myanmarese Armed Forces)

The Myanmarese armed forces' strength could be in the range of 400,000 active soldiers. For the military, fighting internal threats has been a key reason for its oversized presence—and a justification for its rule, which stretched from 1962 to the advent of Thein Sein's government in 2011. However, authors such as Mary P. Callaham have indicated that the most of these forces have little combat experience. She suggests that the country's military might not be as effective a fighting force as it was once believed to be: 'Officers as high-ranking as majors and in some cases lieutenant colonels today probably have less experience fighting wars than trying to build roads'.[22]

The army's growth over the course of more than a decade has been affected by the introduction of new units, such as light infantry divisions, expanded armour divisions and artillery forces, and engineering battalions. It is also alleged that the army employs a large number of children as soldiers, often using them as shields in the asymmetrical fighting with the insurgents.

In June 2012, the Myanmar government, through a Joint Action Plan signed with the United Nations (UN), had pledged to end the recruitment and use of children into its armed forces. It also promised to take steps to ensure that children would be protected from recruitment in the future and to clear the military of anyone under age 18 by 1 December 2013. However, allegations of ongoing recruitment continue to be made. Children continue to be recruited into the Myanmar military and non-state armed groups. In December 2013, international media ran stories of children who had escaped the army camps after years of servitude and forced enlistment.[23]

---

[22] Mary P. Callaham, *Making Enemies, War and State-Building in Burma* (Cornell: Cornell University Press, 2004).

[23] 'Burma Continues to Enlist Child Soldiers', *CBS News*, 2013, available online at http://www.cbsnews.com/news/burma-continues-to-enlist-children-soldiers/ (accessed 18 December 2013).

With the expansion in its numbers, the army's presence has increased throughout the country, especially in the ethnic regions. The ceasefire agreements brokered during former Prime Minister Khin Nyunt's tenure facilitated a much larger presence for the military in the country's ethnic regions. In Shan state alone, the number of battalions has increased from 40 to 200 in the last 18 years, while in Kachin state, new artillery battalions have been deployed to neutralize local insurgent groups. Myanmar has acquired new weapons systems from India, Singapore, Pakistan, North Korea, Ukraine and Israel. The country's principal supplier, however, has been China.[24]

Moreover, the political power exercised by the *Tatmadaw* remains paramount and undisturbed. It controls 25 per cent of seats in both houses of the Union Parliament and the regional assemblies, which means that it effectively has a veto over constitutional amendments, which require the support of more than 75 per cent of Parliament. Final decisions on all government policies are believed to be made by the 11-member National Defence and Security Council—a seemingly paramount body that includes the Commander-in-Chief of the armed forces, the Defence Minister and three other senior military officials.[25] The military also garners a major chunk of Myanmar's resources. For the financial year 2013–2014, the Defense Ministry was allocated 20.86 per cent of the proposed national budget,[26] a marginally less amount than the previous year.

Myanmar Police Forces

As Myanmar transforms itself from a military state to a quasi-military one, the role of the police force in managing law and order affairs and other civilian duties has become important. It is not clear, however, that the Myanmar Police Force (MPF), created in

[24] Aung Zaw, 'A Growing Tatmadaw', 2006, available online at http://www.irrawaddy.org/article.php?art_id=5537&page=6 (accessed 23 February 2012).

[25] Ba Kaung, 'Burmese Army Chief Defends Political Role', *Irrawaddy*, 2012, available online at http://www2.irrawaddy.org/article.php?art_id=23290 (accessed 22 May 2012).

[26] 'Burma Military to Receive 20.8% of Budget', *Irrawaddy*, 2013, available online at http://www.irrawaddy.org/archives/27244 (accessed 21 February 2013).

1995 and described to be 93,000 men and women strong is geared to handle the responsibility. Its role, for example, in the Rakhine state came under criticism for failing to stop the wave of religious unrest between the Buddhists and the Muslims. It lacks basic equipment and only has about a year of training.[27] However, over the coming years, things have been projected to improve through externally funded police reforms programmes. In November 2013, the European Union (EU) introduced an 18-month project worth US$ 13.6 million for community policing and best practice in crowd management as part of its support of the Myanmar's police reform.[28]

External Powers

China: Growing Influence

Strategy and economics govern China's interests in Myanmar, with which it shares a 2,204-km-long international boundary. Over the years, China has invested billions of dollars into the Myanmarese economy. Myanmar remains critical for China's soaring energy requirements. The US$ 30 billion worth Shwe oil and gas pipeline project which passes through the insurgency-ridden central Myanmar territories before entering the Yunnan province became operational in July 2013. The project has been criticized as being extractive with little benefit for the local population.[29]

Outpouring of migrants from Myanmar, fallout of the army operations against the insurgents, has remained a critical issue for China. To that extent, China has, over the years, pursued a policy of engaging with and pressurizing Naypyidaw. In 2013,

---

[27] Didier Lauras, 'Myanmar Police Struggle to Adapt to Post-junta Era', 2013, available online at http://sg.news.yahoo.com/myanmar-police-struggle-adapt-post-junta-era-035335362.html (accessed 9 January 2014).

[28] 'EU Supports Police Reform in Myanmar', *Mizzima News*, 2013, available online at http://www.mizzima.com/mizzima-news/myanmar/item/10684-eu-supports-police-reform-in-myanmar (accessed 9 January 2014).

[29] Burma Partnership, (2013). 'Drawing The Line: The Case against China's Shwe Gas Project, For Better Extractive Industries in Burma', available online at http://www.burmapartnership.org/2013/09/drawing-the-line/ (accessed 09 January 2014).

China played a critical part in brokering a ceasefire agreement between the KIA and the Myanmar government. At the same time, however, it continued supplying arms to the UWSA. On 21 January 2013, the *Democratic Voice of Burma* reported the supply of armoured vehicles by the Chinese to the UWSA. Quoting the *Janes Intelligence Review*, the report said that the 'transfer of Chinese-made PTL02 Wheeled Tank Destroyers is believed to have taken place in the middle of 2012', thus, marking 'a significant escalation in the equipment supply to the UWSA'[30] from China. The report surmised that this could be Beijing's attempt to use the UWSA as leverage as Myanmar develops its relations with the United States. The report termed the supply as unprecedented both in the quantity of munitions and in the type of systems delivered, and concluded that the delivery is highly likely to have stemmed from a high-level decision made in Beijing.

Myanmar's ungoverned areas also reportedly provide refuge to criminals and anti-state elements from China. Liu Yuejin, the Director of China's Ministry of Public Security's Anti-drug Bureau, told the media in February 2013[31] that Beijing had planned to use a drone strike targeting Naw Kham, the leader of a drug gang, who was thought to be in hiding in the mountains of northeastern Myanmar. Naw Kham reportedly led one of the biggest armed gangs in the 'Golden Triangle' region near the Mekong river and was responsible for killing 13 sailors in October 2011. The plan, however, was abandoned.

Thailand: The Spill-over State

With Thailand, Myanmar shares a 2,107-km-long border. In the past, ethnic insurgents operating in the southern part of Myanmar, such as the KNU and its military wing, the KNLA, found it convenient to escape into the safety of Thailand, thus, making the army operations ineffective. Myanmar on several occasions tried putting pressure on Bangkok by linking border trade between the two countries with its southern neighbour's cooperation to clear out its border towns of Myanmarese rebels. Myanmarese refugees

---

[30] Francis Wade, 'China Ups Weapons Transfers to Wa Army', 2013, available online at http://www.dvb.no/news/china-ups-weapons%E2%80%99-tranfers-to-wa-army/25895 (accessed 21 January 2013).

[31] Ananth Krishnan, 'China Planned Drone Strike in Myanmar', *Hindu*, New Delhi, 19 February 2013.

also often sneaked into Thailand to avoid being caught in the crossfire between the Tatmadaw troops and the rebels. Myanmar alleged that the rebels too find refuge in the refugee camps. The KNU, on the other hand, denied the charge, and maintains that 'We are based and operating in our own territory [in Burma]'.[32]

Besides armed conflict, refugees as well as drugs from Myanmar have regularly spilled over into Thailand. Thailand launched its official war against drugs in February 2003 and killed 2,275 people including many drug lords in the first three months.[33] The campaign reduced the volume of illicit drug flow. But owing to the continuing demand for drugs that still exists in Thailand, the flow of drugs continues.

The longevity of the conflict situation appears to have created a band of stakeholders within the Thai military who benefit from such cross-border problems. On 20 January 2013, Thai news media reported that a police investigation had found that army officers, some as senior as Major and Colonel, were involved in the smuggling of Rohingya Muslims from Myanmar into Malaysia via Thailand and that the trafficking had been going on for several years.[34]

India: The Impact State

With regard to the armed conflict situation in Myanmar, India is more of an *impact* state rather than a *cause* state, unlike China and, to some extent, Thailand. India shares a 1,338-km-long international border with Myanmar, most of which has been porous and unguarded. Moreover, India's northeast, abutting on the international border, has been insurgency-ridden for the past several decades. While none of the Myanmarese insurgent groups

---

[32] Naw Noreen, 'Burma Tells Thailand to "Clear Out" Rebels', 2011, available online at http://www.dvb.no/news/burma-tells-thailand-to-%E2%80%98clear-out%E2%80%99-rebels/16751 (accessed 23 February 2012).

[33] Human Rights Watch, 'Not Enough Graves: The War on Drugs, HIV/AIDS, and Violations of Human Rights', 2004, available online at http://www.hrw.org/sites/default/files/reports/thailand0704.pdf (accessed 21 February 2013).

[34] 'Army Officers Linked to Rohingya Smuggling', *Bangkok Post*, 2013, available online at http://www.bangkokpost.com/news/local/331655/army-officers-linked-to-rohingya-smuggling (accessed 22 January 2013).

benefit from their alliance with their Indian counterparts, Indian insurgents, especially those operating in states such as Nagaland and Manipur, have not only set up camps inside Myanmar but also have benefited from their nexus with the Myanmarese insurgencies as well as the army. The trade in drugs and small arms in Myanmar has been a constant source of turbulence in India's northeast. India also faces the problem of the refugees, especially the Chins from Myanmar, disturbing the demographic profile of states like Mizoram.

Cooperation from Myanmar remains a critical factor for India's counter-insurgency campaign in its northeastern region. To achieve that, India has been assisting the capacity building among the Myanmarese army and providing assistance for building border roads to facilitate Myanmarese action against the Indian insurgent camps. Notwithstanding the 2012 controversy in which India's military assistance to the Myanmar military came under close scrutiny after reports of use of the India-supplied Swedish anti-tank 84 mm Carl Gustaf rocket launchers by the Myanmar military against the Kachins,[35] India reportedly stepped up its supplies of 'rocket launchers, mortars, rifles, radars, night-vision devices, Gypsies, bailey bridges, communication and Inmarsat sets'[36] to the country in 2013.

Armed Conflict in 2013

Major Trends

The Long War Ends

On 30 May 2013, KIA's political wing, the KIO, signed a seven-point agreement with the Myanmar government, following three days of hectic negotiations in the Kachin state capital of Myitkyina.

---

[35] Bertil Lintner, 'Svenska vapen', 2012, available online at http://media1.dougmorton.com/apms/SVD_A_NYHETER_2012-spread.pdf (accessed 11 December 2012).

[36] Rajat Pandit, 'India Steps Up Military Aid to Myanmar to Offset China's Might', *Times of India*, New Delhi, 1 November 2013.

Both sides pledged to decrease military tensions and to commit to work towards a future peace agreement. The agreement was witnessed and signed by UN General Secretary's special advisor Vijay Nambiar, Deputy Chief of Mission from the Chinese Embassy and representatives of eight armed ethnic groups. While the KIO had originally insisted that a ceasefire alone was not enough and favoured the presence of international monitors and the starting of political negotiations on autonomy for the Kachin, the agreement indicated a settlement around ceasefire, with a promise of political talks in the future. Statements released on the occasion also said that the two parties agreed in principle to establish Joint Monitoring Committees, to continue to discuss on internally displaced persons' (IDPs) resettlement, to establish a technical team based in Kachin's capital Myitkyina and to continue to allow the participation of observers.

The signing of the ceasefire was marked by two distinct developments: the critical role played by the Chinese and the exclusion of the western powers from the peace talks. Two rounds of peace talks under the Chinese auspices were held in the border township of Ruili in China's Yunnan province on 4 February and 10 March. It was marked by a dramatic decline in the intensity of fighting between the KIA and the Myanmarese military, prompting President Thein Sein to claim during his European tour in March, 'There's no more hostilities, no more fighting all over the country, we have been able to end this kind of armed conflict'.[37] A third round of talks between the government's peace team and the rebel representatives, scheduled to be held in early April in Myitkyina, was deferred. While the Kachin NGOs blamed the Chinese's interference, objecting to the proposed presence of the representatives of the United States and the United Kingdom in the peace talks, the government-affiliated Myanmar Peace Centre said that the Kachins had asked for a rescheduling. Hectic negotiations and bargaining in the end led to the exclusion of the United States and the United Kingdom. The UN's role as a signatory had managed to receive the approval of the Chinese.

---

[37] 'Kachin Group Says Violence Continues While President Claims Peace', *Irrawaddy*, 2013, available online at http://www.irrawaddy.org/.z_kachin/kachin-group-says-violence-continues-while-president-claims-peace.html (accessed 10 January 2014).

Intermittent Clashes

Notwithstanding the ceasefire agreements, intermittent clashes between the government troops and ethnic armed groups such as the KIO, the SSA-South and Ta'ang National Liberation Army (TNLA) continued in Kachin and Shan states. In October, for example, clashes broke out between the military and the SSA.[38] In September and October, the KIO and the military clashed in the Mansi township, not only creating a humanitarian crisis but also preventing the relief agencies and the UN from reaching the affected civilian population.[39] The northern Shan state-based TNLA, armed wing of the PSLF, said in a statement in August that it would be unable to proceed with peace talks with the government due to continued fighting between its cadres and the Myanmar army.[40]

Such armed confrontations, however, have occurred more due to misunderstandings and misfires, rather than a concerted effort on part of the military to keep the fire burning. A source close to the rebels, however, indicated that, 'There may have been a misfire, or misunderstanding. So, whenever clashes break out we can't say that it has an effect on the ceasefire agreement'.[41] This remained one of the positive outcomes of the ceasefire agreements, with both sides committed to protect the achievements made thus far. Allegations of abuse by the military continued, although on certain instances[42] the latter instituted inquiries to investigate into the charges.

---

[38] Democracy for Burma, 'Myanmar: Fighting Continue between RCSS/SSA and Government Army', 2013, available online at http://democracyforburma.wordpress.com/2013/10/15/myanmar-fighting-continue-between-rcssssa-and-government-army/ (accessed 16 December 2013).

[39] 'UN Deeply Concerned as Fighting Worsens in Southern Kachin State', *Kachin News*, 2013, available online at http://www.kachinnews.com/news/2588-un-deeply-concerned-as-fighting-worsens-in-southern-kachin-state.html (accessed 17 December 2013).

[40] 'Ta'ang Army Suspends Talks with Govt as Clashes Continue', *Democratic Voice of Burma*, 2013, available online at http://www.dvb.no/news/taang-army-suspends-talks-with-govt-as-clashes-continue/31933 (accessed 17 December 2013).

[41] See note 38.

[42] Lawi Weng, 'Burma Military Investigates Alleged Rape of 13-Year Old Girl', *Irrawaddy*, 2014, available online at http://www.irrawaddy.org/burma/burma-military-investigates-alleged-rape-13-year-old-girl.html (accessed 08 January 2013).

Buddhist-Rohingya Clashes

Over 200 people lost their lives in a wave of violence between the Muslim Rohingyas and the Buddhists in 2012. Clashes, which attracted international attention, continued well into the first half of 2013, with the Central Government favouring the Buddhists and portraying the groups like the 969 movement as a cultural movement. Another 45 people lost their lives in 2013. In November, a delegation of the Organization of Islamic Cooperation (OIC) toured Sittwe to investigate allegations of human rights abuses against Rohingyas, and visited camps housing mostly displaced Rohingya refugees as well as some ethnic Rakhines and met local officials. In December, the OIC Secretary General, Professor Ekmeleddin İhsanoğlu termed the Rohingyas as indigenous people of the country.[43] On 12 November, the UN General Assembly released its draft annual resolution against Myanmar, calling on the government to address the communal violence. On 21 November, the UN passed a resolution calling on Myanmar to grant Rohingyas the citizenship denied them under a 1982 law.

Such activism, however, has little prospect of success, amid unanimity of views among the Bamar-dominant civil society, the opposition parties and the government. During the OIC delegation's visit, Buddhists protesters staged demonstrations across the country, calling on the OIC not to interfere in the country's affairs and objecting to any plans for the group to open a domestic office in the country, saying that the organization was only interested in providing aid for Rohingyas and other Muslims.[44] Myanmar also rejected the UN's November resolution. The Presidential spokesperson, Ye Htut, used his Facebook page to declare, 'We cannot give citizenship rights to those who are not in accord with the law, whatever the pressure. That is our sovereign right'.[45]

---

[43] Colin Hinshelwood, 'Rohingya Are an Indigenous People of Burma: OIC Sec-Gen', 2013, available online at https://www.dvb.no/interview/rohingya-are-an-indigenous-people-of-the-land-oic-sec-gen-burma-myanmar/35165 (accessed 17 December 2013).

[44] Radio Free Asia, 'Peace in Myanmar's Rakhine State Will "Take Some Time"', 2013, available online at http://www.rfa.org/english/news/myanmar/peace-12162013164550.html (accessed 17 December 2013).

[45] Channel News Asia, 'Myanmar Rejects UN Rohingya Citizenship Appeal', 2013, available online at http://www.channelnewsasia.com/news/asiapacific/myanmar-rejects-un/895184.html (accessed 17 December 2013).

Anti-Rohingya sentiment is one of the common threads that run through both the government and the opposition, thereby indicating a grim future for this sizeable population. The opposition, National League for Democracy (NLD), endorsed the official position by posturing that, 'The Rohingya do not exist under Myanmar's law'. Aung San Suu Kyi, the opposition leader, has rejected report of the Human Rights Watch published in April 2013 that the plight of the Rohingyas amounts to ethnic cleansing.

Explosions: An Aberration?

In October, several bombs exploded in northeastern Myanmar, including one in a plush hotel in the country's commercial capital. Three people were killed and 10 others were injured in the string of attacks in the country's four different regions (Yangon, Pegu, Mandalay and Sagaing), including the two biggest cities — Yangon and Mandalay, and Sagaing. The last of the explosions struck Namkham, a town in Shan state bordering China.

The government interpreted the explosions as an attempt to 'alarm the public and raise doubts in the international community that Myanmar can guarantee security when it takes the rotating chair next year of the Association of South East Asian Nations (ASEAN)'.[46] Possible groups suspected to have carried out the bombings included the faction within the military, disgruntled with the reforms process, the Muslim groups trying to take revenge for the anti-Muslim riots and the ethnic minorities, unhappy with the pace of reforms and the peace process. Four suspects were arrested over the bombings.

Police sources claimed that the bombers were financed by a businessman linked to the KNU, who was 'unhappy with economic and political changes that have attracted foreign investors'[47]

---

[46] Aung Hla Tun and Jared Ferrie, 'More Bombs Explode in Myanmar; Police Arrest Four Suspects', 2013, available online at http://www.reuters.com/article/2013/10/17/us-myanmar-bombings-idUSBRE99G0D820131017 (accessed 12 December 2013).

[47] 'Myanmar: Police Have Theory for Blasts', *New York Times*, 2013, available online at http://www.nytimes.com/2013/10/19/world/asia/myanmar-police-have-theory-for-blasts.html?_r=0 (accessed 15 December 2013).

to the country. They also indicated that the arrested confessed to have carried out the bombings. Although Myanmar is no stranger to bombings, such attacks have been rare since Thein Sein's government took power in 2011. In 2010, three explosions during the New Year festival had killed at least 10 people. Prior to that, in 2005, three bombs at a convention centre and markets had killed 23, an attack blamed on ethnic minority rebels and an exiled political group.

The Ambit of Reforms

That the much lauded reforms have not touched the lives of all of Myanmar's citizens, especially those in the periphery, has remained one of the persistent critiques by the Myanmar watchers. While to a large extent such an outlook reflects the on-ground reality, it also demonstrates a continuation of scepticism regarding the abilities and intentions of the Central Government. Moreover, such interpretations also tend to glorify the role of the ethnic militia.

Ethnic groups interpret that the ceasefire agreement is merely as an instrument to dominate their land, which is resource-rich and almost central to Myanmar's economic progress. In March 2012, the government passed two new land bills, designed to help farmers with land rights. However, these legislations, in the words of the activists, provide little protection and could make more farmers landless.[48] These laws do not address shifting cultivation practised by many ethnic groups. Under the laws, the government could consider such land vacant and give it to companies for large-scale infrastructural development.

Indeed, it is feared that in combination with the ceasefires with armed ethnic groups, the laws can facilitate land grabbing in conflict-affected areas. A report by the Karen Human Rights Group (KHRG) indicated that such exploitative land acquisitions by local and foreign players have gathered pace following the January 2012 ceasefire that ended more than six decades of war between the government and the KNU. In Kachin province,

---

[48] 'Ethnic Minority Land Rights Next Hurdle for Myanmar Peace', *Reuters*, 2013, available online at http://www.trust.org/item/20130508071750-b1jne/ (accessed 11 December 2013).

landlessness and ongoing clashes between the army and ethnic Kachin rebels have exacerbated food insecurity.

The slow pace of peace talks has created fissures even within the ethnic groups such as the KNU, giving rise to *hardline* and *pragmatic* factions.[49] While the pragmatic faction, dominated by the current KNU leadership, favours moving forward quickly with the peace process, despite complaints that little has been done to protect civilians, implement a code of conduct for cease-fires, or withdraw government troops from KNU territories, the hardline faction, dominated by KNU Brigade 5, does not want to follow the government's plans so easily. In addition to protection for civilians, the faction, allied with the UNFC alliance, wants a guarantee that development projects in the state should benefit local people.

Opium Cultivation

According to the UN Office on Drugs and Crime (UNODC), in 2013, the area under opium poppy cultivation in Myanmar increased 13 per cent compared to 2012 to reach 57,800 hectares. About 870 tons of opium, compared to 690 tons in 2012, were produced in the country in 2013. In the Golden Triangle area, where the borders of Laos, Myanmar and Thailand meet, Laos produced 41 tons and Thailand 3 tons.[50] This indicates that despite eradication efforts, opium poppy cultivation in the region continues to increase. After significant decreases in opium cultivation in the region between 1998 and 2005, when UNODC and local governments initiated crop substitution and eradication programmes with some initial successes, cultivation of the crop has increased annually since 2006.

---

[49] Saw Yan Naing, 'Who's Behind the Bombings in Burma?', 2013, available online at http://www.irrawaddy.org/burma/news-analysis/whos-behind-bombings-burma.html (accessed 12 December 2013).

[50] 'Myanmar's Opium Cultivation Up 13 Per Cent, UN Says', *Nation*, 2013, available online at http://www.nationmultimedia.com/breakingnews/Myanmars-opium-cultivation-up-13-per-cent-UN-says-30222386.html (accessed 18 December 2013).

Conflict Management

Dialogue Processes

The ceasefire with the Kachins brought to culmination the first phase of the government's objective of concluding individual ceasefire agreements with the insurgent groups. This would be followed by a national ceasefire agreement with the groups signing a common agreement with the government, before the initiation of a political dialogue. In 2013, especially in the second half of the year, a large number of negotiations, both among the insurgent groups themselves and with the government representatives took place.

The UNFC in September held peace talks with the government peace delegation in Chiang Mai. Afterwards, UNFC leaders said a nationwide ceasefire agreement between the government and all ethnic rebel groups was unlikely to be signed anytime soon because the meeting had ended in disagreement.[51] In October, the ethnic groups met for a meeting in the KIO stronghold of Laiza, where they drew up an 11-point agreement outlining their position on a nationwide ceasefire with Naypyidaw. This meeting resulted in the establishment of a Nationwide Ceasefire Coordination Team (NCCT) to represent the groups in a dialogue with the government to reach a nationwide ceasefire agreement. The second round of the meeting, planned to be held to discuss a government-proposed nationwide ceasefire, was postponed to the third week of January 2014.

A national dialogue was held on 4 and 5 November between the Government and ethnic armed groups in Myitkyina, the capital city of Kachin state. This was the first ever meeting of this nature and represented, in the words of Vijay Nambiar, the UN Secretary General's Special Adviser on Myanmar who participated as observer in the talks, 'a significant move forward in the

---

[51] 'UNFC—Government's Offer of a Nationwide Ceasefire not Acceptable Now', *Karen News*, 2013, available online at http://karennews.org/2013/09/unfc-governments-offer-of-a-nationwide-ceasefire-not-acceptable-now.html/ (accessed 17 December 2013).

national reconciliation process'.[52] At the Myitkyina congregation, the Government negotiator Aung Min gave ethnic representatives a draft of a government ceasefire proposal. As the year ended, no significant progress towards a national ceasefire appeared to have been made, although the continuous process of dialogue crated adequate conditions for some of the IDPs to return home.

Issue of a Federal Army

During the dialogue, creation of a federal army that would incorporate the rebel fighters into a national military or a federal army became a contentious issue between the government and the ethnic groups. The KIA, for example, insisted that the 'military recruitment process should be reformed to accommodate the integration of ethnic commanders and senior soldiers into a federal union army'.[53] In fact, this issue was one of the many incompatibilities between both the parties, other issues being the demand for a federal Myanmar and recognition of the 1947 Panglong Agreement, which set out a recipe for autonomy of ethnic groups within a united Myanmar, by the ethnic armed outfits.

Government figures put the number of cadres in the insurgent armies at 200,000. Since any such absorption into a federal army would mean these cadres retaining their weapons, the condition has been unacceptable to the government. Although on 14 November, Minister of the President's Office demonstrated some flexibility and said that armed forces that are in conformity with the federal union could be considered, additional problems of this being acceptable to the military remained. It needs mention that these peace negotiations did not witness attendance by the

---

[52] United Nations News Centre, 'Myanmar: UN Adviser Lauds Peace Talks in Kachin', 2013, available online at http://www.un.org/apps/news/story.asp/www.iaea.org/html/www.sealthedeal2009.org/petition/story.asp?NewsID=46425&Cr=myanmar&Cr1=#.Uqf5GPQW2Sp (accessed 11 December 2013).

[53] Nyein Nyein, 'Peace Talks Turn to Future Federal Army Structure', *Relief Web*, 2013, available online at http://reliefweb.int/report/myanmar/peace-talks-turn-future-federal-army-structure (accessed 11 December 2013).

Myanmar army's Commander-in-Chief and regional commanders. If the statement of a Lt. General of the Myanmar army provides any indication, the road ahead is bound to be turbulent. Lt. Gen. Myint Soe expressed concern that a federal army, which would likely see ethnic armed leaders granted a degree of operational autonomy in ethnic regions, could cause the military to 'collapse or become divided'.[54]

It remained to be seen whether a common ground could be arrived at, although experts are largely pessimistic. In the words of Bertil Lintner,

> Of course the military cannot accept this. Their idea about the future of this country is entirely different. They want the non-[Burman] ethnic groups to accept the 2008 Constitution, to obey laws imposed by the state, and not to be a burden on the local people—which means no recruitment or tax collection.[55]

Winning the Rebels Over

As the government attempted to bring armed groups on its side, it indulged in the controversial awarding of car import licenses to some ethnic leaders, raising fears that such lucrative deals benefiting the top leadership of the armed groups would have a corrupting effect and would alienate them from their constituency. According to local Myanmar media, all the ethnic insurgent groups received such licenses, which were distributed during the 66th Union Day ceremony on 12 February. In the subsequent months, photographs of such cars also appeared in the local media and on the Internet, detailing the import of expensive luxury cars such as brand-new 2013-model Rolls-Royces, Bentleys and Lexus by the KNU and the KNLA.[56] Some

---

[54] Nyein, 'Peace Talks Turn to Future Federal Army Structure', 2013.

[55] Simon Lewis, 'Burma Expert Doubtful That Current Talks Will Bring Peace', *Irrawaddy*, 2013, available online at http://www.irrawaddy.org/burma/burma-expert-doubtful-current-talks-will-bring-peace.html (accessed 17 December 2013).

[56] 'Buying Peace in Burma with Rolls-Royce Import Permits', Hlaoo1980.blogspot.com, 2013, available online at http://hlaoo1980.blogspot.sg/2013/11/buying-peace-in-burma-with-rolls-royce.html (accessed 9 January 2014).

of the groups resold these permits to car dealers, car brokers and private owners at more than 50 million kyats (US$ 50,000) for each permit. Some used the licences to legalize the vehicles they had imported illegally, and the rest bought vehicles for their own use. The only group which had not received the license was the KIA, which during the license distribution in February was still in a fighting mode. Not surprisingly, in November, General Gwan Maw, Chief of Staff of the military wing of the KIO, accused other groups of signing ceasefire agreements with the government in exchange for lucrative car import permits. 'To those making efforts for peace, I urge them not to exchange peace for car permits', he said.[57]

Apart from such offers, local interests of the individual outfits have also been accommodated by the Central Government. The KNU, for example, has reportedly been given 'a site for a factory in a special economic zone outside Hpa-An (capital of the Kayin state in southern Myanmar); and a licence to open a tour company of its own'.[58]

Such attempts to win over the rebel leadership have several parallels in conflict theatres all over the world. However, apart from short-term benefits, these measures can be counter-productive. Experts argue that such deals could 'cause a lot of resentment among the ordinary people. There would be a backlash, which would make the situation even more complicated'.[59] It could fracture the unity among the rebel organizations as well. From a different point of view, the eagerness with which each of these ethnic outfits have accepted and benefited from the government's offers is a narrative of their farcical claim of representative status. They seem to be driven more by personal gains rather than good of the community they claim to represent.

---

[57] Radio Free Asia, 'Myanmar Political Parties Set to Hold Talks With Armed Rebel Groups', 2013, available online at http://www.rfa.org/english/news/myanmar/peace-talks-11212013183055.html (accessed 12 December 2013)

[58] 'If You're Karen and You Know It', *Economist*, 2013, available online at http://www.economist.com/blogs/banyan/2013/11/myanmars-longest-war (accessed 15 December 2013).

[59] See note 55.

Trust Deficit

Even after the military campaigns came to a close, the Tatmadaw did not evoke much trust among the ethnic population. Apart from the long-held beliefs that the military is anti-democracy and is only a reluctant partner in the reforms project, its involvement in large-scale land grabs added to its negative image. A report by the Asian Human Rights Commission (AHRC) documented the instances of such land grabs 'under a false veneer of legality' and said that 'the actions cast doubt on the country's commitment to political reform after decades under military rule'.[60] The instances cited were

> [T]he decades-old military land grab in Migyaungkan village in the outskirts of Yangon, the expansion of the China-backed Letpadaung copper mine in Salingyi township in northern Myanmar, a land conflict with police in Ma-Ubin and a police land grab in Nattalin township—both in the country's south.[61]

Those protesting against the land grabs were imprisoned.

Challenges for the NLD

In the past years, the opposition, NLD in general and its supreme leader Aung San Suu Kyi in particular, were criticized for refusing to take stand on issues such as the ethnic conflicts and the Rohingya versus Buddhists issue. Such silence came at a cost. Suu Kyi's image suffered both internally and among the pro-democracy activists outside Myanmar. Aung Zaw, the founder of *Irrawaddy*, summed up in his autobiography, *The Face of Resistance: Aung San Suu Kyi and Burma's Fight for Freedom*. He wrote,

> She has become silent on the issue of sanctions and is no longer increasing pressure on the generals, or speaking out about current

---

[60] Radio Free Asia, 'Myanmar Military's Land Grabs "Cast Doubt" on Commitment to Reform', 2013, available online at http://www.rfa.org/english/news/myanmar/land-grabs-12172013183620.html (accessed 18 December 2013).

[61] Ibid.

and past abuses and allegations of crimes against humanity. Some of her recent decisions have, in fact, harmed those she claims to represent.[62]

Over time and under pressure, both NLD and Suu Kyi attempted to traverse a path of rectification, by projecting an inconsistent image of greater involvement in the peace process. Representative of NLD Nang Khin Htwe Myint participated in the meeting between 11 political parties of Myanmar and the UNFC in Chiang Mai on 22 November 2013.

Realizing that her silence has been less fruitful in making the military accede to the demands for constitutional reforms, Suu Kyi became more vocal and forthright regarding the need to bring about the change. In the last quarter of 2013, the NLD took to conducting road trips and public events in Yangon and other cities about the controversial 2008 constitution and the party's desire to have it either amended or rewritten. In December, speaking to party supporters in Yangon, she said that her endeavours to amend the constitution should not be seen as opposition to the military, but rather as an attempt to unify the military and the public. 'Our endeavour to amend the constitution, to take a leadership role in the national politics, does not mean we oppose the Tatmadaw and we would like everyone to know our intention is to unify the Tatmadaw and the public', she said.[63] The rally was attended by 35,000–40,000 people. The NLD later claimed that a survey carried out in the rally indicated that 95 per cent of the attendees supported an amendment to the constitution. A similar rally by the NLD in November in Naypyidaw reportedly had returned a result of 88 per cent approval for constitutional reforms.

---

[62] Bertil Lintner, 'Images of a Dark Era', *Asia Times*, 2013, available online at http://www.atimes.com/atimes/Southeast_Asia/SEA-01-221113.html (accessed 14 December 2013).

[63] 'Suu Kyi Says Constitutional Reform Will Unify Military and People', *Democratic Voice of Burma*, 2013, available online at http://www.dvb.no/news/suu-kyi-says-constitutional-reform-will-unify-military-and-people-burma-myanmar/35319 (accessed 17 December 2013).

Conclusions and Outlook for 2014

In his New Year speech on 2 January 2014, Myanmar President Thein Sein claimed that the country achieved some important developments in 2013 with a new political culture emerging within the society. He credited the different political groups for avoiding direct confrontation and trying to overcome challenges through negotiation and dialogue. He also described the country's reform process as stronger, attributing the achievement to the government's working collaboratively on various issues.[64] The president's claims are true only to an extent, as the country's progress is still tentative and hinged on actors, institutions and incidents alike.

A lot of importance has been ascribed to the role of the Parliament. According to a report,[65] the legislative body 'has turned out to be far more vibrant and influential than expected'. Both its lower and upper houses have a key role in driving the transition process through the enactment and amendment of legislation needed to reform the outdated legal code and are acting as a real check on the power of the executive. In the two years of operations, even while being hampered by the 25 per cent military bloc assured by the 2008 Constitution, the Parliament has been instrumental in legislating on important subjects, including some controversial ones that shape the country's progress. At the same time, however, as an instrument of change, the Parliament faces several challenges. These include the representatives' lack of experience and institutional weaknesses, lack of knowledge of democratic practice, no policy and research help and committees lacking internal experts to report on and analyse the issues. As a result, 'efficient, effective lawmaking is impossible', the report concludes.[66]

---

[64] 'Myanmar President Underlines Important Developments Achieved in 2013', *Xinhua*, 2014, available online at http://www.globaltimes.cn/content/835591.shtml#.Us_xmp6SySp (accessed 12 December 2014).

[65] International Crisis Group, 'Not a Rubber Stamp: Myanmar's Legislature in a Time of Transition', 2013, available online at http://www.crisisgroup.org/en/regions/asia/south-east-asia/myanmar/b142-not-a-rubber-stamp-myanmar-s-legislature-in-a-time-of-transition.aspx (accessed 12 December 2014).

[66] Ibid.

This creates additional challenges for constitutional reforms. In June, a 109-member parliamentary review committee was formed, which began accepting proposals for amending the constitution from the public. Irrespective of its report, whether the Tatmadaw would support reforms in the 2008 Constitution and pave the way for a free and fair parliamentary election in 2015 remains an important question. Such steps would curtail the military's wide-ranging influence in Myanmar's politics. Apart from the controversial Article 59(F), which bans citizens whose spouse or children are foreign nationals from holding the nation's top office, and hence effectively debars Aung San Suu Kyi from running for the President's Office, the reforms process would have to make the country a truly federal entity.

Experts opine that socio-economic progress and peace in Myanmar will come only if the government grants the ethnic groups in its border areas a degree of self-government.[67] It has to recognize the indigenous land tenure systems practised by ethnic groups and take their concerns on land seriously. Land, with 70 per cent of the population depending on agriculture, is a politically and economically sensitive issue in Myanmar. However, settling debates over the business interests of the military in the conflict zones could well mar the peace processes. In November, a senior member of Myanmar's ruling Union Solidarity and Development Party (USDP), Hla Swe, questioned whether ethnic rebel leaders were 'really representing the interests of their people' in the negotiations.[68] He warned the government against giving in to rebel demands, saying that President Thein Sein's negotiating team led by Minister Aung Min had been too patient already.

And lastly, much of the future would also depend upon the influence of the external powers. While countries like the United States would try pushing for constitutional reforms and a free and fair poll in 2015, a lot would depend on the position China takes on Myanmar's reforms processes. Analysts indicate that China is

---

[67] Thin Lei Win, 'In Kachin, Myanmar's Reforms Seem a World Away', 2013, available online at http://www.trust.org/item/20131112034416-c28j5 (accessed 11 December 2013).

[68] See note 57.

unsure about the reforms process and blames President Thein Sein for the falling Chinese investment in that country.[69] On the other hand, Suu Kyi has publicly indicated her support for a robust relationship with China, helping to somewhat mitigate Beijing's concern about her future international alignment choices.

[69] Yun Sun, 'China Adapts to New Myanmar Reality', 2013, available online at http://atimes.com/atimes/Southeast_Asia/SEA-04-231213.html (accessed 12 December 2013).

5

Northeast India: Bordering on Renewed Conflict or Building on the Peace?

Mirza Zulfiqur Rahman

A Short History

Northeast India has been witness to numerous insurgencies and remains one of the most enduring contested spaces, not only in independent India, but also in the overall South Asian context. The often raging and simmering insurgencies in Northeast India have been viewed in isolation and as somewhat internal to India, but they sit in the centre of a truly transregional context, connecting the dynamics of irregular warfare spanning South Asia and Southeast Asia. Insurgent contestations in Northeast India date back to prior to India's independence from British colonial rule, and subsequently have marked over six-and-a-half decades in India's post-independence nation-building process, and continuing.

It is important to note that insurgencies in Northeast India were set in the backdrop of World War II, with the region being one of the active theatres of the war in Asia. The revolutionary Naga leader, Angami Zhapu Phizo, who founded the Naga National Council (NNC) as the forbearer of the Naga insurgency, had trained with the Japanese forces fighting against the British in the warfront in Burma, along with Mizo and Manipuri groups. Such an exposure and training in jungle warfare and guerrilla tactics during World War II helped in sustaining the initial insurgencies in Northeast India.

The Naga insurgency started with the formation of the NNC under the leadership of Phizo in 1946, and the subsequent declaration of Naga independence from British colonial rule on 14 August 1947. This came after the rejection of a 'Nine-point Agreement' known as the 'Akbar Hydari Agreement', which was signed between the moderates in the NNC and Sir Akbar Hydari, the then Governor of Assam, on 29 June 1947.

The following three decades leading to the Shillong Accord of 1975 were marked by violent armed conflict between the Naga rebels and the Indian Army, leading to innumerable deaths and human rights abuses. The Shillong Accord signed between the embattled leadership of NNC and the Government of India on 11 November 1975 was described as a sell-out by a section of the NNC. Prominent among the rebels of the NNC, Thuingaleng Muivah, Isak Chisi Swu and S.S. Khaplang broke away to form the National Socialist Council of Nagaland (NSCN) in 1980 at Myanmar. Subsequent rivalries within the NSCN led to another split in the year 1988, with Khaplang breaking away to form the NSCN (K), while Muivah and Swu formed the NSCN (IM). The armed violence continued unabated, both against the state and inter-factional, until the Government of India entered into ceasefire arrangements with NSCN (IM) in 1997 and with NSCN (K) in 2001. The NSCN (IM) split on 23 November 2007, with the formation of NSCN-Unification (NSCN (U)), which resulted in violent factional clashes. NSCN (IM) and NSCN (K) have managed to strengthen themselves during the ceasefire period in terms of arms, funding sources and increased cadre base.[1]

The United Liberation Front of Assam (ULFA) was founded by some Assamese youths led by Paresh Baruah and Arabinda Rajkhowa in Sibsagar district of Assam on 7 April 1979. ULFA moved ahead with violence against the Indian state and the sovereignty of Assam was the main plank on which it conducted its armed rebellion. The Indian Army carried out operations against

---

[1] For more on the Naga conflict, see Prasenjit Biswas and Chandan Suklabaidya, *Ethnic Life-Worlds in North-east India: An Analysis* (New Delhi: SAGE Publications, 2008); Sanjoy Hazarika, *Strangers in the Mist: Tales of War and Peace from India's Northeast* (New Delhi: Penguin, 1995).

ULFA in quick succession between 1990 and 1992, which included Operation Bajrang and Operation Rhino.[2] Operation All Clear was launched in 2003 by the Indian Army along with the Royal Government of Bhutan against ULFA camps in Bhutan, the operation being termed as highly successful. The anti-talks faction[3] of the ULFA continues to operate in Assam from bases in Bangladesh, Myanmar and Bhutan, although its modus operandi has changed considerably in the past decade.

The Bodo insurgency started with the formation of the National Democratic Front of Bodoland (NDFB) under the leadership of Ranjan Daimary on 3 October 1986 in Assam. The 1990s saw a lot of violence in the Bodo heartland of Assam, as another group called the Bodo Liberation Tigers (BLT) under the leadership of Prem Singh Brahma was formed on 18 June 1996. The Bodo Accord of February 2003 constituted the Bodoland Territorial Council (BTC), and the BLT cadres led by their Chief, Hagrama Mohilary, surrendered arms to form the council. However, the NDFB have been continuing with their armed rebellion, in spite of a split between the moderates and the hardliners in 2008.

Assam has been witness to Karbi, Dimasa, Hmar, Muslim and Adivasi insurgencies over the past two decades. Various insurgent groups claiming to represent these communities have been fighting against the security forces and numerous factions have emerged, which has resulted in a lot of insurgent activity, including sporadic inter-ethnic clashes.

Manipur has been one of the most troubled states in the region, with Naga, Meitei and Kuki insurgent groups operating from the state. The Manipur hills, which are dominated by various Naga tribes, had a sense of participation in the Naga insurgency. The first Meitei insurgent group, United National Liberation Front (UNLF), was formed on 24 November 1964, and was right from the beginning besotted with factionalism. This factionalism, accompanied by divergent ideological orientations and support bases,

---

[2] For more on the ULFA, see Hazarika, *Strangers in the Mist*.
[3] The ULFA had split between the pro-talks and the anti-talks factions with the surrender of the A and C companies of its powerful 28th Batallion on 24 June 2008. Paresh Barua heads the ULFA anti-talks faction.

ensured a number of insurgent groups in Manipur, such as the People's Liberation Army (PLA), People's Revolutionary Party of Kangleipak (PREPAK) and the Kangleipak Communist Party (KCP), all between 1977 and 1980. Another rebel group called the Kanglei Yawol Kanna Lup (KYKL), formed in 1994 with a radical agenda of moral and social reform, contributed to the existing violence. Several Kuki groups were formed in the 1990s which were based primarily on inter-ethnic rivalry in the Manipur hills with the Naga tribes. The Manipuri Muslims known as *Pangal Meiteis* formed the People's United Liberation Front (PULF) in 1993, given the overall ethnic violence in Manipur.

The Mizo insurgency had its origins in the devastating famine, locally known as *Mautam*, of 1959, and the Mizo National Front (MNF), which was formed under Pu Laldenga, started the insurgent movement on 22 October 1961 against governmental apathy during the famine. One of the most intense and violent insurgencies in Northeast India, it lasted for over two decades and ended with the formation of the separate state of Mizoram in 1987, where the MNF came overground to form the state government. However, Mizoram has witnessed insurgency by Reangs who formed the Bru National Liberation Front (BNLF) in 1996 following ethnic clashes with the Mizos. The Hmar People's Convention-Democracy (HPC-D), formed in 1995, have been active in Mizoram, apart from Manipur and Assam, fighting for the rights of the Hmar tribe.

Tripura saw armed struggle by the tribal people soon after India's independence, primarily against the Bengali settlers who came from East Pakistan following the Partition of 1947, which led to a change in the demographic character of the erstwhile princely state. The 1960s saw the Sengkrak movement against the displacement and alienation of tribal lands in Tripura. The Tribal National Volunteers (TNV) was formed in 1978, which continued its insurgent activity until 1988, when it entered into an accord with the Indian government. The All Tripura Tiger Force (ATTF) was formed in 1990 under the leadership of Ranjit Debbarma, and consolidated the tribal base to become a powerful insurgent group in Tripura. The National Liberation Front of Tripura (NLFT) was formed in 1989, under the leadership of Dhananjoy Reang, with similar objectives, of armed struggle for the protection of tribal rights, as the ATTF. NLFT has been plagued by intense factionalism and leadership contestations, with many splits occurring in the past decade among its leaders Nayanbasi Jamatiya, Biswamohan Debbarma and Joshua Debbarma.

The state of Meghalaya saw the rise of insurgency with the formation of the Hynniewtrep Achik Liberation Council (HALC), which had the participation of all the three major tribes of the state, Khasis, Jaintias and Garos, and their common goal of fighting the outsiders. However, ethnic differences resulted in a split in 1992, when the Hynniewtrep National Liberation Council (HNLC), representing Khasis and Jaintias, and the Achik Matgrik Liberation Army (AMLA), representing Garos, were formed out of the HALC. Armed struggle has continued for a separate Khasiland with close coordination with other insurgent groups of Northeast India having bases in Bangladesh. Several top leaders of the HNLC have surrendered, including its Chairman, Julius Dorphang, in July 2007, but the outfit still continues to be strong in the border areas linking Meghalaya with Bangladesh. The demand for a separate Garoland has intensified with two new insurgent groups formed in the Garo hills of Meghalaya over the past decade, the People's Liberation Front of Meghalaya (PLF-M) and the Liberation of Achik Elite Force (LAEF). Former Deputy Superintendent of Police in the Meghalaya government Champion Sangma formed the Garo National Liberation Army (GNLA) in 2009, and has been instrumental in reviving the insurgency in Garo Hills, demanding a sovereign Garoland.

Various insurgent groups operating in other parts of Northeast India, which have seen violent insurgencies in the past and continuing, have used the state of Arunachal Pradesh as an operating base, although relatively calmer than the other six northeastern states. The easternmost districts of Tirap, Changlang and Longding of Arunachal Pradesh prove to be the hotbed of inter-factional rivalry between the NSCN (IM) and the NSCN (K), given a large Naga population in these districts. The other insurgent groups, such as ULFA and NDFB, are believed to have bases in Arunachal Pradesh, particularly in Lohit, West Kameng and East Kameng districts adjoining Assam, using the state's dense forest cover effectively.

Major Actors in the Conflict

Insurgent Groups

The principal insurgent groups in Northeast India are NSCN (IM), NSCN (K) and NSCN (U) (three Naga factions spanning Nagaland, Manipur, Arunachal Pradesh and Assam); ULFA Anti-talks Faction (led by Paresh Barua), NDFB (Ranjan Daimary and IK Songbijit factions), Karbi People's Liberation Tigers (KPLT), Dima Halam Daogah-Jewel (DHD-J), United People's Democratic Solidarity (UPDS), All Adivasi National Liberation Army (AANLA), Muslim United Liberation Tigers of Assam (MULTA) and Kamtapur Liberation Organization (KLO); UNLF, PLA, KCP, PREPAK, KYKL, PULF (Meitei groups from Manipur); Kuki National Front (KNF) and Kuki National Army (KNA) (Kuki groups from Manipur hills); ATTF and NLFT (Tripuri groups from Tripura); BNLF (Reang group in Mizoram); HNLC (Khasi group in Meghalaya); Achik National Volunteer Council (ANVC), GNLA, PLF-M and LAEF (Garo groups in Meghalaya) and HPC-D (Hmar group spanning Assam, Manipur, Nagaland and Mizoram).

The NSCN (IM) remains the strongest insurgent group in Northeast India, given the number of states it operates in as well as the wide range of activities it is involved in. Its political objectives of unification of all Naga-inhabited areas and self-determination based on the historical Naga narrative, along with a 'Nagaland for Christ' slogan since early 1990s, have contributed to its dominance over the decades. It has entered the 14th year of ceasefire and peace talks with the Union Government of India and projects itself as the sole representative of the Naga peace process. NSCN (IM), although with similar objectives, has overshadowed the NSCN (K) and NSCN (U), which has resulted in their activities being confined to their pockets of influence in Northeast India and Myanmar.

The ULFA in Assam has suffered a lot of setbacks with almost all of its top leadership being arrested in 2009, and had suffered a split in 2008 when two companies of its 28th battalion had surrendered for peace talks. The outfit, being in a disarray, has in the past few years changed its modus operandi, using mercenary tactics of sabotage. The NDFB also suffered a split in 2008, with the anti-talks faction led by Ranjan Daimary continuing its activities from bases along the Assam–Arunachal Pradesh border and Bangladesh. The arrest of DHD-J Chief Jewel Gorlosa in June 2009 from Bangalore and the killing of its Foreign Secretary in Guwahati dealt a severe blow to the outfit which is also known as Black Widow. The group, claiming to represent the Dimasa tribe in North Cachar hills district, along with the UPDS participated in a mass surrender soon after, paving the way for peace talks. Karbi Longri National Liberation Front (KLNLF), the Karbi insurgent outfit, also surrendered en masse in February 2010. The AANLA, MULTA and KLO, however, are operating in various parts of Assam, with sporadic insurgent activity, but with limited impact.

The valley groups in Manipur have been very active in the past few years, resulting in a lot of violence in the state. UNLF has been leading the charge against the security forces, with PREPAK, PLA, KYKL and KCP stepping up their activities in various parts of the valley, particularly targeting the Hindi-speaking people living in Manipur. The Meitei Pangal group PULF has been engaged in sporadic incidents in its pockets of influence in the state. The Kuki insurgent groups have been under a Suspension of Operations (SoO) with the government, but they are active in the Manipur hills bordering Myanmar, often engaging in violent clashes with Meitei and Naga insurgent groups in the state. Most of the informal arms-, ammunition- and narcotics trade go through this region and are controlled amongst the Naga, Meitei and Kuki groups, thereby resulting in an intense turf war between the various ethnic insurgent groupings. NSCN (IM) is particularly active in the Manipur hills dominated by Thangkhul Nagas, taking advantage of the fact that their ceasefire with the Government of India in the state of Nagaland does not extend to Manipur.

The NLFT and the ATTF in Tripura have continued their insurgent violence in the state, but with limited success and operational mobility. This is due to a huge number of cadres of both the insurgent outfits surrendering before the security forces in the state. This has been referred to as a success of the counter-insurgency strategy of the state in Tripura, whereas in most other parts of Northeast India, insurgent activities had actually seen a rise. The NLFT and the ATTF now have a hugely depleted cadre base, and many of them are in the jungles, attempting a regrouping in the face of strong counter-insurgency measures.

Meghalaya and Mizoram have seen insurgent groups operating from their territory, but these groups are relatively small in their cadre base and operational abilities. Khasi group HNLC of Meghalaya has seen most of the cadres laying down arms, along with its Chairman, but still continues to operate along the Meghalaya–Bangladesh border, with sporadic attacks on security forces and government establishments. The Garo insurgent groups PLF-M and LAEF are relatively new to the insurgency scene, yet have managed to make their presence felt in the Garo hills region of Meghalaya through their sporadic attacks. The Reang group BNLF have developed their operational base in Mizoram and Tripura border, consolidating on the increasingly hostile ethnic relations between the Mizos and the Reangs in Mizoram, often leading to ethnic clashes. The Hmar group HPC-D has concentrated on a strategy of assimilating their tribal base spanning across Assam, Manipur and Mizoram, and fighting for the rights of their community. There are reports of Communist Party of India (Maoist) [CPI (Maoist)] influence in parts of Northeast India, but its impact is not seen.

Arunachal Pradesh has been the scene of activity for some of the major insurgent groups of Northeast India such as NSCN (IM), NSCN (K), NSCN (U), ULFA and NDFB. The state which does not have any insurgency of its own has seen these groups make their operational and training bases in its territory, given a dense forest cover and its proximity to the Myanmar border, providing an exit route during counter-insurgency operations.

Government Actors

The Government of India and the state governments of the respective states of Northeast India have been engaged in tackling the countless insurgencies that have taken place in the region ever since Independence. The Indian Army, central paramilitary forces, the state police forces and intelligence and security agencies have been engaged in counter-insurgency operations in Northeast India, with varying degrees of operational success. The state governments in each of the states are important actors in the entire conflict scenario, as they have to coordinate with the army in the operations against the insurgent groups, and the efficacy of such coordination holds the key to the success of any counter-insurgency measure. The individual state governments in Assam, Nagaland, Manipur and Tripura have an important role to play in providing the space and conditions for any peace process with insurgents to come about or to be a success in their respective states.

The Border Security Force is an important actor in Northeast India, as they play a crucial role in monitoring and controlling the insurgent movements and activity across the large stretches of international boundary Northeast India shares, especially with Myanmar, Bangladesh and Bhutan, given the presence of insurgent training facilities and camps in these countries and existing supply lines of arms, ammunition and narcotics. The army has the use of the much controversial Armed Forces Special Powers Act (AFSPA) of 1958 in the conduct of its counter-insurgency operations in certain government-designated *disturbed areas* of Northeast India. The states of Assam, some parts of Arunachal Pradesh, Manipur and Tripura have in place a Unified Command structure to fight insurgency, which is headed by the state Chief Minister and consists of the army, paramilitary forces and the state police forces, to ensure better operational coordination.

Civil Society Actors

A large number of civil society actors have played an important role in how conflict has progressed and peace processes are being shaped in Northeast India. The Mizo National Famine Front (MNFF) started as a civil society group, later became an insurgent outfit, and after its surrender, became a local political party in Mizoram. The BLT and NDFB are seen to have emerged out of a student organization spearheading the Bodo agitation in Assam which is still active in promoting peace in the region, the All Bodo Students Union (ABSU). The All Assam Students Union (AASU) and the Asom Jatiyatabadi Yuva Chatra Parishad (AJYCP) were forerunners in the anti-foreigners agitation in Assam, at the time when ULFA was formed, and still continue to play an important role in rallying public opinion. The Asom Sahitya Sabha (ASS) and the Bodo Sahitya Sabha (BSS) are important civil society actors in Assam. The Naga Hoho and other tribal hohos, Naga Mothers Association (NMA), Naga Student's Forum (NSF) and United Naga Council (UNC) are important civil society actors in the ongoing peace process in Nagaland where the Indian government is in negotiations with the insurgent group NSCN (IM).

Apunba Lup, a conglomerate of civil society organizations fighting against human rights violations and the use of AFSPA by the government, and Meira Paibis are key stakeholders in the state of Manipur. The Khasi Students Union (KSU) and Garo Students Union (GSU) in Meghalaya are important civil society actors. The Young Mizo Association (YMA) and Mizo Zirlai Pawl (MZP) are key actors in Mizoram and have a history of rallying public opinion on issues related to ethnic minorities living in the state.

The local political parties in Northeast India are important players in the conflict and peace processes in the region. Asom Gana Parishad (AGP), Bodoland People's Front (BPF), Autonomous State Demand Council (ASDC) in Assam, Democratic Alliance of Nagaland (DAN) in Nagaland, MNF in Mizoram and Communist Party of India-Marxist (CPI-M) in Tripura are all key political parties which have a critical stake in the conflict and peace processes in the region. The Church as an institution is another key actor in the conflict and peace processes in Nagaland, Mizoram and Meghalaya.

Major Development during 2013 and Trends

The year 2013 was quite a mixed bag for the overall conflict scenario in Northeast India, with minimal gains for the counter-insurgency efforts by the state. Manipur, Meghalaya, Assam and Nagaland were the states in Northeast India which saw considerable violence and high incidence of insurgent attacks in 2013. On the other hand, there was a decrease in insurgency-related attacks and fatalities in Tripura and Mizoram. There were a number of surrenders across insurgent groups in Assam, Manipur and Meghalaya. The strategies used by the insurgent groups were mercenary in nature, and included hit-and-run attacks and other forms of sabotages. The year was marked by various incidents which included bomb blasts, ethnic clashes, fratricidal killings, attacks on migrant communities, especially Hindi-speaking and Bengali-speaking communities, attacks on public infrastructure and government symbols such as highway projects, dam projects, railways, government offices and security establishments, kidnappings of officers and contractors on government duty and increased kidnappings and extortion demands.

Insurgent Activity in 2013

There is a trend of return to a renewed conflict cycle in Northeast India after a decline in violent activities over the past five years. It can be described to be a situation which is bordering on a renewed cycle of conflict and violence, which can go either way. Several fragmented and low-intensity incidents of conflict were witnessed all across the major states of Northeast India, with a sustained assertion by the ULFA Anti-talks Faction, the NDFB Anti-talks Factions and the NDFB (IK Songbijit faction) across the state of Assam. The Songbijit faction of the NDFB has been seen as a highly organized criminal gang across Assam and Arunachal Pradesh, frequently carrying out sabotage activities and kidnappings for ransom. It has managed to recruit new cadres and send them to Myanmar and Chittagong Hill Tracts for training purposes. The factions, who have chosen to be outside the ambit of the ongoing peace talks in Assam, have chosen a modus operandi of engaging in arms and drug trafficking and fake currency networks in the region.

The large-scale violence in the run-up to the Rabha Hasong Autonomous Council elections in Lower Assam, and the involvement of Garo and other non-tribal groups along the Assam–Meghalaya state border, is a worrying trend. This must be analysed in the backdrop of the increase in insurgent activity by Garo insurgent groups such as the GNLA, in the Garo Hills region of Meghalaya, even after its chief was apprehended in mid-2012. The availability and use of sophisticated arms and ammunition in such incidents of inter-ethnic violence, which was also seen in the Bodo–Muslim riots in Kokrajhar in 2012, points towards the active involvement of armed insurgent groups who, taking advantage of such ethnic divide, recruit more people and gain coinage.

The factional fights in various insurgent organizations in Nagaland, Manipur, Assam and Meghalaya have led to many splinter groups which have been operating across these states, and have led to the increase in violent incidents, albeit on a low scale. The rise of criminal gangs in Northeast India has been of late seen as a major trend, and the year 2013 saw their base increase in the region. On the other hand, the CorCom, which is an umbrella organization of seven insurgent organizations of Manipur, have been fighting on a united base in the Manipur Valley. The strong network of interdependency among various insurgent organizations of Northeast India has been evident in the year 2013, with various linkmen being active across the region, raising funds and acquiring weapons of various types, their strength based on illicit arms, drugs and fake currency networks.

The year 2013 has seen an increase in anti-outsider movements in Assam, Meghalaya, Nagaland, Manipur and Mizoram, with the Inner Line Permit demand gaining momentum, which has been seen as advantageous to the divisive agenda of insurgent groups in the region. The anti-outsider attacks, seen mainly in the blasts in Manipur and the killings in the Garo Hills area in the year 2013, are indeed ominous signs, which must be stemmed immediately. The tribal and non-tribal, hill–valley and inter-state divide in parts of Assam, Manipur and along the Assam–Meghalaya border, Assam–Nagaland border and Assam–Arunachal Pradesh border have the potential to turn into conflict flashpoints in the future. This was evident in the clashes between the Karbi and Rengma Nagas in December 2013, where the involvement of armed insurgent groups was a major trigger.

Counter-insurgency Operations in 2013

The counter-insurgency operations against the Naga insurgent groups remained ineffective in the states of Assam, Arunachal Pradesh and Manipur, as they had used their ceasefire status in Nagaland to their maximum benefit. The army has been engaged in operations against the NSCN factions in various parts of the Karbi Anglong hills where they are supporting the Rengma Nagas against the Karbis, but has not been able to control them, given their mobility across the Assam–Nagaland border and ground ceasefire rules.

The inability of the security forces to operate effectively in parts of Arunachal Pradesh, especially Tirap and Changlang districts where Naga factions dominate, and in West Kameng, East Kameng and Lohit districts where ULFA and NDFB dominate, has severely dented the counter-insurgency efforts in the overall conflict situation. The porous international borders with Myanmar and Bangladesh and the security forces' inability to monitor them effectively for arms, ammunition and insurgents' movements have severely impeded the counter-insurgency efforts. This ground situation has not changed much in 2013, and much needs to be done to improve the army presence and monitoring along the borders. In many cases, the security forces have been late in responding to the new contours of conflict in many parts of Northeast India, especially in the face of an ineffective policing infrastructure at the local level. The year 2013 saw violence spiral out of control in the Assam–Meghalaya and the Assam–Nagaland state borders, while the security agencies could not respond in time, and were caught off guard.

The increase in insurgent activities in Arunachal Pradesh, parts of Nagaland, Assam and Manipur has demonstrated the ineffectiveness of the counter-insurgency policy over the past many decades, which has measured its success or failure based on the fluctuations in insurgent-related incidents in the region, but have failed to move beyond in building trust.

The modernization of the capabilities of the state policing system has been long overdue, and this has affected the effectiveness of the Unified Command system in some of these insurgent-affected states. There is a need to build on the relative peace in Northeast India by security forces, instead of allowing the situation to border on renewed conflict cycles.

Conflict Management Efforts

Northeast India has seen protracted conflict between the various insurgent groups of the region and the government actors over the past three decades, and particularly in the past decade, nothing much has drastically changed in the overall conflict scenario. It is a continuing scene of insurgent conflict versus counter-insurgency measures adopted by the government, year after year in the past decade, interspersed with some peace processes, which have seen no positive direction. Apart from protracted conflicts in various states of Northeast India, there are some protracted (or prolonged) peace processes in some of the key insurgency affected states of the region, which are the result of a mix of reasons, ranging from governmental policy design to insurgent group's strategies and the role of the civil society actors amidst the dynamics of the overall peace negotiation process.

The protracted conflict we witness in Northeast India has social, political, economic and strategic tones, which is also true of the protracted peace processes, which makes for a vicious cycle. The protracted character and dynamics of the conflict feed into the protracted character and dynamics of the peace processes, and vice versa, making peace and stability in the region difficult to achieve. The sense of stagnancy that we see in the conflict management scenario in Northeast India is the inability of the stakeholders to break away from this vicious cycle. The sense of stagnancy has been a concern for many in India and around the world, but there has been little analysis of the underlying reasons.

Rising Threat of Islamist Militancy in Northeast India

The demonstration by Muslim advocacy groups, which resulted in violent clashes in Mumbai's Azad Maidan on 11 August 2012, leaving two dead and over 65 injured, was held to protest against the killings of Muslims in Kokrajhar (the inter-community clashes between Muslims and the Bodo community) and in the Arakan state of Myanmar (the inter-community clashes between the Rohingiya Muslims and the Rakhine community). The linkage of these two separate inter-community clashes in one single protest march in Mumbai may be symbolic, but the threat of the rise of Islamist militancy in parts of Northeast India and the larger international neighbourhoods encompassing Myanmar and Bangladesh has to be seen in context. It has been well documented that Islamist militant groups and networks have had links with insurgent groups in many states of Northeast India, especially in Manipur, Assam and Nagaland, and this had been oscillating between tactical support in arms dealing, narcotics and illegal and fake currency networks and anti-government sabotage activities over the past few decades. This trend, however, does not indicate by itself the threat of Islamist militancy. While many commentators have described the threat of the rise of Islamist militancy in Northeast India as unfounded and being alarmist, the ground conditions in the larger region cannot be ignored.

The PULF has been operating in parts of Manipur, Assam and Nagaland for the past two decades, and has been splintered, as has been the trend with many other insurgent organizations in Northeast India, into many smaller factions over time; it is one of the major Islamist militant organizations already active. Apart from this, the role and support of Pakistan's Inter-services Intelligence (ISI) and Bangladesh's Directorate General of Forces Intelligence (DGFI) to many insurgent organizations and networks in Northeast India has unabatedly continued. There is a sort of a ideological vacuum in many of the *home-grown* insurgent organizations in Northeast India; they have suffered huge losses in tactical and public legitimacy accounts in the past decade-and-a-half, and are not in a position to prevent the growth of Islamist militancy in Northeast India, to guard their own turf in the region.

The entry points for Islamist militancy in Northeast India are not hard to comprehend. The presence of a large *illegal* Muslim immigrant community in Assam, which has been a source of much political activism in the past and continuing, and was one of the motivations for the formation of the ULFA, provides a fertile ground as an entry point for Islamist militant groups. The political uncertainty that has engulfed this migrant community for over four decades now has made them vulnerable to such militant influence, as a way to survive the political threat. Further enhancing the political aspect of an ever-looming *threat to their survival* versus their responses to *surviving the threat* over the past decades, the instances of large-scale riots and inter-community clashes in the past, such as the Nellie riots and the recent instances in Udalguri in 2008 and Kokrajhar in 2012, have made the case for militant responses, a usable instrument in the evolving politics of ethnic divisions of demography.

The recent riots in Kokrajhar saw the use of sophisticated weapons by the anti-talk Bodo militant groups who took advantage of the situation, also a result of the flawed surrender policy of the Indian counter-insurgency establishment; there is the possibility of such weapons coming into the hands of the Muslim groups by jihadi groups across the border. The threat of the rise of militancy amongst the Muslims affected by the Kokrajhar violence was raised by the National Commission for Minorities (NCM) in its report to the Assam Government after a field visit to the violence-affected areas of Bodoland Territorial Autonomous District (BTAD) areas in August 2012. The overall political, economic and living conditions of the Muslim community in BTAD areas have been described as a fertile ground for jihadi influence by monitoring groups and field studies.

This brings into context the rise in militant activities amongst the Rohingya Muslims in the larger region of Arakan state of Myanmar, South Bangladesh, and parts of Tripura and Mizoram, where they are trying to push, in the face of deportation by the Border Guards Force along the Bangladesh border and political and ethnic clashes in Myanmar. The links of Rohingya militant organizations with Al-Qaeda and Lashkar-e-Taiba have been substantiated in the past. There have been reports of Rohingya Muslims trying to make way into Northeast India, and this seems not a distant possibility, given the state of our borders and the manner we treat our sensitive and *peaceful states* borders, especially in Mizoram, Manipur and Tripura. The Government of India needs to brace itself to counter the threat of Islamist militancy in the larger region through proactive diplomacy and understanding of larger issues and linkages, and not be content on *managing* the home situation. The trends that are emerging cannot be ignored, for the lack of actual ground instances, but we must prepare and remedy the conditions for such entry points for Islamist militancy. The elections in Bangladesh in 2014 have brought uncertainty and turmoil in the country, and the rising illicit trans-border networks cannot be ignored.

Ceasefires, Government Surrender Policy and Protracted Peace Processes

The Naga peace process between the NSCN (IM) and New Delhi, which has entered its 16th year in 2013, is a classic case in point. The Ceasefire Monitoring Group (CFMG) formed in 1997, entrusted with maintaining the ground ceasefire rules in Nagaland and consisting of security forces, intelligence agencies, government functionaries and members of the NSCN (IM) and NSCN (K),[4] has failed in its objective. The NSCN (IM) and NSCN (K) do collect *taxes* (extortions), and a glance at the NSCN (IM) will reveal that between 1997 when the ceasefire started and 2009, the outfit managed new recruitment, increasing its armed cadres from 1,000 to 5,000.[5] The NSCN (IM) has managed to consolidate its existing pockets of influence, and use its *ceasefire status* in Nagaland to operate in neighbouring states of Manipur, Assam and Arunachal Pradesh. It is apparent that New Delhi has favoured NSCN (IM) over the NSCN (K) in implementing the ceasefire ground rules in their pockets of influence in Nagaland and elsewhere in Northeast India,[6] the reason being the ongoing peace negotiations with NSCN (IM), and the comfort level New Delhi shares with its top leadership. The carrying of arms under the cover of jackets and shawls everywhere during ceasefire, which has been done by NSCN (IM) and NSCN (K), defeats the very rationale of having a ceasefire, as such violation has the potential to intimidate and incite violence anytime, as has been demonstrated in the *peacetime factional fights* which has killed many combatants and non-combatants in various parts of Nagaland and other states as well.

The NSCN (IM) and the Indian government have not been able to finalize a concrete peace deal, even after numerous rounds of peace negotiations, with the peace talks stumbling on two major issues—one, on the Greater Nagalim project[7] and two, on the issue of a solution under the ambit of the Constitution of India.

---

[4] New Delhi entered into ceasefire with the NSCN (K) in 2001, although the peace negotiations are going on with importance accorded primarily with the NSCN (IM), the powerful of the two groups.

[5] Namrata Goswami, 'The Naga Intra-community Dialogue: Preventing and Managing Violent Ethnic Conflict', *Global Change, Peace and Security* 22, no. 1 (2010): 93–120.

[6] Field observations by the author and informal interactions with army officials in the Pangsau Pass area of Arunachal Pradesh, where both the Naga insurgent factions operate.

[7] Contentious issue of territoriality floated by NSCN (IM), which involves the integration of Nagaland and all Naga-inhabited areas of Manipur, Assam, Arunachal Pradesh and even parts of Myanmar. This issue has led to violence in Manipur and Assam in the past, and forms the core of the ideology of the NSCN (IM).

The entire peace process is trapped in stagnancy and the talk of an interim peace deal has been talked of since 2004, and one can imagine if an interim peace deal takes more than five years to take any shape, how long will the final solution take. The central government peace interlocutor in the Indo-Naga peace talks was removed in 2009 and another appointed in February 2010. What was termed by the central government to be a Christmas gift for the Naga people in December 2012 has yet to fructify even after the Christmas of 2013 has passed by.

The long-drawn peace process has enabled the NSCN (IM) to work towards establishing its dominance and eliminating other insurgent factions claiming to be representing the Naga cause before any final political solution with New Delhi. The conspiracy theories may be many, accusing the central government, the state government, NSCN (IM) or NSCN (K) of delaying the peace or derailing the peace, but the fact remains that the ultimate casualty is the peace process itself. The huge obsession with the formalized processes with these aforementioned actors results in the increasing marginalization of the civil society's initiatives and bearings on the overall peace process and a lasting solution.

The civil society organizations in Nagaland such as the Naga Hoho, NMA, NSF and UNC are playing an important role in laying the groundwork for the emergence of lasting peace in the region. These are the actors who are working as a bridge between various regions in the proposed Nagalim, reaching out to communities, both Naga and other ethnic tribes, and promoting dialogue and understanding between them, assuaging and understanding contesting aspirations between communities of the region, which the conflicting parties in the political talks process have not been able to do. They have joined efforts to talk to top rebel leaders to stop fratricidal killings between Naga insurgent factions, extortions and threats, and they have been termed as being largely successful. They have tried to bring in more participation of women in the dialogue process and this definitely must be replicated in other parts of Northeast India as well.

Assam has witnessed the almost decimation of ULFA as an insurgent group, with the surrender of its top leadership excluding Commander-in-Chief Paresh Baruah, as well as the mass surrenders of DHD-J and UPDS in 2009 and KLNLF in February 2010. The past decade has seen various insurgent groups in Assam divided along lines of ideology, pro-ceasefire and anti-ceasefire, pro-peace talks and anti-peace talks, important pro-talks groups and non-important pro-talks groups, which have made the atmosphere of peace talks murky. Pro-talks groups of the ULFA, NDFB, DHD (Dilip Nunisa faction), Birsa Commando Force (BCF) and Adivasi Cobra Militant Force (ACMF) are living in designated camps in Kokrajhar, Karbi Anglong, North Cachar hills and Tinsukia for periods varying from one to six years.[8] The Assam government categorizes most of these groups as being non-important, and that explains the uncertain future of peace talks with these groups.

These pro-talks groups live in designated camps for years on end, living on government expenses and amidst a prevailing sense of frustration at the non-initiation of peace talks or any roadmap for their rehabilitation, often engaging in illicit activities, moving out of their designated camps to extort money, conduct kidnappings and issuing threats. Most of the top surrendered leaders living in designated camps manage to move out and live in civilian areas with arms, creating an atmosphere of fear and insecurity in such places.

The peace talks with the recently surrendered leadership of the ULFA, DHD-J, UPDS and KLNLF, as also the SoO with a number of Kuki groups recently in Manipur, can in all likelihood fall into the same trap of unending cycles of negotiations, without resulting in any lasting political solution for the insurgency-affected states. This reflects a lack of commitment and will on the part of the government actors for a lasting political solution to the various insurgencies in the region. The existing surrender policy and the consequent lack of tangible progress in peace talks in Northeast India have made insurgents potentially willing to enter talks desist from coming forward to surrender.

Another facet of the surrender policy is that the precedent of such protracted peace talks has made insurgent groups who come forward to surrender opting to keep arms and ammunition in reserve, thereby ensuring an option open for themselves to go back to the jungles if they are not able to achieve tangible gains out of the peace process. Insurgent surrenders in recent times have shown that the number of arms and ammunition deposited

---

[8] 'Stuck in Camps, Surrendered Militants Wait for Road Ahead', *Indian Express*, 13 August 2009.

with security forces at the time of their surrenders are minimal compared to their estimated levels of insurgent operations earlier. The various insurgent groups in Northeast India are adopting a strategy to withhold some arms and ammunition at the time of surrendering, by hiding or by creating proxy splinter groups, in order to protect their interests from other factions or insurgent groups during the period of ceasefire.

The central government's surrender and ceasefire policy in Northeast India has certain flaws, and to make things more complicated, it has employed different yardsticks in terms of peacetime operational conduct of the security forces towards different insurgent organizations, depending on the varying status of peace talks with them. The highest number of surrenders over the past few years has come from Assam and Manipur, leading to a mushrooming of designated camps, occupying much of the government's energies and resources over protracted peace talks. Moreover, there have been token surrenders by various insurgent groups in Northeast India, either to dispose some of the mercenary elements in their organizations, or to avail of the benefits of the surrender policy in the form of monetary compensation and lucrative government contracts. There have been reports of some insurgent organizations in Manipur which have formed and then summarily surrendered to benefit from such governmental largesse.

The increased factionalism in most of the insurgent groups in Northeast India is a serious concern, and the conscious policy of the government to *split and rule* and avoid any sincere attempt to solve any insurgency politically, hoping that they will weaken and fade away with time, has been instrumental in promoting this trend. Northeast India has been fast turning into a maze of insurgent factions, which is neither a positive sign for the future, and nor are the government actors fully aware of the implications it may hold for Northeast India and mainland India as an extension. These factions provide the fertile ground for radical jihadi outfits, sponsored by elements from Bangladesh and Pakistan, to wage war on India, as they become easy to infiltrate, given their divisions and want of resources to run the outfit. These insurgent factions, *ceasefire* or anti-ceasefire, are easily corruptible, and they are thriving on the illicit arms and ammunition, narcotics and fake currency networks in the region. Some factions have been ideologically and operationally hijacked by jihadi elements. The presence of a large illegal Bangladeshi migrant population in Assam has provided the jihadi groups a fertile recruiting ground internally. The government has painfully delayed the settlement of the illegal Bangladeshi migrants issue in Assam, and these migrants, faced with an uncertain political future in the state, are easily tempted to join these jihadi groups, which they feel will secure their interests against other ethnic communities in the state in the future.

Armed Forces Special Power Act (AFSPA)

The contentious AFSPA of 1958 forms the very basis of the counter-insurgency operations in *disturbed* parts of Northeast India. The alleged human rights violations during the use of the AFSPA in Manipur and Assam, and the civil society movement against it, makes for a critical analysis of this Act. The AFSPA has been the symbol of military and government presence for the people of Northeast India, and in many ways, the domination that it represents has fuelled many insurgencies. The security forces offer the rationale for AFSPA by saying that they are fighting an unequal battle, and extraordinary situations require special laws to handle them. However, in democratic India, the survival and operation of a exceptional law for over 50 years, without much debate in the national mainstream, reflects the construction of Northeast India, which is portrayed as endlessly and incurably violent, and is ruled by a binary which depicts that the ethnic tribes of Northeast India cannot be mainstreamed as other people in mainland India have been, further reinforcing the state of exceptionalism which dominates interaction between the military and the society.[9] The success or failure of the AFSPA in the past 50 years can be judged by the fact that insurgencies and violence have considerably increased in Northeast India even during the operation and continuance of this Act, and while other such extraordinary acts in the country have been reviewed and modified, this has continued to be in force. The central government must demonstrate sincere commitment to review and streamline the AFSPA, in view of the rising unrest against it in several states.

[9] Duncan McDuie-Ra, 'Fifty-year Disturbance: The Armed Forces Special Powers Act and Exceptionalism in a South Asian Periphery', *Contemporary South Asia* 17, no. 3 (2009): 255–270.

Peaceful *States in Northeast India*

The states of Arunachal Pradesh, Mizoram and Meghalaya are considered to be *peaceful* states in Northeast India; Assam, Nagaland, Manipur and Tripura have been the focus of conflict analysis and counter-insurgency attention. However, these relatively *peaceful* states in Northeast India, if overlooked, cannot explain the conflict dynamics of the region in totality. Every state in the region is connected in terms of the overall conflict dynamics and insurgent activity, and Arunachal Pradesh, Mizoram and Meghalaya have seen insurgent activity in the recent past, with insurgent groups operating across borders. In fact, it becomes easier for insurgent groups in Assam and Nagaland to have bases in Arunachal Pradesh or to conduct their activity across Meghalaya and Mizoram to connect to critical logistical supply networks in Bangladesh and Myanmar. Also, after insurgency has ended in Mizoram and been controlled in Meghalaya, new groups such as BNLF, HPC-D, PLF-M and LAEF are emerging which can grow big with time and consolidation of their respective ethnic bases. It is also known that bigger insurgent organizations such as NSCN (IM), NSCN (K), ULFA and NDFB are supporting smaller outfits in other states, to help maintain their logistics and increase their operating base. Some ethnic groups have reportedly been targeted by bigger insurgent groups in these *peaceful* states, for purposes of recruitment in their own organizations, as in the case of NSCN factions in Arunachal Pradesh, as it does not require watertight ethnic affinity in cadre composition to operate illicit arms and ammunition, narcotics and fake currency networks. The counter-insurgency establishment cannot ignore such spaces, in the face of an already complex conflict scenario and illicit trade network in Northeast India.

Securitization through Development

The overarching focus on security and counter-insurgency operations has made Northeast India the policy prerogative of the Ministry of Home Affairs (MHA) and the Ministry of Defence (MOD). However, India's Look East Policy and the possibility of connecting Northeast India with the economies of Southeast Asia, along with providing overall development and capacity building in the region, have opened new strategies to tackle conflict in the region. The Ministry of External Affairs (MEA) and Ministry of Commerce have taken considerable interest in the region, and in finding ways of unlocking borders, which have been long used by the insurgents to carry out their activities against the state. There needs to be some alternative for the people of the region to engage in purposive activity and defeat one of the sources of insurgency in the region, the fight against neglect by New Delhi. However, this should not be done in a manner which is seen as externally imposed, and development policy inputs must be sought from communities in order to be sustainable and more participatory. The border areas must be studied well and prepared before opening them, as there are extremely complex networks and dynamics along the proposed border to be opened for trade, especially the Moreh border, which, if overlooked, can create huge problems for both, the communities living in the border areas and the security forces engaged in monitoring these borders.

Future Trends

The government actors must be ready to think innovatively to unlock the solutions for a sustainable peace to be created in Northeast India, and one critical element of this is to elicit policy inputs from within the region, thereby filling the *trust deficit* that is often seen in New Delhi–Northeast India interactions. Imposed solutions are neither acceptable to people nor effective in their outcomes. The civil society actors in the region must be harnessed to create a platform where purposive dialogue can happen to resolve insurgencies, conflict situations and other concerns facing society, instead of the largely formalized processes of peace negotiations between the state and insurgent groups. This formalized approach, on the one hand, lacks transparency in protracted peace process negotiations between the state and the insurgent groups, and on the other, undermines and neglects civil society efforts to bring about peace in the society. This lack of transparency leads to social and ethnic discord and mistrust, which further fuels new insurgencies. This is now being seen as increasingly true in cases of renewed ethnic violence in the region, as was evident in the ethnic clashes in Rabha Hasong, Karbi Anglong and Bodoland areas. There appears to be a premium by the government actors on conflict rather than peace in Northeast India. A peaceful ethnic community is not important and is most likely subject to governmental neglect, but once it picks up arms and announces its insurgency, it becomes important and an interlocutor is sent by New Delhi to broach peace with the group representing the ethnic community. Instead, there should be a concerted effort to build platforms of dialogue across Northeast India, and peaceful communities should be heard, without them being pushed to insurgency. The government must initiate the shift from protracted peace negotiations to the creation of sustained dialogues in Northeast India.

The spread of corruption and linkages between politicians, government officials and insurgents, particularly in an insurgency-affected region like Northeast India, must be addressed with utmost urgency. The arrest of North Cachar Hills Autonomous Council's chief Mohet Hojai, for allegedly having links with DHD-J and the aspect of diversion of government development funds to insurgent organizations, is a marker of how complex the conflict situation has become in parts of Northeast India. This will not be a standalone case, and more such instances of corrupt nexus will be unearthed if proper investigations are carried out in other states of Northeast India, especially in Nagaland and Manipur.

Given the interconnectedness of the conflict scenario in Northeast India, special counter-insurgency attention must be focused on certain insurgent *hotspots*, which is characterized by complex insurgent networks and insufficient governmental presence. The identifiable insurgent hotspots in Northeast India are Karbi Anglong–North Cachar Hills region of Assam, Lohit–Tirap–Changlang region of Arunachal Pradesh, West Kameng–East Kameng–Baksa–Udalguri–Sonitpur region encompassing Assam and Arunachal Pradesh and Ukhrul–Senapati–Chandel region of Manipur and Southern Mizoram. Rapid modernization of police forces to continually monitor these *hotspots* is required.

6

Left-wing Extremism in 2013: A Mixed Bag

N. Manoharan

Introduction

Left-wing extremism (LWE) continued to remain as one of the major challenges to India's internal security in 2013 as well. Its intensity persisted especially in three states—Chhattisgarh, Jharkhand and Orissa—apart from significant presence in West Bengal, Bihar and Maharashtra. At the same time, Left-wing extremists have successfully managed to penetrate into some of the states of the northeast and south of India and into few of the urban areas. Compared to 2012, the number of violent incidents and killings due to LWE has come down in 2013. However, though less in numbers, the attacks by Maoists in 2013 have been intense and brutal. The year, interestingly, witnessed a shrink in the number of middle- and top-level Maoist leaders due to killings or arrests or surrenders. Yet, one cannot assert with absolute confidence that the LWE is on the wane.

Conflict management efforts by both central and state governments have been focused on a two-pronged approach—security and development—with moderate success. Central Armed Police Forces (CAPFs) persisted with their operations along with State Police Forces. However, coordination between the two continued to be problematic. Development initiatives have not been optimally implemented. Analysing trends of LWE in 2013, it is clear that the conflict is going to continue in 2014 and beyond, thus, keeping the government on its toes.

Major Actors

Of the actors pertaining to LWE, at least three can be identified as prominent:

Communist Party of India (Maoist) [CPI (Maoist)]

According to the Ministry of Home Affairs, the CPI (Maoist) continues to remain the most dominant and violent group, accounting for more than 80 per cent of the violence and killings in the LWE areas.[1] For these reasons, it has been included in the Schedule of Terrorist Organizations, along with all its formations and front organizations under the Unlawful Activities (Prevention) Act, 1967.[2]

Formed in September 2004 with the merger of the Maoist Communist Centre (MCC) and People's War Group (PWG), the aim of the CPI (Maoist) is to establish a 'people's democratic state under the leadership of the proletariat' that will 'guarantee real democracy for the vast majority of people while exercising dictatorship over a tiny minority of exploiters'.[3] Its 'ultimate programme is socialism and then advancing towards communism on a world scale'.[4] Maoists call the Indian state as 'reactionary' and 'autocratic' and seek a 'worker–peasant alliance' to overthrow 'imperialism, feudalism and comprador bureaucratic

---

[1] Government of India, Ministry of Home Affairs, *Annual Report – 2012–2013*, 2013, p. 3.
[2] 'CPI (Maoist) Included in List of Terrorist Organizations to Avoid Any Ambiguity', *Press Information Bureau*, 22 June 2009.
[3] CPI (Maoist), *Party Programme*, issued by the CC of the CPI (Maoist), available online at http://www.bannedthought.net/India/CPI-Maoist-Docs/Founding/Programme-pamphlet.pdf (accessed 4 January 2014).
[4] Ibid.

capitalism' via an armed revolutionary struggle.[5] In a joint press statement, General Secretaries of the Central Committee (CC) of the two outfits, Kishan of the MCC and Ganapathy of the PWG, declared:

> The immediate aim and programme of the Maoist party is to carry on and complete the already ongoing and advancing New Democratic Revolution in India as a part of the world proletarian revolution by overthrowing the semi-colonial, semi-feudal system under the neo-colonial form of indirect rule, exploitation and control.... This revolution will be carried out and completed through armed agrarian revolutionary war, i.e. protracted people's war with the armed seizure of power remaining as its central and principal task, encircling the cities from the countryside and thereby finally capturing them. Hence the countryside as well as the Protracted People's War will remain as the 'center of gravity' of the party's work, while urban work will be complimentary to it.[6]

The organizational structure of the Maoists is hierarchical. The highest decision-making body is the CC, which is formed every five years by the party congress. Next in the hierarchy are Special Area/Special Zonal/State Committees; Regional Committees; Zonal/District/Divisional Committees; Sub-zonal/Sub-divisional Committees; Area Committees and local-level committees such as Village/*Basti*/Factory/College party committees.

The Central Military Commission (CMC) controls the military setup, which is the People's Liberation Guerrilla Army (PLGA). The structure of the PLGA closely resembles a standing professional army with formations of platoons, companies and divisions. It is constituted by three force levels: the primary force that consists of platoons, companies and central/state special action teams, which move anywhere to participate in the war depending on the needs of the movement under the instructions of the commissions/commands; the secondary force that comprises of local guerrilla squads, special guerrilla squads,

---

[5] The Indian Maoist's strategy and tactics are clearly spelled out in a document issued by the Central Committee of the CPI (Maoist) titled *Strategy and Tactics of the Indian Revolution* dated September 2004.

[6] CPI (Maoist), 'Press Statement', issued by the Central Committee of the CPI (Maoist), 14 October 2004.

platoons and district-/division-level action teams; and the base force that is the people's militia, which forms the bulk of the Maoists' strength and is constituted by tribals and adivasis. Maoists are estimated to have strength of some 8,500 armed cadres, and about 45,000–50,000 part-timers.[7] However, of late, they have been facing leadership crisis. In a 7,000-word letter to party members, General Secretary, CPI (Maoist), Muppalla Laxmana Rao, aka Ganapathy, admitted to the crisis within the party. The crisis, according to Ganapathy, was not just due the lack of leaders at the top, but also within the party ranks.[8]

The Government of India

The central government closely monitors and supplements the effort of the state governments in dealing with LWE. The Union Ministry of Home Affairs is the nodal ministry. A separate division for Naxal Management was created in October 2006 to 'monitor the Naxal situation and counter-measures being taken by the affected States'.[9] The role and responsibilities of the division include the following:

- Deployment of CAPFs in LWE-affected states.
- Reimburse security-related expenditure (SRE) incurred by the LWE-affected states on anti-Naxal operations under the SRE Scheme.
- Provide assistance to the state governments to fill up critical infrastructure gaps under the Scheme for Special Infrastructure (SIS) in LWE-affected states.
- Provide assistance to the state governments for construction/strengthening of fortified police stations under the

---

[7] Government of India, Ministry of Home Affairs, 'Left Wing Extremist Violence in the Country', Rajya Sabha, Unstarred Question No. 2248, 21 February 2014.

[8] Ushinor Majumdar, 'Top Maoist Leader Ganapathi Admits to Leadership Crisis in Party', Tehelka.com, 19 September 2013, available online at http://www.tehelka.com/top-maoist-leader-ganapathi-admits-to-leadership-crisis-in-party/ (accessed 4 December 2013).

[9] Government of India, *Annual Report – 2012–2013*, p. 3.

Scheme for Construction/Strengthening of 400 Fortified Police Stations in LWE-affected districts.
- Review the security situation in the LWE-affected states and issue advisories and messages to the state governments concerned.
- Provide assistance to state governments for the creation of operational infrastructure and logistics required to combat LWE.
- Media and public perception management.
- Coordinate the implementation of LWE-related schemes of other central ministries, especially the Integrated Action Plan (IAP) for 82 districts and Road Requirement Plan for 34 districts.
- Coordinate the implementation of various development schemes, flagship programmes and distribution of titles under the Scheduled Tribes and Other Traditional Forest Dwellers (Recognition of Forest Rights) Act, 2006, in LWE-affected states.[10]

Apart from the Ministry of Home Affairs, Ministry of Rural Development, Ministry of Tribal Affairs, Ministry of Youth and Sports and the Planning Commission are involved in various aspects of the issue involving enormous resources. Yet, how far they are working in a coordinated manner to achieve the common objective is highly questionable.

Concerned State Governments

As per the Indian Constitution, state governments are primarily responsible for countering LWE, though the central government closely monitors the situation and supplements the effort of the state governments in dealing with LWE.[11] In terms of geographical

---

[10] Government of India, Ministry of Home Affairs, 'Naxal Management Division', 2013, available online at http://mha.nic.in/naxal_new (accessed 1 January 2014).

[11] The federal division of powers is found in Seventh Schedule of the Constitution. Under List II, Entry 2, 'public order' is vested with the state governments.

spread, the worst LWE-affected states are Chhattisgarh, Jharkhand and Odisha. The LWE problem also exists in certain pockets in the States of Maharashtra, West Bengal, Andhra Pradesh, Madhya Pradesh, Karnataka and Uttar Pradesh. In the recent years, the Maoists have been trying to spread to states like Assam and Arunachal Pradesh in the northeast and Kerala and Tamil Nadu in the south. The state actors include police, intelligence and special forces of each of the states. Since these LWE-affected states are ruled by different parties, there is a problem of coordination among them.[12] Yet another issue is that many of the states take double stands when it comes to declaring themselves as *Naxal-affected*. To attract the Centre's SRE, Scheme, they tend to show themselves as *affected*. But, when it comes to projecting their image, they maintain it as *free of LWE*.

Major Trends in Conflict during 2013

On analysing Naxal conflict during 2013, three broad trends could be discerned. The conflict claimed 394 lives involving 1,129 incidents. However, when compared to 2012, both the number of incidents and killings fell marginally in 2013.[13]

Swarming Attacks

The Maoists continued to effectively use the method of swarming attacks on targets, be it in Bihar, Orissa, Jharkhand or Chhattisgarh, apart from ambushes and gunfire during encounters. Landmine blasts too have become a frequent method of attacking security forces. One of such ruthless attacks was made on a convoy of

---

[12] Eight different parties rule each of these states: Congress, Bharatiya Janata Party, Biju Janata Dal, Samajwadi Party, Janata Dal (United), All India Anna Dravida Munnetra Kazhagam (AIADMK), Trinamool Congress, and Jharkhand Mukti Morcha (JMM).

[13] Ministry of Home Affairs, 'Statewise Extent of Naxal Violence During 2008–2013', 2014, available online at http://www.mha.nic.in/sites/upload_files/mha/files/NaxalStats-100114.pdf (accessed 10 May 2014).

Congress leaders and workers at Jeeram Ghati in Jagdalpur district of Chhattisgarh on 25 May 2013 that claimed 28 lives and injured scores of others. Those killed included Mahendra Karma, former Minister of Chhattisgarh and former Lok Sabha member, Nand Kumar Patel, the state's Congress chief, his son Dinesh Patel, and former Member of Legislative Assembly (MLA) Uday Mudliyar; former Union minister Vidya Charan Shukla and Konta MLA Kawasi Lakhma were critically injured. The convoy was an ideal target because of the presence of many high-profile leaders in one place, and that too with less security cover, passing through a most vulnerable area.[14]

Assessing the incident, some key issues are worth examining. It is surprising why so many top leaders decided to travel together in one convoy on a route that traverses through areas dominated by Maoists. The convoy was huge, comprising about 25 vehicles, thus, limiting their mobility and getaway in case of an ambush or even at a slight disruption. The Standard Operating Procedures (SOPs) were simply ignored. The route was indeed sanitized, but only cosmetically. There was no area-domination exercise, neither were there attempts to use unmanned aerial vehicles (UAVs) to monitor the convoy route.

There were, indeed, intelligence alerts on a possible attack, but they were ignored for being *generic* in nature.[15] But one wonders how even a general build-up before the attack of that magnitude could have gone unnoticed. Most importantly, attacks from Maoists are anticipated during that part of the year when trees shed maximum part of their green before monsoon sets in. Moreover, due to the assembly elections in the state, Maoists were out to deter and disrupt election campaigns to undermine any democratic process. Maoists also had their own reasons to attack each of the Congress leaders who were part of the convoy. In a four-page note sent to the media houses, a spokesperson of Dandkaranya Vishesh Zonal Committee, Gudsa Usendi, noted that Nand Kumar Patel was targeted because he approved 'Operation Green Hunt'

---

[14] Suvojit Bagchi, 'Maoists Attack Congress Convoy in Chhattisgarh', *Hindu*, 26 May 2013.

[15] Rahul Tripathi, 'Chhattisgarh Govt Ignored Advice to Move Forces to Bastar, Indicates Centre', *Indian Express*, 28 May 2013.

when he was Chhattisgarh's Home Minister, and Mahendra Karma was 'punished' for his 'misdeeds' as the founder of the Salwa Judum.[16] In fact, Mahendra Karma, who was under *Z-plus* security cover, was high on the Maoists' hit list, having escaped their attack five times earlier. This time he was not lucky.

Soft Targets

The Maoists also indulged in attacking soft targets such as trains and civilians. On 13 June 2013, around 150 Maoists attacked the Patna–Dhanbad Intercity Express near Jamui railway station, killing three and injuring five, and took away AK-47 and INSAS rifles from the cops before escaping in the dense forest area. On 30 November 2013, Maoists attacked Sahebganj–Danapur Intercity Express in Bihar's Munger district, killing three cops and injuring two, including a civilian.[17] It was the 13th such attack on trains in Bihar and Jharkhand in the last eight years.

Apart from attacks on trains, the Maoists also targeted civilians suspected to be *exploiters* and *state agents*, including suspected police informers, traders, local political leaders and government officials. Such attacks tend to be very brutal and are concentrated in areas with a heavy presence of security forces, and are intended to deter people from any resistance to the Maoist authority. The Maoists also indulged in kidnapping to warn villagers from helping security forces. This was unlike the trend of kidnapping high-profile persons (legislators, administrators and foreigners) in 2012 to demand the release of fellow militants who are interned in various prisons. On 13 December 2013, seven villagers were kidnapped in Kalimela area of Odisha's Malkangiri district. A village panchayat ward member, Tulasi Behera, was kidnapped from Chintanwada village and six others from Ramaguda.[18]

---

[16] Suvojit Bagchi, 'Our Target Was Only Karma, Other Congress Leaders: Maoists', *Hindu*, 28 May 2013.
[17] '3 GRP Jawans Killed as Maoists Attack Train in Bihar', *Hindu*, 30 November 2013.
[18] 'Reds Kidnap 7 in Malkangiri', *Times of India*, 13 December 2013.

Spread beyond the Red Corridor

The problem of the LWE has been like a shifting pain that moved from West Bengal to Bihar in the 1970s and then to Andhra Pradesh in the 1980s. After nearly two decades, when there was pressure in Andhra Pradesh, the Naxals found suitable sanctuary in the Central Indian areas comprising parts of Jharkhand, Chhattisgarh, Orissa, Maharashtra, Karnataka, Bihar and West Bengal. Now, there are reports that the Maoists are spreading to the northeast and the south of India. Why? Are they moving in search of new *safe zones* because of military action in Central India? Or, are they spreading because they have found new breeding grounds for LWE? Or, is the shift to a *new theatre* because of some other reason?

It is known that the Indian Maoists have good network with several key militant groups of Northeast India that commenced in roughly the mid-1990s. In fact, with some groups like People's Liberation Army of Manipur, the exact modalities of working—formal, semi-formal and informal—are spelled out through *memoranda of understanding*.[19] The linkage ranges from getting arms, ammunitions and communication devices to training from the northeast militant groups such as the National Socialist Council of Nagaland (NSCN-IM), anti-talk faction of the United Liberation Front of Asom (ULFA) led by Paresh Barua, People's Liberation Army (PLA), People's Revolutionary Party of Kangleipak (Prepak), Revolutionary People's Front (RPF), Kamtapur Liberation Organization (KLO), Gorkha Liberation Tiger Force (GLTF), Gurkha Liberation Organization (GLO), Adibasi National Liberation Army, Adivasi People's Army (APA), and National Democratic Front of Bodoland (NDFB). Maoists, in turn, are said to be providing explosives (ammonium nitrate) and funds to the northeast groups. Chinese small arms find their way to the *Red Corridor* mainly through these groups. It is through the northeast groups that the Maoists have good access to militant groups of Myanmar. The mutual support between Naxals and northeast militant groups is not just restricted to material, but extends to moral aspects as well. While Naxals have strongly supported *people's movements* of the Northeast, the northeast militant groups have stood by *revolutionaries*. 'Enemy's enemy is a friend' is

---

[19] 'PLA, Naxals Signed MoU in 2008 for Fighting Govt: Cops', *Indian Express*, 2 April 2012.

the guiding maxim in this case as well. ULFA leader Paresh Baruah once remarked, 'The Indian colonial government is also viewed as an enemy by the Maoists. Our enemy is also the same and so there is an understanding with them'.[20]

But what is more concerning is attempts by the Maoists to push the boundaries of the *Red Corridor* and set up support bases in upper Assam and some of the tribal areas in the hilly interiors. The presence of Maoists is felt in pockets of Tinsukia, Dibrugarh, Lakhimpur, Dhemaji, Sivasagar, Golaghat and Karbi Anglong districts of Assam and Lohit district of Arunachal Pradesh (adjoining Tinsukia). The hub of Maoist activities is said to be in Sadiya area, situated at the Assam–Arunachal Pradesh border. Governments of Assam and India have recently admitted to this.[21] How deep is the penetration? This is where the ULFA chief Paresh Barua went partly wrong when he observed: 'We have a definite strategy and we do not think Maoism will be able to strike deep roots in Assam'.[22] Maoists have a clear-cut objective: capture of power, as against ULFA's secession from India. Northeast India has now become a new *strategic area* for the Maoists. To the Maoists,

> The 'strategic areas' are hilly regions with dense forest cover, have sufficient economic resources, a vast population, and a vast forest area spreading over thousands of square kilometers. In such areas the enemy is weak, and these areas are very favourable for the maneuvers of the people's army. In these strategic areas we can defeat the enemy completely by fulfilling the tasks of building and consolidating a strong proletarian party and a strong people's army; procuring the people's support and economic resources, while developing the guerrilla war aiming at the building of liberated/base areas in these areas.[23]

[20] 'ULFA C-in-C Paresh Barua Confirms ULFA–Maoists Links', *Shillong Times*, 3 February 2012.

[21] 'Will Take Steps to Curb Maoist Menace: Tarun Gogoi', *Daily News and Analysis*, 23 April 2012; 'Maoists Will Be Dealt With Firmly: Chidambaram', *Times of India*, 12 May 2012.

[22] 'Drug Menace: Narcotics Control Bureau Tightens Screw', *Daily News and Analysis*, 6 April 2011.

[23] CPI (Maoist), CC, 'Strategy and Tactics of Indian Revolution', Chapter 7, p. 51, available at http://www.bannedthought.net/India/CPI-Maoist-Docs/Founding/StrategyTactics-pamphlet.pdf (accessed 28 December 2013).

Therefore, apart from military utility of training, arms procurement and sanctuary, the Maoists also found parts of the northeast of India as a new zone of *revolution* to establish what they call *base areas*. In this regard, two major causes are being exploited: deprivation among the tea workers of Assam and anti-dam sentiments in Arunachal Pradesh. Since there is political vacuum in both cases, Maoists are more than willing to fill them. Interestingly, adivasis in tea gardens are descendants of migrants from present-day Jharkhand, Bihar, Odisha, Chhatisgarh and Madhya Pradesh during the British times. The Maoists have already set up local committees in these areas. From there, it will become easy for them to link up to southern parts of Bhutan, where Nepali refugees are populated.

The Maoists have also been trying to extend their presence in southern India. In an internal communication, the Ministry of Home Affairs has observed that the CPI (Maoist) has been expanding its organizational base in the Western Ghats, especially around the tri-junction of Tamil Nadu–Kerala–Karnataka. In 2013, the presence and movement of the armed cadres of CPI (Maoist) have been noticed on over two dozen occasions in Malappuram, Wayanad and Kannur in Kerala and Mysore, Kodagu, Udupi, Chikmagalur and Shimoga in Karnataka. Though adjoining areas of Tamil Nadu have not witnessed any movement of armed Naxal cadres, activities of its front bodies have increased in Erode district.[24] Confirming this, the Maoists in a document released to celebrate the ninth anniversary of their formation, observed: 'Our comrades are putting determined and tireless efforts facing some of the toughest conditions that our movement had ever faced in new areas of extension in the strategic tri-junction area between Tamil Nadu, Karnataka and Kerala'.[25] As is their wont, the Maoists try to exploit the local grievances to gain influence. In the tri-junction area, they smelt an opportunity in the eviction of forest dwellers and tribals from

---

[24] 'Naxals Trying to Expand in South: MHA', *Hindu*, 24 November 2013.

[25] CPI (Maoist), 'Revolutionary Greetings for the 9th Anniversary Celebrations of Our Glorious Party', issued by the Central Committee of CPI (Maoist), 1 September 2013, available online at http://www.signalfire.org/?p=25832 (accessed 5 January 2014).

the Western Ghats under the National Park Act and the government's move to implement the Kasturirangan report on conservation of the Ghats.[26]

The year also witnessed Maoists increasing their presence in the urban areas of India. Significant Maoist activities, especially of its front organizations, have been reported from places like Delhi and the National Capital Region, Gurgaon, Noida, Mumbai, Chennai, Kolkata, Bangalore, Pune, Nagpur, Surat, Ahmedabad, Bhopal, Ranchi, Jamshedpur, Raipur, Durg, Patna, Hyderabad, Rourkela, Bhubaneswar, Guwahati and Chandigarh. The urban fronts comprise organizations involved in *revolutionary democratic* activities, opposition to *war on people*, displacement and *violence on women* and in *cultural* activities.[27] Also significantly, CPI (Maoist) is systematically penetrating the student community as well as the workers in the unorganized sectors and this could have a large impact on the future course of the movement.[28]

What are the reasons for a major urban push by the Maoists? Due to a depleting tribal cadre base, Maoists have to turn somewhere for replenishment. They find urban regions a good catchment area. The main advantage with the urban cadres, which is absent in their tribal counterparts, is that they come with enough intellect to take the movement forward. They may find life in the forest too difficult to sustain, yet the Maoists wish to cultivate them 'to lead militant activities that are facing a leadership crisis due to depleting recruitment, elimination of the existing cadres due to security operations and large-scale surrenders by senior cadres'.[29] Immense financial and human resources are being invested in running 'urban activities and guidance on how to develop better coordination among the urban frontal organisations of the party'.[30]

---

[26] Gururaj A. Paniyadi, 'Naxals on the Comeback Trail?' *Deccan Chronicle*, 2 December 2013.
[27] Vivek Deshpande, 'The "Urban Maoist" Front', *Indian Express*, 23 September 2013.
[28] Ibid.
[29] Ibid.
[30] Ibid.

External Linkages

The external linkages of Maoists with both state and non-state actors within and without India were also conspicuous in 2013. Contextualizing and justifying external linkages within the Maoists' thought, the Naxals hold that

> There are two different kinds of United Fronts. One, between people, and the other between people and enemy (a section/group/persons from enemy classes) using the contradictions among the enemy. [Maoist] Party has to do that. This scope is there to some extent on some issues. We call it the indirect reserves of the revolution which can be used carefully. If we have clear understanding that they are not our class allies, then we would not have right opportunist deviations. We need united fronts of this kind for the success of the revolution.[31]

The Inter-services Intelligence (ISI), in its attempts to rope in India-based militant groups, has found Indian Maoists more than suitable for its agenda. For this, the ISI has made use of underworld dons like Dawood Ibrahim and Chhota Shakeel to facilitate the linkage.[32] Naxals are now part of ISI's 'Karachi Project' that aims to bleed India, both militarily and economically, without leaving any evidence of its involvement—a *plausible deniability* operation. Can the ISI get better 'Fifth Columnists' than Maoists? The overall intention of the ISI is to give an impression to the outside world that all terror attacks in India are home-grown.[33] The Pakistani intelligence agency has also facilitated contacts between Maoists and anti-India terror groups based in Pakistan such as Lashkar-e-Taiba (LeT), Jaish-e-Muhammad (JeM) and Harkat-ul-jihad-al-Islami (HuJI), Bangladesh-based Islamic militant groups and those that operate in India such as Indian Mujahideen and Student Islamic Movement of India

---

[31] Jan Myrdal and Gautam Navlakha, Interview with Ganapathy, General Secretary of the CPI (Maoists), January 2010, available online at http://www.bannedthought.net/India/CPI-Maoist-Docs/Interviews/Ganapathy-Myrdal-100100.pdf (accessed 2 January 2014).

[32] 'ISI Had Instructed Chhota Shakeel to Rope in Maoists', *Deccan Herald*, 13 August 2010.

[33] Sandeep Unnithan, 'Karachi Project', *India Today*, 18 February 2010.

(SIMI).[34] Indo-Nepal and Indo-Bangladesh borders are being used by these groups as transit routes to reach out to Naxals. These external contacts have opened a wider world for the Naxals in terms of new ways of fund-raising that includes trafficking of drugs and counterfeit currencies, arms procurement and training. Some of the training camps are located in Bangladesh, funded by the ISI and run by Bangladeshi Left-extremist groups.[35] These apart, as Maoists are now expanding into urban areas, they are keen to harness latent existing infrastructure of militant Islamist groups like the Lashkar. In their own admission, Naxals are presently 'weak in urban areas', but have identified it as one of the 'most important urgent tasks'.[36] The alliance between the 'major source of external threats' with the 'bigger internal security threat' cannot be more deadly.[37] At the same time, Naxals are a bit cautious in their liaison with jihadist groups because of long-term consequences. Therefore, the Naxal leadership is said to be in favour of 'specific and need-based exchanges' with these groups that could be restricted to 'consequential solidarity'.[38] The Maoists are aware of the fact that if the LeT–Maoists alliance is comprehensive and deep, it would be easier for the Indian state to club LWE also under anti-terrorism and respond accordingly. Naxals would not wish such a state response that could be more ruthless than the present *holistic* one. At the end of the day, the ideology and objectives of these groups are quite different. However, even limited cooperation is a cause for concern, as Naxals are desperately looking outwards to enhance their military potential vis-à-vis the Indian state's ongoing military push.[39]

Involvement of the ISI and some militant groups of Northeast India in facilitating the drug trade for Naxals is also noted.

[34] 'Naxals May Have Links with LeT: Chhattisgarh CM', *Deccan Herald*, 19 May 2010.

[35] Anupam Dasgupta, 'Lethal Enemy', *Week*, 17 April 2011.

[36] See note 31.

[37] Ben West, 'Edge of Terrorism: Tracking the Pakistani Origins of Naxalite Maoists Terror in India', *STRATFOR*, 22 November 2010.

[38] See note 35.

[39] Dubbed as 'Operation Green Hunt', the ongoing joint anti-Naxal move by the central and state governments commenced in 2009 in the states of Jharkhand, Chhattisgarh, Orissa and West Bengal. But the government never used such a phrase to describe the present push.

Naxal-dominated areas are not only rich in minerals and inhabited by tribals, but also popular drug-cultivating tracts (cannabis and poppy in particular) in the states of Madhya Pradesh, Maharashtra, Chhattisgarh, Bihar, Jharkhand, Orissa and Andhra Pradesh. Apart from being the world's largest producer of licit opium and the only authorized user of the gum method of opium production for pharmaceutical preparations, India is also sandwiched between the 'Golden Crescent' and the 'Golden Triangle', the two major drug-producing and drug-trafficking regions of the world.[40] This geo-economic factor has not only helped Maoists to collect protection money from drug cultivators, traders and traffickers, but also to involve themselves directly in drug trafficking. This is evident from the seizure of large contrabands of marijuana that were being brought from states and specifically areas which are Naxal-infested.[41] They are the latest entrants in this trade to fund their activities. Drugs like marijuana from Naxal areas are found for street sale even in remote areas of southern states like Kerala. The marijuana cultivated in the Naxalite-dominated forests bordering Orissa and Andhra Pradesh (called *Sheelavathi* in the local dialect) is said to have higher tetrahydrocannabinol content, a psychoactive compound, than that of locally produced drugs (locally called *Neelachadayan*). These drugs are peddled by Naxal-linked middlemen in large quantities by rail and road, including on buses conducting interstate services.[42]

The Maoists' strategy is expansion by mergers and networking with like-minded revolutionary organizations to 'fight against the common enemy: Imperialism'.[43] They call this the *second wave*.[44] They have clearly stated that it is 'part of our policy to have

---

[40] Bureau of International Narcotics and Law Enforcement Affairs, *International Narcotics Control Strategy Report (INCSR) – 2011* Vol. 1, 3 March 2011.

[41] See note 22.

[42] 'Ganja Trail Leads to Naxal Belt', *Hindu*, 24 August 2010.

[43] Interview with Ganapathy, 7 October 1998, available online at http://www.rediff.com/news/1998/oct/07gana.htm (accessed 26 December 2013).

[44] The *first wave* was said to have begun with the Russian Revolution under Lenin and ended with the Cultural Revolution in China under Mao.

relations with all communists and nationality struggles'.[45] They believe that CPI (Maoist) is part of the world proletariat revolution and is not independent. If it succeeds, then one part of the revolutionary world will succeed. It will work as a part of the world socialist revolution and is strictly related to the success or failure of the world socialist revolution. At the same time, more working-class struggles in the imperialist/capitalist countries will have a favourable impact on the Indian revolution as well. They are mutually reinforcing. Therefore, according to the Maoists,

> It is important for the success of the Indian revolution as an inseparable part of great world socialist revolution to actively defend Maoism, fight imperialism and support the class struggle throughout the world and also take the support of the International Maoist Parties/Organizations/Forces, proletariat and people.[46]

It is for this purpose that they maintain fraternal relations with Maoist and anti-imperialist forces and firmly believe that it is important to extend help as well as take international help for the success of any revolution, but because of the ongoing repression, the relations are maintained through several umbrella organizations that exist at regional and global levels.

Prominent among them is CCOMPOSA (Coordination Committee of Maoist Parties and Organizations of South Asia), which was formed in July 2001 with a purpose to unify and coordinate the activities of *genuine* Maoist parties and organizations in South Asia. Nepalese Maoists, PWG, MCC, Purbo Banglar Movement (Bangladesh), Communist Party of Ceylon (Sri Lanka) and other Indian LWE parties became its members. The present constituent parties of CCOMPOSA are United Communist Party of Nepal (Maoist), Poorba Bangladesh Sarvahara Party (Coordination Centre), Communist Party of East Bengal (Marxist-Leninist), Red Flag Communist Party of Bhutan (Marxist-Leninist-Maoist), CPI (Marxist-Leninist-Maoist), CPI (Marxist-Leninist) (Naxalbari) and CPI (Maoist). The CCOMPOSA members have agreed to share each other's experiences and strengthen one another in 'fighting back the enemies in the respective countries' and 'making South

[45] See note 43.
[46] See note 31.

Asia a blazing center of world revolution'.[47] The aim of the organization was identified to 'develop mass movements against the common enemy, i.e. Indian Expansionism, the world imperialist system, particularly US imperialism, the No. 1 enemy of the world people; and to overthrow the existing system in the countries of South Asia'.[48] Conferences are held from time to time to take stock of the situation and plan responses. So far, only five such conferences have been held since the formation of the body—once in two years on an average. However, CCOMPOSA received a setback with the Nepali Maoists joining the political mainstream renouncing violence.

At the global level, FOIR (Friends of Indian Revolution) is an important umbrella organization whose representatives abroad seek to raise finances in several countries, especially those of the West, for the *cause* of the Indian *revolution*. Then, there are bodies like ICMLPO (International Conference of Marxist-Leninist Parties and Organizations), RIM (Revolutionary Internationalist Movement), World People's Resistance Movement (WPRM) and ICM (International Communist Movement) that link LWE groups located all over the world stretching from Peru in the west to Philippines in the east. They sustain fraternal ties and jointly conduct programmes that are mutually beneficial.[49] This does not mean that the Maoists are unanimous in their opinion on linkages with international communist movements. For instance, before the merger of MCC and PWG to form CPI (Maoist), the MCC had joined RIM in 2002, but PWG opposed the idea. After the merger, MCC pulled out of RIM as per the decision of the new Party. RIM went out of action anyway.

The *outreach efforts* of Maoists are more of recent phenomena unlike in the past when the movement remained more local in scope. Connecting to larger international communist movements commenced only in the 2000s particularly after the formation of

---

[47] CCOMPOSA, Press Release of 5th Conference of CCOMPOSA, 23 March 2011, available online at http://revintcan.wordpress.com/2011/03/29/ccomposa-5th-conference-press-release (accessed 27 December 2013).

[48] 'Press Statement of CCOMPOSA', *People's March*, Vol. 4, No. 8, August 2003.

[49] 'Support for Naxals Goes Global', *People's Review*, 24 February 2011.

CPI (Maoist). It was the PWG that initiated relations at different levels with different militant communist organizations across the world that follow the same ideology; but relations with other groups were to be at functional level.[50] They have been participating in international debates and sending delegations to international forums, though, according to them, much progress needs to be made on this front.

Conflict Management

Efforts by both the central and the state governments to deal with the LWE are *holistic* in nature. Here, *holistic* means addressing the areas of security, development, ensuring entitlement of local communities and promoting good governance. In view of this, the Government of India, in close consultations with the states, has identified 106 districts in nine states for special and focused attention in the areas of security and development.[51]

The view and the policy of the government is to effectively deal with the LWE insurgency by primarily facilitating capacity building of the state governments concerned on both security and development fronts.

On the security front, the Union Government has been supplementing the efforts of states that include providing CAPFs and Commando Battalions for Resolute Action (CoBRAs), sanctioning of India Reserve (IR) battalions, setting up of Counterinsurgency and Anti-terrorism (CIAT) schools, modernization

---

[50] Maoist leader Ganapathy, in this regard, explained that

> Our support to any nationalist movement does not mean that we support all the activities of that organisation. We will support an organisation only if they support the ongoing revolutionary movement. We support only those struggles that we know are genuine nationalist struggles. There are struggles in Jammu and Kashmir, the struggles of the Nagas in the northeast. We assure all of them the right of self-determination. On this basis alone, we would hold relations with these people.

[51] Government of India, *Annual Report – 2012–2013*, p. 18.

and upgradation of the State Police and their intelligence apparatus under the Scheme for the Modernization of State Police Forces (MPF Scheme), reimbursement of SRE under the SRE Scheme, filling up critical infrastructure gaps under the SIS in LWE-affected states, providing helicopters for anti-Naxal operations, assisting in the training of State Police through the Ministry of Defence, the Central Police Organizations and the Bureau of Police Research and Development, sharing of intelligence, facilitating interstate coordination, assisting in community policing and civic action programmes, etc. The underlying philosophy is to enhance the capacity of the state governments to tackle the Maoist menace in a concerted manner.[52]

The government is implementing schemes related to improving the security environment, viz., the SRE Scheme, the SIS Scheme, the Scheme of Construction of Fortified Police Stations, etc. Following the internal security meeting of chief ministers, the Centre has decided to step up its counter-Naxal operations. Over 537 companies of CAPFs personnel drawn from the Central Reserve Police Force (CRPF), Border Security Force (BSF), Indo-Tibetan Border Police (ITBP), Central Industrial Security Force (CISF) and Sashastra Seema Bal (SSB) are deployed at present in the states for anti-Maoist operations along with State Police Forces.[53] These deployments are dynamic in nature and are based on three factors: requirements projected by state governments, availability of force and the security situation in a particular location. In addition, UAVs stationed at the Begumpet airport have been helping the ground forces to track Maoist movement. The UAVs are under the command of the CRPF, but the footage relayed by them is being used by all the partner states. Efforts are also being made to set up another UAV base at Bhilai in Chhattisgarh.[54]

Simultaneously, focused attention is also paid to development and governance issues particularly at the cutting-edge level. As rightly pointed out by the Ministry of Home Affairs, Left-wing extremists operate in the vacuum created by functional

[52] See note 10.
[53] Lok Sabha Unstarred Question No. 895, 2013, answered on 10 December.
[54] 'UAVs to Log More Hours to Counter Maoist Challenge', *Hindu*, 17 June 2013.

inadequacies of field-level governance structures, espouse local demands and take advantage of prevalent dissatisfaction and feelings of perceived neglect and injustice among the underprivileged and remote segments of population.[55] In this context, the funds allocated to the states under various central schemes such as the Backward Regions Grant Fund, Mahatma Gandhi National Rural Employment Guarantee Scheme, Prime Minister's Gram Sadak Yojna, National Rural Health Mission, Ashram Schools, Rajiv Gandhi Grameen Vidhyutikaran Yojna and Sarva Siksha Abhiyan acquire special significance.

In addition, the government is implementing the IAP to address development deficit in public infrastructure and services in 82 selected districts. The government is also implementing an ambitious Road Development Plan in 34 worst-LWE-affected districts through the Ministry of Road Transport and Highways. The implementation of the Forest Rights Act, 2006, especially the provisions pertaining to the allotment of title deeds to individuals and communities, is also an area of priority.[56]

The Union Government instituted a number of review and monitoring mechanisms for different aspects of the LWE problem and the measures needed to deal with it. These include:

- A Standing Committee of Chief Ministers of States concerned, under the chairmanship of the Union Home Minister, to work out a coordinated strategic policy and tactical measures to deal with the problem simultaneously on political, security and development fronts.
- A Review Group (earlier called Task Force) under the Cabinet Secretary to review efforts across a range of development and security measures.
- A Coordination Centre chaired by the Union Home Secretary to review and coordinate the efforts of the state governments, where the state governments are represented by the Chief Secretaries and the Director Generals of Police.
- A Task Force under the Special Secretary (Internal Security), Ministry of Home Affairs, with senior officers from

---

[55] Government of India, Ministry of Home Affairs, *Annual Report 2009–2010*, 2010, p. 17.

[56] Government of India, *Annual Report – 2012–2013*, pp. 18–19.

Intelligence Agencies, CAPFs and State Police Forces, to monitor and coordinate counter-LWE efforts.
- An Empowered Group of Officers under the chairpersonship of Member Secretary, Planning Commission has been set up by the government to override or modify existing instructions on implementation of various development programmes and flagship schemes, with regard to the local needs and conditions in LWE-affected areas. The affected states have been asked to constitute an Empowered Group at the state level.[57]

However, in countering LWE, both central and state governments face numerous challenges. For one, the modernization of the police force which this strategy requires is wanting in the heavily-affected states. Most of the states are found wanting in the utilization of police modernization funds. They do not even have perspective action plans for modernization. As the Parliamentary Committee rightly points out,

> [W]hen it comes to the control and superintendence of police forces, the States do not want to yield even an inch of their jurisdiction. But at the same time when it comes to improve and strengthen their police forces, they simply raise their hands expressing their inability to do so because of financial constraints.[58]

The Centre also has to share blame for releasing funds in delay. Partly, the reason for delay is due to states' failure to submit *utilization certificates* on time. But, overall, the scheme has undoubtedly made some positive impact on strengthening the *first responders*.[59]

Besides, the training imparted to the police has been limited to the *military* aspects for neutralizing the cadres as opposed to

---

[57] See note 10.

[58] Rajya Sabha, Department-related Parliamentary Standing Committee on Home Affairs, 98th Report on the Demands For Grants (2003–2004) of the Ministry of Home Affairs, presented to the Rajya Sabha on 8 April 2003, p. 42.2.

[59] Om Shankar Jha, 'Impact of Modernisation of Police Force Scheme on Combat Capability of the Police Forces in Naxal-affected States: A Critical Evaluation', *IDSA Occasional Paper* No. 7, December 2007.

the *civic* aspects such as strengthening ties with the local population. Recognizing the limitations of this approach, the states are expanding their civic action programmes by initiatives such as holding health camps, distributing food and clothes and holding sports tournaments and tribal festivals, but much more will need to be done to overcome the years of distrust of state institutions and policies.

Apart from counter-guerrilla operations, poor state resources also impede the effective implementation of other strategies to supplement hot pursuit. A good example is the surrender policy implemented by individual states. The central government provides them assistance by reimbursement of expenditure up to ₹10,000 for a person surrendering without arms, and up to ₹20,000 with regular weapons, under the SRE Scheme.[60] However, the rehabilitation of the surrendered militants remains of primary concern and a weakness in the surrender policy. This problem is particularly acute in Maharashtra where the surrendered Naxals have come under repeated attacks.

Non-optimal fund utilization by the states is another issue. In its Action Taken Report to the parliamentary panel, the Ministry of Home Affairs said that ₹445.82 crore were released to nine states between 2008–2009 and 2011–2012, but only ₹258.26 crore (57 per cent) were utilized for improving infrastructure in these places. The money was earmarked for the states under the SIS, which was approved during the 11th Plan. The 'progress of works under this scheme has been slow due to serious security problems created by the Maoists, reluctance of contractors to operate in these areas, difficulty in mobilisation of material and machinery resulting in slower utilisation of funds'.[61] Further, it said that paramilitary forces are required to shift their bases often owing to *changing situations* in the Maoist *theatre*, which necessitate change of works approved under the scheme leading to delays.

In the absence of proper coordination with the CRPF, the state police are finding it difficult to keep pace with the Maoists. For instance, in 2013, a coordination issue erupted in Bihar in a major

---

[60] '1550 Naxalites, Militants Surrendered in 2008', *Zee News*, 24 February 2009.

[61] Shemin Joy, 'Funds for Core Upgrade Less Used in Maoist Areas', *Deccan Herald*, 13 December 2013.

way. It started when the state police instituted an inquiry by an IG-rank officer into the killing of one Arvind Bhuiyan by the CRPF in an encounter at Baltharwa village located on the border of Gaya–Aurangabad districts and inside Chakarbanda forest in June 2012. The CRPF was held guilty. Though the local police did not initiate any follow-up action, it did hurt the Central Force, which in turn decided to restrict its job to only guarding its camp in Maoist-infested areas. The differences, however, turned uglier when the Bihar police headquarters lodged a case and subsequently jailed an assistant commandant, Sanjay Kumar Yadav, of CRPF after taping his phone call which revealed he was passing operational details to Maoists in Aurangabad. The case just highlights the extent of difficulties in cooperative efforts of central and state forces in the LWE-affected states.[62]

The Road Ahead: Countering the Naxal Threat

In 2007, Prime Minister Manmohan Singh characterized LWE, otherwise known as Naxalism, as 'India's greatest internal security threat'.[63] At a later date, he said, 'The problem of Left Wing extremism is indeed a complex one'.[64] The then Home Minister dubbed it as a 'threat to our way of life'. The issue of Naxalism started as an agrarian rebellion in the aftermath of a police firing incident in Naxalbari village of West Bengal in May 1967.[65] Now, the LWE has reached a critical phase and there is a paradigm shift in how Naxals operate.

Looking ahead, the conflict is going to continue. Some of the pointers emanating from the Maoists should be taken note of. In a recent letter to his cadres, CPI (Maoist) leader Ganapathy

---

[62] Gyan Prakash, 'Strained Ties with CRPF Hamper Anti-Red Operations', *Times of India*, 4 December 2013.

[63] 'Communist Rebels Pose the Single Biggest Threat to India, Says PM', *Hindu*, 20 December 2007.

[64] Prime Minister Manmohan Singh, Address at the Chief Ministers' Conference on Internal Security, 17 August 2009.

[65] Sumanta Banerjee, *In the Wake of Naxalbari* (Kolkata: Subarnarekha, 1980), pp. 111–112.

asked his men to 'explore all legal and illegal ways' to get the jailed leaders out—either by breaking in or by obtaining bail. On urban expansion, Ganapathy, in an interview at a different date, observed:

> It is not true that we have been completely eliminated from the urban areas and plains as some people are propagating or as some others believe. [...] We have gained many experiences in the urban areas. We have enriched our policy on urban work. [...] it is ridiculous and unreal to say that we would never be able to extend to urban areas. If rural areas are liberated first, then basing on its strength and on the struggles of the working class in urban areas, cities would be liberated later. Along with the liberation of cities the comprador rule and imperialist control would also be forced to end in our country.[66]

Therefore, it is not enough to just assess the incident and move on; the important question should be: What should be done to counter the LWE?

Despite being dubbed as 'India's greatest internal security threat', the threat assessment of LWE has not been realistic. The nature of LWE has substantially transformed. From an ideologically driven movement, it has transformed itself into a guerrilla force with its own army, sophisticated arms, weapons-manufacturing capabilities, funding sources—internal and external, rigid organizational structure, fertile recruiting base, ideal terrain to hide and thousands of sympathizers across India and even among civil society. What is more worrying is their need-based linkage with both state and non-state actors within and without India. Rapid economic development and improvement of transport and communication infrastructure have added new dimensions to the threat.

However, the present anti-Maoist strategy of 'Clear–Hold–Develop' has not taken the real gravity and dynamics of the menace into consideration. LWE is no more a *public order* issue and falls well within the innermost circle of what Justice Hidayatullah

---

[66] Interview of Ganapathy, General Secretary, CPI (Maoist). The text of this interview was released by the Central Committee, CPI (Maoist) in November 2010 in response to the questions sent to him by some media persons after the death of Azad.

calls 'three concentric circles' of threats.[67] Given the inter-state and global nature of the threat, the Union Government is duty bound under Article 355 to 'protect every state against external aggression and internal disturbance'.

What is required, at the outset, is a political desire, if not the political will, to deal with the entire gamut of the threat. All political parties have to rise above narrow electoral consideration to fight the Naxals. As long as the political consensus on the issue is not achieved, a long-lasting solution to the problem will remain evasive. Leading national parties, along with the concerned state political parties, have to take the lead in arriving at a common understanding on the causes, consequences of and counter-measures to LWE. It should also be noted that the rise of LWE can also be attributed to the failure of moderate political parties in articulating the rising expectations and grievances of the people at the right time in an adequate manner.

The parties, therefore, have to get on to their primary task of *interest aggregation*. It is important to develop a strong participatory mechanism. Grassroots democracy would ultimately prove to be the ideal foil to militancy. They give enough space—for mainstream and regional political parties, civil society groups, or even dissidents—for political action. Provisions under the Sixth Schedule of the Constitution and the Panchayat (Extension to Scheduled Areas) (PESA) Act that mandates tribal advisory councils to oversee tribal affairs and empowers governors of each state to intervene in matters where they see tribal autonomy being compromised are hardly used. The PESA not only accepted the validity of 'customary law, social and religious practices, and traditional management practices of community resources', but also directed the state governments not to make any law which is inconsistent with these.[68] Accepting a clear-cut role for the community, it gave wide-ranging powers to *Gram Sabha*s to approve plans, programmes for social and economic development, identify beneficiaries under poverty alleviation programmes, certify

[67] Supreme Court of India, *Dr Ram Manohar Lohia vs. State of Bihar and Others*, Supreme Court Judgement, 7 September 1965.
[68] PESA, 1996, No. 40 of 1996, available online at http://tribal.nic.in/WriteReadData/CMS/Documents/201211290242170976562pesa6636533023.pdf (accessed 5 January 2014).

utilization of funds by *Gram Panchayats*, protect natural resources, including minor forest produce, and be consulted prior to land acquisition. The full-fledged implementation of the PESA Act will empower the marginalized tribals and, in turn, deal a bigger blow to the Maoists.

Instead of slackness on account of the prevailing disturbed environment, the administrative apparatus should work overtime to ensure that all socio-economic development and poverty alleviation programmes are implemented with high efficiency and honesty and within an urgent timeframe. Good governance is the key. Attention is also required in making sure that the criminal justice system functions with speed, fairness, transparency and honesty; it is difficult to bring down the prevailing *crisis of legitimacy*. Overhauling is required in all three stages of the criminal justice system—investigation, prosecution and adjudication.

At the operational level, it is only valuable intelligence that will help in finding the *invisible enemy*. The key to success in fighting Naxals effectively lies in obtaining accurate and reliable intelligence. In short, it is enhancing the ability to *expect the unexpected* that holds the key. Although the local police forces are first responders, they are considered the weakest link in the entire response chain. What India requires is, as the Padmanabhaiah Committee advocated, a 'highly motivated, professionally skilled, infrastructurally self-sufficient and sophisticatedly trained police force'. Although the Army's successful track record in counter-insurgency is well established, its primary role is to safeguard the country's territorial integrity from any external aggression. The Army, therefore, can be best utilized in training Central Police Organisations and State Police Forces in counter-insurgency tactics, techniques and procedures.

In doing so, the human rights aspect should not be ignored. The core counter-Naxal strategy should revolve around *less fear-mongering* and *more confidence*. Adhering to human rights obligations when combating Maoists helps to ensure that advocates of violence do not win sympathy from the ranks of those harmed and alienated by the state.

PART II
Peace Audit

7

Peace Process in Jammu and Kashmir 2013: Hope to Simmering Discontent?

Ashok Bhan

The Indian State of Jammu and Kashmir (J&K) has witnessed relative calm in terrorist violence, and law-and-order situation has remained stable for three successive years since 2011, notwithstanding the sharp increase in ceasefire violations from Pakistan, moderate increase in infiltration, a spurt in targeting security force (SF) personnel and resumption of civil strife and protest *hartal*s (strike) beginning with the hanging of Parliament attack accused Mohammed Afzal Guru during 2013. Indeed, these years have been marked by development and hope. The relatively peaceful environment has allowed infrastructural and economic development, addressing un-employment and empowerment of women, working on harnessing hydroelectric (hydel) power aimed at economic self-reliance and focus on health, education and water supply.

Those who believe that *positive peace* can return in J&K through development alone miss the point that the situation cannot be kept under control for a long time by military means without timely and desirable political interventions. The Government of India did extend the hand of friendship in February 2011 and gave unilateral concessions to Pakistan despite continued cross-border terrorism and inaction on bringing the perpetrators of 26/11 to justice. India had hoped that such concessions will reduce the trust deficit and help in resolving bilateral issues through dialogue.

Unfortunately, relations between the two neighbours again soured towards the end of 2012, and the year 2013 was marked by a standoff in any meaningful bilateral contact. Pakistan's attitude shows that it is not interested in promoting positive and lasting peace in J&K. The civil government in Pakistan has made abundantly clear its intent to use the *Kashmir card* to hit India where it hurts her the most. This has become evident by the democratically elected government in Pakistan reiterating moral, material and political support to Kashmiri separatists in international fora, increase in ceasefire violations and pumping in of more terrorists.

For Readers to appreciate the progress, if any, made in the peace process in J&K during 2013, it will be useful to recapitulate the following important conclusions that the author had drawn in the essay last year on the peace process during 2012:[1]

- In the context of the worrying situation which prevailed during 2008–2010, the past two years have been marked by hope and development.
- The escalation of Indo–Pak hostilities towards the end of 2012, elections due in Pakistan in May 2013 and US drawdown from Afghanistan make it difficult to predict how soon a meaningful dialogue can be resumed between India and Pakistan.
- Trade and economic activity, development, employment generation, etc., are positive developments, but hopes were belied by status quo on a political solution, winning *hearts and minds* and creating an institutional mechanism to end perceived discrimination between regions and communities.
- There is a need to address the internal dimension to run up in the state assembly elections by starting an informed debate on the report of Interlocutors/Working Groups, forward movement on confidence building measures, including trans-LoC trade and travel, revisiting the phased withdrawal of Armed Forces Special Powers Act (AFSPA), engaging separatists, empowering panchayats to strengthen grass-roots level democracy, etc.

[1] Bhan, Ashok, 'Jammu and Kashmir—Peace Audit 2012: A Need to Focus on the Internal Dimension', in *Armed Conflicts in South Asia 2013*, eds. D. Suba Chandran and P.R. Chari (New Delhi: Routledge, forthcoming).

- Improve intelligence, strict check on infiltration, strengthening security grid for continued operations against terrorists and avoiding collateral damage in CI ops and maintenance of law and order.
- A favourable environment needs to be created for holding free, fair and peaceful elections to the Lok Sabha in mid-2014 and to the state assembly towards the end of 2014.

Unfortunately, nothing tangible was achieved by addressing the external dimension or by way of political interventions to address the internal dimension. The past three years (2011–2013) have, therefore, been years of missed opportunities as far as finding a lasting solution to the vexed J&K issue is concerned. While Pakistan has spurned all Indian overtures and refused to discontinue using its soil for terror attacks in J&K and elsewhere, the Indian handling of the internal dimension has been lacklustre. Consequently, as we approach the next assembly elections in J&K, Pakistan has made itself available the undiminished support base to give boycott calls, increase terrorist violence and vitiate peaceful holding of elections. The biggest challenge for the Indian State will be to ensure free, fair and peaceful polls to the Lok Sabha and more importantly to the state assembly due in December 2014.

In this chapter, this year the progress made on the peace process in the three intertwining reconciliation pathways, namely, dialogue with Pakistan, political interventions to attend to the internal dimension and the issues of governance will be discussed. Some other important areas bearing on the peace process such as political consensus, strengthening of democratic institutions, recent incursions by China, preparedness to fight terror, and communal and regional fault lines will also be addressed.

Changing Nature of Violence

The year 2013 began in the backdrop of an increase in cross-border firing incidents from Pakistan, ostensibly to infiltrate terrorists. Numerically speaking, the downward trend in violent incidents continues since the year 2001 (Table 7.1). In 2013, there were 113 incidents of terrorist violence as against 124 incidents

Table 7.1:
Terrorist violence in Jammu and Kashmir (1996-2013)

Year	Violent Incident	Civilian	Deaths SF Personnel	Terrorist	Total	Political Activist Killed	Suicidal Attack	Car Bomb
1996	4,499	1,424	189	1,209	2,822	61	0	0
1997	3,101	1,030	216	1,075	2,321	58	0	0
1998	2,894	967	268	999	2,234	58	0	0
1999	2,989	937	407	1,082	2,426	42	2	0
2000	2,948	942	482	1,520	2,944	35	17	0
2001	4,118	1,098	613	2,020	3,731	76	28	0
2002	3,594	1,050	539	1,707	3,296	101	10	2
2003	3,023	836	384	1,494	2,714	55	11	4
2004	2,330	733	330	976	2,039	62	10	1
2005	1,791	556	244	917	1,717	40	8	13
2006	1,438	410	182	591	1,183	17	2	5
2007	897	170	122	472	764	9	2	2
2008	534	147	85	339	571	4	0	0
2009	385	83	79	239	401	4	0	1
2010	368	164	69	232	465	4	0	0
2011	195	40	33	100	173	4	0	1
2012	124	24	15	72	111	5	0	0
2013	113	34	65*	67	166	3	2	0

Source: Jammu and Kashmir CID.
Note: *Including 12 soldiers killed on LoC/IB.

in the year 2012, 195 in 2011 and 368 in 2010. But behind these figures lie some ground realities which do not augur well for the peace process. The nature of violence has changed with terrorists having been tasked to demoralize police and the SFs and also not to allow the grass-roots democracy to strengthen by targeting elected panchayat members. For analysing the violence figures, the year 1996 has been deliberately chosen as it was towards the end of this year that assembly elections were held after a long spell of the central rule.

The net infiltration ending November 2013 (as per Multi-agency Centre of the Government of India) was 97 as against 121 during 2012, 52 in 2011 and 95 in 2010 (Table 7.2). What is more significant is that after many years, both in 2012 and 2013, the

Table 7.2:
Hartal calls by separatists, ceasefire violations by Pakistan, infiltration and terrorists killed (2006-2013)

Year	Hartal Calls	Ceasefire Violations	Attempted Infiltration	Net Infiltration	Terrorist Killed
2006	26	–	573	317	591
2007	13	–	535	311	472
2008	33	26	342	57	339
2009	35	18	485	113	239
2010	132	44	489	95	232
2011	22	51	247	52	100
2012	19	93	264	121	72
2013	37	151	277	97	67

Source: Jammu and Kashmir State CID and Multi-agency Centre GOI.

number of terrorists infiltrated was many more than those neutralized, thus adding to the numbers on ground. The number of terrorists killed in relation to fresh infiltration was 67:97 in 2013, 72:121 in 2012, 100:52 in 2011 and 232:95 in 2010 (Table 7.2). The increase may not be very large, but it reveals a trend that Pakistan wanted desperately to increase the number of terrorists and add to weapons to be used at the time of her choosing. The recovery of a huge cache of arms and ammunition including 20 AK rifles and an equal number of pistols hidden within 1 km of LoC in Kupwara district on 29 December is an indicator in this direction.

There can be no doubt that terrorists those infiltrate are trained by the Pakistan Army and are well aware of the topography. 'Significantly, the new brands of infiltrants coming across are much better trained, well equipped and battle-hardened', observes former Special Secretary, Cabinet Secretariat Rana Banerjee.[2] Banerjee adds further:

> They not only had accurate data about the *gulleys* and *nullahs* in this difficult Shamshabari terrain but seemed well aware of precise Indian military post locations and troop strengths deployed in the 15 Corps northern grid. This knowledge could not have been obtained

---

[2] Banerjee, Rana, 'Intrusions along the LoC/IB in J&K: Pakistani Objectives', *Institute of Peace and Conflict Studies*, Article No. 4140, New Delhi, 15 October 2013.

by any rag tag outfit of infiltrators without assistance of serving military personnel on the other side.

There are also indications that 'educated young Kashmiris are joining terrorist ranks and this thinking on their part is a serious matter', laments Dr Shujaat Bukhari,[3] a well-known journalist and the Editor of a daily—*Rising Kashmir*. He also cautions about the increasing alienation of the youth as revealed by 'reactions of Kashmiri young men and women to different situations on social network'.

Incidents of ceasefire violation have increased to 151 in 2013, the highest in a year since ceasefire came into force in 2003. There were only three incidents of violation from 2004 to 2007, 26 incidents in 2008 (largely after General Musharraf quit as President), 18 in 2009, 44 in 2010, 51 in 2011 and 93 in 2012. Towards the end of 2012, a series of ceasefire violations began. The most serious violations during 2013 leading to heightened tension were brutal beheading of an Indian soldier and mutilating body of another on 8 January in Mendhar sector and killing of one Junior Commissioned Officer (JCO) and four Indian soldiers in an ambush within the Indian Territory by Pak troops and infiltrators in the Chakan Da Bagh in Poonch sector during early hours of 6 August.

The casualty of SFs has increased suddenly to 65 (including 12 in border firing incidents) in the year 2013 as against 15 in 2012, 33 in 2011 and 63 in 2010. There were targeted killings of police and SF personnel and daring attacks on them. Thirty-four civilians got killed during the period under review as against 24 in the year 2012, 40 in 2011 and 164 in 2010. Here again, members of panchayats and those having contacts with SFs were targeted. To better appreciate the modus operandi and changed nature of violence, the important terrorist acts in J&K during 2013 are chronologically summarized as follows:

- An Indian soldier was beheaded and body of another mutilated on 8 January 2013 in Mankote sector of Poonch district.

[3] Bukhari, Shujaat, 'Conflict Early Warning: Political Challenges ahead in J&K', paper presented at the seminar on Contemporary Regional Environment & Implications on J&K, IIPA, J&K Regional Branch, Central University of Jammu and IPCS New Delhi, Jammu (J&K), 23 December 2013.

- Terrorists shot dead Sarpanch Habibullah of Goripora Bomai Sopore in Baramulla district on 11 January.
- Bullet ridden body of Mohammed Shafi Dar @ Shafi Mukdam of Aglar Kandi, PS Rajpora, District Pulwama, who had earlier been kidnapped by terrorists, recovered on 11 January from village Akhal
- On 14 February, terrorists shot dead Sarpanch Javid Ahmed Wani of village Kalantara in Baramulla district.
- Two Constables of IR 16 Battalion of J&K Police Santosh Singh and Azad Chand shot at and killed by terrorists at Handwara Chowk on 2 March.
- Two terrorists hurled a grenade and fired indiscriminately upon a CRPF party at Bemina in the outskirts of Srinagar on 13 March killing 5 CRPF personnel on the spot. 6 CRPF personnel and 5 civilians were injured. The two terrorists were killed in the retaliatory action.
- Terrorists fired upon a BSF vehicle at Methan bye pass in Srinagar on 21 March injuring three BSF jawans, one of whom Krishan Kalita, succumbed to his injuries.
- On 24 March, terrorists fired at an IRP Constable and a civilian at Iqbal market Sopore (District Baramulla). The civilian Abdul Rashid succumbed to his injuries. Service rifle of the injured constable was taken away.
- Terrorists shot dead Sarpanch Ghulam Mohammad Lone (aged 40/45 years) resident of Kulpora, Pulwama in his house on 8 April.
- Terrorists fired upon a patrolling party of Police Division Putkhah (stationed at Churoo) at Peer Mohalla, Village Haigam (Sopore) on 26 April, causing death of four Police personnel. Terrorists took away their 3 AK rifles.
- After Friday prayers on 10 May, terrorists shot dead ASI Farooq Ahmed, posted in P/S Pulwama, at Rajpora Chowk, Pulwama where he was performing duty.
- Terrorists shot dead two Police personnel at Hari Singh High Street in Srinagar on 22 June.
- Terrorists on 24 June, riding a motorcycle, fired indiscriminately at an Army convoy at Hyderpora By-Pass in Srinagar, causing death of eight Army Jawans.
- On 26 June, terrorists shot at Kifayat Hussain Mir (35/36 years) at Shanger Gund Bohripora in Baramulla district.

The deceased was running an NGO and had contested 2008 Assembly Elections as an independent candidate.
- Former Director of SKIMS and noted cardiologist Dr Jalal-ud-din was seriously injured and two of his PSOs killed when on 18 July terrorists attacked the vehicle in which he was travelling near Pampore in Pulwama district. Dr Jalal later succumbed to his injuries.
- Khazir Mohammed, a Sarpanch, was shot at and injured when he was coming out of a mosque after offering Friday prayers on 26 July in Kranki Shivan village of Sopore, District Baramulla. Khazir had resigned as Sarpanch in 2012 but later withdrawn the resignation.
- One JCO and four Indian soldiers ambushed and killed within Indian Territory by Pak troops and infiltrators in the Chakan Da Bagh in Poonch sector during early hours of 6 August.
- One policeman killed and a civilian injured in a terrorist attack in Arwani, Anantnag on Aug 26.
- Three terrorists in Army uniform infiltrate from across and carry out twin strikes at Hiranagar police Station in Kathua district and 16 Cavalry Unit of Army near Samba on 26 September killing 10 persons including Lt Col Bikramjeet Singh, three soldiers, four policemen and two civilians. Terrorists were later gunned down after an 11-hour gun battle by the Army.
- SHO Police Station Chadura killed and six persons including three policemen injured in a terrorist attack on 2 December.
- A CRPF Assistant Sub Inspector was killed and a jawan injured on 11 December in a militant attack in Nowgam bye pass area in the outskirts of Srinagar.

On top of it, there is the revival of protests and demonstrations with 37 *hartal* calls by separatists in 2013 as against 22 in 2012 and 19 in 2011. The separatists are once again proactive in exploiting each incident including when terrorists are killed in encounters.

Hanging of Indian Parliament attack accused Mohammad Afzal Guru on 9 February evoked protests from the mainstream political parties as well as separatists bringing the latter together on the platform of Mutahida Majlis-e-Mashawarat (MMM) which issued a weekly calendar of protests and *hartal*s. In the state assembly and outside, battle lines were drawn, along regional and communal lines, between those critical of the hangings and those opposing any concessions to those involved in terrorist activities. While tension over the hanging subsided after a while, observers in Kashmir feel that the scars left in the minds would continue to haunt the state. On the other hand, security analysts describe *disproportionate* sympathy of the Indian media and intelligentsia in this case as the soft belly of India's approach to combat terrorism. Advance information on hanging, it is argued by government circles, would have evoked widespread protests and mayhem to stall due process of law.

It will be useful to recapitulate the following more important incidents that evoked protests and led to disturbances during the year:

- Mohammed Afzal Guru, an accused in the case related to the attack on Indian Parliament, was hanged in Tihar Jail on 9 February 2013 and his body was buried in the jail premises.
- Liaquat Shah, a former terrorist based in Pakistan was arrested by Delhi Police on 20 March 2013 from near the Indo-Nepal border on allegations of planning a terror attack in Delhi.The J&K authorities, however, claimed that he was returning to surrender under the rehabilitation policy. Case is being investigated by the National Investigation Agency (NIA).
- In a firing incident, allegedly by the SFs, at village Markundal, Sumbal during the night intervening June 29/30, two civilians namely Irfan Nabi Ganai and Tariq Ahmed Leharwal lost their lives. Police registered a case and investigation taken up.
- Four civilians killed and 40 injured when BSF and JKP opened fire on protesters outside a BSF camp at Darham Sharti village in Gool Tehsil of Ramban district on 18 July. This led to widespread protests in the state and authorities had to impose curfew in the valley. Large-scale arrest of suspects involved in stone pelting began.
- Four persons including two terrorists killed in Gagran Shopian in cross firing with CRPF on 7 September leading to *hartal* calls and curfew in Shopian, Pulwama and Kulgam.

- Another civilian killed in firing on 11 September. Shutdown continued for three weeks.
- A complete shutdown observed in Chadoora (Badgam district) and adjoining areas after killing of the Lashkar-e-Taiba Commander Omar Bilal in Hushroo village on 26 December. Agitators claimed that the killed person was a local youth Showkat Ahmed Lone who had gone missing. However, mother of Showkat who was taken by police and shown the body categorically denied that it was that of her son.

Terrorist violence is once again raising its head with the net increase in the number of terrorists and targeting SFs and police personnel. There is enough evidence of the continued support of Pak establishment including the civil government in keeping the pot simmering if not boiling. These developments attain significance in the backdrop of forthcoming elections to the Lok Sabha and state assembly of J&K.

India-Pakistan Bilateral Dialogue Addressing the External Dimension

The composite dialogue between India and Pakistan was consigned to the backburner by the 2008 Mumbai terror attack planned on the Pakistani soil and carried out by Pakistani terrorists and non-cooperation of Pakistan to bring Pak-based perpetrators to justice. There was also a sudden increase in ceasefire violations towards the later part of the year 2008. Financial aid and moral support to the Hurriyat Conference had already been resumed in March 2008. India agreed to resume a comprehensive bilateral dialogue at a meeting of the Foreign Secretaries in Thimphu, Bhutan on 6 February 2011. According to foreign policy analysts, there were several positive developments in India–Pakistan relations, including the liberalization of trade and travel. Cross-border terrorism saw a decline even though major terrorist outfits such as Lashkar-e-Taiba and Jaish-e-Mohammed continued to operate freely in Pakistan, spewing hatred against India.

The ceasefire along the border and LoC remained in place even though stray incidents did occur.[4]

Unfortunately, the composite dialogue meant to settle outstanding issues did not make any head way. Instead, Pakistani Parliament passed a resolution in early 2012 invoking United Nations (UN) Resolutions to solve Kashmir, a stand reiterated by Pakistan President Zardari in his UN Security Council speech in September 2012. Pakistan Interior Minister Rehman Malik during his India visit equated Mumbai attack to Babri Masjid. Towards the end of 2012, there began a series of ceasefire violations to provide cover to infiltrators. The tension heightened with the cruel act of beheading an Indian soldier and mutilating body of another on 8 January 2013. Tongue lashing by Pak Foreign Minister accusing India of war-mongering, using contemptuous language and taunting India with investigation by UNMOGIP, whose role India does not recognize since 1971 added to the tension. 'If the exercise of the last eight years and more was for building trust between the two countries', argues Kanwal Sibal, 'then the kind of tongue-lashing that Ms Khar has given India hardly demonstrates that it has been successful. She represents the civilian government of Pakistan, which is supposed to be more committed to improve ties with India'.[5]

Pakistani Army continued to consider jehadi groups operating in India as their strategic assets, and the Pakistan Prime Minister Raja Parvez Ashraf received Kashmiri separatists promising them support in their *struggle for right of self-determination*. None of this could help reduce trust deficit. A sense of outrage in India on the cruel beheading incident compelled the government to end unilateral concessions and base Pak policy strictly on reciprocity. Indian Prime Minister Manmohan Singh's statement that 'It can't be business as usual with Pakistan' adequately captured the public mood.

Pakistan did not stop there. Two days before its term was to end, National Assembly of Pakistan passed a resolution on

---

[4] Saran, Shyam, 'Deciphering Pakistani Adventurism', *Business Standard*, 16 January 2013.

[5] Sibal, Kanwal, 'Nettlesome Neighbour', *Deccan Herald*, 21 January 2013.

14 March 2013 condemning hanging of Indian Parliament attack convict Afzal Guru and demanded the return of his mortal remains to his family. This attitude continued with another similar resolution passed by the Pakistan National Assembly on 13 August even after Nawaz Sharif took over as the prime minister. The Indian Parliament on 15 March rejected the first Pak resolution as interference in its internal matters and reiterated that entire J&K is an integral part of India. The group visa scheme for Pak nationals was put on hold and India–Pakistan hockey series shelved. Indian Parliament also reacted to Pakistan by passing another similar resolution on 14 August.

In his address to the United Nations General Assembly (UNGA) on 28 September, Prime Minister Manmohan Singh asked Pakistan to shut down *terrorist machinery* on its soil while making it clear that there can be no compromise on the territorial integrity of India of which J&K is an integral part. He stated, 'State-sponsored cross-border terrorism is of particular concern to India, also on account of the fact that the epicentre of terrorism in our region is located in our neighborhood in Pakistan'. The Indian Prime Minister rejected the demand made a day earlier by Pakistan Prime Minister Mian Nawaz Sharif that Kashmir issue be resolved on the basis of UN resolutions, terming them as outdated and instead favoured the resolution of bilateral issues in accordance with the Simla agreement.

The current bitterness in India–Pakistan relations makes the resumption of dialogue highly unlikely any time soon. Prime Minister Manmohan Singh expressed disappointment with his Pakistani counterpart for failing to keep his promise made during their New York meeting to stop ceasefire violations in J&K[6] which views he reiterated while meeting Shahbaz Sharif, Chief Minister of Pakistan's Punjab province and brother of the Pak Premier.[7] Manmohan Singh also strongly reacted to a statement (later denied) by Pakistan Prime Minister that 'Kashmir is a flashpoint that can trigger a fourth war with India'. The Indian Prime Minister reacted strongly by stating, 'there is no scope of Pakistan

[6] Deshpande, Rajeev, 'PM Disappointed with Sharif over Ceasefire Violations', *TNN*, 25 October 2013.

[7] 'PM Raises LoC Violations in J&K with Sharif', *Daily Excelsior*, 13 December 2013.

winning any war in my lifetime'.[8] Nawaz Sharif while receiving the new Indian High Commissioner did express his desire for peaceful relations with India and suggested institutionalizing of National Security Advisor (NSA)-level talks to discuss matters related to terrorism,[9] but it will be naïve to expect any breakthrough in the current atmosphere.

It took more than two months for the Directors General of Military Operations (DGMOs) to meet and take a decision to honour the 2003 ceasefire. Rana Banerjee, a noted security analyst and former Special Secretary in the Cabinet Secretariat opines

> as long as the fundamental approach to achieve tactical or strategic objectives does not change, it would be naïve to expect any mechanism of joint interaction between the Directors General of Military Operations of the two Armies to provide succour, either as short-term redress for any specific incidents or to prevent recurring ceasefire violations.[10]

Indian security analysts and Pakistan watchers do not expect any dramatic changes in India–Pakistan relation during 2014. 'The Army will not allow Nawaz Sharif to take over the policy agenda on Kashmir or bilateral relations with India at present', comments Rana Banerjee and cautions India against lowering guards 'till we detect any incremental change in this equation'.[11] The former Indian Foreign Secretary Kanwal Sibal fears that the relations between India and Pakistan may worsen in 2014 as Nawaz Sharif is focusing on Kashmir, knowing that it is a dead end issue. According to him,

> His strong links with Punjab-based jihadi groups, the continuing grip of the Pakistani military on policies towards India, his adviser Sartaz Aziz's new environmentalist twist that India vacate Siachen to cease polluting Pakistan's waters, Pakistan's prevarication on DGMO talks to end LoC firings, relegating the MFN issue to the back-drawer are all negative portents'.[12]

[8] 'Pak Can't Win War—PM', *Daily Excelsior*, Jammu, 5 December 2013.
[9] 'Sharif for NSA Level Talks', *Daily Excelsior*, Jammu, 12 December 2013.
[10] See note 2.
[11] Ibid.
[12] Sibal, Kanwal, 'Fixing the Fault Lines in 2014', *Mail Today*, 30 December 2013.

Fears have been expressed that Pakistan wary of Indian influence in Afghanistan may raise level of violence in J&K to keep Indian troops engaged. The existing nexus between the Lashkar-e-Taiba and Haqanni groups presently used to target Indian interests in Afghanistan can with receding US influence extend to J&K. Shujaat Bukhari, a noted journalist of Kashmir, does not agree that Afghan Mujahideen will come to J&K. He argues 'they have not come to J&K in last 23 years and this is not their battlefield'.[13] 'There may be an "Ugly stability" for at least 2 years in Afghanistan as Taliban are weaker today and ANSF is much better trained and equipped', argues D. Suba Chandran, Director of the New Delhi-based think tank Institute of Peace and Conflict Studies (IPCS) and adds, 'there is likelihood of Punjabi Taliban finding their way to J&K than Afghan Taliban'.[14]

Pakistan Army's orientation has not changed despite talk of focus changing from fighting India to internal situation. 'There may be a new Army Chief but the army remains the same', says Sushant Sareen, Senior Fellow at the New Delhi-based Vivekananda Foundation.[15]

With national and state elections due for 2014 in J&K, Pakistan will try to increase terror-related incidents to disturb the situation. Increased infiltration and targeting SF personnel may be an early warning towards the Pakistani designs. Any meaningful forward movement in addressing the external dimension will thus have to wait for quite some time.

Political Interventions to Address the Internal Dimension

While Pakistan has spurned Indian overtures for making a new beginning, India has also taken a *wait and watch* posture in handling the internal dimension. New Delhi has made efforts, albeit

[13] See note 3.
[14] Suba Chandran, D., 'Afghanistan After 2014 and Regional Security', paper presented at the seminar on Contemporary Regional Environment & Implications on J&K, IIPA, J&K Regional Branch, Central University of Jammu and IPCS New Delhi, Jammu (J&K), 23 December 2013.
[15] Sareen, Sushant, 'New Army Chief, TTP and Regional Security', paper presented at the seminar on Contemporary Regional Environment & Implications on J&K, IIPA, J&K Regional Branch, Central University of Jammu and IPCS New Delhi, Jammu (J&K), 23 December 2013.

feeble, at least in their appearance to the outside world, to bring separatists to the negotiation table. On the eve of the prime minister's visit (24–25 June), Track II activists thronged Srinagar but were told by separatists that there was no scope of a meeting until the previous *commitments* were fulfilled. A new demand of return of Afzal Guru's mortal remains was added to preconditions such as the release of political detainees, booking of police personnel for the deaths of over 100 civilians in 2010 during street fights, withdrawal of AFSPA, etc.

The visit of the prime minister and Smt. Sonia Gandhi to the state in June had purely a developmental agenda. The prime minister reiterated the government's willingness to talk to anyone who shuns violence and made it clear that it would not succumb to terrorists' efforts to destabilize the state. He stated that the entire nation stood united against terrorism and would not tolerate it. Not that anyone expected the prime minister to announce a political package or revocation of AFSPA. The visit was ill timed, according to noted columnist Shujaat Bukhari as the prime minister 'came at a time when peace constituency has shrunk, dialogue both at the internal and external levels is stalled and the efforts to reach out to the people at the political level is completely absent'.[16]

During the prime minister's visit, Chief Minister Omar Abdullah urged for the resumption of internal dialogue for the political resolution of grievances and aspirations of pluralistic and diverse state, resumption of dialogue with Pakistan and comprehensive review on cross LoC trade and travel. He showed satisfaction over the rehabilitation policy with 422 cases having been approved for return out of 1,094 applications received.

The National Conference (NC) delegation which met the prime minister demanded greater autonomy in pursuance to the state assembly resolution and implementing recommendations of the Working Groups and Interlocutors. The delegation did not press for the withdrawal of AFSPA on this occasion but made it clear that the party's views on the issue remained unchanged.

It may be recalled that frustrated by New Delhi's silence, Chief Minister Omar Abdullah on the floor of the state assembly on 25 March had said that the state had only acceded and not merged

---

[16] Bukhari, Shujaat, 'J&K: Mr PM You Failed to Talk Peace', *Institute of Peace and Conflict Studies*, Article No. 4013, New Delhi, 26 June 26 2013.

with India and that the political status of J&K cannot be changed by repeatedly using the words *atoot ang* (integral part of India). He repeated these views when interacting with a European Union delegation on 25 September.[17] However, he toned down his stand by telling the media persons on the sidelines of reopening of move offices in Jammu on 4 November that he had not used the words like *conditional* or *incomplete* regarding the accession of J&K to India and said that the state is an integral part of India. 'Jammu and Kashmir acceded to India. If we accede to India are we not integral part of India … of course, we are', said the Chief Minister.[18] Omar Abdullah has rightly been pushing for the resolution of J&K's political concerns adding that economic development alone cannot settle issues confronting the state. Addressing a rally in Bandipora district in north Kashmir, Omar said, 'The three wars fought by India and Pakistan over Kashmir, militant violence and different political voices reverberating in the skies of J&K were not for construction of roads, educational institutions or hospitals'.

In the absence of dialogue with Pakistan and refusal of separatists to talk, New Delhi is in a dilemma how far it will be productive without taking Pakistan on board to address the internal dimension, more particularly, the centre–state relations in terms of the demands of mainstream parties and recommendations of the Working Groups/Interlocutors. This is well demonstrated by the go-slow approach of the J&K Government's Cabinet Sub Committee on Justice Sagheer Ahmed Working Group recommendations on centre–state relations despite the mandate of the group being within the ambit of the Constitution of India and not touching upon the demands of separatists. The term of the sub-committee, which has representation from the ruling coalition partners, the National Conference and Congress parties, has been extended for the eighth time and it failed to meet even once during 2013. In previous 17 meetings, consensus has eluded the coalition partners on autonomy. While National Conference strongly advocates autonomy, the Congress party has stuck to its stand for making 1975 Indira–Sheikh accord as the basis for any solution.

[17] Pandit, M. Saleem, 'J&K Never Merged with India: Omar Abdullah', *TNN*, 26 September 2013.
[18] 'Jammu and Kashmir integral part of India says CM Omar Abdullah', *PTI*, New Delhi, 4 November 2013.

The separatists found handy material to exploit the sentiments after hanging of Afzal Guru and alleged incidents attributed to SFs listed earlier. The frequency of *hartal* calls and number of protest demonstrations have suddenly increased. The state government has been exercising restraint in dealing with street fights. Once again it became necessary for the law-and-order machinery to restrict movements of separatist leaders and resort to the arrest of agitators pelting stones. Despite the lukewarm response of the people to *hartal* calls and agitations, they did affect normal life and trade.

Pakistani leaders visiting India have made it customary to meet Kashmiri separatists and exchange views and also give directions on expectations from them. Syed Ali Shah Geelani, Mirwaiz Umar Farooq, Asia Indrabi and Yaseen Malik had separate meetings with Pakistan Prime Minister's Advisor on National Security and Foreign Affairs Sartaj Aziz on November 10 when he was in New Delhi. Hina Rabbani Khar had also similarly met separatists during her visit to New Delhi in July 2011. It may be recalled that a delegation of separatist leaders from Kashmir led by Mirwaiz Umar Farooq visited Pakistan and met Prime Minister Raja Parvez Ashraf. Media also reported on their meetings with Hafiz Saeed and Syed Salauddin, both wanted in India for terrorist acts. These meetings coupled with Pakistan's open support to Kashmir cause in International fora including UN and Organisation of Islamic Cooperation (OIC) provided much needed motivation to separatists. The continued funding of separatists and terrorists from across has ensured that separatists increase their activities in the election year propagating their stand against democratic processes.

Syed Ali Shah Geelani in recent public meetings continued to take the hardline that no solution of the dispute would be acceptable except independence. He has started wooing the minorities to join the *freedom movement* assuring them that their lives and properties will remain safe. He opposes the four-point formula of General Musharraf saying that no roadmaps including autonomy, self-rule, status quo, etc., mooted by political mainstream is acceptable to his faction of the Hurriyat Conference. Mirwaiz Umar Farooq has similarly been describing the state as an internationally accepted dispute and favours referendum to decide the future of the state. There arises a window of hope occasionally with moderate Hurriyat faction leader Professor Abdul Ghani

Bhat describing the UN resolutions on J&K as *dead* but hardliners are quick to reject such claims.

The issues related to internally displaced Pandits continue to remain largely unattended. It would be travesty of justice if the authorities are following a wait and watch approach in this regard. The prime minister's package has not been fully implemented. The recruitment process needs to be expedited. The usurping of lands and damage to temples and shrines of pandits has not abated. The much talked about Temples and Shrines Bill to manage these religious places remains in a limbo. And then the long-term issue of the return of the community with dignity and honour cannot be achieved as the *sense of security* of the community has not yet been restored.

There is a view that the absence of serious political thinking on these and other issues can lead to the resurgence of violence. According to this school of thought, silence should not be mistaken as a sign of contentment. They feel that it needs to be seen as a strong means of communication. Media reports of educated young Kashmiris joining the terrorist ranks and increase in alienation as symbolized by views of youth on social networking sites are all indicative of hope turning into cynicism. While no one can find fault with the development agenda, its predominance to eclipse the political resolution of grievances of the three geographic regions is a hindrance in the peace process.

The issues which need political intervention urgently include centre–state relations in terms of reports of working group/interlocutors and demands of mainstream parties, fulfilling regional aspirations by an institutionalized mechanism, problems faced by displaced Kashmiri Pandits including their return, reducing footprints of SFs from hinterland including revisiting AFSPA and empowering Panchayati Raj Institutions including the adoption of 73rd and 74th amendments of the Constitution of India and elections to local bodies.

In addition, Pakistan will have to be taken on board with regard to addressing bottlenecks and security concerns of trans-LoC travel and trade as well as the return and rehabilitation of surrendering Kashmiri youth presently in Pakistan. Meanwhile, efforts to bring separatists to the negotiation table must continue. It would be of interest if more of them like Sajjad Lone of People's Party are willing to test the waters during the next assembly elections. It may be of interest to note that the Peoples Conference (Sajjad) has organized 59 public meetings during 2013 and others can take a cue from them.

Internal Dimension of the Conflict-Development and Governance

During 2013, the central and state governments have gone about full throttle towards the development of infrastructure, skills development, employment generation and empowerment of women. Prime Minister Manmohan Singh and United Progressive Alliance (UPA) Chairperson Sonia Gandhi during their visit to J&K on 25–26 June promised full support to the state for its holistic and inclusive development. The prime minister announced ₹1,629 crore Srinagar–Leh power transmission line and ₹710 crore package for the rural road network package in the state under Pradhan Mantri Gram Sadak Yojana (PMGSY). Prime minister laid the foundation stone of 850 MW Ratle Hydroelectric Power Project in Kishtwar and inaugurated the Banihal–Qazigund rail link joining the two provinces of J&K across the Pir Panchal Range.

Under prime minister's special scholarship scheme 3,747 students of the state were found eligible during 2013–2014. The scheme launched in 2011 had attracted only 38 students in the first year, and in 2012–2013, the number of eligible candidates rose to 3,340. Under this scheme, ₹30,000 per annum is paid to students pursuing general degree courses, ₹1.25 lakhs for engineering students and ₹3 lakhs for medical students. Rupees 1 lakh is also paid towards hostel fee.[19]

In the last 10 years, only a little over 50 per cent of the targets set for implementing a ₹24,467 crore package under Prime Minister's Reconstruction Plan (PMRP) to raise infrastructure damaged during the conflict have been achieved. The PMRP announced in November 2004 by the prime minister was to be implemented in the central and state sectors, the former

[19] 'PMs Special Scholarship Package: 3,747 J&K Students Found Eligible', *Kashmir Times*, Jammu, 12 December 2013.

including the power-generating hydel projects. The centre has already released ₹7,214 crores, and ₹600 crores are due to be released this fiscal under the state sector. It may take another 3–4 years, according to media reports,[20] to complete the projects but meanwhile due to delays the revised cost is now estimated at ₹34,800 crores which the centre is committed to provide to take the plan to its logical conclusion.

The chief minister handed training-cum-placement letters to 300 J&K youth selected under UDAAN—Programme for skills development and employment—by the Canara Bank in Jammu on 31 December. Director UDAAN revealed on this occasion that 59,000 youth of J&K are being trained and placed in as many as 42 private organizations in rest of India during the next five years for which required memorandum of understandings (MoUs) have been signed by concerned parties. He said as many as 2,385 youth are presently under training with 30 private partners in the country.[21]

The state government under the UMEED programme plans to empower 9 lakh poor women by organizing savings and credit-based self-help groups and their federation at village and block levels to address their socio-economic problems.[22] In a phased-approach spread over five years, 143 blocks and 4,098 gram panchayats would be covered under the scheme with an estimated outlay of 755 crores including ₹248 crores as seed money to be made available to the self-help groups. The central government will provide 90 per cent of funds for the scheme.

The state government claims to have provided 100 thousand jobs, supported the creation of 2,500 entrepreneurship units and provided skill upgradation training to 40,000 youth in the last five years. One hundred thousand more jobs are in the pipeline.

Power projects to generate 1400 MW were launched in the last five years and 9,000 MW of power generation is expected in next 7–8 years to give financial autonomy to the state. Major strides

[20] Pargal, Sanjeev, 'Ahead of Elections, N Command Chief Puts Troops on High Alert', *Daily Excelsior*, Jammu, 5 January 2014.
[21] 'Process of Job Creation in Full Swing: Omar', *Daily Excelsior*, Jammu, 1 January 2014.
[22] 'Omar Favours Empowerment of Women', *Daily Excelsior*, Jammu, 12 December 2013.

have been made in providing water supply, road connectivity, education and healthcare in the state.[23]

Despite institutional mechanisms created by the state government during the last five years, the public perception about governance deficit, lack of accountability and institutionalized corruption has not changed. Steps taken by the government in this regard include the constitution of Information and Vigilance Commissions, re-constitution of Accountability Commission, third-party monitoring, Public Service Guarantee Act, e-purchasing and Result Framework Document.

A high-level committee set up by the government with much hype to weed out the *deadwood* in the state administration has not given any recommendations. Despite directions of the J&K High Court, the state government has been reluctant to make provisions of the Prevention of Corruption Act more stringent. Over 60 per cent of power energy is lost in transmission and distribution in the state. Last fiscal the state government imported power worth ₹3,100 crores, whereas the revenue collected was only ₹1,800 crores.

Enquiries initiated by the State Accountability Commission have been stayed by the Hon'ble High Court. No effort has been made to break the impasse by either getting stays vacated or amending the relevant Act. The State Vigilance Commission is yet to get its required complement of staff. With the state entering into the election year, it is pretty much clear that the current pace and complexion of governance will not show any significant change for the better.

The development agenda of the state fully supported by the Union Government has provided succour to the people of the state. Unfortunately, the governance deficit impinges on the benefits derived from developmental agenda and impairs the peace process. It dents the writ of the democratic institutions which have been so assiduously nursed during the last 17 years since the 1996 assembly elections. The coalition government will find it very difficult to take any stringent measures during the last year of the current assembly in this regard.

---

[23] 'Let Facts Speak—DIP/J-7684 Dated January 4', *Daily Excelsior*, Jammu, 5 January 2014.

Incursions by China

During the past one year, a number of Chinese incursions have been reported in Leh, with the most significant one being the Depsang plains incident of 15 April to 6 May 2013 when Chinese troops intruded 19 km inside the Indian territory. The standoff was resolved before the visit of External Affairs Minister Salman Khursheed to China. Yet again Chinese troops are reported to have apprehended five Indian nationals in the Chumar area of Ladakh, well from inside the Indian territory, in early December in an apparent bid to lay claim on the area. They were returned following the efforts made through existing border mechanisms between India and China. These trespasses due to their frequency and dimension cannot be called isolated in nature.

It needs to be noted that no significant progress in the critical border issue has been made despite many rounds of talks. If the special representative (SR) mechanism was intended to find a solution to the border issue, the statements by the top Chinese leadership that the border issue will take a very long time to resolve and that a complete solution may not be possible do belie such expectations. These views came from the former Chinese Premier Wen Jiabao during his trip to India in 2010 and were reiterated by the new Chinese President Xi Jinping soon after he took over, though subsequently he and others have spoken of resolving the issue as soon as possible and directing the SRs to do so. Meanwhile, the Chinese also modified the mandate of the SRs by enlarging it to cover all the issues rather than the border issue alone.

The new Chinese leadership appears to be in a combative mood. The former foreign Secretary Kanwal Sibal writes, 'China's focus is on maintaining peace and tranquillity along the border rather than settling the border issue. China has also stepped up its claim on Arunachal Pradesh since last over seven years. China has begun calling Arunachal Pradesh as South Tibet'. These along with firming its hold on the territory of J&K ceded to it by Pakistan and the issue of stapled visas to Kashmiris to give a political message are termed by Sibal as 'indicators of new Chinese leadership to be in a combative mood toughening its tone on territorial and sovereignty issues following its enormous economic success and growing military strength'.[24]

Professor S. Kondapalli had cautioned[25] on the eve of Prime Minister Manmohan Singh's recent visit to China that he would come across phrases such as multilaterism, against trade protectionism, climate change proposals and there will be anaemic attention to bilateral issues. China is averse to take up bilateral issues including the boundary issue, the occupation of 20,000 km of the territory of Gilgit and Baltistan, *stapled* visas and the presence of Chinese troops in Pak-occupied Kashmir (PoK).China's relations with Pakistan are acquiring even more strategic dimensions with China's decision to take over Gwadar. Significantly, the Pakistan Premier Nawaz Sharif was in Beijing at the same time when our Defence Minister Antony was there.

Former Special Director in the Indian Intelligence Bureau R.N. Ravi after a weeklong visit to border areas in Ladakh draws a very dismal picture of grabbing of pastures and land by China and Indian indifference in providing basic necessities to the people in these remote areas.[26] He warns that caught between a *strong* and *aggressive* China and a *weak* and *indifferent* India the locals have 'begun discovering deeper meaning in the common cultural co-ordinates and shared sociological bonds with their kin across the border, and, of course not so dark a future in China...'. This can have very serious repercussions for the state and the integrity of India if not addressed.

Defence Minister A.K. Antony had himself conceded in Parliament in September 2013 that 'China is superior in terms of border infrastructure as India was late in deciding on building roads and other capabilities near the line of actual control (LAC)'. The raising of a new mountain *strike* Corps with two independent infantry Brigades and two independent Armoured Brigades for

---

[24] Sibal, Kanwal, 'Great Wall of Discontent', *Force*, July 2013.

[25] Kondapalli, Srikanth, 'Limits of India's Engagements with China', *rediff.com*, 21 October 2013, available online at http://www.rediff.com/news/column/limits-to-indias-engagement-with-china/20131021.htm.

[26] Ravi, R.N., 'Indifferent India allows Chinese land grab on the border', *rediff.com*, 20 December 2013, http://www.rediff.com/news/column/indifferent-India-allows-chinese-land-grab-on-the-border/20131220.htm.

deployment along the LAC will provide offensive teeth against China. The construction of road and rail infrastructure in these areas is also a welcome step. Bottlenecks on these projects on political and environmental considerations must be resolved.

It needs a closer analysis whether the increase in the intensity of incidents of terror and trespasses along India's Northern Borders both by Pakistan and China, during the current year in particular, are indicative of any meeting of minds between the two hostile neighbours to contain India. The answer to new Chinese belligerence will lie in preparedness, both military and infrastructural, along the borders.

Strengthening of Democratic Institutions— Elections in 2014

Strengthening of democratic institutions in J&K has been the most important positive political intervention post-Pak-sponsored asymmetric warfare which began in the late 1980s. The successful holding of assembly elections in 1996, 2002 and 2008; periodic Lok Sabha polls and elections to panchayats in 2011 were all landmark developments. Pakistan would not like to see democratic processes and institutions snatching the influence of its separatist support base and will do all that is necessary to disturb the forthcoming parliamentary and the state assembly elections. Hardliner Hurriyat leader Syed Ali Shah Geelani has already started to harp on the boycott of elections in his public meetings.

When General K.V. Krishna Rao took over as the Governor of the J&K in March 1993, his focus was on the resumption of the political process and handing over the reins to a duly elected government in the shortest possible time. Assembly elections were held in 1996 after a prolonged period of governor/president's rule in the state. This and following elections in 2002 and 2008 have thrown up different possibilities and allowed elected governments to meet the expectations of the people. The democratic institutions have provided enough opportunity for the people to raise their grievances before their elected representatives. The performance of successive governments and achievements can be a subject matter of debate but that democracy has taken roots

Table 7.3:
Votes polled in elections to the Jammu and Kashmir assembly

Year of Poll	Seats Contested	No. of Candidates	Poll %
1987	76	528	74.9
1996	87	547	53.9
2002	87	709	43.1
2008	87	1,354	61.5

Source: Chief Electoral Officer, Government of Jammu and Kashmir, http://ceojk.nic.in/

cannot be disputed. This is a positive development. It is high time to consolidate on these gains by ensuring peaceful, free and fair elections in the state.

It would be useful for the reader to get a feel of how people of the state have responded to the assembly elections since 1996. Despite Pakistan inspired calls for poll boycott by separatists, the turnout has been sizeable and sometimes overwhelming (Table 7.3). The number of participating candidates has increased successively. Over 80 per cent voters exercised their franchise in the elections to panchayats held in 2011. It is true that poll percentage need not be taken as an index of the resolution of the conflict but it does reveal the people's faith in democracy and rejection of poll boycott calls.

Constituencies shown in Table 7.4 are those which at least on one occasion in the last three elections to the state assembly polled less than 20 per cent votes. There are some constituencies in the Kashmir valley where low turnout is recorded partly because of the genuine influence of separatists and partly because conditions are created where even those who want to vote prefer to remain indoors. There are only six constituencies, all within the city of Srinagar, which polled less than 25 per cent votes in all the three assembly polls (Table 7.4). This table also reveals that separatists' writ does not always run, for instance, even Sopore assembly constituency, the home turf of the hardliner Syed Ali Shah Geelani, polled 38 per cent in 1996 and 20 per cent in 2008. The area of influence of separatists even within the Kashmir valley, as would be clear from Table 7.4 is very limited. Their claim of representing even Kashmiris becomes highly questionable, the voters of Jammu province and Ladakh region having remained predominantly steadfast in their allegiance to the Indian state.

Table 7.4:
Low voter turnout constituencies during assembly polls in J&K

Constituency	% Votes Polled		
	1996	2002	2008
Sopore	38	8	20
Hazratbal	24	7	29
Zadibal	13	5	17
Idgah	20	5	22
Khanyar	13	4	17
Habba Kadal	17	3	12
Amira Kadal	13	3	15
Sonwar	35	10	37
Batmalloo	20	4	21
Anantnag	35	7	41
Tral	59	12	49
Pampore	61	19	43
Pulwama	51	18	40
Kookernag	41	15	70
Bijbihara	37	17	61

Source: Chief Electoral Officer, Government of Jammu and Kashmir, http://ceojk.nic.in/

This is not to belittle the existence of a conflict situation that needs to be resolved, howsoever small be the separatists' constituency. They retain the capacity to sway the people in the valley by their emotive appeal on issues that arise from time to time.

The challenges that the government is likely to face in run up to the assembly elections include keeping in check any attempts by Pakistan to escalate terrorist violence, dealing imaginatively with protests sponsored by separatists and providing security to candidates, political activists and public meetings.

It would be naïve to think that the role of the security grid has in any way lessened in this election than in the previous three. Any such thoughts must be laid to rest right away. This time the regional and communal tensions and their exploitation for political gains will be an additional challenge. The cut-throat competition among the two regional parties—National Conference (NC) and People's Democratic Party (PDP) — in the valley and the two national parties (Congress and BJP) in Jammu will throw up debates and controversies on the relationship between the state and the Union of India. These issues will be played up in a big way to the detriment of the security and law-and-order situations. The social media will play a crucial role in the elections for the first time and mischievous elements may use it to spread rumours and incite trouble.

The state government employees have been agitating for quite some time for improvement in their service conditions and emoluments. It may not be possible for the government to accept their demands. The agitating state government employees may exploit the situation and refuse to carry out poll duties. This must be kept in mind by the state government and the election authorities.

Mainstreaming of separatists by encouraging them to participate in the electoral process will be a positive step forward for the peace process. Having failed to capture power by gun, some separatists are not averse to participating in the elections. Such aspirations have come to the fore in participation in elections of Shabnam Lone and her brother Sajjad Lone of People's Conference as well as a number of proxy candidates with the support of separatists in the recent past. Even Syed Ali Shah Geelani has remained a member of the legislature. Jamaat-e-Islami is known to have allowed its supporters to vote in favour of select candidates. There is a need to encourage separatists to participate in the coming assembly elections. This can be a positive development in the peace process.

Preparedness

The security grid in J&K will have to urgently take remedial steps. The prolonged combat fatigue coupled with the mirage of peace carved by the reduction in incidents of violence and expectations from the newly elected government in Pakistan may have set complacency in the system. To this, add the war of words between the civil government and the army on issues including AFSPA.

The much needed synergy between various colours of uniform as also between civilian government and military is being restored to prevent attacks of the kind witnessed on Hiranagar police station and the Samba-based army unit. Army has claimed the presence of 400 terrorists in the state and efforts by Pakistan to pump in more. Some good results with neutralizing top terrorist commanders in the last two months of 2013 have already set the pace for stepping up antiterrorist operations.

The counter infiltration effort needs to be redoubled in view of recent incidents. Pakistan will use every opportunity to send in more terrorists and weapons. According to reports, militants have concentrated themselves across the LoC at various locations. The border check posts created by J&K police some years back will need to be made functional again. In this regard, the recent upgradation of technology along the fence on the International Border (IB) by the Border Security Force by introducing the state-of-the-art communication and surveillance system and induction by the army of high technology thermal imagers and setting up of special control rooms to analyse the data provided by the thermal cameras will help better surveillance along the IB and LoC.

The Northern Army Commander Lt. Gen. Sanjiv Chachra has put the troops on high alert while visiting formations along the LoC in the Kashmir valley.[27] His call to the troops to exercise utmost restraint during anti-terror operations and ensure that there is no human rights violation and collateral damage is very timely and appropriate. Jammu police has also begun a survey of border villages after arresting two Pakistani nationals and recovering narcotics, currency and Pakistani SIM cards.

The funding of separatists and terrorists needs to be blocked. It is well known that Hawala route, banking channels, human couriers and of late cross-border trade is used as media for bringing in money besides the counterfeit currency. According to a charge sheet filed in a Delhi Court by NIA against Syed Salauddin and nine others, Hizbul Mujahideen (HM) has developed a well spread-out system of distribution of funds to sympathizers, runners, over ground workers, underground workers and to next of kin of its cadres killed/injured. Rupees 80 crores were received in last eight years to fund HM and these funds came from Pakistan and PoK, according to the charge sheet.

---

[27] Pargal, Sanjeev, 'PMRP Cost Escalates to ₹34,858 cr—Only 50 pc Projects Completed in 10 Years', *Daily Excelsior*, 2 January 2014.

Holding free, fair and peaceful elections is a challenge which will require a coordinated strategy between the administration and SFs. Army has with credit provided area dominance for public meetings, road opening in the border belt and important communication links for the travelling of candidates and political activists and made arrangements for poll parties in remote and far flung areas in the past. Immediate security of venues of public meetings, candidates and poll staff will need full mobilization of J&K police and Central Para Military Forces. An environment will have to be created by maintaining peace and keeping terrorists under check so that voters can fearlessly exercise their franchise both in the Lok Sabha and assembly elections. Success in this will be a step forward in the peace process.

Communal and Regional Fault Lines

The communal divide in the wake of Amarnath land row in 2008 and more recently after the execution of Afzal Guru has left its scars. On every issue with communal overtones, the population composition of the two provinces leads invariably to a regional divide between Muslim-dominated Kashmir and Hindu-dominated Jammu provinces. Sectarian violence in Budgam district of the valley and communal violence in Kishtwar district of Jammu province during 2013 pose fresh challenges for the already stretched security apparatus.

There are reports that separatists are making deep inroads into the Muslim-majority Chenab valley and districts of Poonch and Rajouri in Jammu province. Their success in achieving influence in the Chenab valley is cited as one of the reasons for heightened tension between the two communities leading to ugly incidents in Kishtwar.

The political expediency and vote bank politics can further vitiate the atmosphere as the state assembly elections come nearer. There is the likelihood of competitive politicking on each perceived or real incident of violation of human rights between separatists and mainstream political parties in the valley. Issues such as autonomy and self-rule, withdrawal of AFSPA and disbanding of Village Defence Committees will be raised in the valley which will be vehemently opposed in Jammu. Conversely, voices in support of the abrogation of Article 370 of the Constitution and regional autonomy from the south of Pir Panchal will be opposed in the valley.

A case in point is strong reaction to a statement by BJP's Prime Ministerial Candidate Narendra Modi in a public rally in Jammu on 1 December advocating a debate on whether the people of the state had benefitted from Article 370. J&K Chief Minister Omar Abdullah warned that any move to abrogate Article 370, which defines the relationship between the state and the centre, will reopen the issue of the state's accession to India. Omar minced no words in saying that, 'Article 370 of the Constitution was acting as a "bridge" between Jammu and Kashmir and rest of the country and attempts to weaken it would only weaken this relationship'.[28] PDP Supremo Mufti Mohammad Sayeed reacted sharply by saying that the Article was permanent as the Constituent Assembly of the state had ratified it. He advocated Modi to 'steer clear of the divisive issues and follow Atal Behari Vajpayee in building bridges rather than spark off controversies that have no relevance except trying to reap votes at the cost of National interest'.

A strong reaction came from Hurriyat Conference (M) Chairman Umar Farooq who advocated Modi to go through history. 'Kashmir is an internationally accepted dispute. A referendum should be held and India will get to know what Kashmiris want', he added in an interview. Hurriyat (G) Chairman Ali Shah Geelani labelled Modi as a *killer of humanity* and added during a public meeting in Kulgam in south Kashmir that 'his candidature is in total contrast to India's claim of being a democratic and secular country'. Without going into the merits of the proposition, these reactions are being cited to illustrate the nature of discourse that can be expected on issues which are perceived differently in the two regions and by the two largest communities.

The possibility of raking up of such issues is further illustrated by the BJP National Spokesperson Nirmala Sitharaman speaking to the media in Jammu on 27 December and reiterating that the Article 370, Kishtwar communal violence and re-induction of Sajjad Ahmed Kitchloo into the J&K ministry and Kashmiri

---

[28] 'Art 370 Foundation Stone of India, J&K Relations: Omar', *Daily Excelsior*, Jammu, 5 December 2013.

Hindu Shrines and Temple Bill will be among host of other issues during the Lok Sabha and assembly elections due next year.[29]

The communal situation will have to be closely watched in run up to the elections, and the civil administration and security apparatus must prevent the recurrence of a Kishtwar-like situation. It would require close coordination between the civil administration and the army to respond to any situation in far and remote hilly areas. The troops deployed in these areas must respond under a well-drafted strategy as help from district headquarters or state headquarters takes a long time to reach. The standard operating procedures must provide for quick response to the requests of civil administration to deal with a communal situation in such areas.

Political Consensus at National Level

There is lack of political consensus at the national level to deal with terrorism, engagement with Pakistan and even on defining the contours of conflict resolution between the centre and the state. First and foremost, India must have in place a credible machinery to collect intelligence, prevent terror acts and investigate these crimes. It is of no use blaming Pakistan after each incident. The National Counter Terrorism Centre mooted by the Union Government needs to be revisited after taking the states on board. There is no substitute for preparedness. State police forces in terror prone states must be trained and provided adequate infrastructure to prevent terror strikes.

There must be continuity at the level of the central government on its Kashmir policy. This can be achieved by a consensus among important political parties about what people of India want so that any change at the centre does not impair the conflict resolution process. Loose press statements by political parties on a serious subject like Kashmir tend to send signals about the non-seriousness of the political leadership to resolve the issue. After the visit of all-party parliamentary delegation to J&K following

[29] Bhat, Avtar, 'Article 370, Kitchloo, Shrine Bill Major Issues of BJPs Poll Plank: Sitharaman', *Daily Excelsior*, Jammu, 28 December 2013.

disturbances in the state in 2010, there has been no consensus on the follow-up. The report of interlocutors advocating resolution within the framework of the Indian Constitution is also gathering dust for want of consensus.There are divergent views between the two main national political parties on Article 370 of the Constitution of India which gives special status to the state of J&K. Such differences seem to have held up the conflict resolution.

Conclusions

Security situation in J&K in recent years has been a vast improvement over the conditions that prevailed in early 1990s under the onslaught of Pakistan-sponsored proxy war to dismember India. Except for the revival of terrorist violence after Pakistani misadventure in Kargil in 1999, there has been a steady fall in violence since 2001. All credit must go to the SFs, J&K police and the people of the state who were fed up of disturbed conditions and yearned for the return of normalcy.

While violence is under control, there has been for a variety of reasons no progress in bilateral talks between India and Pakistan to find a lasting solution nor has the internal dimension more importantly the centre–state relations and regional aspirations of the people been addressed. This makes the peace process fragile despite reasonable success of the development agenda of the state and central governments. Raising heads of terrorists particularly in targeting SFs and police personnel during 2013 must be seen in this backdrop. Any relapse at this stage will seriously hurt the peace process.

The year 2014 is an election year with Lok Sabha and assembly elections due to be held. It will be a test for the stability of the peace process in the state. While auditing the peace process in 2013, it has become necessary to look ahead at the challenges and early warnings. Pakistan has made its intentions clear by increasing ceasefire violations and sending in more terrorists. Hardliner separatists have begun propaganda for poll boycott.

A free, fair and peaceful elections will strengthen the democratic institutions in which the people of the state have shown faith. This will need strengthening of the security grid and gearing up of the civil administration and election authorities. The political parties will have to resist the temptation of exploiting regional and communal sentiments for electoral gains. Meanwhile, it would be unreasonable to expect any significant forward movement in addressing the external and internal dimensions till a new government is formed in New Delhi and later in the state of J&K.

8

Peace Processes in Manipur: A Perspective

Chitra Ahanthem

A Turbulent Historical Background

Manipur, a sovereign kingdom came under British rule as a princely state in 1891 after its defeat in the Khongjom war. Following the defeat, the Assam Rifles occupied the Kangla, and Manipur became the last independent kingdom to be merged into British India. When the British left the Indian subcontinent in 1947, Manipur also regained its independence with the Manipur Constitution Act 1947, leading to the establishment of a government with an elected legislature and the Maharaja Bodhchandra as the Executive Head. However, in 1949, Maharaja Bodhchandra was summoned to Shillong, the capital of the then Indian province of Assam, and on 21 September 1949 signed a Treaty of Accession under which Manipur was to be formally merged to India on 15 October 1949. Manipur was a union territory from 1956, becoming a full-fledged state in 1972.

But the signing of the merger agreement was considered to be under duress by the majority, and the first seeds of rebellion were sowed when Hijam Irabot, who opposed the merger, went underground and raised a band of revolutionaries. Irabot sought the support of Communist Party of Burma but died before his efforts could bear fruit in 1951. The first Meitei revolutionary movement ended with Irabot. It was not until the mid-1960s that Manipur experienced another upsurge in violent, anti-government activities. On 24 November 1964, the first resistance group was formed with the emergence of the United National Liberation Front (UNLF) which stated as its aim not only an independent, socialist republic in Manipur but also that it had a *historic mission* to liberate Manipur 'from colonial occupation in the larger context of liberating the entire Indo-Burma region, for a common future'.[1] But since the UNLF was not the sole group that would espouse the cause of a *sovereign Manipur* for over a period of time, there came into being other major groups such as the People's Liberation Army (PLA), People's Revolutionary Party of Kangleipak, Kangleipak Communist Party (KCP) and offshoots from these groups due to ideological differences, leadership issues, etc.

Apart from the Meitei outfits that are active in the Imphal Valley, the major Naga insurgent group—National Socialist Council of Nagaland-Isak–Muivah (NSCN-IM)—has a strong base in four of Manipur's five hill districts, namely, Ukhrul, Senapati, Tamenglong and Chandel. The Nagas who have had a long struggle for their unique place in history and sovereignty with its insurgent movement fragmenting in the journey into the Naga National Council, NSCN-IM and the NSCN-Khaplang (NSCN-K), of which the latter two are more active politically and in terms of their role in prevailing the armed conflict in the state. The ongoing talks between the NSCN-IM and the Government of India have meanwhile triggered off an active civil response from various groups from among the Meiteis and the Kukis with the main spotlight being territorial integrity.

The demand for Kukiland (land for the Kukis) is a direct challenge to the demand for Greater Nagaland by the NSCN-IM. *Greater Nagaland* as projected by the NSCN-IM would have to be inclusive of all Naga-inhabited areas, thereby forking out major chunks if not the entire districts of Chandel, Senapati, Tamenglong and Ukhrul, to be integrated with the neighbouring Nagaland state.

The intention to drive out Kukis from these four hill districts, in fact, led to an intense and prolonged *ethnic cleansing* by the

---

[1] Bertil Lintner, *Great Game East* (New Delhi: Harper Collins, 2012), pp. 146–147.

NSCN-IM in the 1990s. While Meiteis oppose the creation of either a Kuki homeland or a greater Nagaland, the Kukis and Nagas are unable to establish any kind of coordination or cooperation. Thus, the ethnic conflict between the Nagas and the Kukis constitutes another problem of the state. Clashes between the two groups are now not heard of. A number of Kuki outfits like Kuki National Army (KNA), Kuki National Front (KNF) and many others had been struggling for a separate state within the Indian Union since the late 1980s.[2]

Peace in Manipur?

The very idea of *peace* in Manipur in its current situation is layered. If at one level, we are to look at the frequency and number of occasions now in which armed groups or non-state armed actors (various armed groups) have engaged with state armed actors (security personnel) or undertaken attacks and ambushes, there is indeed a decline of such confrontations as compared to the early 1980s and 1990s. Such confrontations between the state and non-state forces lead to a state of fear, harassment and trauma for security personnel would undertake what are called *combing operations* in the immediate vicinity of sites where attacks took place or where there was suspicion of the movement of the non-state actors. It was in the context of such *combing operations* undertaken by paramilitary forces who were protected under the impunity of the Armed Forces Special Powers Act (AFSPA) that the civilian population of Manipur came to grapple with numerous cases of their civil rights being violated: with numerous cases of forced disappearances, torture in custody, illegal detention, rape and fake encounters even as human rights groups and civil society took to the streets and various other forums to protest against the arbitrary actions. It was the public outrage and agitations, but more specifically the Kangla protest where 12 Meira Paibi women stripped themselves to protest in the wake of the brutal rape and

---

[2] SATP, Manipur Backgrounder, available online at http://www.satp.org/satporgtp/countries/india/states/manipur/backgrounder/index.html.

murder of Thangjam Manorama, an alleged former underground care that the situation in the state came under national and international media and human rights groups. Though *combing operations* still continue, they are done so under an arrangement called *joint operations* where paramilitary forces and state police forces work in tandem. Such a move is aimed at deflecting criticism of paramilitary forces and their manner of operations and to co-opt the state police force into the battlefront. This circumstantial marriage has now brought about a situation where the state police force now stands accused of being responsible for a majority of extra judicial killings. Even as the number of confrontations between the state and non-state security forces has decreased, there has been a rise in the number of cases where the civilian space has been terrorized by bomb blasts, extortions, kidnappings for ransom and kidnapping of minors for induction as child soldiers. On the other hand, the triangular conflict status quo arising in the state due to the demands of political identity and territorial status among the Meiteis, Kukis and Nagas has led to a situation where the civil sphere has been infringed. The state highways, which are predominantly in areas inhabited by Kukis and Nagas and hence under their control, are often used to hold the state to ransom over various *demands* ranging from Kuki statehood calls to protests over the entry of the NSCN-IM leadership to Ukhrul and other Naga-inhabited areas.

The State of Peace Talks

According to the Governance and Social Development Resource Centre (GSDRC), a partnership of research institutes, think tanks and consultancy organizations with expertise in governance, social development, humanitarian and conflict issues:

> Peace agreements are formal agreements aimed at ending violent conflict and creating the conditions for durable peace. They include ceasefire agreements, interim or preliminary agreements, comprehensive and framework agreements, and implementation agreements. The way in which the conflict ends — whether by compromise, or a one-sided victory, for example — typically has implications for the nature of the peace. The signing of a peace

agreement is often considered to signal the end of the conflict. Much of the literature argues instead that this signals only the beginning of a process toward ending the conflict given that relapse into violence is common, full implementation of the peace agreement is seen as another key milestone. Key parties to the conflict may agree to peace agreements for tactical reasons, without being genuinely committed to the peace process.[3]

In the context mentioned previously, the various *peace process* or *peace talks* as they are described are at best in a convoluted state in Manipur. Manipur's armed and political conflict is a mix of the fight between armed state actors and non-state actors, on one hand, and the infighting between the various non-state forces, on the other. Broadly speaking, the non-state forces constitute two main groups: the valley-based groups and the hill-based groups. Of these two categories, the hill-based ones are again sub-divided into the Naga insurgent groups and the Kuki groups, while a new entrant that is making its presence felt is a Zeliangrong armed group.

With the Kuki groups, the first suspension of operations (SoO) was signed in 2005 with only the Indian army, a fact that speaks volumes of the manner in which the civil administration is kept aside by the armed forces in the region. It was only in 2008 that the existing tripartite agreement came to be signed between the Government of India and the Manipur state government on one side and various Kuki underground groups on the other side. The Kuki groups that are in a tripartite SoO with the central and the Manipur state government are again splintered into two umbrella groups: the Kuki National Organization and the United Peoples Front (UPF). Official sources stated that more than 30 militant groups from both the hills ands the valley have entered the peace process since 2008.[4]

However, there is no real information available on the public domain about the exact number of groups. Interestingly, the term

---

[3] GSDRC, 'Ending Violent Conflict: Peace Agreements and Conflict Transformation', available online at http://www.gsdrc.org/go/conflict/chapter-3-preventing-and-managing-violent-conflict/ending-violent-conflict-peace-agreements-and-conflict-transformation

[4] Telegraph, 'Over 150 Manipur Rebels Surrender', 10 September 2013, available online at http://www.telegraphindia.com/1130910/jsp/northeast/story_17330230.jsp#.Um6WN4Xem1v

used for peace talks with the valley-based groups is *Memorandum of Understanding* (MoU), though the terms of agreement are along the same lines and similarly not disclosed to the public. A few of the hill-based groups have a designated camp area where the cadres who have laid down arms are put up, but mostly the cadres who have *given up arms* are put up in what are called *designated army camps* in Assam Rifles camps. Out of the scratchy terms of ground rules that are in public knowledge, it is mentioned there that the cadres are not to carry arms and ammunition out of their designated camp area and that they be present in the camp every day. These ground rules are flouted with total nonchalance as are evident from the various media reports that have documented all too clearly the manner in which cadres from designated camps have indulged in extortion bids, physical harassment to civilians, etc.

The very nature of the peace talks is suspected for a variety of reasons. On 24 February 2013, one day after top cadres of the Kanglei Yawol Kanna Lup-Military Defence Force (KYKL-MDF) were arrested for violating the recently signed peace talks agreement by trying to barge inside the office chamber of the Regional Institute of Medical Sciences Director's office; two persons came forth to claim that they were unwittingly made to join in the surrender and signing of the MoU programme as cadres of the United Revolutionary Front (URF).

The MoU in question was signed on 13 February at the First Manipur Rifles Banquet Hall between representatives of the state government, centre and three militant outfits—KYKL-MDF; URF, Manipur and the Kangleipak Communist Party, Lamphel. In a press conference, the two said that they had no idea that they would be made to join in the surrender programme and had been hired by one person for masonry work at the Headquarter of 57 Mountain Division, Leimakhong.[5]

The process leading to SoO and MoUs or the requirements specified for armed groups to be a part of the *peace talks* in Manipur are not made clear, and also there is no specification on what happens in the case when ground rules are flouted. In a Kuki-designated camp located in Churachandpur district,

---

[5] Imphal Free Press, 'Two Claim They Were Made Part of Surrender Drama', 25 February, available online at http://www.ifp.co.in/nws-12668-two-claim-they-were-made-part-of-surrender-drama/

this author saw the presence of child soldiers, thereby throwing up the issue of whether numbers are the sole criteria for armed groups to be recognized as one that can enter into the *peace process*. In another camp in the interiors of the Imphal East district, there were two very cramped rooms meant to house 40 cadres each when it was clear that not more than 10–12 cadres could fit into them. A separate room with double locks was meant to house the arms and ammunition of the armed group but the few cadres at the designated camp carried the most sophisticated assault rifles. With a paltry sum of ₹4,000 made out for every cadre made out that armed groups say is supposed to cover the monthly food rations and other essential items, there is a growing incidence of cadres who have taken part on the *laying down of arms* which incidentally the media has been asked not to term as *surrender programmes* taking to extortion. If there is any criteria at all for insurgent groups to enter into *peace talks* with the state and central governments are in place that information is out of the public domain. Apart from the Kuki armed groups, the valley-based Meitei armed groups have not entered into peace talks with the government as a unified party but rather as factions with cadres of the same group operating actively.

In another incident that mirrors the lack of transparency and any seriousness on the part of the government to regulate how former insurgents are being paid their stipends, newspapers in the state reported that Lallumba, the President of the KCP (MC) Lallumba group, decamped from the 7th MR Khabeishoi camp on 9 June along with a huge amount of ₹19,268,800 meant for a one-time rehabilitation package from the government. The amount including monthly allowance of eight months, bank deposits of 114 cadres and 10 polit buro members of the outfit which had signed a tripartite peace talk with the central and the state governments on 6 August 2010 at the First Manipur Rifles Banquet Hall.[6]

Even as the remaining cadres submitted *complaints* to the state Principal Secretary Home with copies being submitted to the Joint

---

[6] Imphal Free Press, 'Lallumba of KCP (MC) Lallumba Group 'Decamps' with ₹1.92 Crores', 8 July 2013, available online at http://www.ifp.co.in/nws-15474-lallumba-of-kcp-mc-lallumba-group-decamps-with-rs-1-92-crores/

Secretary Home, IGAR (S), GOC 57th Mountain Division, IGP (CRPF) and DIG, there has been no word from the concerned over the fate of the cadres in the camp or in terms of the whereabouts of the former leader of the group. There have been numerous incidents when residents in the areas around the AR camps where cadres of various underground groups are kept after entering into SoO and MoU have demanded that the cadres be shifted out of their areas. Such calls have come up on the basis of the cadres *disturbing the peace* with their involvement in cases of the harassment of people in the area, physical intimidation and extortion. To cite an example here: when it came into the public domain that cadres of the KYKL (MDF) who were earlier lodged with the 20th Assam Rifles camp at Chandel Headquarter would be shifted to the Khongjom area of Thoubal district, locals of Khongjom and surrounding villages in Thoubal district including from Sapam, Chingtham, Samram, Langthabal, Langathel, Tekcham took to the streets protesting the move. This came about even as the people of Chandel head quarter district were protesting against the said cadres of the group being stationed at the district.[7] The modalities of the ongoing *peace* processes in the state clearly show that what are being undertaken are only superficial events centred *signing ceremonies* that are dressed up under the term *home coming ceremonies* with no real meaning or value in the life of the common man or any perceptible step towards limiting the level of violence arising out of the conflict situation. Rather, the ambiguity of the terms of the various peace initiatives taken up by the state and central governments with the armed groups on one hand and the fact that major valley-based armed groups are yet to bite the peace bait shows that such initiatives do not look to be bringing about any tangible change to the theatre of conflict in the state. The political gains if any of the ongoing *peace process* in Manipur with various armed groups of the hills and the valley are yet to emerge but already the fissures arising out of the overlapping demands by the Kukis, Nagas in terms of carving out territorial areas with the Meiteis insisting on their territorial integrity have

---

[7] Imphal Free Press, 'Cadres in 'Peace Talks' Unwanted in Both Chandel and Khongjom', 7 May 2013, available online at http://www.ifp.co.in/nws-14106-cadres-in-peace-talks-unwanted-in-both-chandel-and-khongjom/

changed the tone of various civil society groups on community lines. On 10 October 2012, when the Union Home Minister Sushil Kumar Shinde hinted that a *solution* to the *Naga issue* was likely before March 2013, when Assembly polls in Nagaland were due, the Kukis opposed the talks, threatening to renew their demand for statehood, even as the Meiteis vehemently rejected the talks, claiming that settlement proposals would disturb the *unity of Manipur or its territorial integrity*. Furthermore, on 2 November 2012, the Kuki National Organization (KNO), an umbrella organization of 16 Kuki militant groups, threatened to resume armed struggle and to *secede from Manipur* if the centre did not begin talks with them.

On the other hand, the United Committee Manipur (UCM), an apex body of the Meiteis, on 18 October 2012, categorically stated that it would demand *pre-merger status* of Manipur if the ongoing political dialogue between NSCN-IM and GoI disturbed the unity or territorial integrity of Manipur in any way. On 26 October 2012, the United Naga Council (UNC), the main apex body of the Nagas, asserted that a peaceful parting of the Nagas in Manipur and the Meiteis as good neighbours, was the only way to avert a catastrophic situation that would arise out of the prolonged 'forced union of the two'.[8]

Overtures and Responses

Apart from the major Naga groups and the Kuki armed groups, none of the major Meitei insurgent groups have come forth to the peace table with ritual appeals being made by the government on occasions such as Republic Day and Independence Day observations and the groups dismissing the offer.

In September 2006, during a session of the Manipur Assembly, Chief Minister Okram Ibobi Singh made a clarification on the floor of the Assembly that in the 16 years that the state government had introduced a surrender policy for insurgents, only 377 underground activists from 19 different organizations had actually

[8] SATP, Manipur Assessment—Year 2013, available online at http://www.satp.org/satporgtp/countries/india/states/manipur/index.html

bitten the bait, an average of 20 persons per organization in the said 16 years or a little over one person in a year, per organization.[9] Earlier, while responding to the then Manipur Governor S.S. Sidhu's appeal to militant groups to come to the negotiation table, the UNLF Chairman Sana Yaima (now in NIA custody) in a press statement in Imphal on 31 January 2005, came up with a four-point proposal to *end the conflict satisfactorily once and for all.* The proposals mooted were as follows:

1. To hold a plebiscite under the aegis of the United Nations aegis so that the people of Manipur can exercise their democratic right to decide on the core issue of the conflict—the restoration of Manipur's sovereignty and independence.
2. To deploy a UN Peace Keeping Force in Manipur to ensure free and fair conduct of the Plebiscite.
3. UNLF to deposit all its arms to the UN Peace Keeping Force and India to withdraw all its regular and para military forces from Manipur before a deadline prior to the Plebiscite date to be decided by the UN. Also, the UN Peace Keeping Force to call upon all other armed opposition groups in Manipur to follow suit.
4. The UN to hand over political power in accordance with the result of the Plebiscite.[10]

The state government rejected the proposals and that was the end of the peace offer. Similarly, when the Manipur Chief Minister Okram Ibobi Singh reached out to the PLA to shun violence and came forward for peace talks in 2012, the PLA President Irengbam Chaoren rejected the offer and instead appealed to all armed groups in the northeast to join in a united fight against the Indian state.[11]

[9] Pradip Phanjoubam, 'Northeast Problems as a Subject and Object', in *Beyond Counter-Insurgency* (New Delhi: Oxford University Press, 2009), p. 149.
[10] SATP, 'UNLF Response to Manipur Governor's Appeal for Dialogue', 31 January 2005. http://www.satp.org/satporgtp/countries/india/states/manipur/documents/papers/unlf2005.htm
[11] Sangai Express, 'RPF's Chief Greets on Outfit's 29th B'Day', 25 February 2014, available online at http://e-pao.net/GP.asp?src=6..250208.feb08

According to Ceety Khongsai in the Manipur Chapter of 'Liberation Movements in the North East in the *Journal of NE India Studies*':

> The Peace initiative of the Government of India in the northeast suffers from ambiguities. The matter becomes more confusing when the GOI-NSCN (IM)'s Ceasefire Agreement intentionally nullifies the repeated Manipur Territorial Integrity Bills' passed in the Manipur Legislative Assembly by appending the words, 'without territorial limits'. Sensing the impending inter community fracas the GOI was left with no other options but delete the controversial words from the text of the agreement. However, the public are still in disbelief regarding the sincerity and honesty of the central government in handling the fluid social atmosphere in Manipur; in the backdrop of the UNC's Alternative Arrangement for the Nagas gaining momentum fresh clouds of apprehensions grips the entire northeast by questioning New Delhi's honesty on the issue. On the other hand, the announcement made by Indian Prime Minister Dr Manmohan Singh that 'there's enough room in the constitution to accommodate the demands of the northeast insurgents' categorically invalidate the hypothesis of possible outside-the-constitution solution to the decades old Naga political problem.[12]

Road to Peace

Given the context of the ongoing peace initiatives in the state, it is no surprise that there is no real change on the ground. The absence of any of the major armed groups stepping forth to enter into peace talks with the government casts shadows on the intent of the government and its various ongoing processes. Writing under the pen name of Yenning (Manipuri word for *spring*), a leading columnist writing in the Sangai Express on the nature of *Peace talks as counter insurgency measure* has this to say:

> If at all the government is interested to resolve the conflict in Manipur through peaceful and democratic means, then the first and the foremost step is initiation of a process for identifying the common problems, which are acceptable to both the conflicting groups, through an inclusive mechanism. Mere appeals for peace talks from

[12] Ceety Khongsai, 'Liberation Movements in the North-east: The Manipur Chapter', *Journal of North East India Studies*, 2012, available online at http://www.jneis.com/?p=350

time to time along with military engagements cannot bring about any tangible solution and least of all, addressing the problem. A charter of demands submitted by United NGOs Mission-Manipur, a conglomerate of over 100 grass NGOs operating in both the hill and valley areas pointed out specific pre-negotiating measures to be adopted by the government: (i) 'Constitute an Independent Commissions for Conflict Resolution in the state; (ii) develop a framework on pre-negotiation, negotiation and post negotiation with special monitoring mechanisms with due representation from civil society, NGOs and also by engaging International Community as a Third Party to settle the long standing political conflict in the state'. The most important one is to constitute the committee to identify a possible common meeting point within a time frame. However, the process of constituting the committee should be done under the Prime Minister Office or Ministry of External Affairs with the state government particularly the Home Minister and/or elected legislators as facilitators. This will increase the commitment of the government to the AOG (armed opposition group).[13]

Writing for the Institute for Defence Studies and Analyses (IDSA), Namrata Goswami asks this rather pertinent question: what could be a feasible formula for peace talks in Manipur? For one, it has to deeply engage with the societal issues that have led to these multiple armed conflicts. Fears of loss of land, demands for political empowerment and economic development, ethnic identity assertion, cultural exclusivity, hill–plain divide, divide between the ethnic communities and the rest of India further fuelled by the absence of an inclusive politics, have created a web of alienation and loss of self-worth. Moreover, the politicization of ethnic differences for electoral gains, rampant corruption in development projects, fears of discrimination and ethnic distrust creates the structural conditions for armed conflicts aligned along exclusivist ethnic lines. Merely, a mechanical process of peace talks may not salvage years of traumatic experience of conflict, killings, kidnappings and social stress in Manipur since the 1960s.[14]

[13] Yenning, 'Hoi Polloi and Mundanity: Peace Talks as Counter Insurgency Measure', *Sangai Express*, 27 May 2013, available online at http://www.thesangaiexpress.com/tseitm-26603-peace-talks-as-counter-insurgency-measure/
[14] Namrata Goswami, Peace Gestures in Manipur: Will It Work? September 2013, available online at http://www.idsa.in/idsacomments/PeaceGesturesinManipur_ngoswami_230913

A scan of daily newspapers of the year 2013 reflects the uncertain nature of the *peace talks* in the state. There is no clarity over the nature of the various *tripartite agreements* signed between various armed rebel groups, the state government and the central government in terms of the mandates for these agreements and frameworks for a road map to mainstreaming insurgents/armed cadres who have given up arms. What is being portrayed on the ground are the sheer number of insurgent/armed cadres taking part in *home coming ceremonies* even as there is a lack of clarity and intent to lay down political talking points of bringing about a resolution to the armed conflict in the state. A summary of news reports published in Manipur in the public domain details how the year 2013 went by in terms of the *peace talks*. The media coverage ranges from public apprehending *surrender agents* who take in unsuspecting civilians to take part in surrender programmes (*Surrender agents* held, house dismantled: *Sangai Express*); to lack of co-ordination between security forces (UPPK cadres run away from their camp; state police fumes as AR takes away the fleeing cadres: *Hueiyen News Service*); to numerous incidents of cadres part of *peace initiatives* like MoUs and SoO being apprehended by the public or police forces for harassment to people, extortion attempts, robbery charges and drug dealings; to charges of *ground rule violations of talks* levelled against cadres and security personnel, to threats by armed cadres to give up *peace talks* over the non-payment of their stipends, etc.

With various *civil society groups* and pressure groups already taking their stands on the nature of peace processes operating in the state on ethnic lines and their affiliations, the road ahead for real term peace looks challenging to say the least, given the number of armed groups operating in the state and the ethnocentric politics driving them. The onus lies with the government to come clean on the mandates of the peace talks that they are currently engaged in along with a time frame and what concrete steps the talks are aiming to arrive at for without these in place, the event-centric approach of SoO and MoU being signed and armed cadres being left to languish in army camps can only backfire, putting the talks and the fragile *peace* in peril.

9

Auditing Peace and Conflict in India's Northeast: Do We Need a 'Peace Policy'?

Nani Gopal Mahanta

Theorizing Peace in India's Northeast

The terminology of peace is a contested domain. Noted peace scholar Johan Galtung developed a concept called 'violence triangle' to understand the notion of peace.[1] Galtung refers to the distinction between three separate forms of violence, all of which are closely related to each other. Three forms of violence that Galtung refers to are—direct violence, structural violence and cultural violence. In order to achieve peace in the holistic or positive sense, society has to overcome all forms of direct, structural and cultural violence.

However, the achievement of peace in India's security paradigm is generally understood to be what Johan Galtung says to be the absence of violence, which falls under the domain of negative peace.

The typical security attitude of the Indian State to peace was best reflected by a statement of the governor of Assam in an All

---

[1] Johan Galtung, Carl G. Jacobsen and Kai Frithjof Brand-Jacobsen, *Searching for Peace* (London: Pluto Press, 2000), pp. 17–18.

India Police Golf Tournament at the Shillong Golf Club where he talked about his version of bringing peace to Assam. His approach to the peace making process is 'dialogues should be on or our terms and pressure should be maintained on the ULFA'. His point was militancy in the region has substantially declined due to fatigue and disintegration amongst the militants groups, and now seeing no other alternative, they were coming forward to the peace talks.[2]

Therefore, peace in the region is overwhelmingly understood in terms of the following three manifestations:

1. Absence of violence
2. Physical disappearance of militants
3. Marginalization of insurgent groups through hot chase and peace talks

Peace in India's northeast is singularly understood as bringing an insurgent/terrorist group to one of the following broad parameters of the Home Ministry's bureaucratic vocabulary:

1. Ceasefire
2. Suspension of Operation (SoO)
3. Memorandum of Settlement (MoS)
4. En-masse joining of mainstream
5. Talk in progress
6. Unilateral ceasefire
7. En-masse surrender.[3]

This chapter makes an attempt to audit the conflict dynamics and peace process in two important conflict-ridden states of India, i.e., Assam and Nagaland. The chapter provides a critical analysis of the Indian State's approach to the conflict resolution process in the region. Three most important states where insurgency is still very active are: Nagaland, Manipur and Assam.[4] Assam and Nagaland have been witnessing serious peace efforts between the

---

[2] *The Sentinel*, 31 October 2004.

[3] These are some of the terminologies used by the Home Ministry to refer to the peace process with the insurgent outfits. Obtained from intelligence officials.

[4] As per report given by Institute of Conflict Management, see http://www.satp.org/ (accessed 10 May 2014).

Government of India (GoI) and the insurgent outfits. Peace efforts in Manipur have still not acquired much success. This chapter also addresses a serious question that has been hogging limelight in the security circle and among some scholars regarding the desirability of peace dialogues in the region. In contrast to the existing cynical viewpoints about peace talks, this chapter argues for the selective opening up of dialogues for the sake of sustainable peace in the region. Towards the end, this chapter argues for a comprehensive peace policy in the region.

The crux of the argument is that the problem does not lie with the peace process per se but the way peace accords have been arrived at. A major revision of peace efforts is the need of the hour, the chapter argues.

Peace Process in Bodoland

The 2003 Bodo Accord created the first plain tribe in the Sixth Schedule of Indian Constitution known as Bodoland Territorial Council (BTC) in Assam that would comprise four new contiguous districts—Kokrajhar, Baska, Udalguri and Chirang—on the north bank of the Brahmaputra. The area of these eight districts is a little over 27,100 square kilometres, about 35 per cent of the total area of Assam which fell sort of divide Assam fifty–fifty by the Bodo leaders. The Bodos are the largest plain tribes of Assam out of the nine plains tribal people of the Brahmaputra and Barak Valley of Assam. They are the dominant minority in Bodoland, and the granting of socio-political and economic rights to the Bodos has created anxieties, tensions and contradictions to the other non-Bodos such as the Koch Rajbongshi, the Assamese-speaking Hindus, the indigenous Muslims, the Muslims of east Bengal origin, the Adivasis, etc.

The Accord for the creation of the BTC was reached at a tripartite meeting held in New Delhi on 10 February 2003 between the representatives of Union Government, Assam government and a Bodoland Liberation Tigerss (BLT) delegation. The objectives of the agreement were very clear:

> [T]o create an Autonomous self governing body to be known as Bodoland Territorial Council (BTC) within the State of Assam

and to provide constitutional protection under Sixth Schedule to the said Autonomous Body; to fulfil economic, educational and linguistic aspirations and the preservation of land-rights, socio-cultural and ethnic identity of the Bodos; and speed up the infrastructure development in BTC area.[5]

In 1993, the Bodos had a different memorandum, signed by the All Bodo Students Union (ABSU) — a representative of the non-violent civil society (CS) organization of the Bodo society. In contrast, the 2003 Accord was signed by Hagrama Basumatary, Chairman, BLT, hitherto a clandestine outfit which was once banned by the Union Government as a terrorist outfit. I have argued somewhere else:

> The BTC Accord has failed in two areas. First: The very nature of 'hegemonic peace' as has been conceptualised by the Indian State is objectionable. Durable peace is based on the notions of fairness, justice, representation to various stakeholders, etc. The BTC Accord could give them nothing. Secondly: The Accord could not solve the twin structural issues for which the Bodos have been fighting since pre-independence period, i.e. protection of tribal belts and blocks and settlement of the illegal migration issue. [6]

The Accord is primarily unrepresentative and created a big hiatus between the Bodos and non-Bodos, particularly among the Adivasis, the Koch Rajbongshis, the Rabhas, the Assamese, etc. The Bodoland area witnessed serious group clashes in 1993 that had displaced about 3,568 families consisting of 18,000 persons. In another gruesome killing in the relief camp in Bashbari in the Barpeta district, more than 100 East Bengal immigrant Muslims were killed, hundreds of houses were torched and 70,000 were rendered homeless on 24 July 1994. From 1996 till 1998, in a series of killings, hundreds of Muslims, *Santhal*s, Bodos and Assamese-speaking Hindus were killed.

From 2008, the immigrant Muslims have become the sole target of the Bodo extremists. In 2008, in the Darrang–Udalguri

---

[5] Bodo Accord — Clause 2.

[6] For detailed account see, Nani Gopal Mahanta, 'Politics of Space and Violence in Bodoland' (Special Article) *Economic and Political Weekly* XLVIII, no. 23 (2013).

clash, nearly 80 people got killed and 2 lakh people got displaced; majority of them again happened to be the Muslims. In 2012 group clash, more than 100 people got killed, 4,85,921 people got displaced—primarily in the districts of Kokrajhar, Chirang, Baksa, Dhubri and Bongaiogoan in Western Assam, mostly belonging to the immigrant Muslims and the indigenous Bodo people.[7] Ninety per cent of the victims again happened to be the East Bengal immigrant Muslims. Once again on the aftermath of 15th General Election in the country in a matter of 36 hours on 1–2 May 2014, more than 50 Muslim people, mostly women and children, were killed by trigger-happy extremists in the areas of Baksa, Narayanguri and Basbari areas of the BTC.

All those group clashes or attacks by the militants on the innocent civilians clearly demonstrate the fact that peace achieved in the Bodoland area is very fragile and short lived. Ethnic and group clashes have been erupting at regular intervals. The analysis of a fragile peace in the area will remain partial if we do not look at the role of various militant outfits in the Bodoland area.

Militancy Scene in Bodoland

In the Bodoland area, apart from the erstwhile BLT, the former National Democratic Front of Bodoland (NDFB) was committed to the establishment of an independent Bodo homeland. The NDFB is an offshoot of the Bodo Security Force (BdSF) which was subsequently re-designated as the Bodoland Army, and the NDFB was established as its political wing at Udalguri on 3 October 1986.[8]

Subsequently, the NDFB has got divided into following three factions:

1. NDFB (progressive) under the leadership of Govinda Basumatary (a breakaway group from NDFB).
2. NDFB-RB—led by Ranjan Daimary Faction (arrested in Bangladesh and handed over to Assam in 2009).

[7] Data computed from the Deputy Commissioner office, Kokrajhar, released on 20 August 2012.
[8] The BdSF was rechristened as NDFB on 18 April 1993. Since then, the organisation is known as NDFB.

3. NDFB—Songbijit group who declared the formation of an interim national council with Songbijit as the president on 20 November 2012 after the arrest and subsequent surrender by Ranjan Daimary.

All the NDFB factions have come a long way from their original demand of an independent Bodoland to some form of political arrangement within the broad framework of the Indian Constitution. The NDFB (P) has already submitted its charter of demand to the GoI. The main demand of the outfit is to divide Assam 50:50 which is also the motto of the ABSU. Of late, the group has been reported to be working in tandem with CS groups of the Bodos including the ABSU. A leader of the faction said that anything from the union territory to an autonomous state would give them a face-saving formula. The group has also been trying for the incorporation of the left-out Bodo villages and areas within the framework of Bodoland.

NDFB-R faction is yet to start the formal talk process with the GoI, although they have formally agreed to surrender their arms and equipments to the authority. According to a report, Ranjan Daimary's demand for peace would be something different from all the other factions. They would demand for a special relation or some sort of special federal relations with India. Ranjan Daiamry's demand would come closer to the Nationalist Socialist Council of Nagaland (Isak-Muivah) (NSCN-IM)'s demand. Songbijit's group, particularly its Christian members, is likely to merge with the Ranajan faction and the Hindu cadres are likely to be the members of the existing ruling establishment, i.e., erstwhile BLT members.

The NDFB-Songbijit's group is said to be responsible for the present law-and-order problem in the state. Extortion, kidnapping, multiple taxation, etc., have become some of the important devices for the militant outfit to cause havoc in the state, particularly in the districts such as Sonitpur, Baksa, Udalguri, Chirang, etc.

The gruesome killing of Muslim people on the aftermath of election in the early part of May 2014 reflects a deeper level of animosity between the Bodos and the non-Bodos. The Kokrajhar parliamentary constituency is said to be the hub of Bodoland politics in which there were two dominant candidates from the Bodos. The Bodo votes got divided between the ruling Bodoland People's Front (BPF) candidate Chandan Brahma and Urkha Brahma who was supported by the powerful ABSU, NDFB (Govinda Basumatary) and other CS organizations. On the other hand, 20 non-Bodo ethnic and linguistic groups under the banner of Sanmilita Janagostiya Aikyoamancha (SJA) came together to support an independent candidate and an ex-United Liberation Front of Assam (ex-ULFA) leader Naba Sarania. The selection of the ex-ULFA leader as the candidate from the Kokrajhar constituency was very symbolic as the non-Bodos wanted to give a message that they too would no longer be at the receiving end and can project someone who could challenge the Bodos if need be. Immediately after the election, a former Minister of the Government of Assam and a leader of BPF Pramila Rani Barhma blamed the Muslims for not voting the Bodo candidate.[9]

The state Director General of Police (DGP) has held the Songbijit faction responsible for the killing of more than 50 persons in Baksa and Kokrajhar districts on 1–2 May 2014.[10] However, a deeper analysis would reveal that the various forces (including anti-talk faction of the Songbijit group and a section of ex-BLT) have come together ostensibly to teach the Muslims a lesson for not voting for the Bodo candidate in the 14th Lok Sabha election from the Kokrajhar constituency.[11] The Bodos took the non-Bodo's interest for granted and could never believe that there would be such huge collective defiance and mobilization against the Bodo candidates. The non-Bodo-supported candidate got elected with one of the highest margins in the country and the Muslims had to pay a heavy price for their collective defiance.

Conflict Scenario and Peace Process in Nagaland

The oldest peace negotiation in the region has been going on between the NSCN-IM and GoI since 1997. More than 80 rounds of dialoguing have taken place between the two. The 16-year plus long negotiations between the NSCN-IM and the GoI without

[9] See *Assam Tribune*, 29 April 2014.
[10] See *Assam Tribune*, 3 May 2014.
[11] See Kaustubh Deka, 'Bodo Hopes and Minority Rights', *Hindu*, 12 May 2014.

yielding any positive results has resulted in frustration and discontent among the masses. Apart from its negotiations with the IM and Khaplang groups, the GoI has also proposed to open up doors of negotiations with the new faction of NSCN-Khaplang (NSCN-K), i.e., NSCN-Khole/Kitovi (NSCN-KK) group.[12] This has irked NSCN-IM and expressed their anguish through Joint Council as an effort to sabotage the peace effort.

The demand for Naga's sovereignty and the integration of Naga-inhabited areas still remain the two most important demands for the Naga groups. The common people are tired of factional killings, extortion in the name of 'revolutionary taxation' and the fruitless negotiations with the GoI. Everyone is eager to see an amicable settlement of the six-decade-old conflict that pre-dates India's independence. This opinion has also been expressed by various other CS groups such as the Naga Hoho and the Naga Students Federation.

In this period, the Naga political insurgent groups (NPIGs) such as NSCN-IM, NSCN-K, NSCN-KK and NSCN-Unification have effectively erected parallel government structures collecting elaborate taxes from the people in the name of Naga nationalism. One of the appalling aspects of the Naga movement after the split in 1988 is the increased flurry of factional warfare between the IM group and the Khaplang group. Each group claims to be the true representative of the Naga nation and accuses the other of being reactionary force. Moreover, there are many people who are talking about the functionaries of the NPIGs making easy money through extortions in the name of 'revolutionary taxation'. Some are of the view that factional warfare is caused because of the attempt by the underground factions to protect their respective revenue turfs.

The cause of sovereignty is either lost or overshadowed by greed factors as these groups are more interested in personal gratification. They are engaged in collecting huge funds as taxes from the people and business houses and even engaged in factional warfare to control their revenue turfs. Another cause of disenchantment among the people is the spate of killings between various factions

---

[12] For example, the Joint Secretary of MHA, Government of India, said: 'If we don't take all three factions into account, no kind of agreement is going to succeed'. For details, see 'NSCN (IM) Cautions, Government of India', *Sangai Express*, 20 May 2012.

of the NSCN which has increased since their split in 1988 clauses of ceasefire notwithstanding!

The rebel groups run their respective parallel governments with the power of gun, and people are generally scared to speak about their high-handedness and autocratic behaviour in the name of Naga nationalism. As a retired Naga IAS officer writes,

> Define the present reality carefully ..... How do you read into a situation where the total populace lives in fear of our own freedom fighters? Just think .... We fear our own more than our adversary! It is obvious that something somewhere has terribly gone wrong. No matter what the constraints, the people ought to be standing behind our national workers if their efforts were transparent and honourable.[13]

Intense factionalism is a very important feature of Naga nationalism. The people in Nagaland are apprehensive and disillusioned by the present leadership of the NSCN-IM that is mostly dominated by the Tangkhul tribe of Manipur. Significantly, the NSCN-IM does not enjoy the support of many tribes from eastern Nagaland such as the Konyak, Chang, Phom, Khemnuingan, etc. Occasionally, efforts have been made to unite various factions of NSCN. The so-called Home Minister of NSCN-IM Azheto Chophy and C. Singson of NSCN-K made efforts to unite various factions of NSCN which was, however, discarded by top-ranking leaders of NSCN-IM. In recent times, there are reported alliances between the NSCN-KK group and the NSCN-Unification group.

The Konyak-dominated NSCN-K recently made efforts in Myanmar to bring various insurgent outfits of the northeast into one umbrella to be known as Northeast Alliance Force. Some of the constituents of this united front are: ULFA (I), NDFB (Songbijit), People's Revolutionary Party of Kangleipak, NSCN-K and other Manipuri insurgent outfits. The NSCN-K is dominant in the eastern Nagaland districts of Tuensang, Mon, Longleng and Kiphire. The group has a wide

> following among the Konyaks of both India and Myanmar, the Pangmeis of Myanmar, the Aos of Mokokchung district, the Phoms

---

[13] Khekiye K. Sema, 'Transition', *Eastern Mirror*, 26 February 2014, available online at htpp://easternmirrornagaland.com/2014/02/transition/ (accessed 28 May 2014).

and Yimchungers of Tuensang district, the Angamis, the Semas and the Lothas. It commands influence in parts of Nagaland, Tirap and Changlang districts of Arunachal Pradesh, as well as the Hemei and Pangmei settlements in Myanmar.[14]

Eastern Nagaland has added a new dimension to the conflict of northeast India by demanding a separate state within Nagaland. The Eastern Nagaland Public Organization (ENPO) has demanded the formation of a separate state to be known as Frontier Nagaland. The demand has been raised across party lines that included 20 MLAs of the last legislative assembly. CS organizations in Nagaland believe that the eastern Nagaland demand is more accentuated by the GoI intelligence wings in order to encounter the powerful NSCN-IM.

NSCN-IM remains the most dominant organization in Nagaland, although its impact has come down in recent times. The secret nature of negotiations with the GoI has caused suspicion over the intentions and designs of NSCN-IM. With the Indian government ruling out the demand for Naga sovereignty and integration in its political negotiations with the NSCN-IM, the question of Naga nation and Naga integration have reached a stalemate.

There is a proposal for alternative arrangement for the Nagas of Manipur that has come up in the context of Naga political conflict. The settlement of Nagas in Manipur remains a serious demand for the NSCN-IM. Some people whom I interacted in the course of my fieldwork in Nagaland have expressed the fear of a civil war in case the GoI tries to impose any solution with just one faction. Concerned citizens have expressed the view that the peace process cannot be regarded as the NSCN-IM peace process as it includes only one faction whose standing is in doubt in the eyes of many Nagas.

Recently, there has been a healthy nurturing of CS activism and awareness on the 'Indo–Naga conflict'. Till now the insurgent groups and the armed nationalists exercised a sort of monopoly over the issue. The enlightened minds have increasingly started to voice their concerns about the harm done to the Naga movement by the self-indulgent and reckless behaviour by the armed groups. The armed groups had been treating the Naga national

---

[14] http://www.satp.org/satporgtp/countries/india/states/nagaland/ (accessed 29 May 2014).

cause as their sole prerogative and exercising a monopoly over the issue suppressing any attempt from other quarters. As a noted intellectual Abraham Lotha writes, 'A positive thing emerging is the fact that Nagas are not as gullible as they were at earlier times. We are becoming more critical of the various factions who are claiming to champion the cause of the Nagas'.[15]

Members from the CS are increasingly concerned at the future of Naga political movement and have voiced their opinions and concerns about the current political situation and the need to create common platforms to give emphasis on the views and opinions of the masses. Till now the dominant political group, the NSCN-IM, has not been willing to include the opinion of any other faction or of the common masses in its negotiations with the GoI. Many members of the CS have confided in front of us that the main objective of the GoI in entering political negotiations with the NSCN-IM was to tackle the 'mother of all insurgencies', instead of finding an amicable settlement of the 'Indo–Naga' political conflict that predates India's independence.

Peace Process with ULFA

From 1985 to 2009, ULFA has been one of the most 'dreaded' insurgent outfits in the country. I have argued elsewhere:

> ULFA represents a mindset, a suppressed voice which is deeply engrained in Assam's psyche. ULFA is the last source of Assam's protest against New Delhi … the declining support base of ULFA is not to be seen in its numerical strength. It represents the unmet aspirations of the innumerable tribal and ethnic groups of Assam.[16]

There were six conflict settlement attempts as far as ULFA and GoI is concerned.[17]

---

[15] Abraham Lotha, *The Raging Mithun* (Barkweaver Publications, 2013), p. 32.
[16] See Nani Gopal Mahanta, *Confronting the State: ULFA's Quest for Sovereignty* (New Delhi: SAGE Publications, 2013, preface, XVI).
[17] Ibid., p. 255.

The first effort for peace talks was made in 1991 by the ULFA Chairman on the eve of army operations. However, when the major leaders failed to surrender, the peace process was abandoned. A section of ULFA leaders in 1991–1992 made the second effort for peace talks which was known as the pro talk group, under the leadership of Sunil Nath. The third major effort for talks between the GoI and ULFA was made in 2005 by the constitution of People's Consultative Group (PCG). In the midst of army operations particularly in Dibru–Saikhowa, ULFA constituted a CS team to facilitate peace talks between the GoI and itself. Skeptics, however, argue that ULFA was never serious about a conflict settlement; PCG was constituted to gain some immediate respite from military operations. Amongst all the dialogues that had taken place between ULFA representatives and the GoI, this was the most serious effort which began by the participation of the Prime Minister, Home Minister and Defence Minister of India at various levels. However, mutual mistrust, conditionality's for surrender by ULFA top leaders, extortion and recruitment drive by ULFA, etc., had derailed the peace process. The fourth abortive attempt for peace talks was made by the ULFA's 28 Battalion in 2007. However, the GoI was never serious for talks with a splinter group of ULFA, although the 28 Battalion was the most powerful military wing of ULFA. After the surrender by the Battalion, ULFA had gradually lost its military grip in Assam. An unsuccessful fifth attempt was made by Arabinda Rajkhowa in 2009 which, however, did not proceed further as a result of arrest of the chairman himself. The last major initiative for conflict settlement was made by Assam Jatiya Masabha which began by holding a National Convention on 24 April 2010. This can be considered to be the first genuine civil society effort in Assam for the settlement of the ULFA issue.[18]

After the arrest of the major leaders of the organization in Bangladesh in December 2009, civil society organizations played an important role in initiating peace talks between the GoI and ULFA. Nearly 109 organizations, activists and intellectuals of Assam gathered in Guwahati on 24 April 2010 to finalize the

[18] For the detailed account of the peace process of ULFA and the role of civil society organizations, please see note 17, pp. 251–290.

modalities for talks. Here the opinion of the chief architect of peace talks Professor Hiren Gohain is significant:

> The Assamese community is in crisis due to external pressure which we have failed to tackle. In the last 30 years, over 12,000 ULFA members and 18,000 others were killed. This apart, many ULFA leaders have been missing. There are blasts in various parts of the State and that has made individual liberty very fragile. If the peace process is stalled, we won't get rid of the problems afflicting the State. Now both the ULFA and the government have shown positive gesture for peace talks, but a sense of mistrust pulls them back.

Professor Gohain's comment on the peace initiative under the leadership of Mamoni Raisom Goswami is noteworthy:

> The peace overture taken by Mamoni Raisom Goswami with the formation of the People's Consultative Group (PCG) is a chapter of history and the participation of the Prime Minister generated lot of enthusiasm. However sincerity on the part of the government was lacking and the PCG too split later on. We need to learn a lesson from that incident – that an individual's view can't be above that of the masses.

In order to establish his neutral credential Professor Gohain made it clear that the conveners[19] have had nothing to do with the government or ULFA; they are neutral in their approach. He said,

> [W]e are distressed by the present state of affairs in the state and on behalf of the people of Assam; we would like to attempt for a negotiated settlement of ULFA issue.... We have had informal discussions with some ULFA leaders, but that led various quarters to undertake a false propaganda against us. However, the ULFA leaders who have got the chance to feel the pulse of the people of Assam from a close range haven't misunderstood us. The ULFA has to bury the differences within itself.[20]

---

[19] The convention, chaired by a presidium was headed by Dr Hiren Gohain. The other members of the presidium were Dr Nirmal Kumar Choudhury, Dr Mamoni Raisom Goswami, Hiranya Kumar Bhattacharya, Harekrishna Deka (absent), Rohini Baruah, Indibor Deuri, Khursed Alam and Ratneswar Basumatary. Dilip Patgiri and Lachit Bordoloi were the secretaries.

[20] Speech of Hiren Gohain, *Asomiya Pratidin*, 25 April 2010.

Various scholars, educationists and representatives of political parties demanded that the talks between the two should be held on all issues raised by ULFA including sovereignty.[21] Even the representatives of the national political parties wondered why sovereignty should be a hinder for talks. As the Communist Party of India's central executive committee member Promode Gogoi said:

> Talks should be without any preconditions. The Government of India held talks on sovereignty with the Mizo National Front (MNF) of Mizoram and the NSCN-IM of Nagaland. What is the problem to hold talks on sovereignty with the ULFA? This doesn't mean that sovereignty should be given to Assam. There shouldn't be any opposition to provide special rights to Assam as given to Jammu & Kashmir'. The written statement of the Axam Xahitya Xabha (AXX) — the premiere literary body of the state urged the government to initiate talks even on the issues raised by ULFA: 'All core issues of the ULFA, including the issue of sovereignty, can be discussed. However, both the government and the ULFA should shun violence.

Not all those issues including the claim of sovereignty ever figured prominently in the peace talks. The convention formed a steering committee for facilitating the peace process. The steering committee would also help the ULFA in the process of negotiations with the government. The steering body constituted expert committees for studying basic issues such as the right of the indigenous people over the natural resources, economic development, problems such as flood and erosion and infiltration, etc. The expert committees were asked to finalize reports within two to three months so that the same can be placed before the centre during talks.

Professor Gohain and his team painstakingly prepared a voluminous report — elaborating demands and justifications for the same. However, most of the suggestions have been discarded as ULFA's objective was not for placing those demands but to legitimize their comeback, and they were in great need of some

---

[21] Noted among them are ex-Vice-Chancellor of Gauhati University Debo Prasad Barooah, noted journalist Radhika Mohan Bhagawati and many others.

respectable intellectuals to back them in their efforts to lead a respectable life. Finally, ULFA demanded 12-point charter:

- A discussion on 'grounds for ULFA–PTF's struggle and their genuineness'
- Status report on missing ULFA leaders and cadres
- Constitutional and political arrangements and reforms, protection of the identity and material resources of the local indigenous population of Assam
- Financial and economic arrangements
- Settlement of all royalties on mines/minerals including oil on a retrospective compensatory basis and rights of independent use for a sustainable economic development in future
- Illegal migration—its effect/impact and required remedies including sealing of international borders, river patrolling, development of a native force to man the borders
- Ethnic issues—problems and constitutional restructuring including settlement of border disputes and removal of encroachment
- Education and health-reforms as required to preserve the identity of the people of Assam and benefits, agricultural and rural development
- Land and natural resources—including right of natives to the land, flood control and management, industrial growth, development of infrastructure, removal of transport bottleneck, development of entrepreneurial skill and efficiency in labour, availability of credit, infusion of capital-leading to industrial take off
- Right to engage in specific relationship with foreign countries for promotion of mutual trade, commerce cultural relationship, restoration, protection, preservation and spread of indigenous culture of Assam in all its variety
- Amnesty, reintegration and rehabilitation of ULFA members and affected people[22]

---

[22] Prabin Kalita, 'Ulfa Drops Its Primary Demand of Secession from India', *Times of India*, 5 August 2011, available online at http://timesofindia.indiatimes.com/city/guwahati/Ulfa-drops-its-primary-demand-of-secession-from-India/articleshow/9495173.cms

On the basis of the charter, the ULFA narrowed their demand into the following three main demands:

- Creation of an upper house giving representation to the ethnic communities of the state
- Update of National Registrar of Citizens (NRC) — in a time bound manner
- Recognition of scheduled tribes (ST) status to six communities of Assam — Motok, Maran, Chutia, Ahom, Koch Rajbongshi and the Adivasis (tea tribes original).

Meanwhile, ULFA further got divided into pro-talk and anti-talk factions, with the former being led by its chairman Aurobindo Rajkhowa. The anti-talk faction expelled its chairman Aurobindo Rajkhowa and declared itself to be ULFA independent in April 2013 under the leadership of Paresh Barua.

Among all the peace talks that we have been discussing here, the ULFA peace talk with the present set of leaders under Aurobindo Rajkhowa is actually a non-starter. After having five rounds of preliminary talks, the Ministry of Home Affairs (MHA) has put the entire exercise into cold storage. It is because in the opinion of MHA, ULFA has lost its credibility in the eyes of Assamese people.

Peace Process in Karbi Anglong

The state formation demands by various organizations had started in the period of 1960s. The Karbi Riso A-Darbar (KRA-D), Separate State Demand Committee and Central Autonomous Demand Committee (CADC) spare-headed the movement. However, it is Autonomous State Demand Committee (ASDC) that had given a concrete shape to the demand. In recent times, various organizations have come together under the banner like Joint Action Karbi Anglong Union (JAKASU) for a unified fighting for the Karbi state. The emergence of insurgent groups has drastically changed the autonomous demand movement in Karbi Anglona and NC Hills. Various extremists' organizations have been constituted to put forward the Karbi demand. Some of them are Karbi National Volunteers (KNV), United People's Democratic Society (UPDS),

Karbi-Longri National Liberation Front (KLNLF), KNPR, KLNLF-ATF better known as Karbi People's Liberation Tiger (KPLT), etc. Groups like KLNLF demanded a separate Karbi state to be known as Karbi Longri. Needless to say, various political and civil outfits are attached to various militant groups. A researcher has argued, 'It is even realized by many that this kind of radical exclusivist sentiments are deepening during the movement for separate state, where different political elites or the political parties backed the militant movements in the district ... by all means they are assisting one another'.[23]

The major demand of the Karbi insurgency groups is the demand of a separate and autonomous state exclusive to the Karbis, known as the Karbi Hemprek. One contradiction in the separate Karbi state is that the other ethnic groups of the district have been demanding separate homeland and concession. Dima Halam Daogah (DHD) subsequently divided into various factions have been demanding a separate homeland for Dimasa, known as the Dimaraji Kingdom comprising NC Hills, Karbi Anglong (KA) and parts of Nagaon. The Kuki Revolutionary Army (KRA) vouches for political concession to the Kukis mostly living in the Singhason Hills of KA district. There were substantial clashes between the Kukis and Karbis over land and resources. In 2003 and 2004, 85 people were killed out of which 23 were Kukis and 54 were Karbis.

The Karbis seek to unite both the North Cachar Hills (now known as Dima Haso district) and KA in their proposed separate state demand. However, in recent times, both the communities have fought with each other under the banner of their respective militias. KA has witnessed various group clashes in 2001, 2003, 2004 and again at the beginning and end of 2005. Those clashes had involved various communities; however, major clashes have occurred between the Karbis and Dimasa which began on 26 September 2005. It is estimated that till 6 November 2005, 90 people were killed—that include 76 Karbis, 11 Dimasas, 1 Bodo, etc. Three thousand houses were torched, destroyed or looted as per the report by the Asian Centre for Human Rights. The report also cited the displacement of 44,016 of both the communities.

[23] Chao Suseng Fa gogoi, 'Contested Ethnicity in Karbi Anglong', *Unpublished Thesis* (Gauhati University).

Various factors are discernible from those clashes — these include increasing inward looking demand by the Karbis, feeling of superiority of one community over others (known as *panasa*), identity consciousness of smaller identities (Kukis), overlapping of homeland space between the Karbis and the Dimasas, scarce resources and claim over them, rumour of being killed by one group and subsequent retaliations by the other and a gradual loss of a shared space which emanate from the lack of representation to various communities. Meanwhile Memorandum of Settlement (MoS) was arrived at with insurgent outfits such as UPDS, KRA and United Kuki Democratic Front. The MoS signed with the UPDS have brought about more decentralization to the Karbi Anglong Autonomous Council (KAAC). As a part of agreement, it was decided,

> As part of this process, several rounds of tripartite discussions were held with the representatives of the UPDS. As a result of this consultative process, it has been agreed to initiate time bound steps to bring about greater devolution of power to the grass root level in Karbi Anglong while ensuring increased capacity building for developmental activities at all levels.

As part of the restructuring and empowerment process, the existing KAAC will be renamed as Karbi Anglong Autonomous Territorial Council (KAATC). In 2010, UPDS in collaboration with around 30 CS groups constituted a platform known as Peoples' Alliance for Peace Agreement (PAPA) and through this platform they fought in the assembly and council elections, although they could not achieve much success.

However, the peace process in KA has created its own fissures. Various breakaway groups have been formed. Important among them who are present in KA are Karbi People's Liberation Tiger (KPLT), Karbi National Liberation Army (KNLA), Dimasa Jadi Naiso Army (DJNA), United People's Liberation Army (UPLA), Adivasi National Liberation Army (ANLA-Binod Tanti faction) NDFB (Songbijit), etc. Even some pro-talk groups have been divided like KRA has been divided into pro-talk and KRA general. KPLT has been demanding the recognition of KA under Article 244A of the Indian Constitution. It was formerly known as the anti-talk faction of the Karbi-Longri North-Cachar Hills Liberation Front (KLNLF) which was later on re-named as KPLT. Even KPLT has been divided into two factions — one led by supposedly the pro-talk leader Ran Rongpi and the antitalk faction led by Kangtphur with around 40 cadres. The new group of KPLT is said to be Karbi National Protection Force (KNPF) formed in the mid of 2011. However, many cadres and leaders of KPLT including its chief were killed in an encounter with police in May 2014.

Most of these groups are backed by NSCN-IM and NSCN-K. They provide their old arms to these outfits which they need to recycle from time to time in return of providing huge financial incentives to the IM group. These fringe outfits project the ideological or identity issues of their community as a means of legitimization process. Police sources as well as media reports suggest that the cadres of these outfits have been arrested in a number of anti-social activities, such as smuggling, car theft, kidnapping and rhino poaching in the Kaziranga National Park.

Peace Process in North Cachar Hills

The GoI can claim to have achieved major success in Dima Hasao district (formerly known as North Cachar Hills) as both the important factions—DHD (J) and DHD (N)—have signed the MoS. The memorandum has talked about enhanced autonomy and specific economic packages for the speedy development of the region. A committee will be constituted to look into the functioning of the Sixth Schedule in the area, and it has also been decided that the North Cachar Hills Autonomous Council (NCHAC) will be renamed as the Dima Hasao Autonomous Territorial Council (DHATC). In order to pay focus on development, a special economic package of ₹200 crore (₹40 crore per annum) over and above the plan fund over the next five years will be provided to the DHATC. One noticeable feature of the MoS is the adequate protection to the non-Dimasa tribes; their culture and economic interest are to receive priority in the proposed reformed council.

However, like in other parts of Assam, the NC Hills too has witnessed the consolidation and split of existing outfits after the peace accords have been signed. 'Dimasa Action' has refused to accept the peace process and is engaged in extortion, kidnapping and killing. Its top leaders David Kemprai and Niput Rajiung are mostly operating in the Umrangsu area. Their main demand is a separate homeland called Dimaraji.

The Dimasa Action group is backed by the NSCN-IM. Until the issue of IM is amicably resolved, the ripple effect will be felt in various districts of Assam, particularly in NC Hills and KA. The IM takes these outfits as their cohorts to fulfil their insatiable demand for money and to convert the majority Hindu Naga (the Zeliangrong and the Zeme tribes who are mostly from Harakka Hindu cult) and other tribal to Christianity. Surrendered militants have held many Baptist Christian groups responsible for the present impasse in the district and accused them of working in tandem with NSCN-IM for the process of conversion. Perhaps a larger prognostication is required to authenticate the role of such socio-religious organization and their link with militant outfits.

One such splinter group in the Dima Hasao district is Dimasa National Revolutionary Front (DNRF) with Sandip Maibong as its main leader. Dimasa National Liberation Front (DNLF) is another post-accord insurgent outfit; however, many of the cadres of both the outfits including the chairman of the DNLF have been arrested. Apart from the Dimasa group, there is one non-Dimasa outfit known as the Hill Tiger Force (HTF), which represents the interest of non-Dimasa tribes such as the Kuki, Hmars, Zeme Nagas, etc. The outfit is regarded as the underground faction of the Indigenous Peoples Forum (IPF) who has been fighting for the rights of the non-Dimasa people in the district.

Should There be a Moratorium on Peace Talks

Innumerable insurgent outfits and endless peace talks with the GoI have generated substantial cynicism among the scholars' regarding the utility and desirability of peace talks. Recently, a scholar has argued:

> The challenge for the Government is to carry on multiple peace processes to the next level—an indeed complex process, since in many cases, demands of one insurgent group contradict the others'.... Again, it has to be seen whether peace talk with any particular rebel group is indirectly providing a status of legitimacy to that group.[24]

[24] Rani Pathak Das, *Insurgent Politics & Negotiations: Is a Moratorium on Peace Talks Needed*? available online at http://cdpsindia.org/ne_insurgency.asp (accessed 30 May 2014).

The notion that should there be a moratorium of the peace process in India's northeast emanates from the following premises:

- Peace process has not yielded any desirable result. Violence is going on unabated. Killing, arson and extortion are in full spate.
- Nor has it succeeded in containing the growth of new outfits or fringe outfits.
- Peace agreements are taken as shield by the surrendered outfits to carry on their subversive activities.
- How long the GoI and state governments would keep on signing peace agreements as there are many outfits within one ethnic group such as the Bodos and the Nagas?

The question of having moratorium on peace talks also came from the government sources. The then Union Home Minister P. Chidambaram also expressed his reservation for opening up of doors of negotiation with new insurgent outfits.[25] This was followed by a series of discussions and debates among the scholars of the region regarding the moratorium on peace talks.[26] Some commentators went to the extent of blaming the government for encouraging insurgency in the region.

> Is the Government actually encouraging insurgency by talking peace or agreeing to talk peace with each and every insurgent group, big or small, ones with some sort of an ideology or without..... Thus, while on one hand, the Government is giving legitimacy to the demands raised by the rebels, on the other, it seems to be clueless as to what could be offered to the different groups in their respective peace deals.[27]

We have no problem if we provide a critical analysis or interrogate the nature of peace process in the region. I believe that it is indeed necessary to scrutinize the nature and character of peace accords and agreements in the region. Peace per se is not an end

---

[25] Nishit Dholabhai, 'PC Rules Out Talks with New Outfits', *Telegraph*, 16 July 2010.
[26] The Centre for Development and Peace Studies, Guwahati organized a round table titled *Policy on Peace Talks* in Guwahati on 15 September 2010.
[27] See note 24.

in itself. Peace is a value which needs to be linked to the larger issues of democracy, justice and equity in the society. Peace may be achieved by hot chase or even by military means, compromising certain basic notions of fairness and justice. But is it a sustainable or democratic peace or militarized peace? What kind of peace is desirable in a society? These are certain questions which perhaps require larger debate and discussions. However, to say that there should be a moratorium of peace process in India's northeast region is like throwing the baby in the bath tub. The manifestation of a crisis must not be diagnosed with a treatment which is more dangerous than the disease itself. This is not only undemocratic but is also not based on the sound principle of Conflict Resolution. The doors of dialogue, negotiation and mediation must not be closed forever for the alternative of it would be to engage in a perpetual war.

Today Indian State is fighting on two fronts: (1) one with the insurgents and (2) with the idea of secessionism. It is the systematic and sustaining engagement that has helped to win over the psyche of the people in the region—certain structural bottlenecks notwithstanding! In fact, this is what makes Indian state different from the rest of the institution called state in other developing countries such as in South Asia, Africa and Latin America. The accommodative character of India has compelled many scholars to cite India as the successful model of managing diversity and insurgency—does not matter howsoever faulty it could be. In fact, as I have suggested elsewhere, there is a substantial decline of insurgency in northeast India particularly in the states of Nagaland, Assam and Tripura.[28]

The CS is coming in large numbers against the dictates of insurgents—the recent being a huge gathering in Kohima whereby thousands of people have thronged in to protest against the functioning of the insurgent outfits which was unthinkable in previous years.

If we analyse the transitional peace process in Nagaland, the incidents of violence which we consider as a yardstick for the success or failure of the peace process is not very depressing.

---

[28] For details please see, Nani Gopal Mahanta, 'Conflict Dynamics in a "Shatter Zone"', in *Shifting Terrain-Conflict Dynamics in North East India*, ed. Nani G. Mahanta and Dilip Gogoi (New Delhi: DVS, 2012) pp. 17-29.

From the period of 2000–2012, there is a substantial decline of civilian death. In fact, 20 civilians have been killed in last four years (2009–2012), which is, though tragic, is a smaller number in relative terms. In the same period, there is not a single death of SF personnel. Of course, it is the casualty of militants which has seen a disturbing trend. The violence in Nagaland has been mainly in the form of inter-factional clashes between different groups.

As MHA report says 'The number of incidents of interfactional violence between major insurgent groups, viz., National Socialist Council of Nagaland (Isak Muivah) (NSCN-IM) and National Socialist Council of Nagaland (Khaplang) (NSCN-K) has marginally increased during the year 2012'.[29]

It is the clash between NSCN-K and NSCN-KK that had shown an upward trend of militant casualty. This is not something unnatural in Nagaland as they have a long history of such inter-group and intra-group clashes. Skeptics may argue: Why then a peace process? However, a pertinent question may be raised: Where is the mighty role of the state and why the state equipped with AFSPA remains silent? Is it because they do not want to enforce the terms of ceasefire agreements strictly? Besides, there are allegations of the diabolical role by the intelligence agencies in terms of balancing the pendulum by supporting one group against the other. It has been argued that the demand of the Eastern Nagaland and the emergence of new militant outfit could be a part of that balancing pendulum. Therefore, the peace process in the region must not be seen in terms of the simplistic analysis of a visible peace process without understanding the underlying nuances.

The Need for a Peace Process Policy

What northeast India requires is not a moratorium on peace talks but a comprehensive peace process policy that goes beyond the immediacy of ceasefire, suspension of operations and agreements. The present peace craft in the region is somehow to coerce, cajole or co-opt the leaders of the insurgent outfit into some temporary ceasefire framework. Under the existing system, the leaders and

[29] Ministry of Home Affairs Report on Northeast—2013.

important cadres receive material help for their livelihood and in due course of time they are conveniently discarded and handed over to the CS for their well-being. Peace talk in India's northeast is not a mechanism for structural conflict resolution, but it is a temporary means to rehabilitate the leaders and cadres. The state primarily relies on the conflict fatigue of the leaders and hence the dependent variables for which insurgency emerge find no prognostication in the corridor of policy makers. Perhaps that is the basic reason why there is an unending saga of insurgency in the region. In the light of a comprehensive peace process policy in the region, the following points hold significance.

The first step of the peace process policy in the region should be to go beyond negative peace, i.e., peace must not be understood only as the absence of violence but it should also address some structural issues for which insurgency becomes a recurring phenomenon in the region.

The proper crafting of peace agreement and the involvement of stakeholders are the two important criteria for a sustainable peace in the region. Negotiation in Nagaland can be referred here. The entire peace talks in Nagaland must not be hogged by one insurgency outfit, i.e., the NSCN-IM. The exclusion of various stakeholders both of violent and non-violent nature has caused serious dissatisfaction among the masses.

Besides, it is imperative that the GoI gives due recognition to genuine non-violent voices. There must not be a message from the GoI that it is only violence that pays or there must not be an impression that the GoI gives credence only to a violent discourse.

Bodoland has become a typical case that demonstrates the utility of violence for settling political scores. The very logic for the creation of Bodoland was a series of violence and ethnic outbidding of the non-Bodos which led to massive displacement, killing and destruction of property. The recognition of Telengana as the 29th state has opened up the debate for a Bodoalnd state in Assam. The assumption is that another series of violence and killing against the innocent ones would hasten the process of state recognition.

Most of the time, accords are signed hurriedly for political expediency. Here, the opinion of ex-Chief Minister of Assam, Hiteswar Saikia, is significant regarding the 1993 Bodo Accord:

> I know such a situation would develop ... I requested Pilot not to sign the Accord in haste.... I made it clear that the Boro dominated

areas of Lower Assam were not contiguous. So if the non-Boro areas to be included in the BAC area for the sake of contiguity, the consent of the non-Boros would have to be obtained. Mr Pilot, however, refused to listen and told me the draft had the blessings of Prime Minister Narasimha Rao. Thus I had no choice but to agree.[30]

A comprehensive peace process policy must be based on the notions of fairness, justice and representation to various stakeholders. The Bodoland accord of 2003 is the best example of how not to make an accord. One of the basic objectives of the peace policy should be to address the structural issues for which a conflict occurs. The Bodo accord was neither representative nor it could solve the structural problems of the people, i.e., the land question and the settlement of the illegal immigration problem.

Peace agreement are not an end in itself; they facilitate a process which needs to be carried forward very diligently. Post-conflict reconstruction (PCR) such as disarming the militants, accord implementation and rehabilitation of the ex-militants are some effective ways for sustainable peace. The enforcement of strict terms is most essential so that surrendered militants cannot create the law-and-order problem. Reconciliation among contending groups and sustained dialogue among the communities could be effective ways of a durable peace process in the region. Bodoland, KA and Dima Hasao are such areas in the region which witness serious mistrust among the communities, particularly among the Bodos and the non-Bodos, Karbis and the Dimasas, etc. Such an unbridgeable gap among the communities is one of the main reasons for the recurrence of violent conflict. Till now, no effective means of dialoguing has ever been taken up for addressing mutual apprehensions.

For a sustainable peace process in the region, it is essential for a proper implementation of promised Accords. Accords or MoS are some of the legal, institutional means of coming into some agreement through which a stalemate is resolved. However, it becomes clear that many of the Accords and MoS signed between the GoI/GOA and other parties are not honoured or blissfully forgotten. Two such examples are the non-implementation of the Karbi Accord and Assam Accord. Main provisions of both the accords are yet to be implemented.

---

[30] Kalyan Chaudhury, 'The North-East Area of Darkness: Accord Unclear of Territories', *Frontline*, 26 August 1994, pp. 30–31.

The 1995 Karbi agreement promised to provide more autonomy to the KAAC. The non-implementation of the accord has become the reference point for many insurgent outfits in the region. For the Assam Accord, which was signed in 1984, a series of accord implementation and evaluation meetings were held. For example, in 2000, a tripartite talk took place between the AASU, GoI and GOA. Another round of accord review meet took place in July 2005 where the PM of India was also present. A time-bound resolution was made to start some of the works including the NRC, provisions of which are yet to be honoured.

There is no denying the fact that there is a tangible reflection of peace dividends in the region. The number of direct violence by the insurgent outfit has substantially been declining. Secessionist and exclusivist forces have been fast losing their ground. With economic progress and globalization, the younger generation has been more interested in their career. They are more concerned about economic development and good governance of the state. Young people in Nagaland are coming in large numbers against illegal multiple taxations.

> Several Dimapur-based Naga civil society groups, frontal organisations, student and youth organisations and business associations have resolved to oppose rampant and multiple 'tax' collection by Naga insurgent groups. At a meeting of these groups, held under their aegis of Naga Council, Dimapur on Monday, to discuss 'rampant, unabated taxation by underground factions' in Nagaland's Dimapur district, it was decided that the Council would convey their resolution to all Naga insurgent groups and urge them to immediately abolish 'back-breaking multiple taxes' on goods imposed at check gates, godowns and shops.[31]

Coming out of nearly a lakh people against the armed groups in Nagaland holds tremendous significance as it was unthinkable only a few years back. A whole young generation is emerging whose primary interest is not to go out of India but to develop within the liberal framework of the Indian political system.

But this is not to suggest that insurgency is over. Issues for conflict and confrontation with the Indian State have drastically

[31] 'Civil Society Says No to Insurgents' Tax Collection System', *Hindu*, 30 May 2013.

changed in the post-2005 period. Issues of governance, land allotment, rehabilitation, displacement and transparency in administration, people's participation and community resources have become more crucial than before. People want development, but have started asking critical questions: 'development by whom, for whom, who will be the beneficiaries and at what cost'. Movements that have addressed these people's issues have become more popular and sustainable in comparison with the armed groups who have perennially neglected these issues for a dream of independent sovereign homeland. The resolution of the structural issues that confront the region for so many decades along with good governance will usher a sustainable peace process in the region.

We can conclude in the words of P.C. Halder, the interlocutor with various insurgent outfits in the region:

> Peace agreements, irrespective of their nomenclature and scope, are aimed at facilitating peace and stability through consensus building through evolving agreed protocols or political arrangements. These agreements, by themselves, are not be seen as an endpoints or final destinations ... despite various peace processes, the conflicts in the region have not ended but there are valid reasons to be optimistic'.[32]

---

[32] P.C. Haldar, 'Understanding Peace Processes', in *Enchanting North-East India-Issues and Way Forward* (Guwahati: Shyam K Mahanta, 2013), pp. 38–41.

10

Elections 2013 and Peace Process in Nepal

Nishchal Nath Pandey

The year 2013 was relatively peaceful for the Nepalese in comparison with the previous years. The breakaway party from the Unified Communist Party of Nepal (Maoists) (UCPN-M), the CPN–Maoists led by Comrade Kiran could not enjoy much public support to disrupt the Constituent Assembly (CA) elections that was held successfully on 19 November 2013. The various factions of the militant parties in the terai also could not garner the support of the Madhesi people throughout the course of the year. The number of casualties from violent clashes between the state security forces and the insurgents or criminal elements in the countryside had drastically dwindled ever since the end of the Maoist people's war in 2007, and this year also saw the final commissioning of People's Liberation Army (PLA) cadres into the Nepal Army which marked a watershed in the history of Nepal.

But Nepal's woes lie elsewhere. Unable to draft an all-acceptable, democratic and inclusive constitution, the first CA had to be dissolved in May 2012. It was a culmination of selfish interests over national interests, partisanship over consensus and greed over sacrifice and marked an unfortunate episode in which a bulky, expensive body of 601 MPs could not agree on a single document even after wrangling for more than four years. The promise of Nepali people giving a constitution by themselves and for themselves which they had envisaged a long ago ever since the first democratic movement of 1951 lay in shatters. Several parties including the Nepali Congress (NC) began demanding the resignation of Prime Minister Dr Baburam Bhattarai but devoid of an acceptable candidate to replace him, the country dillydallied for several more months. Ultimately, analogous of the *Bangladeshi model* the incumbent Chief Justice (CJ) was chosen as the head of a caretaker administration to conduct elections to another CA Chief Justice Khil Raj Regmi's appointment as the head of the executive sparked yet another round of protests. Even the Nepal Bar Association vowed not to permit him inside the Supreme Court premises as it was against the *separation of powers* to have the single person as the head of the executive as well as the judiciary. In fact, after assuming the position of the Chief Executive, Regmi also started amending the interim constitution and began forwarding it to the President. This made him the head of the legislature branch also, something unheard and unseen in any modern day functioning democratic state. But this experiment had to be done because of the inability to select an acceptable prime minister at a time when the country did not have a constitution, an elected parliament, and even the local bodies remained dissolved for more than a decade.

The Election Commission (EC) began preparatory works in earnest and also for the first time issued voter IDs. The threat of violence, intimidation and incessant strikes and *bandh*s called by the Kiran-led Maoist party, although successful in creating a psychology of panic, was unable to stop the voters from exercising their fundamental right on the day of the polls. Nepalese rural folk have generally regarded the poling day as a festive day, in which the entire adult members of one's family went out and voted. A record turnout of approximately 78 per cent was remarkable in the region. But one has to take into account the fact that due to the obstacles created by the Kiran-led party, a lot of voters did not even register themselves. For instance, in the district of Gorkha with the constituency of Dr Baburam Bhattarai, the total number of voters this time was lesser than the number of votes received by Dr Bhattarai in the CA elections held in 2008. In other mountainous districts, Maoist party cadres destroyed computers belonging to the EC. However, despite the *bandh* called by the party, such a big turnout on the elections day was certainly a political setback for the Kiran-led party.

The CA election results came as a surprise to many, as the largest party the Prachanda-led UCPN-M emerged as the third largest party. The NC emerged as the biggest party. What was most astonishing was the rout of Madhesi parties mostly due to their infighting and backbiting. It must not be overlooked, however, that the total number of votes that all the Madhesi parties have received is still the same as the votes they received in 2008. But their political positioning vis-à-vis the rest of the parties inside the CA has diminished considerably this time.

The international community mainly the European Union (EU), US, India and China hailed the smooth conducting of elections and less number of violence compared to what was initially feared. The EU stated,

- Voting was conducted in an orderly and generally calm atmosphere. Polling procedures were followed consistently in the polling stations observed by the EU EOM and the performance of polling staff was mostly assessed to be good. The integrity of the vote was sufficiently protected in 97 per cent of the polling stations observed as efficient processing of voters and appropriate use of controls and safeguards were implemented. The EU EOM continues to observe the counting and aggregation of results and will follow any consequent complaints and appeals before reaching a final conclusion.
- The Election Commission of Nepal (ECN) has enjoyed public confidence throughout the whole election process, acting, thus far, in an independent and impartial manner. Technical electoral preparations were completed in a timely manner despite considerable logistical challenges and time constraints. The ECN demonstrated competence in conducting key operations of the electoral process. The delivery of election material to the districts was concluded well in advance of election day, as were staff deployments.
- The Final Voters' List, as announced by the ECN, includes 12,147,865 voters capturing an estimated figure of around 75 per cent of the potential Nepalese electorate. One of the main challenges faced by the electoral administration was the provision of voter ID cards. However, EU observers reported that on election day, generally voters did not face difficulties regarding their identification as those without these cards were facilitated on production of other documents.
- Freedoms of speech and assembly were respected as candidates campaigned actively across the country. Several incidents of a violent nature took place throughout the campaign period, attributed variously to both participating parties as well as to

those parties boycotting the elections. However, this did not have a significant impact on the unfolding of the campaign. Electoral campaign activities were largely manifest through small meetings.[1]

With the successful completion of the CA elections, the aimless drift seen in Nepali politics throughout the course of 2012–2013 came to an end. Nepal just completed one of the major events of the last year. In the mixed electoral system of Nepal, there are two components. The first one is First-Past-The-Post (henceforth FPTP) and the other one is Proportional Representation (henceforth PR).

There are total 601 seats available in the constituent assembly. Nepal is divided into 240 constituencies. One from each of those constituencies will get seats for the constituent assembly. In the PR system, the entire country is considered as a single constituency. For the PR system, 335 seats are allocated and representatives are selected on the basis of the proportion of the vote that their party gets. The remaining 26 seats are there for distinguished personalities and indigenous nationalities. Table 10.1 represents the chart of the election results:

The results show that Nepal will yet again have a hung parliament. But the structure of the parliament will be quite dissimilar than that in 2008. The NC is the largest party instead of the Maoists and the Madhesi splinter groups are no longer the King makers. With the Communist Party of Nepal (Unified Marxist–Leninist) (CPN (UML)) as the second largest party, its support is imperative. In fact, the Maoist party can still run the roost if it can play its cards well. Unfortunately, it is the same type of political one-upmanship that led to the collapse of the first CA Parties busied themselves with forming and dismantling governments than focusing on constitution drafting. Coalitions were formed and dismantled in Nepal forgetting that during India's tryst with its CA, a single prime minister had ruled the country since 1947–1964. This provided stability to the Indian republic during its nascent phase.

---

[1] European Union Election Observation Mission, 'Well-conducted Elections with High Participation Allow for Continuation of Democratic State Building', Kathmandu, 21 November 2013, available online at http://eeas.europa.eu/delegations/nepal/documents/press_corner/2013.11.22.en.pdf (accessed 29 January 2014).

Table 10.1:
The result of constituent assembly 2013 of Nepal

Party	FPTP			PR			Nominated Seats	Total Seats	+/-
	Votes	%	Seats	Votes	%	Seats			
Nepali Congress	2,694,983	29.80	105	2,418,370	25.55	91			
Communist Party of Nepal (Unified Marxist–Leninist)	2,492,090	27.55	91	2,239,609	23.66	84			
Unified Communist Party of Nepal (Maoist)	1,609,145	17.79	26	1,439,726	15.21	54			
Rastriya Prajatantra Party Nepal	252,579	2.79	0	630,697	6.66	24			
Madhesi Jana Adhikar Forum, Nepal (Loktantrik)	283,468	3.13	4	274,987	2.91	10			
Rastriya Prajatantra Party	238,313	2.63	3	260,234	2.75	10			
Madhesi Jana Adhikar Forum, Nepal	206,110	2.28	2	214,319	2.26	8			
Tarai-Madhesh Loktantrik Party	171,889	1.90	4	181,140	1.91	7			
Sadbhavana Party	140,930	1.56	1	133,271	1.41	5			
Communist Party of Nepal (Marxist–Leninist) (2002)	98,091	1.08	0	130,300	1.38	5			
Federal Socialist Party	108,683	1.20	0	121,274	1.28	5			
Rastriya Janamorcha	66,666	0.74	0	92,387	0.98	3			
Communist Party of Nepal (United)	24,808	0.27	0	91,997	0.97	3			
Rashtriya Madhesh Samajwadi Party	76,392	0.84	0	79,508	0.84	3			
Nepal Workers Peasants Party	54,323	0.60	1	66,778	0.71	3			

Party					
Rastriya Janamukti Party	39,352	0.44	0	63,834	0.67	2
Terai Madhes Sadbhavana Party	65,047	0.72	1	62,746	0.66	2
Tharuhat Tarai Party Nepal	38,972	0.43	0	62,526	0.66	2
Nepal Pariwar Dal	14,546	0.16	0	51,823	0.55	2
Dalit Janajati Party	33,508	0.37	0	48,802	0.52	2
Akhanda Nepal Party	12,590	0.14	0	36,883	0.39	1
Madeshi Janadikar Forum (Gantantrik)	35,289	0.39	0	33,982	0.36	1
Nepali Janata Dal	6,816	0.08	0	33,203	0.35	1
Khambuwan Rashtriya Morcha, Nepal	6,451	0.07	0	30,686	0.32	1
Nepa Rastriya Party	9,377	0.10	0	28,011	0.30	1
Jana Jagaran Party Nepal	3,510	0.04	0	27,397	0.29	1
Sanghiya Sadhbhawana Party	20,395	0.23	0	25,215	0.27	1
Madhesh Samata Party Nepal	8,130	0.09	0	23,001	0.24	1
Samajwadi Janata Party	4,661	0.05	0	21,624	0.23	1
Sanghiya Loktantrik Rastriya Manch (Tharuhat)	4,622	0.05	0	21,128	0.22	1
Sanghiya Gantantrik Samajwadi Party Nepal	8,950	0.10	0	18,631	0.20	0
Nepal Communist Party	8,291	0.09	0	18,140	0.19	0
Nepal Yuwa Kisan Party	2,457	0.03	0	16,204	0.17	0
Nepal Janata Party	2,441	0.03	0	15,650	0.17	0
Nepal Sadbhawana Party	12,572	0.14	0	15,578	0.16	0

(Table 10.1 Continued)

(Table 10.1 Continued)

Party	FPTP			PR			Nominated Seats	Total Seats	+/-
	Votes	%	Seats	Votes	%	Seats			
Khas Samabeshi Rashtriya Party	6,035	0.07	0	15,225	0.16	0			
Terai Madhesh Pahad Himal Ekata Party	2,212	0.02	0	12,466	0.13	0			
Akhanda Sudhur Pashchim Party	5,548	0.06	0	12,334	0.13	0			
Madhesh Terai Forum	3,632	0.04	0	11,286	0.12	0			
Rashtriya Swabhiman Party Nepal	1,550	0.02	0	11,270	0.12	0			
Lok Dal	748	0.01	0	10,953	0.12	0			
Janata Dal Nepal	350	0.00	0	10,645	0.11	0			
Nepal Loktantrik Samajwadi Dal	1,552	0.02	0	10,359	0.11	0			
Janata Dal Loktantrik Party	1,478	0.02	0	10,018	0.11	0			
Jana Prajatantrik Party	1,318	0.01	0	8,645	0.09	0			
Shiva Sena Nepal	3,479	0.04	0	8,416	0.09	0			
Picchada Barga Nishad Dalit Janajati Party	255	0.00	0	8,332	0.09	0			
Mongol National Organization	4,669	0.05	0	8,215	0.09	0			
Nava Nepal Nirman Party	1,398	0.02	0	8,119	0.09	0			
Chure Babar Rashtriya Ekata Party	2,410	0.03	0	7,975	0.08	0			
Nepal Shanti Chhetra Parishad	41	0.00	0	7,757	0.08	0			
Nepal Gantantrik Ekata Party	0	0	0	7,178	0.08	0			
Sanghiya Limbuwan Rajya Parishad	3,063	0.03	0	7,063	0.07	0			

Party				
Bishwa Satyabadi Party	111	0.00	6,666	0.07	0
Sahakari Party Nepal	847	0.01	6,141	0.06	0
Rashtriya Janata Dal Nepal	2,569	0.03	6,097	0.06	0
Shanti Party Nepal	1,659	0.02	6,032	0.06	0
Sanghiya Samabeshi Samajwadi Party, Nepal	65	0.00	5,978	0.06	0
Garib Ekta Samaj Party, Nepal	421	0.00	5,859	0.06	0
Madhesi Janadikar Forum Madhesh	2,197	0.02	5,814	0.06	0
Rashtriya Yatharthabadi Party Nepal	953	0.01	5,505	0.06	0
Nepal Ama Party	1,542	0.02	5,491	0.06	0
Janata Dal United	522	0.01	5,396	0.06	0
Rashtriya Shiva Sena Party	1,959	0.02	5,371	0.06	0
Rashtriya Madhesh Bahujan Samajwadi Party	869	0.01	5,301	0.06	0
Samyukta Rashtrabadi Morcha Nepal	812	0.01	5,225	0.06	0
Rashtriya Mukti Andolan Nepal	167	0.00	5,216	0.06	0
Churebavar Loktantrik Party	566	0.01	5,085	0.05	0
Nepal Nagarik Party	691	0.01	4,861	0.05	0
Nepal Labour Party	982	0.01	4,837	0.05	0
Nepal Sadbhawana Party (Gajendrawadi)	1,679	0.02	4,824	0.05	0
Rashtriya Nagarik Party	290	0.00	4,668	0.05	0

(Table 10.1 Continued)

(Table 10.1 Continued)

Party	FPTP			PR			Nominated Seats	Total Seats	+/-
	Votes	%	Seats	Votes	%	Seats			
Churebavar Rashtriya Party	577	0.01	0	4,650	0.05	0			
Nepal Sadbhawana Party (United)	1,285	0.01	0	4,578	0.05	0			
Bahujan Samaj Party Nepal	460	0.00	0	4,522	0.05	0			
Jantantrik Terai Madhes Mukti Tigers	2,755	0.03	0	4,370	0.05	0			
Hindu Prajatantrik Party, Nepal	178	0.00	0	4,215	0.04	0			
Naya Nepal Rashtriya Party	55	0.00	0	4,140	0.04	0			
Jana Unity-Cooperative Party of Nepal	2,125	0.02	0	4,066	0.04	0			
Nepal Samabeshi Party	131	0.01	0	3,882	0.04	0			
Deshbhakta Samaaj	703	0.01	0	3,866	0.04	0			
Limbuwan Mukti Morcha	398	0.00	0	3,748	0.04	0			
Liberal Democratic Party	407	0.00	0	3,721	0.04	0			
Nepal Jana Sambeshi Ekata Party	142	0.00	0	3,674	0.04	0			
Nepal Communist Party (ML-Socialist)	788	0.01	0	3,661	0.04	0			
Janata Party Nepal	1,354	0.01	0	3,595	0.04	0			
Rashtriya Churebavar Party	403	0.00	0	3,484	0.04	0			
Nepal Gauravshali Party	116	0.00	0	3,388	0.04	0			
Nepal Rashtriya Bikash Party	550	0.01	0	3,373	0.04	0			
Rashtriya Ekata Party	750	0.01	0	3,365	0.04	0			

Social Republican Party	541	0.01	3,360	0.04	0
Deshbhakta Paryavaraniya Samajik Morcha	217	0.00	3,293	0.03	0
United Green Organization	94	0.00	3,229	0.03	0
Jana Morcha Nepal	876	0.01	3,181	0.03	0
Nepal Rashtra Sewa Dal	183	0.00	3,127	0.03	0
Loktantrik Party – Nepal	249	0.00	3,107	0.03	0
Rastriya Jana Bikas Party	67	0.00	3,102	0.03	0
Matribhumi Nepal Dal	440	0.00	3,099	0.03	0
Naya Sanghiyata Janadharana Party	0	0.00	3,007	0.03	0
Nepal Rashtriya Yatayat Bikash Dal	12	0.00	2,952	0.03	0
Rashtrabadi Ekata Party	394	0.00	2,905	0.03	0
Limbuwan Mukti Morcha Nepal	741	0.01	2,844	0.03	0
Nepal Samajwadi Party (Lohiaite)	743	0.01	2,743	0.03	0
Sanghiya Bikashbadi Party Nepal	0	0.00	2,652	0.03	0
Rashtrabadi Janata Party	762	0.01	2,505	0.03	0
Nepal Janabhawana Party	28	0.00	2,439	0.03	0
Nepal Nyayik Dal	146	0.00	2,379	0.03	0
Tamangsaling Rashtriya Janaekta Party	36	0.00	2,308	0.02	0
Samyukta Jana Morcha	147	0.00	2,225	0.02	0
Shramik Janata Party – Nepal	45	0.00	2,034	0.02	0

(Table 10.1 Continued)

(Table 10.1 Continued)

Party	FPTP			PR			Nominated Seats	Total Seats	+/-
	Votes	%	Seats	Votes	%	Seats			
Rashtriya Madhesh Ekata Party, Nepal	850	0.01	0	2,031	0.02	0			
Om Sena Nepal	18	0.00	0	2,011	0.02	0			
Hariyali Party Nepal	251	0.00	0	1,927	0.02	0			
Nepal Madhesi Janata Dal (S)	334	0.00	0	1,902	0.02	0			
Nepal Shramjivi Dal	40	0.00	0	1,891	0.02	0			
Yuwa Shakti Nepal Party	22	0.00	0	1,820	0.02	0			
League Nepal Shanti Ekata Party	435	0.00	0	1,813	0.02	0			
Loktantrik Janata Party Nepal	135	0.00	0	1,729	0.02	0			
Terai Pahad Himal Samaj Party	81	0.00	0	1,697	0.02	0			
Rashtriya Loktantrik Yuwa Party	34	0.00	0	1,191	0.01	0			
Nepali Janata Party	0	0.00	0	996	0.01	0			
Garib Janatako Kranti Party	682	0.00	0	0	0.00	0			
Communist Party of Nepal (MLM) Communist	247	0.00	0	7,781	0.00	0			
Independents	107,764	1.19	2	–	–	–			
Total	9,044,908	100	240	9,463,862	100	335	26	601	0

Source: Election Commission, Nepal.

The CA elections have been a powerful lesson to all political formations in Nepal, with a clear popular mandate against the fractious and obstructive politics of the past. Any political party choosing to ignore the public mood can only attract further, and potentially permanent marginalization. While the mandate remains somewhat fractured, it has created conditions that, with a measure of political sagacity on the part of the main players, could result not only in stable arrangements for governance, but, crucially, a final resolution of the issues that have obstructed the drafting of the Constitution.[1]

After a lapse of two months post elections, a government was formed under the President of the NC Sushil Koirala with the support of the CPN (UML). The UML also decided to send some ministers to the Koirala Cabinet. In fact, important portfolios such as Home and Foreign went to the UML party. The Koirala government has already ruled for more than 100 days but has been criticized for its slow decisions on critical matters. However, it has made some headway on drafting the constitution which is a positive sign.

As per Arjun Bhandari:

One of the major challenges for the CA is to draft a constitution within a year as per the promise of the parties represented in the High-level Political Committee. Adopting a new constitution will be an uphill task if the UCPN-M stays away from the constitution drafting process.[2]

In actuality, the EC had never stated that this was the elections for a 'second C.A'. This is a new sovereign body in itself. As the president of Rastriya Prajatantra Party (Nepal) (RPP-N) Kamal Thapa said in the first session of parliament, 'this is not the extension of the previous C.A.' His party has emerged as the fourth largest party and will emerge stronger if the major three parties continue to fight among themselves in trivial issues of power sharing. What the Nepali electorate desperately want is electricity, water, better infrastructure and a better life. They have seen

---

[1] 'Nepal Assessment—2014', available online at http://www.satp.org/satporgtp/countries/nepal/index.html (accessed 2 February 2014).

[2] Arjun Bhandari, 'Logic behind Second CA and Its Future', *Himalayan Times*, 31 December 2013.

the economic developments in neighbouring countries and want the same in their own. Due to prolonged political instability, vital institutions of the state such as Nepal Airlines, universities, hospitals and even embassies are either lying headless or politicized to an extent that has made them annexes of various political parties. The new government must not only correct these malpractices but also provide good governance. Moreover, the constitution must be drafted and promulgated within the reaming months of this year 2014.

The previous CA had discussed at length on various tenets of the constitution but could not agree on main issues of federalism. In fact, it also struggled on issues such as what type of a political system to adopt? In their election manifestos, major parties such as the NC and the UML do not want the French model of the hybrid political system. The NC has clearly aligned itself with parliamentary democracy. The previous CA had the following thematic committees:

1. Constituent Assembly Committees
   a. Constitutional Committee
   b. Thematic Committees
      i. Committee on Fundamental Rights and Directive Principles
      ii. Committee on the Protection of the Rights of Minorities and Marginalized Communities
      iii. Committee on State Restructuring and Distribution of State Power
      iv. Committee for Determining the Structure of the Legislative Body
      v. Committee for Determining the Form of the Government
      vi. Judicial System Committee
      vii. Committee for Determining the Structure of Constitutional Bodies
      viii. Committee on Natural Resources, Financial Rights and Revenue Sharing
      ix. Committee for Determining the Base of Cultural and Social Solidarity
      x. National Interest Preservation Committee

c. Procedural Committees
      i. Committee on Citizen
      ii. Public Opinion Collection and Coordination Committee
      iii. Capacity Building and Source Management Committee
2. Legislative Parliament Committees
   a. Legislative Committee
   b. Thematic Committees
      i. Committee on Finance and Labor Relations
      ii. Committee for International Relations and Human Rights
      iii. Committee on Natural Resources and Means
      iv. Development Committee
      v. Women Children and Social Welfare Committee
      vi. State Affair Committee
      vii. Public Account Committee
   c. Special Committees
      i. Security Special Committee
      ii. Parliamentary Hearing Special Committee

Whether or not to stick with these committees remains an issue. Most problematic is the controversy on whether or not to 'own' the decisions of the previous CA. Since this new House is a sovereign, independent body in itself, it is not constrained or binded by any previous commitments or obligations. But if all things were to start afresh, there would be a risk of losing precious time making this new body a repetition of the first one. Parties must rise above narrow partisanship and come together this year for the sake of their nation. It was finally decided in March 2014 to own up the decisions of the previous CA, although some parties such as the RPP-N were against it.

Just how poor is country's economic performance is depicted by a latest statement by the World Bank (WB) which has expressed concerns over poor implementation of seven projects in the country in which the multilateral lending agency has invested close to US$ 500 million. These projects include Emerging Towns

Project, Road Sector Development Project, Bridge Improvement and Maintenance Programme, Kabeli Transmission Project, Enhanced Vocational Education and Training Project, Nepal Health Sector Programme and Community Action for Nutrition Project (Sunaula Hazar Din). The WB officials during quarterly portfolio performance review meeting held at the Ministry of Finance (MoF) said:

> These projects have not been able to utilise the allocated funds, conduct financial audits and procurement works on time, and prepare comprehensive action plans for execution. These projects have also been witnessing frequent transfer of staff and have been victims of red tape and bad governance.[3]

With an annual gross domestic product (GDP) growth of 3.4 per cent, Nepal's economy is hardly moving. It survives on remittances sent by Nepalese labourers working in the Gulf and Malaysia. But the plight of these workers is getting bad every month. News reports of hundreds of Nepalese dying in the Gulf due to extreme weather conditions have rocked the headlines and continue to trouble human rights activists. Even the Malaysian government has begun cracking down in illegal workers.

> In the face of an intensive crackdown on illegal migrant workers in Malaysia and Saudi Arabia and an ever increasing number of passport seekers, Nepal's missions in major labour destinations are in desperate need of additional staffers to handle an unprecedented crisis. The under-staffed embassies cannot cope with many working ten hours a day, seven days a week.'[4]

This may impact this crucial constituent of Nepal's economy. In case, foreign-based Nepalese youth start returning, it may create a social problem since the country does not have job opportunities.

The tourism sector too has slowed down. Sri Lanka which comprehensively defeated terrorism after Nepal started its peace process has already managed to cross the million mark in its

---

[3] 'WB Not Happy with Seven Funded Projects', *Himalayan Times*, 4 February 2014.

[4] 'Migrants in Lurch as Embassy Staff Overworked', *Kathmandu Post*, 30 January 2014.

Table 10.2:
Summary of tourism scenario, 2011-2012

Indicators	2011	2012	% Change
Tourist arrival by			
Air	545,221	598,258	9.70
Land	190,994	204,834	7.20
Total	736,215	803,092	9.10
Average length of stay	13.12	12.16	–7.3
Sex			
Male	352,059,439	27,024	.80
Female	384,156	363,822	–5.3
By age groups			
0–15 years	32,795	35,468	8.2
16–30 years	171,081	181,558	6.1
31–45 years	212,176	231,117	8.9
46–60 years	177,983	201,835	13.4
61+ years	82,726	109,239	32.0

Source: Nepal Tourism Board.

tourist inflow. This is important in the context of economic recovery of Nepal. Tourism has become the second largest source of revenue for the treasury after remittances sent by foreign-based Nepalese labourers. Table 10.2 depicts the chart of tourist arrivals.

Table 10.2 shows that Nepal's tourism sector is reeling under lack of promotional activities, lack of leadership at the Tourism Board, affected negatively by bad publicity abroad and impacted severely by frequent *bandh*s and strikes. To top all the negatives, the EU banned all Nepali airlines to fly to European destinations in 2013, and this came as a big blow to Nepalese tourism industry. The EU blamed Nepal's notorious air safety record which has witnessed several deadly crashes in the last couple of years. If the Europeans do not fly by Nepali domestic carriers, then the rural tourism mainly mountain tourism will greatly suffer. The new government needs to actively lobby and try to persuade the European friends to restore the status quo ante. Before this, we need to urgently take concrete steps to ensure that Nepal is a safe destination for air travellers.

As of 2013, the following nationalities are the largest number of tourists in the country. The Chinese have emerged as the second largest component of tourists in Nepal which is a phenomenon rise in itself. Currently, Nepal is directly connected by air to Kunming, Lhasa, Guangzhou, Hong Kong, whereas Shanghai is connected by Nepal Airlines which does not have enough aircrafts to fly the route. Another observable fact is that the Sri Lankans have become the third largest tourist cluster to visit Nepal. Most Sri Lankans visit Lumbini through the land route in Bhairahawa.

Top Five Country of Nationality
Rank 1: India
Rank 2: People's Republic of China
Rank 3: Sri Lanka
Rank 4: US
Rank 5: UK

While Nepal has strived its level best to emerge as the most attractive destination in South Asia for conference and meetings, incentives, conferences and exhibitions (MICE) tourism due to its comparatively easy visa policy, this has not seen such a draw due to a high expense of air travel and also due to political instability in the country. Most foreigners still come to Nepal for holiday. We could also have capitalized in religious tourism but have not been successful due to various factors.

Purpose of Visit of Tourists (2012)
Holiday/pleasure
Pilgrimage
Trekking and mountaineering
Official
Business
Study/research/employment
Conference/conv.

Tourist Arrival by Major Five Airlines
Rank 1: Spice Jet Indian Airlines
Rank 2: Jet Airways
Rank 3: Qatar Airlines
Rank 4: Thai Airlines

Given the trade relations with India, covering two-thirds of Nepal's international trade, inflation in India was bound to hit Nepal hard. 'The rising cost of production on the back of energy crisis, soaring prices of imported raw materials and supply constraints in the domestic market are all set to continue which has already spiralled beyond the government's target of 8 percent'.[5] As double-digit inflation was hitting the public hard, the budget of FY 2013 had set a target of containing inflation to 8 per cent — an ambitious target when the Nepali currency is at a record low against the US dollar.

Nepal's energy woes are also infamous and a tragedy for the Nepali people who are actually the title holders of 83,000 MW of hydro potentials. During the winter, 14 hours of crippling load shedding grips the Nepali household and most people rely on inverters, generators and cheap emergency lights imported from China.

> In the present context, the demand of power supply in the evening hours stands at 1176 MW but Nepal has been producing 620 MW only. That includes the 190 MW power which is directly imported from India, which means only 394 MW is generated via domestic hydropower.[6]

There are 130 private companies holding license for 8,000 MW power generation, but most of these companies are for the sake of names only. There is also an additional problem of too many licenses given without ensuring the market for the power generated through these projects. This has cast doubt in the minds of potential investors. It is an irony that, whereas there is a shortage of power, there is growing apprehension that domestic market may not be able to use all the power generated from the numerous projects in the offing.

Although Nepal is likely to miss targets on halving poverty and achieving universal primary education, it still stands among the countries that are close to fulfilling millennium development goals (MDGs). *Global Monitoring Report 2011: Improving the Odds of Achieving the MDGs* released by the WB and the IMF this year

---

[5] 'Waning Hope of Achieving Budget Targets', *Republica*, 24 January 2013.

[6] 'Dark Future', *Himalayan Times*, 26 January 2014.

notes that Nepal is not going to halve poverty and hunger prevalence by 2015 as its leaders committed [but] the good news is that it belongs to the region that has achieved more than 50 per cent of the target on those fronts. Nepal is also set to miss the target on universal primary education with just more than 50 per cent of students completing the last year of primary education. Nepal is also lagging behind in halving maternal mortality and under five mortality rates by 2015, says the report. 'The maternal mortality rate is declining, but only slowly', it reads. However, the report lauds Nepal for already achieving the target of halving (by 2015) the proportion of people without sustainable access to safe drinking water. It also rates Nepal as close to the target of halving the proportion of people without sustainable access to basic sanitation by 2015.[7]

In the final analysis, the year 2013 was a year when people have started dreaming again for the Nepalese. Unable to draft a constitution, the year 2012 saw a major drift in the democratic process when an unelected government headed by the CJ comprising retired bureaucrats had to be formed. But at least, the dawn of 2014 has witnessed the major political parties agreeing to form a majority government and re-committing themselves to promulgate the new statute within the year 2014. Nepalese have been given these promises before. Hopefully, the new year will not go wasted. Because, when the winds of change blow, unimaginable things can happen.

---

[7] 'Nepal Close to Fulfilling MDG Targets: WB IMF', available online at http://archives.myrepublica.com/portal/index.php?action=news_details&news_id=30365 (accessed 4 February 2013).

11

Maoist Insurgency and Peace Process in Nepal: Integration (of the Maoist Combatants) and the Divide within the Maoist Party

Uddhab Prasad Pyakurel

This chapter is a representation of the shades that one can imagine about the split of Unified Communist Party of Nepal-Maoist (UCPN-M) in June 2012 into two parties: UCPN-M and Communist Party of Nepal-Maoist (CPN-M). It focuses on the problems of Marxism as a grand narrative, and the ideological problems within the Nepali Maoists since the signing of the 12-point agreement between the Maoist and the Seven Party Alliance (SPA)[1] on 22 November 2005. This chapter makes an argument that the ideological problems among the different factions within the UCPN-M led to the split, in which the issues of army integration and non-transparent financial mismanagement of peace-process-related budget by Maoist Chairperson Puspa Kamal Dahal became the immediate causes for such a split. The chapter is

[1] This alliance consisted of seven parliamentary parties—Nepali Congress (NC), Nepali Congress (Democratic), Communist Party of Nepal (Unified–Marxist–Leninist), Nepali Workers and Peasants Party, Nepal Goodwill Party (Anandi Devi), United Left Front and People's Front—who were in the street to protest against authoritarian monarchy.

divided into two sections: the first section throws some light on the decade-long Maoist insurgency, and the start of the peace process, whereas the second section deals with the issues related to the intra-party conflict of the Maoists, which eventually invited a formal division of the party.

Change of Image from Hooded Maobadi to City Dwelling Leftists

The image of Maobadi or Maoist as a gun-wielding youth fighting against oppression and feudal order that was created by the CPN-M[2] during the decade-long insurgency starting from 1996 had changed after the first Nepalese Constituent Assembly (CA) election of 10 April 2008 into city dwelling rich politicians among the people. This section analyses the Maoist's journey up to the start of the peace process in 2006. Here, we follow the fragmented approach negating the modernist perspective that views the events or happenings in stages.

If follow the political formation of Nepal after the first *jana andolan* of 1990, it was based on constitutional Monarchy. On 12 May 1991, through the general election to the 'House of Representative', Girija Prasad Koirala (leader of the Congress Party, which had won 114 seats out of 205) was elected as the first prime minister of a democratically elected government in Nepal. An eminent scholar turned politician, Ram Sharan Mahat says that once democracy was established, the country underwent steady improvements in various sectors such as banking, tourism, infrastructure, health, education, etc.[3] However, the Maoists saw this as a sign of bourgeois democracy that needed to be destroyed through a revolution. Nevertheless, the Maoists had already constructed a view that revolution would be successful in Nepal. For instance, Baburam Bhattarai saw that the deteriorating condition of rural

---

[2] During the insurgency, the name of the Maoist party was CPN-M, and it became UCPN-M with the merger of some of the small left outfits during the peace process.

[3] Ram Sharan Mahat, *Defense of Democracy: Dynamics and Faultlines of Nepal's Political Economy* (Delhi: Adroit Publishers, 2005).

economy resulting in the increasing poverty unemployment and inequality in society, in general, should adequately explain the material basis for the raging rebellion of the poor peasant masses over the years.[4]

In 1994, Pushpa Kamal Dahal and Baburam Bhattarai separated from their party CPN (Unity Centre), and they established a parallel party of the same name. Having gone through ups and downs in its organization through splits and unities, CPN (Unity Centre) organized its Third Plenum in March 1995 and the party was renamed as CPN-M. It also came up with a major decision 'for the true liberation of the people all efforts must be concentrated for the development of a people's war that would usher in the new people's democratic form of government'.[5] The party also gave up its policy of taking part in parliamentary elections. In September 1995, the party adopted the 'plan for the historic initiation of the 'People's War' and passed 'seven theoretical premises'. The underground party fixed 13 February 1996 as the date for starting the 'People's War'. On 3 February 1996, the open political wing of the party led by Baburam Bhattarai had presented its 40-point memorandum to the government. It warned the government that the United People's Front of Nepal (UPFN) would begin an armed struggle against the state unless appropriate measures towards fulfilling the demands were initiated by 17 February 1996. Citing the government's indifference to UPFN demands, the party cadres including Bhattarai went underground and launched an attack on 13 February 1996 in four different places in four districts in the name of 'People's War'.

Scholars including Karki and Seddon[6] consider that the demands presented to the government, as well as the issue of the denial of the recognition of the party by the Election Commission, as critical causes for the eruption of 'People's War'. In fact, having a look at the strategic preparation of 'People's War', one can say that those causes are only a farce. It is because the leaders strategically made

---

[4] B. Bhattarai, *The Nature of Underdevelopment and Regional Structure of Nepal: A Marxist Analysis* (New Delhi: Adroit Publishers, 2003).

[5] Deepak Thapa and Bandita Sijipati, *A Kingdom Under Siege: Nepal's Maoist Insurgency 1996 to 2003* (Kathmandu: The Printhouse, 2003).

[6] A. Karki and D. Seddon, *The People's War in Nepal: Left Perspectives* (New Delhi: Adroit Publishers, 2003).

two parties—one underground and the other open—to prepare for the armed conflict. Both the parties aimed to expose the inadequacy of achievements of the 1990s movement. The party, led by Baburam Bhattarai, entered into electoral politics with the explicit objectives 'to expose the inadequacy of the parliamentary system'. Another justifiable evidence for such a position was that the UPFN, without waiting the given deadline that was 17 February, started attack on the government institutions on 13 February 2006. That is why one can say that the attack was guided by the underground party's decision of January 1996 rather than UPFN's given deadline.

The official statement of the CPN (M) in 1996, 'Theoretical Premises for the Historic Initiation of the People's War'[7] clearly shows their aims and plans for their 'People's War'. It states,

> This plan would be based on the aim of completing the new democratic revolution after the destruction of feudalism and imperialism, then immediately moving towards socialism, and, by way of cultural revolutions based on the theory of continuous revolution under the dictatorship of the proletariat, marching to communism—the golden future of the whole humanity.

They started the war by attacking and seizing Bank's cash, loan papers and land registration certificates deposited by peasants at the office of the Small Farmers Development Programme (SFDP) of Chyangli Village Development Committee (VDC) in Gorkha district. They also attacked the Sindhuli Gadhi police post in Sindhuli district and the Athbiskot—Rani police outpost in Rukum district. As per a Maoist report, a multinational company (PepsiCo) situated in the Kathmandu valley, a distillery 'owned by a comprador bourgeois' in Gorkha and the house of a 'notorious feudal-usurer' in Kavre in central-eastern Nepal were also raided in a single day, that is, 13 February 1996. They began to distribute thousands of leaflets and posters, and organized the 'March on' programme, where the slogan raised by the party was 'the path of people's war to smash the reactionary state and establish a democratic state'. This programme was launched

---

[7] SATP *Theoretical Premises for the Historic Initiation of the People's War*, available online at http://www.satp.org/satporgtp/countries/nepal/document/papers/theoretical_premises.htm (accessed 3 January 2014).

in the major cities and headquarters of more than 60 districts in Nepal.[8] One can clearly see that the Maoist insurgency started from the four districts of Gorkha, Sindhuli, Rolpa and Rukum. The first two districts are situated in the central–western and central–eastern hill regions, respectively, and the last two are located in the mid-western Rapti zone in Nepal. Although there might be various factors to examine as to why the Rapti zone became the initiating area of the Maoist movement, the following possibilities are worth mentioning.

There is a narrative among the Nepali communists that since 1957, some districts of the mid-western region such as Rolpa, Rukum and Pyuthan had been exposed to the communist influence. Mohan Bikram Singh, one of the senior and very influential communist leaders, started his communist career in this region. Raising the demand of CA, Singh sensitized people on the issue of their rights and freedom. Because of their political consciousness and value for democracy and freedom, the people of the region contributed a lot to the democratic struggle of Nepal. For example, Thawang, a VDC of Rolpa district, cast only four votes in the 1980s referendum in support of the Panchayat system. The VDC boycotted the election and returned the empty ballot box in the first Rastriya Panchayat election in 1981. Barman Buda, one of the followers of Singh, started leading the Magar people of the region. He, who became a member of the parliament from the UPFN Party, was later imprisoned for five years on the charge of having burnt the picture of the king and queen in the 1980s. In the 1991 election, UPFN won both the seats in Rolpa, and the party was right behind the NC in Rukum district.

There is a little narrative among the educated people and democrats that the antagonism between the UPFN cadres and the ruling NC cadres in Rukum and Rolpa after the first local election of 1992 played a vital role in increasing the Maoist influence in Rolpa and Rukum. In the 1991 election, the UPFN came close to the NC. After the election, the NC started ruling the country with absolute majority in the parliament and the UPFN was busy in the village with the people's awareness campaign. Along with

---

[8] *The Worker*, 1996, cited in *Revolutionary Worker* #894, February 16, 1997, available online at http://revcom.us/a/firstvol/890-899/894/nepal.htm (accessed February 12, 2014).

the campaign, the UPFN began 'taking action against those they considered exploiters, usurers and cheats' in the villages. The so-called enemies of the communists were the NC cadres and the local influential politicians having the background of the previous ruling panchayat system who had joined the NC after the *jana andolan* of 1990. The competition between UPFN and NC became complicated once the NC cadres belonging to the ruling party used the state machinery against their opponents. The police and local government body (the district administration office) in collusion with the local NC leaders started to file 'false accusations' against its opponents. The majority of the accused found that the only solution was to run away into the forest or to the city, or the plains, or even to India, in the hope of passing time until their relatives managed to sort out the dispute.[9] Once the social tension was widening like anything, the Maoist, which was to win people's sentiment, started capitalizing the situation by sending its 'hooded guerrillas' to kill the informers or 'class enemies'. Then some special police operations, that is, Operation Romeo, Kilo Sierra-2 and Operation Search and Kill had been launched in the region. The impact of the operation was later described in Informal Sector Service Centre (INSEC) Human Rights Year Book 1995 reports, which is as follows:

> The government initiated ... suppressive operations to a degree of state terror. Especially the workers of the UPFN were brutally suppressed. Under the direct leadership of the ruling party workers of the locality, police searched, tortured and arrested, without arrest warrants, in 11 villages of the district. Nearly 6,000 locals had left the villages due to the police operation. One hundred and thirty two people were arrested without serving any warrants. The arrested included elderly people of 75 years of age. All the detained were subjected to torture.[10]

For the Maoists, the class enemies were those who made a 'false accusation' on the people. Those who left the village were

---

[9] Anne de Sales, 'The Kham Magar Country, Nepal: Between Ethnic Claims and Maoism', in *Understanding the Maoist Movement of Nepal*, ed. Deepak Thapa (Kathmandu: Martin Chautari, 2003), p. 81.

[10] INSEC, *Human Rights Yearbook* (Kathmandu: Informal Sector Service Centre, 2005).

compelled by circumstances to support the Maoist, and they took part in the attack on villages. Baburam Bhattarai in an interview said that more than 10,000 rural youth, out of a population of 200,000 for the whole district of Rolpa, have been forced to flee from their homes and take shelter in remote jungles. The deplorably cruel situation was created by the government, which sent around 1,550-strong especially trained commando force from Kathmandu.[11]

In fact, along with these operations, the villagers were harassed by the Maoist at night (those who had to be fed) and during the day by policemen. In a way, as Sales (2003) terms, the villages were turned to 'an impossible living situation'. However, villagers, irrespective of their political inclinations, preferred the Maoist rather than the police. It is due to the fact that Maoist, whose atrocious behaviour was similar to the security force in the village, had changed its old modus operandi, and started social work, raised socio-cultural agenda and respected the village elders as their parents. Even while Maoist cadres asked the villagers for food, they used to ask for cheap, simple and easily available things such as maize and salt, whereas the demand of the police was for expensive things like chicken and alcohol. Another cause of the villagers' hostility towards security personnel was that they were often beaten without any prior investigation if the police suspected them. An opinion poll conducted by the then *Himal Khabarpatrika* of March 2001 proved that the brutality of the security force had been seen as one of the main causes of support for the Maoists. According to the poll, 30 per cent of the respondents attributed the rise of the Maoist to highhandedness of the security force.

In their process of war, the Maoists also used the topography of the Rapti zone to their advantage. More than half of the districts of Rukum and Rolpa are forested that gave 'natural surroundings to the guerrillas to hide from state security forces and to launch the training and other sorts of campaigns in the woods. The dense forest and remoteness made it easier for the Maoist to hide their cadres from the state security. It became fruitful for

---

[11] Deepak Thapa, 'Day of the Mao's Boys', *Himal*, 14, no. 5 (2001): 10, available online at http://himalaya.socanth.cam.ac.uk/collections/journals/hsa/pdf/HSA_14_05_2001.pdf (accessed 13 October 2014).

their movement and for supplying their weapons from one part to another. In the case of Terai, where there is 'more influential feudal culture than in the hills', the Maoist realized that 'the geography is negative there to start the insurgency'.[12] Such a natural opportunity has been used by Naxalites of India.[13]

One can raise a question of why the Maoists became powerful in Nepal so that they could make a tacit understanding with the king and even proceeded to have a 12-point agreement with the SPA. The Maoists themselves try to show the causes as those based on 'class discrimination'; however, the 'class' is a traditional and a readymade show card to all who believe in communism. According to the Maoists, they got support from the poor people and assaulted the 'semi-feudal and semi-colonial' Nepali state. They used to say,

> We communists are clear on the scientific facts that it is necessary to raise the flag of just war in order to oppose the unjust war being conducted by the exploiting class and to end war forever amongst the human beings. In the class society, it is impossible to make a forward leap without a revolutionary war'.[14]

Even today, the educated Nepali people with Marxist leanings have a narrative that 'inequality', in its different manifestations (relative poverty, landlessness, unemployment, etc.), was the main cause for the emergence of the Maoist movement. Here, we argue that the main reason for Maoist insurgency was the desire of the Maoists to see the socialist phase that would leap to communism in the linear time as the educated leaders were influenced by Maoism, which is derived from the theory and practice of Mao Tse-Tung in China.

To talk of poverty and suppression, Tharus, one of the major ethnic groups in Terai, and other Terai communities are very poor in comparison with the hill communities such as Bahun, Chhetri,

---

[12] Baburam Bhattarai, 'Janayudda Ka Das Barsha Ra Krishi Kranti Ko Prasna' (Ten years of people's war and the question of agricultural revolution), *Kishan Sandesh*, Vol. 2, December 2005.

[13] Samanta Banerjee, *In the Wake of Naxalbari: A History of the Naxalite Movemnet in India* (Calcutta: Subornarekha, 1980).

[14] Prachanda, 'Some Ideological and Military Questions Raised by People's War', *Problems and Prospects of the Revolution in Nepal* (Nepal: Janadisha, 2004).

Magar, Gurung, Dalits, etc., in the Rapti zone. Again, the situation of Tharus and other Terai communities seem far worse than the Magars or other hill communities on the issue of the exploitation by big landowners. Baburam Bhattarai, the then convenor of the UPFN, accepted this fact and said that the Tharus have to work in a kind of feudal relationship. He wrote, 'the feudal relation in Terai is very much strong'. To him, 'majority of the people are poor peasants and substantial production system is there in the hilly region'.[15] Hence, one can pose a couple of questions, that is, why is the Terai not influenced by the Maoists' activities? If the movement is class based, one wonders as to why the movement became hill based, where, according to the Maoist, the feudal relation is nominal.

It is also a matter of research that how much people supported the CPN (Maoist) until 1998. The Maoists had started the 'People's War' with only 200 cadres in 1996.[16] Until September 1999, the Maoist was busy in 'struggle, propaganda and mobility'. Within that strategy, the Maoist launched some token/small attacks in its area with a view to draw national and international attention. Until May/June 1997, it was assumed[17] that the Maoist preserved and showed its effective influence only in 83 VDCs of four neighbouring districts of Rolpa, Rukum, Salyan and Jajarkot. The Maoists soon saw a major problem in Nepal that the communists have always faced in India. The social hierarchy in Nepal is based on caste just like in India that is different from the idea of social hierarchy in Marxism or Maoism as mentioned earlier. The Nepali Maoists found that it was very difficult to convince the people of their theory of high class and exploited working class (peasants and workers). Therefore, they adopted a strategy in 1998 to take the support of the people, which was to raise the issue of caste/ethnicity.[18,19] Rural Nepal was inhabitated mostly

[15] See note 12.

[16] Liz Philipson, *Conflict in Nepal: Perspective on the Maoist Movement*, May 2002 (An unpublished paper submitted to DFID).

[17] The assumption was based on the Maoist's agenda of boycotting the 1997 local election. The boycott was successful only in those 83 VDCs.

[18] Uddhab Pd. Pyakurel, *Maoist Movement in Nepal: A Sociological Perspective* (New Delhi: Adroit Publishers, 2007).

[19] Uddhab Pd. Pyakurel, 'Political Transition in Nepal: An Overview', in *State of Conflict and Democratic Movement in Nepal*, eds Uddhab Pd. Pyakurel and Indra Adhikari (New Delhi: Vij Books, 2013).

by the semi-literate and uneducated people divided into *jati*s, that is, in the caste system. The Maoists largely capitalized on the issue of *jati* promising the *janajati*s or the communities, who hold the social status below the Bahun–Chhetri castes, that they would grant them *jatiya-rajya* or ethnic federalism after they capture power. To the Dalits or lower untouchable castes, they promised special rights, abolition of untouchability and discrimination. Even today, there are narratives in Nepali society about what the Maoists used to tell the people during the decade long insurgency such as plundering the rich and distributing the money and lands to the poor, giving the states or *rajya* like Magarat, Tamuwan, Limbuan, etc., to Magars, Gurungs and Limbus. They would give employment to all the people in Nepal, untouchability and discrimination free country to Dalits, etc. Baburam Bhattarai, in his interview given to *the Kathmandu Post*, 12 January 2009, said 'To carry your cadres along you had to use certain kinds of rhetoric, you have to pander to their passions at times'.[20] It clearly shows that the Maoists had played with the emotions of the rural masses. Such rhetoric influenced many people in villages, especially the youths who hoped to see changes soon.

The Maoist had formed the 'People's Army' or 'Central Military Commission' under the leadership of Dahal on 13 February 1998 (on the occasion of the second year anniversary); as a result of it, the party could diversify simultaneous attack, which covered at least four zones out of a total of 14 zones of Nepal. Until May 2001, the Maoist-related deaths took place in 52 districts, out of 75, in Nepal.[21] Along with this, the Maoists also found pretexts to criticize the system of parliamentary democracy. In the midterm election of 1994, no party got majority in the Parliament, and people faced five prime ministers within four years. Deuba headed a coalition government from 11 September 1995 to 6 March 1997; Chand headed the government from 12 March 1997 to 4 October 1997. The people had very negative perceptions towards these two

---

[20] Prashant Jha, 'Extremist Factions Derailing Peace Process, Says Nepal Premier', *Hindu*, 17 March 2012, available online at http://www.thehindu.com/news/international/extremist-factions-derailing-peace-process-says-nepal-premier/article3006941.ece (accessed 13 October 2014).

[21] Deepak Thapa, 'Day of the Mao's Boys', 5.

governments. Both the governments were busy in horse-trading in the Parliament. The MPs used the Parliament as a platform to make money and got their bills reimbursed by submitting all sorts of irrelevant dues. Even male MPs submitted pregnancy-related bills and got reimbursement for their expenditure from the state. The state fund was very much misused during that time. The government decided to give 'Pajero and pension' facilities to the MPs, which was severely criticized by the people. Those agendas were picked up by the Maoists and used to show the parliamentary democracy in a negative light among the people.

Between 1998 and 2000, the Maoists shifted its strategy and formed about a dozen ethnic/regional front organizations. The attempt was to mobilize the member of 'marginalized' caste/ ethnic group to support its insurgency. The Maoists, which declared the first district *Janasarkar* (people's government) in Rukum district on 20 December 2000, were able to declare 21 district-level *Janasarkar*s by November 2001. Also, it formed 11 front organizations and nominated all the heads of the fronts from the Janajati communities. In other words, they provided space for a higher proportion of *janajati* and marginalized representation. For example, of the then 55-member Central Committee in 2002, 21 were from Janajati;[22] of the 37 members of the United Revolutionary People's Council, 17 were from Janajati and two from Dalit. Again, of the 23 district 'People's Government' chairpersons, 15 were from Janajati, seven from high caste and one from Dalit.[23]

Expansion in the Name of Peace

On 1 June 2001, there was the royal massacre in Narayanhiti Royal Palace, which led to the change of political scenario in Nepal. Though their position was not against the institution of monarchy until the incident took place, the anti-Gyanendra sentiment

[22] Sudheer Sharma, *The Ethnic Dimension of the Maoist Insurgency*, May 2002 (Unpublished paper).
[23] Harka Gurung, 'Social Exclusion and Maoist Insurgency', Paper Presented at *National Dialogue Conference on ILO Convention 169 on Indigenous and Tribal Peoples*, Kathmandu, 19–20 January.

of the Nepal people was capitalized by the Maoists terming it as 'the official end of the traditional monarchy from Nepal'. Along with that, the Maoists increased their attacks utilizing the power struggles between the politicians and the desire of King Gyanendra to capture power. Once the government led by G.P. Koirala tried to deploy the army to free the abducted 69 policemen from the Maoist, but he failed in the attempt owing to the king's 'non-co-operation'. Since the 'non-co-operation' increased the antagonism between the king and the then government on the issue of the deployment of the army, Koirala resigned from the post of prime minister on 19 July 2001, and Deuba was elected the prime minister on 23 July 2001. By the time of Deuba's appointment, the government announced truce. The Maoist, too, reciprocated the truce, which was enforced until 21 November 2001. In between, there were two rounds of talks between the government and the Maoists; one was on 30 August in Kathmandu and the other on 14 September in Bardiya. However, after the Maoist attacked two district headquarters—Dang and Syangja—on 23 November 2001, the truce was suspended and the country again witnessed violent activities. There is a narrative that the truce was used by the Maoist to raise funds as well as people's support by asking for donations, addressing mass meetings and extending the memberships.

The Maoist insurgency had already caused the devastation of rural economy, and stifled development works in rural areas as the rural masses were caught in the fire between the security forces and Maoists. This led to the migration of rich people to urban areas, and mostly poorer youths to Gulf countries, Malaysia, etc., just to escape the insecurity created by insurgency, and to earn money. Another point to be noted is that the Maoists did not get the social condition in Nepal as envisioned by Mao for the success of revolution. Mao says that any ideology even Marxism–Leninism is ineffective unless it is linked with objective realities, meets objectively existing needs and has been grasped by the masses of the people.[24] However, the Maoist

---

[24] The Bankruptcy of the Idealist Conception of History, *Selected Works of Mao Tse-Tung* (Peking: Foreign Language Press, 1949), avaialble online at http://www.marxists.org/reference/archive/mao/selected-works/volume-4/mswv4_70.htm (accessed 13 October 2014).

theory could not be linked with Nepali 'reality' because the idea of social hierarchy is *jati* or caste in Nepal differing from the Maoist idea of class. This is also the main reason why the Maoist theory could not be grasped by the Nepali masses; Maoism says something very different from the social 'reality' of Nepal. The Maoist leaders had understood this fact; hence, they had brought the uneducated people into their ranks raising the *jati* issue, and rhetoric of looting and distribution wealth to the poor. As the insurgency raged, the Maoists soon found that the majority of the people were unconvinced and did not support them. Consequently, they could not get the support of the masses for an urban insurrection, and, thus, state institutions in Kathmandu seemed too powerful for them to take over by force.

By then, King Gyanendra was already on his way of establishing absolute monarchy in Nepal. In October 2002, he dismissed Prime Minister Sher Bahadur Deuba and consolidated his power. The move of the king to discharge the Deuba government gave birth to a new era of struggle. After dismissing the elected prime minister, the king maintained a distance with the major political parties which had more than 90 per cent seats in the dissolved parliaments and tried to forge alliance with his loyalists and the extremist left—the then Maoists. He not only started searching his loyalists to be appointed as prime ministers,[25] but also involved in negotiating with the rebellion Maoists in the dark room. That was the time when Maoist declined Deuba's offer to negotiate with his government but they had shown their inclination to negotiate with the king saying that they believed that the real power vested with the institution of monarchy. Then onwards people including the author[26,27] raised the question about the intention of the Maoist, doubting whether the Maoist actually wanted to accept the king's active role.

---

[25] Two successive governments—the first under Lokendra Bahadur Chand (11 October 2002) and the second under Surya Bahadur Thapa (4 June 2003) as prime ministers—were appointed. However, the king himself sacked both the governments on 30 May 2003 and 7 May 2004, respectively.

[26] See note 18.

[27] Uddhab Pd. Pyakurel and Indra Adhikari (eds), *State of Conflict and Democratic Movement in Nepal* (New Delhi: Vij Books, 2013).

Interestingly, the relation of the monarchy and the rebellion Maoist party was exposed more once King Gyanendra dismissed the Deuba government and declared a state of emergency in the country by a proclamation on 1 February 2005. When mainstream political parties showed their unity to go against the king's move, and civil society, especially the lawyers, journalists, university teachers and students also gave a boost to their peaceful protest to restore the democratic system in the country by announcing a nationwide peaceful protest programme calling it as *jana andolan*, the Maoist party was busy in an internal debate whether to support the king to sideline the political parties.[28] Surprisingly, a majority of the members of the Maoist party along with Prachanda were of the view to alienate the political parties and share the power under the king's regime. Once Baburam Bhattarai, his wife, the Central Committee member, Hisila Yami and another Central Committee Member Dina Nath Sharma opposed the idea saying that it would be a suicidal decision; the party had taken action against them by putting under the Maoist's custody, and suspending from party's membership.[29] Once the Maoist corrected the decision by its Rolpa Plenum held in April 2005, and decided to accept the competitive democracy, the parties also accepted to go for the election of the CA. Then signing the much-talked 12-point agreement became possible in November 2005 as a background document of Nepal's peace process.

Now we have arrived at the final section of the chapter that deals with the ideological problems and factional conflicts with the UCPN-M. As hinted earlier, the main cause of the Maoist insurgency was not the issue of poverty or exploitation of the peasantry, but the desire of the Maoist educated leaders who wanted to see socialism under their rule that would leap to communism. In order to understand such a phenomenon, the ideological problems and

---

[28] Uddhab Pd. Pyakurel, 'The Vision of the Jana Andolan II for a Future of Nepal', in *State of Conflict and Democratic Movement in Nepal*, eds Uddhab Pd. Pyakurel and Indra Adhikari (New Delhi: Vij Books, 2013).

[29] Prachanda in a press statement, issued on 12 April 2005, accepted that the party had taken action against Dr Bhattarai. He, in several TV and newspaper interviews, argued that they had tacit understanding with the king.

conflicts within the party, it is perhaps important to discuss the problems in the meta-narrative of Marxism and its cult Maoism — the Chinese version of the meta-narrative.

The Peace Process in Nepal

Coming back to our narrative on Nepal, though the 12-point understanding was a milieu of Nepal's peace process, the Comprehensive Peace Accord (CPA) signed on 6 January 2007 by the interim government formed by the SPA and the then CPN-Maoist can be considered as a formal start of the peace process. It is CPA which not only declared the 'End of conflict' but also directed senior leaders of the parties to be sincere in 'the main policy for the long-term peace'. Since it was an output of the several other important efforts made by the SPA and the UCPN-M in different periods of time and contexts, that is, 12-point understanding, 25-point code of conduct agreed on 25 May 2006, 8-point agreement signed on 16 June 2006, the letter sent to the United Nations by both the sides with the similar viewpoints after the successful mass movement in 2006, its preamble acknowledges many of the previous agreements.

In fact, the CPA is a document that initiates radicalizing the mainstream political parties and mainstreaming the UCPN-M bringing it in the competitive party politics through a peaceful manner.[30] Thus, the peace process of Nepal suggested the UCPN-M to follow a couple of the measures, that is, to return the property confiscated during the insurgency to the owner, to allow other political parties for a political campaign in the country, in general, and in the UCPN-M controlled villages, in particular. Similarly, the high-level special committee for army integration, Truth and Reconciliation Commission, Commission for the Investigation of Disappeared People, State Restructuring Commission, etc., for making the federal structure were other important tasks opened up by the CPA. Furthermore, the election of CA for the making of a new constitution was the major task of the CPA.

[30] See note 27.

The Year '2013' and the Army Integration Process

Since the management of Maoist combatants and their arms were one of the important aspects of Nepal's peace process, the Government of Nepal and the UCPN-M reached on the Agreement on Monitoring of Management of Arms and Armies on 28 November 2006. The United Nations Mission in Nepal (UNMIN), on the request of the Interim Government and the UCPN-M, established its office in Kathmandu on 23 January 2007 in order to facilitate the work of the arms and armies management. The management process of the combatants of the UCPN-M began on 15 June 2007, and the UNMIN announced the first result of the verification of Maoist combatants on 27 December 2007.[31]

The issue of the management of Maoist combatants was politicized to such an extent that it had stopped the whole peace and the constitution writing process for quite a long time. Though advocacy and counter-advocacy were witnessed on the issue of the ex-combatant's management, eventually, the issue had concluded with the integration of former Maoist fighters into the Nepal Army. In fact, the then high-level political mechanism headed by the UCPN-M Chairman Pushpa Kamal Dahal stated on 12 April 2013 that they have concluded the army integration process by sorting out all the debated issues. Dahal's statement came just after all political parties reached to an agreement to dissolve the Special Committee which was formed for the supervision, integration and rehabilitation of Maoist combatants as per the Interim Constitution 2007. As a result, 1422 ex-combatants, out of 17,052 (13,494 males and 3,558 females) regrouped Maoists, were selected for integration. While 15,624 opted for voluntary retirement and six went for rehabilitation. Of these, 1,352 ex-combatants completed basic army training for rank and files along with the other 70 ex-combatants who underwent training for the officer level. They had already performed the 'passing-out' parade on 4 July 2013.[32]

---

[31] The type of weapons registered so far are 91 mortars (of which 55 were locally made), 61 machine guns, 2,403 rifles, 61 automatic weapons, 9 sub-automatic guns, 114 side arms, 212 shot guns, 253 miscellaneous and 244 home-made weapons.

[32] For details, see http://www.nipsnepal.org/uploads/files/A%20Nepali%20Model%20of%20Peace%20Process-%20A%20Policy%20Briefing%20Pape%20in%20English.pdf (accessed 25 May 2014).

The Army Integration Process and Divide within the Maoist Party

Though the successful conclusion of the army integration process by dissolving the Special Committee for the supervision, integration and rehabilitation of Maoist combatants after sorting out all the debated issues has been considered as a major path-breaking event for lasting peace, and democratic consolidation in Nepal,[33] it had become a case of displeasure for the Maoist party leaders and sympathizers. The discontent was due to the formal split of the party along with the integration process was being implemented. Surprisingly, the Maoist, which was a champion in creating and resolving the difference of opinion in the party, failed to handle the same on the issue of army integration, and it had to witness the split of the party on 18 June 2012.

In fact, it was a big surprise-cum-complexity for other than Maoists to understand the intra-party conflict of the Maoist party. It was due to the typical characteristics developed by the Maoist party during the negotiation, according to which they used to show a vertical division within them once they had to implement the provisions of the agreement signed with other counterparts. Those who knew it were in doubt on the much-talked rift between the Baidya faction and the mainstream party led by the Chairperson Dahal on the issue of army integration too. That is why many (including the author) had questioned asking whether such an internal rift of the Maoist party is genuine or artificial just to avoid implementing their earlier promises.[34] Such scepticism had following four major grounds:

- As stated, earlier evidence shows that the entire leadership of the Maoist party (either the so-called hardliner or soft) sits with a united version when there is dialogue/negotiation with other parties. Surprisingly, however, they show

---

[33] Uddhab Pd. Pyakurel, 'Nepal 2013: Constituent Assembly Elections' (New Delhi: IPCS), available online at http://www.ipcs.org/article/south-asia/year-in-review-nepal-2013-constituent-assembly-elections-4243.html (accessed 13 October 2014).

[34] See note 19.

their vertical division after the dialogue gets over and time comes for implementing it. If one takes the Kharipati plenum decision of the UCPN-M (held in the late November 2010) as an example, mainly two strategies were discussed in there and decided by the UCPN-M regarding the management of its combatants. The first one was to try to integrate all verified combatants into the NA, along with the senior combatants into the higher rank of the NA so that the NA as an institution would be either influenced or weakened through infiltration and division. The second was to keep them in the cantonment for long if the UCPN-M could not succeed in integrating all of them into the NA. One may ask the reason behind the Maoist's proposal to prolonging the life of the temporary cantonment with its combatants. The answer was very simple: it was the UCPN-M which wanted not to settle the issue so that it gets benefit financially and politically. In other words, the Maoist which had been receiving a huge amount of money from the cantonments,[35] the ultimate motto of the UCPN-M is to keep its combatants under its command forever, if not at least till the next election, so that the psychological strength of its leadership and bargaining capacity of the party remain high.

- The same thing was repeated during and after 28 May 2011 too; the entire leadership was together to put forward their agenda while their dialogue was on about how to go for another extension of the CA. Dahal himself not only shared the dais with Baidya, but also went on talking in Baidya's line on 27 May 2011. He stated, 'they are not surrendering weapons easily which was exchanged with human blood'.[36] As there were many things to be done by the Maoist party based on the 5-point agreement, a 'serious' rift again developed within the Maoist party.
- Generally, in the Maoist party, Baidya and Dahal used to be together to sideline Baburam Bhattarai. Even if there were differences in opinion between the formers, they used

---

[35] Uddhab Pd. Pyakurel, Maobadi Cantooonment Ko Samajsastha (Sociology of the Maoists' Cantonment) *Kantipur*, 23 January 2008 (in Neplai language).

[36] Prachanda, 'We Are Not Surrendering Weapons Easily Which Were Exchanged with Human Blood', *Kantipur*, May 13, 2011.

to show high regards to each other as they had publicly accepted their *guru–chela* relations. For example, Baidya, even after his group wrote a note of dissent on the party's decision to accept Nepal Army's proposal to go for army integration, and termed it as an 'act of capitulation to regressive forces', mentioned that 'there is conspiracies to create a rift between the chairman and him'.[37]

- Dahal, as a 'dynamic' politician, was acting the role of a peacemaker between the softliners and hardliners by saying that the party was indeed preparing for a revolt. For instance, once there was anxiety shown by the cadres about the Maoist's future along with the end of the peace process, he had said in his controversial video tape of January 2008, 'If we are going to place 10,000 combatants in the army, the whole force will come under our influence...' and that

> The form is very different. But the gist is still the same: we are both taking the revolution forward.... We need money to prepare for the revolt ... the need for 10 crore, to bring it all in a truck. We need money for what the truck carries; nobody gives it for free. We don't have enough money for that. Of the 60 crore, you will take a little bit, and about 20 crore will come to us. Just imagine the preparations we can do with 20 crore.[38]

Those who know such details of the intra-party politics within the party, then, considered the rift of the then Maoist party as an 'acting' or drama.[39] However, all the scepticism and doubts proved wrong, and the rift between Dahal and Baidya more widened ever since the former took the line of peace and constitution on 30 April 2011 and decided to accept Nepal Army's proposal on army integration and ending the dual security system of Maoist leaders. The miffed Baidya faction intensified its campaign countrywide. The mistrust was further intensified with

[37] 'Party Will Ultimately Follow My Line': Kiran, Interview of Maoist Senior Vice-chairman Mohan Baidya 'Kiran', *Republica*, 22 May 2011.
[38] http://bengalunderattack.blogspot.in/2009_05_01_archive.html (accessed 13 October 2014).
[39] Bijay Kumar, 'Rajnaitik Siddhanta Ra Jibanka Pharak Pharak Ranga' (Political Ideology and Different Dimensions of Life), *Kantipur*, 18 June 2011.

the Baidya faction circulating a two-page document to leaders and cadres alleging that Dahal was deviating from the official revolutionary line, putting aside the issue of national independence, heading towards a democratic republic instead of 'people's republic', disarming the combatants in the name of integration, accepting Indian investment in the hydropower sector, abusing party funds and attempting to maintain relations with the Indian intelligence. The document entitled 'Problems of Deviations in Chairman Comrade' has charged Dahal with financial irregularities and misuse of resources.[40] The document also criticizes Dahal for agreeing to make appointments of judges by a commission, not by the federal assembly as demanded by the party. The document expresses dissatisfaction over the party's move to go for 'federal democratic republic' instead of the party's line of 'People's Federal Democratic Republic'. The further points the document read are as follows:

- On the issue of financial discipline, Dahal is seen tilted towards corruption.
- Dahal is seen having the tendency of doing anything—both moral and immoral—for the sake of power, money and prestige.
- Dahal has deliberately left the party without an accounting system and misused financial means and resources in an individualistic way.
- Dahal is of 'self-centric individualistic tendency', intolerance towards those holding dissent and using his power to silence their voices.
- Dahal has developed a 'fascist tendency'.
- Dahal is extending relations with the Indian intelligence agencies.
- On the peace process, the hard-line faction has launched criticism campaigns against Dahal for bringing the Maoist combatants under the control of the Special Committee and accused him of disarming the PLA and emptying the cantonments in the name of 'regrouping' without forging a national security policy, controlling the open border and setting up a border security force.

[40] See note 19.

- Dahal deviated from the party's ideological goals by not launching appropriate programs to counter the party's 'principal enemy' — India — and accused Dahal of extending relations with the sympathizers of 'Indian expansionism and its comprador class'.
- Despite being said that we would go for a federal system with autonomy to ethnicities, Dahal emphasized unitary and centralized system.
- Dahal has agreed to go for bicameral legislature succumbing to the 'bourgeois theory of separation of power, and to minimize the participation of people in the judiciary under the pretext of judicial independence, instead of empowering the "People's Assembly"'.

Once again Maoist Chairman Dahal went to the strategy to convince the Baidya faction by shifting his focus for the time being to the constitution writing process to ensure that it moves ahead simultaneously[41] with the peace process in the next three months. However, Baidya who had disowned the five-point deal that led to the extension of the CA tenure on 28 May 2011 objected to Dahal's decisions, including the one to send Maoist combatants to deploy for the security of Maoist leaders to cantonments and handing over their weapons to the Special Committee. In fact, the Baidya faction lately launched vitriolic polemics against Dahal and registered a series of notes of dissent against the party's decision. The relations between the hard-line faction and the moderators further strained after the party establishment decided to end security being provided by Maoist combatants to the senior party leaders. For the Baidya faction, any move by the party to hand over weapons or combatants to the government would tantamount to a complete 'surrender' and dishonour for the combatants.

When the Baidya faction knew Dahal's position to take any risk to complete the army integration, they saw him as 'steadily sowing seeds of revisionism since long in the guise of the creative application and development of Marxism–Leninism–Maoism'. However, Dahal continued defending his position stating that these decisions were 'in order to prevent counter-revolution in the

[41] http://www.ekantipur.com/2011/06/04/top-story/peace-statute-will-go-side-by-side-dahal/335115.html

21st century it is necessary to develop democracy'. They saw that 'these logics were brought about to pave the way for assimilating bourgeois parliament by the party and consequently reversing revolution in the name of preventing counter-revolution'.[42] Once the rift between Dahal and Baidya took a critical shape, the latter started to hit each and every step taken by Dahal; while he did not issue even a statement when comrade Azad, the spokesperson, and comrade Kishenji, the politburo member, of the CPI-M were killed, but he sent a condolence letter along with a Central Committee representative to attend the funeral of Jyoti Basu, a leader of revisionist CPI-M and the ex-chief minister of West Bengal, Dahal was criticized saying that his attempt was to 'please his masters in India'. In this way, problems went on increasing within the UCPN-M, until the final spark that was given by the issue of the handing over to the Special Committee the keys of the weapons containers kept at the 28 cantonments for Maoist combatants in September 2011.

In the context where their base areas and the local 'people's governments' were already dissolved, the disarmament and dissolving of the Maoist combatants were seen by the hardliners as an act of capitulation to regressive forces. Finally, the Baidya faction launched a public campaign on March 2012 against Maoist Chairperson Dahal and Dr Bhattarai. They demanded the resignation of Bhattarai as the prime minister, accusing his government of being 'anti-national' and 'deviating from the party's core ideology'.[43] On 11 April 2012, the Nepal Army took charge of the cantonments, combatants and the weapons stored in containers inside the camps. On June 2012, the Baidya faction formally announced the formation of a new party, CPN-M. The announcement of the split from the UCPN-M and the formation of the new outfit came at the end of the three-day national gathering of Baidya followers in Kathmandu.

We have seen above that the issue management of Maoist combatants became a spark for the split of the UCPN-M. The reason is that in the Maoist theory, army plays a central role for bringing

---

[42] Mike Ely, 'Nepal's Basanta: Re-evaluating Prachanda and His Path', *Revolution in South Asia*, 31 August 2012, available online at http://southasiarev.wordpress.com/2012/08/31/basanta/ (accessed13 October 2014).

[43] See note 20.

a revolution to establish socialism under the state. Mao considers 'war is a continuation of politics. In this sense war is politics and war itself is a political action; since ancient times there has never been a war that did not have a political character'.[44] He sees the need of the political mobilization of people and the revolutionary army for success. He gives importance to guerrilla warfare as a necessity, 'but loses no chance for mobile warfare under favourable conditions'. Here, one thing becomes clear that the Baidya faction was following the words of Mao so the issue of Maoist army's end gave the last pretext for the spilt in the party. However, the experiences of the various party factions among the Nepali Maoists showed that split was inevitable. Soon after the split, Baidya justified his action by saying that 'the separation happened according to the Marxist philosophy of unity, struggle, transformation and split'[45] implying that the split is seen as a natural process in communist parties. His argument is a way valid as we could count at least four breakaway factions of the Maoist party in Nepal within two decades—from 1994 to 2009.

In conclusion, though the leaders generally cited one reason or the other for the splits, lack of capacity and confidence of the leadership to manage 'opposition and struggle between ideas of different kinds' has become instrumental resulting in the split of the party. It seems that Nepali Maoist followed Mao's idea as mentioned earlier that if there would be no contradictions in the party and no ideological struggles to resolve them, the party's life would end, clearly implying the struggle between the different lines or groups within the party without realizing their own context and limitation. The Maoist is no longer in underground politics, but it has become a part of the democratic system. Here, the people of Nepal expect political groups and leader to behave in a transparent and accountable manner; media including those media houses with their corporate interest become very powerful in creating/defaming the political discourse in an open society; recently, even social media became so powerful to be part of the

---

[44] http://www.marxists.org/reference/archive/mao/selected-works/volume-2/mswv2_09.htm. Mao Tse-tung, On Protracted War (May 1938).
[45] http://www.telegraphnepal.com/headline/2012-06-30/no-treachery-against-mother-nepal-split-was-natural:-mohan-baidya (accessed 13 October 2014).

social interaction. It seems that they are yet to realize these very facts while subscribing some 'ism' in a different context. It is obviously not good for a young democracy like Nepal to witness often split of political parties. However, it can be taken positively if Nepalese leaders tried to learn a lesson from the past and correct themselves by being more transparent, less doublespeak, less populist and more democrats. Once leaders make the practice of democracy as their way of life, politics will not only attract young generations but also help clean the 'dirty' image of politics resulting in a lasting peace and prosperity of the people of Nepal.

12

Sri Lanka: Positive Peace at a Distance

N. Manoharan

Even after five years since the end of *Eelam War IV*, ghosts of conflict continue to haunt Sri Lanka. During the conflict that ended in May 2009, even by conservative estimates, over 20,000 civilians perished, about 6,500 government troops killed and nearly 15,000 rebels lost their lives. This does not include thousands of injured in all the three categories. The conflict also displaced thousands of civilians. According to the United Nations High Commissioner for Refugees (UNHCR), over 300,000 were internally displaced persons (IDPs) and hundreds fled as refugees to other countries, especially to India. The outward flow of Tamils, both legally and illegally, continues, especially to the West. Emigration in the form of *boat people* is a concern. Although the Government of Sri Lanka officially winded up the IDP camps, the resettlement phase is still on. Reconciliation is in progress, but not in an appreciable manner. The most worrying aspect is the long-term political settlement to the ethnic issue, which is on the reverse gear. The defeat of the Liberation Tigers of Tamil Eelam (LTTE) is certainly a big relief not only to Sri Lankans, but also to the whole region. However, how far the demise of the LTTE has translated into peace in the island is a big question.

This is where the purpose of peace audit lies. While performing a peace audit in Sri Lanka, certain crucial questions come to the fore: What is the status of peace since the end of *Eelam War IV*? Does it prevail in the absolute sense or in parts? What are the various hurdles in establishing positive peace in the island state? What should be done about it?

Auditing Peace: Concept and Methodology

Peace is commonly understood in negative sense: the absence of hostility. Such understanding, however, ignores the residual feelings of mistrust and suspicion that the winners and losers of a war harbour towards each other, especially in the post-conflict situation. Hence, it is also important to take into account the positive aspect so as to have a holistic understanding of peace. If looked at in a comprehensive sense, peace (apart from the absence of conflict) is also sincere attempts on addressing reconciliation, the existence of healthy or newly healed interpersonal or international relationships, prosperity in matters of social or economic welfare, the establishment of equality and a working political order that serves the true interests of all.

Apart from this, a comprehensive understanding of peace, the audit exercise here takes into consideration pertinent indicators used in three indices: *Global Peace Index* (GPI), *Positive Peace Index* (PPI) and *Failed State Index* (FSI). They are chosen to reflect *negative* (GPI) and *positive* (PPI) aspects of peace and also institutions that are responsible for maintaining them (FSI). The GPI lists 22 qualitative and quantitative indicators in three broad themes: (a) the level of safety and security in society, (b) the extent of domestic or international conflict and (c) the degree of militarization.[1] The PPI identifies eight key categories known as the *Pillars of Peace*. They include: well-functioning government, sound business environment, equitable distribution of resources, acceptance of the rights of others, good relations with neighbours, free flow of information, high levels of human capital and low levels of corruption.[2] The FSI goes by 12 indicators under three broad categories: social, economic and politico-military. Under social indicators, four are

---

[1] GPI 2013, available online at http://economicsandpeace.org/research/iep-indices-data/global-peace-index (accessed 13 December 2013).

[2] PPI 2013, available online at http://www.visionofhumanity.org/pdf/gpi/2013_Global_Peace_Index_Report.pdf (accessed 13 December 2013).

identified: mounting demographic pressures, massive movement of refugees or IDPs, legacy of vengeance-seeking group grievance or group paranoia and chronic and sustained human flight. Economic indicators include uneven economic development along group lines and sharp and/or severe economic decline. Politico-military indicators comprise criminalization and/or delegitimization of the state, progressive deterioration of public services, suspension or arbitrary application of the rule of law and widespread human rights abuse, security apparatus operates as a *state within a state*, rise of factionalized elites and intervention of other states or external political actors.[3]

The Sri Lankan Case

An attempt is made to audit peace in Sri Lanka using indicators used by the three indices identified above but in three broad categories: security, development and political.

Security

Security has been the topmost priority for the government of Sri Lanka after the end of *Eelam War*. Hence, a *demilitarization* strategy has been put in place that is aimed at preventing any regroup of the LTTE in any form in the near or distant future and internally or externally.[4] In this regard, the *strategy* took care of two things on the ground: maintain large military presence in the Tamil-dominated Northeast of Sri Lanka, and make sure that the surrendered LTTE remnants do not pick up arms once again against the state. The strategy continued in 2013 as well.

---

[3] FSI 2013, available online at http://library.fundforpeace.org/fsi13 (accessed 14 December 2013).
[4] A broad outline of Sri Lanka's 'National Security Strategy' was articulated by the island state's Defence Secretary, Gotabhaya Rajapaksa, during a lecture at Kotelawala Defence University on 13 June 2013. Full text of the speech is available online at http://www.defence.lk/new.asp?fname=Sri_Lanka_National_Security_Concerns_20130613_08 (accessed 14 December 2013).

Military presence in the Tamil-dominated Northeast of Sri Lanka exists in the form of the creation of several *high-security zones* (HSZs) despite recommendations from the Lessons Learnt and Reconciliation Commission (LLRC), and despite calls from the international community to scale them down. In its report, submitted in January 2013, the Army Board on the implementation of the recommendations of the LLRC insisted that 'there is an absolute need to locate our armed forces at strategically important locations'[5] to protect military camps, strategic installations and the lifelines of the security forces. The presence of armed forces is also justified in the name of *development work* in the conflict-affected areas.

The HSZs comprise large chunks of territory in the Jaffna peninsula, districts of Mullaitivu, Kilinochchi and Trincomalee. Since it involves occupying large tracts of residential and agricultural lands, the HSZs have resulted in displacing thousands of residents apart from depriving many farmers of their livelihood. They restrict the freedom of movement to people in surrounding areas, but also remain as a symbol of domination, at least in the perception of Tamils. In terms of numbers, 16 of 19 divisions of the Sri Lankan Army remained in the Northeast of the island. This does not include the presence of Navy and Air Force personnel.[6] Although the government claimed that it has reduced the area of occupation by 40 per cent and the number of troops in the Jaffna Peninsula by 20,000 in 2012–2013, it looks like they will remain as a permanent feature of the region.[7]

Yet another *demilitarization* component that has been followed is in the form of the rehabilitation of the former LTTE cadres. Appreciably, and thanks partly due to international pressure, within months of the formal end of violent ethnic conflict, the 'National Action Plan for the Reintegration of Ex-combatants' was put in place by the Government of Sri Lanka. Called by President

---

[5] See para 15 of chapter 3 of the report. The full report is available online at http://www.army.lk/docimages/image/LLRC_2013.pdf (accessed 1 January 2014).

[6] Nirupama Subramanian, 'Sri Lanka Army Still Has Large Presence in North & East', *Hindu*, Chennai, 19 September 2012.

[7] P.K. Balachandran, 'High Security Zones Cut by 40 Percent, Claims Lanka', *New Indian Express*, Chennai, 24 June 2012.

Rajapaksa as 'Humanitarian Mission-02', the framework of reintegration covered five aspects: disarmament and demobilization, rehabilitation, reinsertion, social reintegration and economic reintegration.[8] The tigers in custody were broadly divided into three categories: those who were forcefully recruited (mostly children), non-combatant members and hardcore combatants. Separate *welfare centres* for each category were set up—24 in all—in the districts of Jaffna, Batticaloa and Vavuniya to rehabilitate them.[9] The first category—comprised of 556 child combatants—was said to be provided with catch-up education classes and allowed family visits and reunion. Nevertheless, free access to specialized independent international agencies such as Save the Child, United Nations International Children's Emergency Fund (UNICEF) and the International Committee of the Red Cross (ICRC) could have made the rehabilitation more successful. Instead of just limiting with secondary education, the programme should go beyond in turning the former child soldiers into useful citizens. Also, their psycho-social problems require bit more attention.[10]

Those identified as *hardcore* cadres were separated out to extract maximum information on the LTTE remnants, their *sleeper cells*, existing network, future plans of revival and hidden weapons/mines. In the initial stages, there were human rights abuses in the rehabilitation process, but they mellowed down later. No distinction was made between leaders and ordinary cadres in this regard. Some of the former LTTE heavyweights are now working with the Sri Lankan Military Intelligence in neutralizing the internal and external networks of the LTTE.[11] They are expected to

---

[8] Interestingly, the work of drafting of the framework commenced in March 2009 itself, over two months before the formal end of war. Full text of the document is available online at http://www.ilo.org/wcmsp5/groups/public/−ed_emp/−emp_ent/−ifp_crisis/documents/publication/wcms_116478.pdf (accessed 10 January 2013).

[9] Bureau of the Commissioner General of Rehabilitation, 'Rehabilitation, Resettlement of Ex-LTTEers, a Success', 2011, http://www.bcgr.gov.lk/news.php?id=108 (accessed 12 December 2012).

[10] UNHCR, 'Sri Lanka: Former Child Soldiers Struggle for a Normal Life', 10 November 2010, available online at http://www.unhcr.org/refworld/country,,IRIN,,LKA,,4cdd263f14,0.html (accessed 14 December 2012).

[11] 'Ex LTTE Cadres Despatched Overseas to Spy for MoD', *Sri Lanka Guardian*, Colombo, 4 December 2011.

undergo legal proceedings after the rehabilitation process, which, in turn, may depend on the *level of cooperation* they render to the government. On the non-combatant front, the government has been bit easy. Releases of those who successfully complete the rehabilitation programme are made from time to time. On 9 September 2013, 107 ex-cadres were released from Maradamadu and Poonthottam rehabilitation centres in Vavuniya. As per government statistics, only 232 cadres remained in the *welfare centres*.[12]

However, despite rehabilitation and reintegration, the stigma as former Tigers remains. The Sri Lankan government has not done much in easing this stain. On the other hand, the government's strategy of releasing the rehabilitated with much media hype has, in fact, increased the stigma factor due to wide publicity and dissemination of their identities. Also, due to their past activities, the physical security of many of the former tigers is in jeopardy. They should be secured. There is also apprehension among the rehabilitated cadres being under watchful eyes of security forces and the chances of them getting detained anytime are high.[13] It is the duty of the government to mellow down such trepidation. The government should also consider the periodic orientation of those reintegrated ex-militants just to make sure that they do not slip away from the right path in the long run. The government has ruled out absorbing them into the armed forces, but about 2,000 ex-cadres have joined Civil Defence Force.[14] Sadly, the plan of action also completely ignores empowering the disabled former Tigers otherwise. It is not too late to address the lacuna. Overall, the proper reintegration of former militants back into the mainstream society is one of the vital components of rebuilding post-conflict societies. If the reintegration

---

[12] Policy Research & Information Unit of the Presidential Secretariat of Sri Lanka, 'Another Batch of Rehabilitated Ex-LTTE Cadres to Be Integrated', 9 September 2013, available online at http://www.priu.gov.lk/news_update/Current_Affairs/ca201309/20130909another_batch_rehabilitated_ex_ltte_cadres_integrated.htm (accessed 1 January 2014).

[13] Charles Haviland, 'Sri Lanka: Former Tamil Tigers Complain of Harassment', *BBC News*, 29 July 2011.

[14] Ministry of Rehabilitation and Prison Reforms, 'Rehabilitated LTTE Cadres Join the Civil Defence Force', 1 October 2012, available online at http://www.reprimin.gov.lk/index.php/en/news/175-rehabilitated-ltte-cadres-join-the-civil-defence-force (accessed 16 December 2013).

programme of the Sri Lankan government is attractive, the dispersed tigers may surface to join the mainstream.

Though the LTTE has been decimated, and most of its leaders and cadres killed or surrendered, its external network persists. There is a fear in the security establishment of Sri Lanka that using this network the Tiger remnants may try to regroup. The priority for Colombo, therefore, is to apprehend LTTE leadership living abroad and smash the international wing of the LTTE completely.[15] To achieve this objective, Sri Lanka appointed military and intelligence officials in key Sri Lankan embassies, especially in Europe, as diplomats to personally oversee the operation and lobby local governments to prevail on LTTE activities, direct appeal for deportation to states where LTTE leaders are held up and highlight to the international community that the international tiger network could be used by other terror groups and mafia. Colombo is also mindful of a million-strong Sri Lankan Tamil diaspora, spread across the world, as a crucial factor for any revival of the LTTE. Although the diaspora is divided on core issues like the end goal of Tamil Eelam and the means to achieve it, it is believed that it may throw a lifeline to militants when in need. Of course, the diaspora continue to lobby for accountability on human rights abuses committed by Sri Lankan armed forces during *Eelam War IV*, but not beyond that.[16]

However, the demilitarization strategy of the government has been one-sided; it did not apply to state forces. Colombo, in fact, did not demobilize the armed forces once the war was over, making Sri Lanka as one of the most militarized societies in the world, roughly at a ratio of one security personnel per 525 subjects; neither there was moderation in the defence budget. In fact, 2013 witnessed a 25 per cent increase over the previous year's budget allocation (about $2 billion). The government also did not

---

[15] Rohan Gunaratne, 'A Post-war Challenge for Sri Lanka: Dismantling the LTTE Overseas and Rebuilding a Sri Lankan Identity', lecture delivered in the auditorium of the Sri Lanka Foundation Institute on the invitation of the Nandadasa Kodagoda Memorial Trust, 2 August 2010, available online at http://www.srilankaguardian.org/2010/08/post-war-challenge-for-sri-lanka.html (accessed 13 December 2013).

[16] International Crisis Group, 'The Sri Lankan Tamil Diaspora After the LTTE', Report No. 186, 23 February 2010.

bother much on the effects such as human rights abuses, prowling of *white van gangs*, media stifling and impact of *HSZs*. It is this securitization, over-centralization and insensitivity towards pluralism that pose dangers for future nation-building and sustainable peace in Sri Lanka.

Development

Development is an important component in establishing sustainable peace in any post-conflict society. Linking the two variables—*peace* and *development*—Sri Lanka President Mahinda Rajapaksa observed: 'Without peace you cannot have development, and without development you cannot have peace. But the biggest achievement of all is the peace itself.'[17] Not long ago, Rajapaksa wished to make Sri Lanka 'a model for by itself... a hub for education, aviation, shipping, communications and tourism'.[18] The United People's Freedom Alliance (UPFA) regime strongly believes that the existing issue is not an ethnic question, but only a problem of development. The belief, therefore, is that the ethnic issue will *wither away* if development is taken care of.

Even after five years of termination of the armed component of the ethnic conflict, the Sri Lankan economy is still reeling under the after-effects of the three-decade-old war. The island is suffering from expensive short-term foreign debt, declining foreign exchange reserves and a high deficit. The global economic crisis has added to the woes by hitting key export sectors such as tea and garments and foreign direct investments. Though Sri Lanka pushes ahead in the transition to a middle-income economy, it has to face 'additional pressure on already stretched resources and economic opportunities, from greater urbanization, environmental degradation, changes in aspirations on the type of employment sought by young people, and changes to the country's epidemiological profile'.[19] Appreciably, inflation has come

---

[17] Greg Sheridan, 'Sri Lanka: A Nation at Peace', Mahinda Rajapaksa's interview, *Australian*, 31 August 2013.

[18] Ravi Velloor, 'A Man Who Loves His Country', Mahinda Rajapaksa's interview, *Strait Times*, 18 March 2010.

[19] Institute of Policy Studies of Sri Lanka, *Sri Lanka: State of the Economy – 2013* (Colombo: Institute of Policy Studies of Sri Lanka, 2013).

down, but is still a cause of concern to the common man whose real income has not kept pace with the inflation. As per the Asian Development Bank, the Gross Domestic Product (GDP) grew at 6.8 per cent in 2013, up from 6.2 per cent in 2012, but down from 8 per cent in 2011.[20] The government is counting on aid flows meant for post-war reconstruction to bail itself out of the crisis. The flow of external aid, however, depends on two factors: how well the global economy revives itself from the current slowdown, and how well the Sri Lankan government reconciles with the international community in addressing the latter's concerns on accountability issues. At the same time, one cannot discount the fact that durable peace can bring a turnaround to the ailing economy.

The Northeast of Sri Lanka is presently the most underdeveloped region in the island. After the *liberation of the East*, in July 2007, the government ventured on the path of its development in the name of *Nagenahira Navodaya* (*Eastern Awakening*). Development programme in the North, after the formal end of conflict in May 2009, has been undertaken in the name of *Uthuru Wasanthaya* (*Northern Spring*) that involves the reconstruction of the war-ravaged areas, resettlement of the conflict-displaced and security. Since the development programme in the East commenced much early, the situation is comparatively better, if not up to the mark.[21]

Under the 'Presidential Task Force for the Development of the Northern Province', the process of development in the North has been proceeding on some logic such as the demining of areas meant for resettlement and reconstruction, and building up of basic infrastructure such as houses, roads, schools, energy grid, telecommunication, etc. Providing livelihood opportunities to all the resettled IDPs is yet another mammoth task before the government.[22] The government finds lack of sufficient resources as the major

---

[20] Asian Development Bank, 'Sri Lanka Economy', 2013, available online at http://www.adb.org/countries/sri-lanka/economy (accessed 16 December 2013).

[21] Sumith Chaaminda, 'Uthuru Wasanthaya and Negenahira Navodaya: Analyzing the Development Discourse', *Colombo Telegraph*, 24 March 2012.

[22] The Task Force, in consultation with the UN, national and international non-governmental organizations (NGOs) and international organizations (IOs), developed a Joint Action Plan for Assistance (JPA) for the Northern Province. Full text of the JPA is available online at http://www.hpsl.lk/docs/2012_JPA_21_February_2012-FINAL.pdf (accessed 26 December 2013).

challenge confronting its reconstruction plans. Initial estimates suggest requirement of over $2 billion for the purpose. Local funds are in short supply, but external sources of finances are reasonable. But Sri Lanka wants them without any strings attached, especially of human rights enquiries, monitoring and accountability. As a result, Sri Lanka has not been able to tap external funds effectively. The government has also not utilized aid and development agencies fearing their help in LTTE's revival, which is an unfound apprehension. In addition to the government of Sri Lanka, three broad categories of actors are involved in the postwar reconstruction: intergovernmental organizations, state actors and local non-governmental organizations. Principal state actors involved in Sri Lanka include India, China, Japan, Libya, Pakistan, Iran, the US and the European Union. Interestingly, Asian countries are dominantly present instead of Western predominance in such tasks. However, there seems to be no proper cohesion in the functioning of these actors in achieving the common objective.

Political

There are two aspects under this component: *democratization* and finding long-term political settlement to the ethnic issue.

Democratization

Although the *democratization* strategy in the post-conflict phase was justified by President Rajapaksa to give 'voice to the people', it was basically to consolidate the power of the ruling coalition — UPFA — at every level: national, provincial and local.

Mahinda Rajapakse, soon after his re-election as the Executive President in January 2010, dissolved the parliament and announced elections scheduled for April 2010. For the first time in two decades, there was no diktat for the Tamil voters from the LTTE. TNA underwent a split between hard-line and moderate leaders. Janata Vimukti Preamuna (JVP), which surprised everyone by emerging as the third largest party in the previous parliamentary polls, also witnessed splits. The main opposition, United National Party (UNP), was also at its lowest point in the political history of Sri Lanka. All these factors, apart from Rajapaksa's charisma, helped the ruling UPFA to secure a landslide victory (144 out of 225 seats). This was the first time in the history of Sri Lanka that a party or coalition got a comfortable majority under the proportional representation system.

Within months after the war, the government conducted elections to local bodies of Jaffna and Vavuniya. In the polls that took place on 8 August 2009, the ruling UPFA won the Jaffna Urban Council and the Tamil National Alliance (TNA), considered as the LTTE proxy, won the Vavuniya Municipal Council. These were the first elections held in the Tamil-dominated areas after the formal end of the ethnic war in the island. In the Provincial Council elections held in September 2012, the UPFA secured a majority along with the Sri Lanka Muslim Congress (SLMC) and formed a government.[23] The elections, however, signified that Tamils still nurture grievances and look forward to a responsible leadership.

Significantly, polls for the entire Northern Province were also conducted in September 2013, for the first time in 25 years. The TNA won 30 out of 38 seats (that included two bonus seats) and formed the government in the Northern Province of Sri Lanka. Interestingly, the UPFA that won in the other two Provinces (Northwestern and Central) got seven seats, and the SLMC got one seat.[24] The fact that the TNA participated in the provincial polls is itself a positive development because it boycotted the Eastern Provincial Council elections in 2008.

In the electoral exercises held thus far, including those in 2013, the use of state resources and power by the ruling coalition was very much evident to the disadvantage of the opposition parties. Then, there were undemocratic actions such as stifling the media, silencing the civil society and splitting and intimidating opposition parties. Those sections of the media that dared to take an independent and objective line were suppressed by various means. Informally, tactics like killings, beatings, kidnappings, intimidations and threats were used to deter media personnel from writing on *sensitive issues*. The aim was to put them on *self-censorship mode*. Those who failed to fall in line were threatened

---

[23] R.K. Radhakrishnan, 'UPFA Leader Becomes CM', *Hindu*, 18 September 2012.

[24] Charles Haviland, 'Sri Lanka's Main Tamil Party Wins Key Vote in the North', *BBC News*, 22 September 2013.

with *dire consequences* and international media personnel were expelled from the country.[25] Crucially, the Rajapaksa regime was not interested in empowering the local and provincial councils enough to take care of the governance at their levels.

But, the most worrying action was when the Sri Lankan President Mahinda Rajapaksa signed an order removing the island state's Supreme Court Chief Justice Shirani Bandaranaike on 13 January 2013. The judiciary usually toed the government line. Even Shirani Bandaranayake, as the Chief Justice, gave several pro-government judgements, notable among them being validating the 18th Amendment and the abolition of independent commissions. However, when she disagreed with the government on the Divi Neguma Bill (that overlooked provinces on managing development funds), trouble started. An 11-member Parliament Select Committee (PSC) found her guilty of three charges that included failing to declare her earnings, of hearing a case in which she had an interest, and of continuing to hold the position of Chief Justice while a case against her husband was pending. Ironically, the PSC became exclusively of ruling members when the Opposition parties pulled out. Shirani Bandaranayake herself boycotted the hearings doubting a fair hearing. Despite Court of Appeal's restraint, and despite Supreme Court's ruling that the PSC had *no legal authority* to declare guilty or pronounce a decision affecting the rights of the judge, the parliament went ahead in impeaching the Chief Justice. The voting count was 155 to 49, with 20 abstentions. The entire impeachment and removal process just took four months, which is unimaginable in India. This was the first time that a serving Chief Justice of the Supreme Court, with over 11 years of service remaining, got removed.[26]

By appointing his Cabinet's legal advisor, Mohan Peiris, as the new Chief Justice, Rajapaksa has now consolidated all powers in the Presidency. *Separation of powers*, the Montesquieun model for governance of a democratic state, is no more. Media, considered as the *fourth pillar* of democracy, has already been subdued. A constitutional dictatorship has set in. What is more concerning, in the

---

[25] United States Embassy in Sri Lanka, 'U.S. Concerned Over Moves to Stifle Free Expression', 29 November 2012.

[26] R.K. Radhakrishnan, 'Rajapaksa Dismisses Chief Justice', *Hindu*, 13 January 2013.

case of the judiciary, is the way in which the Chief Justice was removed. Due process was not followed. President Rajapaksa, however, defended his decision by holding that he had acted in line with the constitution. But, the president himself has admitted that the constitution is *imperfect*. Then, is it not time to correct those *imperfections*? Who else is in a better position with requisite majority than Rajapaksa to do it?

Ethnic Question

Finding a lasting political settlement by taking into account the root causes and grievances of the aggrieved communities is vital to establishing sustainable peace. However, in the Sri Lankan case, efforts to find a long-term political settlement to the ethnic issue are nowhere in sight. Devolution of powers to the minorities seems to be the last priority. The Rajapaksa government has been talking of finding a *home-grown solution* to the ethnic issue. In this regard, President Rajapaksa did indeed appoint an All Party Representative Committee (APRC) in 2006 to 'fashion creative options that satisfy minimum expectations as well as provide a comprehensive approach to the resolution of the national question'. However, instead of exploring *creative options*, the APRC, in its interim report submitted in January 2008, advised the president to implement the 13th Amendment to the constitution.[27] Even after 25 years, ideas for seeking a solution to the ethnic question were back to square one. At last, the APRC reportedly submitted its final report to the president in August 2009. The president, however, chose not to make it public. It is more or less dead now.

At a later date, in an interview, President Mahinda Rajapaksa outlined his thoughts on devolution succinctly when he said, 'We are keen on a sustainable political settlement. But it must have wide acceptance, especially in the context of the post-conflict situation.'[28] With this pronouncement, the writing on the wall was

[27] B. Muralidhar Reddy, 'Sri Lanka: Full Implementation of 13th Amendment Recommended', *Hindu*, 24 January 2008.
[28] Policy Research & Information Unit of the Presidential Secretariat of Sri Lanka, 'Equality of Opportunity Would Be a Better Approach', 29 December 2011, available online at http://www.priu.gov.lk/news_update/Current_Affairs/ca201112/20111229equality_opportunity_better_approach.htm (accessed 1 January 2014).

clear: Colombo would deal with the ethnic issue from the position of strength. Federalism that was once on cards has been ruled out once and for all. Other options such as devolution based on 2,000 proposals, the APRC or even on some features of the LLRC are not under consideration.

At most, what is on cards is some arrangement revolving around the existing 13th Amendment. Through the 13th Amendment, Sri Lanka was divided into nine provinces, each governed by a council headed by an elected Chief Minister. It also merged the North and the East into one province called the Northeast Province, made Tamil an official language along with Sinhala and divided powers under three lists (provincial, reserved and concurrent). Police and land powers were never devolved. The provinces, especially the Northeast, struggled without adequate financial powers. In January 2007, thanks to the Sri Lankan Supreme Court ruling, the Northeast Province was demerged. Amendments to the constitution, such as the 18th, centralized even more powers in the executive (read president), thus, eroding the autonomy and integrity of all other institutions, including the provincial ones. Since Colombo never implemented all the provisions of the 13th Amendment, there have never been *13*, but only *13-minus*.

Personally, President Rajapaksa who initially committed to go 'beyond 13th Amendment' changed track later by holding that 'there is no ethnic issue but only development issue'. Now, the latest move is the appointment of a PSC to review the whole 13th Amendment arrangement.[29] The PSC, however, remains a non-starter because of non-participation of opposition parties such as the UNP and the TNA and even coalition partners such as the SLMC. Hardline parties such as the JVP, National Freedom Front (NFF) and Jathika Hela Urumaya (JHU) have of late started arguing that the Provincial Council system is a divisive mechanism and 'does not suit' a country like Sri Lanka. The system, to them, was not indigenous, but was 'forced on Sri Lanka' by external forces such as India, and hence, the 13th Amendment should go. Unfortunately, a section of the government, led by the president's brother and Defence Secretary, Gotabhaya Rajapaksa, subscribes to this viewpoint. On the other

---

[29] K.T. Rajasingham, 'Sri Lanka: Parliamentary Select Committee on Constitutional Changes Appointed', *Asian Tribune*, 21 June 2013.

hand, a dominant section of the present UPFA government including President Mahinda Rajapaksa support the dilution of the Provincial Council system, termed as the '13th Amendment Minus' framework. The argument is since whatever limited police and land powers that are vested with the provinces were not practically implemented, it is practical to devolve only those implementable portions.

On reconciliation, to pre-empt the United Nations' (UN) move to appoint an experts panel on *war crimes* during the last stages of war, the Sri Lankan President appointed an eight-member LLRC in May 2010. The LLRC is a good step, but its mandate is very limited, and ethnic reconciliation in the real sense has not been looked into seriously. As per the notification, the Commission was mandated to inquire into and report on the facts and circumstances which led to the failure of the ceasefire agreement (CFA) operationalized on 21 February 2002, and the sequence of events that followed thereafter up to 19 May 2009 when the war ended; whether any person, group or institution directly or indirectly bears responsibility; lessons to learn from those events and their attendant concerns in order to ensure that there will be no recurrence; and methodology whereby restitution to any person affected by those events, or their dependents or their heirs, can be effected. The assumption was that the CFA was a failure, which is not correct. Although it is claimed that the LLRC is based on the model of the Truth and Reconciliation Commission of South Africa, there is no mechanism for reconciliation in the real sense. When the LLRC submitted its report in December 2011, things became clear. Although it was not 100 per cent objective, it was not disappointing either. It tried to do a balancing act, containing both positive and negative aspects. On positives, it talked about the need for demilitarization and investigation of disappearances, apart from acknowledging the existence of ethnic grievances; surprisingly, it supported the devolution of powers to minorities, although it did not spell them out. At the same time, it did not fix accountability for human rights abuses during Eelam War IV. The collateral damage, the report reasoned out, was a result of LTTE action and military reaction. Most importantly, the LLRC did not give any action plan on the way forward either on reconciliation or devolution. Yet, the major concern is that the report was not taken seriously and acted upon by the Rajapaksa government.

It was with this concern that a US-sponsored resolution was passed in UNHCR in March 2012 and once again in March 2013. India voted in favour of the resolution. The objective behind the move was not to condemn Sri Lanka, but to 'sow the seeds of lasting peace'. It was pointed out that the 'real reconciliation must be based on accountability, not impunity'. The Court of Inquiry appointed by the Sri Lankan Army was considered to be 'too late and too little'. Since it was not independent, its findings might not be impartial. However, to Colombo, any UN action 'would only lead to derailing the ongoing reconciliation process that has been put in place by the government'. Some in the regime went to the extent of arguing that, 'If we submit to this resolution, Tiger terrorists will raise their head again.' Instead of getting sensitive, Sri Lanka should seriously implement all the recommendations of the LLRC. Thanks to the international pressure, there is some progress in the implementation within a framework of a 'National Plan of Action'. The pace, however, is not encouraging.

Recommendations: For Real and Sustainable Peace

On the basis of audit, it is discerned that post-LTTE Sri Lanka is indeed a far more peaceful country. On the surface, peace prevails in Sri Lanka in the negative sense: absence of conflict. A sustainable peace can only be achieved when Sri Lanka reconciles with its minority communities, reaches out to the Opposition that is presently weak and polarized, practices democracy in the real sense, desecuritizes its functions and makes up with the international community.

Perceptions of what constitutes real and sustainable peace in Sri Lanka differ for the two dominant actors of the island: the government of Sri Lanka under Mahinda Rajapaksa and the Sri Lankan Tamil community presently represented, by and large, by the TNA. To President Rajapaksa, peace prevails in Sri Lanka since May 2009 after the *defeat of terrorism*. To TNA, however, absence of war does not mean that real peace has been achieved. Instead, what prevails is only *negative peace*. Peace in the real sense will be realized only when all displaced persons are resettled, when all the interned Tigers are rehabilitated, when the security apparatus of the state has been wound up and when the ethnic issue is settled to the satisfaction of the Tamil community. It is this perceptional difference that remains the major stumbling block for establishing real and perpetual peace in the island. This should be bridged.

Dubbed as the *greatest terrorist rehabilitation in the world history*, the rehabilitation and re-integration of former child and adult LTTE cadres is yet another issue that requires serious attention of the Sri Lankan government. Child soldiers were looked after well. The government has recently been releasing *innocent* cadres, but the exact nature of their rehabilitation post release should be transparent. The government is also ambiguous about the reintegration of the remaining *hard-core* adult cadres, as there is a concern of re-arrests.

There is an urgent need to find a credible and sustainable political solution to the ethnic issue. So long as the grievances that give rise to militant groups like the LTTE remain, violent resistance will continue. No ethnic strife can be settled without addressing its root causes. President Rajapaksa has to acknowledge this and work in a serious manner. In the present situation, devolution of powers to provinces through the '13th Amendment Plus' is a realistic option. There will be stiff opposition from the Sinhalese hardliners. However, riding on popular support, the president should be in a position to withstand these nationalistic pressures and forge an island-wide consensus for a lasting solution to the ethnic question. Formation of local councils in Jaffna and Vavuniya and conduct of Northern Provincial Council elections are appreciable, but they should be entrusted with sufficient resources and autonomy.

The Rajapaksa government also has to go beyond constitutional tinkering in reaching out to minorities by showing magnanimity. Trust deficit that exists between various communities of the island must be bridged on a priority basis. Talks with TNA were a good move, but they did not take things any further. Any confidence-building measure will go a long way in even convincing the Tamil diaspora that is presently keeping the hopes of Tamil Eelam alive. It is important for the Sri Lankan government to engage the diaspora to make them positively contribute to the development of the country.

For a credible and sustainable political solution, it is vital to acknowledge that more than the military victory against the tigers winning the hearts and minds of minority Tamils is important.

Most importantly, a suitable reconciliation mechanism should be adopted to construct bridges among all the communities in the island. The Rajapaksa government also has to go beyond the constitutional tinkering in reaching out to minorities by showing magnanimity. Resettlement of the displaced, reconstruction of the war-ravaged Northeast and rehabilitation of the LTTE cadres should be done in a more serious and fair manner.

Since the LTTE is now gone, the present moderate Tamil political leadership is unconstrained. But the main issue is the fragmentation of the Tamil polity. There are three different viewpoints among the Sri Lankan Tamils: pro-government, anti-government, and the one in between. However, to gain a viable political settlement, it is important that these three groups unite and negotiate as a single entity keeping in mind the larger interests of the Tamil community.

Reconstructing the war-battered economy should be high on the agenda of the president. The war directly affected the Tamils, but its ill effects impinged on all the other communities. Economically, the island is still recovering. The ongoing global economic crisis has added to their woes by affecting key export sectors such as tea and garments. It is, therefore, important for Colombo to construct bridges with the international community, which has only been asking for an enquiry on human rights abuses during the war. It is important to come clean on the issue in the long-term interests of the country. It is vital to have them as *partners in development* rather than overly depending on countries like China. A small state like Sri Lanka cannot push its development programme with a dented image. The onus now lies on the president to reach out to the international community. The international community also should not push Colombo too far. It should convince Sri Lanka that there is *no torch-carrying* for the LTTE and whatever concerns are raised from time to time are in the interest of the island state and its people.

The Sri Lankan government also should make efforts to win back the international media and organizations, which it antagonized during the war. Such an exercise is crucial in informing the international community of ground realities in the island. Some of the progresses made so far should be highlighted: local elections in Jaffna and Vavuniya, provincial council elections to the Northern Province, participation of TNA in these elections, rehabilitation of ex-child soldiers of the LTTE and the ongoing resettlement process, especially demining. Instead of being defensive, the government can frankly accept the shortfalls and try rectifying them in due course. It should be acknowledged that most of the concerns of the international community are genuine and, if paid heed to, will go a long way in benefiting the island state.

What is also imperative is dismantling of the security state and winning the peace. Sweeping reforms are required in the way emergency regulations are invoked and implemented. The onus of this lies with the three pillars of the Sri Lankan government: executive, legislature and judiciary. Although emergency has been lifted, the Public Security Ordinance should be amended to have inbuilt safeguards against any possible misuse. They range from communication on the arrest of a person to his relatives, production of those arrested before the courts within 24 hours, non-admission of confession made under duress as evidence, institution of checks and balances on the use of special laws such as empowering bodies like the Human Rights Commission, incorporating judicial and parliamentary scrutiny and mandatory periodic review of the Regulations, say once in five or 10 years. Basically, they have to conform to the international standards and commitments made by the island state on the human rights front. As long as the *state of exception* continues, the *state of peace* will be an elusive commodity.

In the same vein, the Sri Lankan government must count in the Opposition's contribution in nation-building. Without bipartisan consensus, any political settlement to the ethnic question would be unsustainable. The political history of Sri Lanka since independence is witness to this.

Overall, it must be realized that this is the historic opportunity for the Rajapaksa regime to not only resolve the ethnic issue once and for all, but also to take the island state to new heights by establishing real and sustainable peace.

13

State, Society and Talks with Taliban: Everywhere and Nowhere

D. Suba Chandran

Since 2012–2013, there have been a series of efforts by the state to initiate negotiations with the Tehrik-e-Taliban Pakistan (TTP), popularly referred to as the Pakistani Taliban. The latest in this initiative is the ongoing initiative[1] between the two sides, started after the killing of Hakimullah Mehsud.

Negotiations between the state and the TTP have been intermittent. In the past, there have been numerous such attempts—led by the political leadership of Pakistan—resulting in some form of an understanding, and the military—resulting in a temporary truce. Neither of these attempts by the political leadership and the military has been long-term. All previous terms negotiations have been short-term and have ended in failure, primarily with the Taliban renewing violence.

A common pattern that could be traced with all the previous attempts by the state to negotiate would include the following: a hurried ceasefire, temporary truce and renewal of violence by the TTP.

Why have the negotiations failed? Will the current round in early 2014 succeed?

---

[1] This essay was written during January–February 2014; negotiations between the two sides have been in progress with both parties announcing specific committees to carry them forward.

Are Both Sides Monolithic? Differences within the Taliban, State and Society

A primary issue that would remain the determining factor in deciding the outcome of any negotiations between the state and the Taliban will be the monolithic nature of both sides. Unfortunately, neither the state nor the Pakistani Taliban is monolithic. There are serious differences in terms of the endgame and strategies, between the actors and within them.

Pakistani Taliban: The Differences Within

Neither the Afghan Taliban on the west of the Durand Line nor the Pakistani Taliban on the east of it is a monolithic entity. The Afghan Taliban consists of two factions — the Quetta Shura, led by Mullah Omar, and the Haqqani Network. Both factions have their own spheres of influences and complement each other. These two groups are not against each other; in fact, the latter, despite its operational independence, owe nominal allegiance to Mullah Omar as its emir. In practice, the Haqqani network is more closer to the Pakistani military and its Inter-services Intelligence (ISI). The Afghan Taliban led by Mullah Omar is considered to be independent, though it is based in Quetta.

The Pakistani Taliban is not a monolithic organization either. The TTP functions more as a franchise, with numerous groups in Federally Administered Tribal Areas (FATA), Swat and the rest of Pakistan owing allegiance to the TTP, but have their own agenda and targets. For example, under Hakimullah Mehsud, the TTP factions in Bajaur, Mohamand and Swat were acting as the TTP franchisees. While the above are Pashtun groups in the FATA and Khyber Pakhtunkhwa (KP), some of the former sectarian groups from Punjab, now referred to as Punjabi Taliban, they also owe allegiance to the TTP.

Political Leadership: Consensus but Differences

Though there appears to be a political consensus based on the All Parties Conference (APC) and its resolutions, as the dialogue process proceeds, cracks have already surfaced within the political leadership.

The Pakistan People's Party (PPP) and Muttahida Quami Movement (MQM) have made clear statements questioning the ongoing process. Imran Khan, who has been championing the cause of the pro-talks faction, seems to be dithering now, with confusing statements. When the Pakistani Taliban announced his name as a part of its negotiating committee, Imran refused to be a part of the same.

The Jamaat-e-Islami (JI) and the Sami-ul-Haq faction of the Jamiat Ulema-e-Islam (JUI), JUI-S, have completely thrown their weight behind the Pakistani Taliban. Both have agreed to be a part of the negotiating committee of the TTP issuing demands and threats to the state.

The Pakistan Muslim League-Nawaz (PML-N) and the Awami National Party (ANP) also favour the talks with the TTP. Nawaz Sharif, leader of the TTP, has been unwavering in his approach ever since his elections. Though the APC recommended strongly opening a dialogue with the Taliban, Sharif led the process to take such a decision. The ANP, one of the most-hit political parties and the victim of Taliban violence, has also agreed in principle to initiate and continue the negotiations with the TTP.

Military: To Strike or Not

Is the military in Pakistan also willing to speak to the TTP? What does the military want vis-à-vis the TTP? It appears that the military and its ISI are divided in terms of whether to neutralize the TTP or wait for the 2014 deadline (for the US withdrawal) and then use both the Afghan and Pakistani Taliban to its advantage vis-à-vis Afghanistan.

Pakistan's military in the past did undertake military operations in the FATA, especially in North and South Waziristan, Kurram, Khyber and Swat. But none of the above operations, except perhaps the one in Swat, was aimed at complete neutralization of the militants. Rather, they appear to be calibrated military offensives, with limited objectives.

On the other hand, the military was continuously attacked by the TTP all over Pakistan. Its posts and camps in FATA and multiple security installations all over Pakistan have been regularly targeted by the TTP. The attacks on PNS Mehran, Kamra Airbase and the General Headquarters in Rawalpindi were bold attacks by the TTP directly taking the fight into military's core.

Civil Society: Heroes of Islam or Villains of Peace?

The civil society is also equally divided in terms of how they perceive the Pakistani Taliban. Though small, the moderate civil society is vibrant in terms of its opposition to the Pakistani Taliban. This section considers neutralization of the Taliban as the only option. Developments within Swat, attacks on minority communities and the growing radicalization are seen as the result of Taliban's onslaught by this section. Hence, they would prefer that the state bring down the Taliban militarily first and negotiate its surrender.

Another section, perhaps larger, but vociferous and with a strong street support led by radical groups and Mullahs, supports the objectives for which the Taliban has been fighting. This section considers the US as an arch-enemy and its presence in Afghanistan as essentially destabilizing; they are also against a liberal–secular approach towards Pakistani polity and society. This section forms the Taliban apologists and overt supporters within Pakistan.

TTP, Maulanas and the Shariah: Is the Religious Leadership Using Taliban as a Strategy?

As one of its demands, during the ongoing negotiation with the state, the Taliban has put forward the imposition of Shariah in Pakistan. In fact, much before the Taliban formally placed its demands, one of the three *maulanas* who have been chosen by the Taliban as its negotiation team—Abdul Aziz (the prayer leader of Lal Masjid in Islamabad which openly revolted against the state in 2007) did mention to the media that he would neither meet the Taliban nor the state committee unless the Sharia was implemented!

What does the TTP mean by the imposition of Shariah and Islamic form of governance, when the Constitution of Pakistan already owes allegiance to the same? Are the maulanas and the religious political parties, after failing to establish themselves in the national polity as a credible political force, trying to create a space for themselves using the Taliban as a strategy? How are the state and liberal constituents in Pakistan likely to respond to this joint assault by the Taliban, its mullahs and the maulanas of mainstream political parties?

TTP's version of Shariah is not difficult to understand. What the TTP wants is simple, based on what they did to the society in Afghanistan and Swat. In terms of Shariah, the mullahs of Taliban are unlikely to engage in a debate in Islamic jurisprudence and provide a well-structured edifice of governance. Rather, it would be narrowly focused on the length of beards, women education and their movement in public, nature of punishment (such as stoning, whipping and beheading), sale and distribution of music CDs and ringtones for mobiles, etc. Besides the above, for Taliban, it would be not only what needs to be decided, but also who would do that. They would want to replace the existing legal system, led by learned judges and lawyers, by a set of mullahs who would issue fatwas and verdicts based on their own world vision, whether justified by the society or not.

Unfortunately for the Taliban, there is no widespread public support in Pakistan for what they consider as Islamic and un-Islamic. From whipping in public to shooting Malala for standing up for girls' education, the civil society, except for a fringe section, has spoken against the Taliban version of Islam and its version of governance. Hence, the TTP is well aware that it will never be able to rule Pakistan just through fire power. It needs an ideological support.

TTP's version of Shariah is easy to comprehend. But what are the maulanas of leading political parties, who are now part of the Taliban's negotiation committee—JUI and JI—along with maulanas like Abdul Aziz battling for? What is in their agenda? Do they believe in Taliban ideology, or are they using the Taliban as a front to reformulate a space for themselves?

Consider the following. Maulana Abdul Aziz, believed to be closer to Zia-ul-Haq, was appointed as the prayer leader of the Lal Masjid in Islamabad. Both he and the Lal Masjid did not gain prominence until the last decade. Suddenly he became famous, or infamous, when he issued a fatwa against the military; he declared those soldiers who gave their lives in their fight against the Taliban as not martyrs, and worse, advocated against any prayers during their funeral. He, along with his brother who was ultimately killed in the military operation in 2007, brainwashed and sent the girl students to vandalize music shops and even imprison a few Chinese women accusing them of prostitution. So did Munawar Hasan, emir of the JI, when he created a controversy recently that the soldiers who lost their lives in fighting the Taliban in Swat cannot be called martyrs.

The JI and JUI-S, whose leaders are also part of the Taliban Committee along with Fazlur Rehman of JUI-F, have been working to establish a political space ever since the founding of Pakistan by Jinnah. In fact, they have been working against a secular Constitution, for it would undermine their position as a leader and a party. The debates between the secular–liberal political parties and the JI, JUI factions would reveal where the religious political parties stand regarding Shariah. The hard reality for these religious political parties is they have been rejected by the nation repeatedly. Except for a short period, that too because Musharraf wanted to undermine the PPP and PML-N during the 2002 elections, these political parties have no public support.

In a free and fair election, the religious parties are unlikely to win sufficient seats to capture power. They should be well aware that under a liberal election and secular constitution, they would have the power to bargain and blackmail, but never to rule and call the shots as the rulers of Pakistan.

Clearly, Shariah is an excuse for the TTP and religious political parties, and maulanas like Abdul Aziz are an excuse. Their convergence is tactical and strategic. Tactically, they find it useful to come together to oppose and undermine the state. Strategically, they would want to capture power and rule Pakistan. Shariah for them is not the objective, but a strategy. The state and liberal society in Pakistan should be aware of this and fight against the same.

Stated Agenda of the TTP: Remove Military, Release Prisoners and Impose Shariah

The first round of talks between the two committees appointed by the state and the TTP has clearly highlighted the negotiating positions of the two sides. Now, the crucial question is how far will the two sides go forward in achieving their objectives? Especially with the TTP presenting a 15-point agenda, how much will the state consider and concede?

The TTP's 15 points are a mixture—some of them are negotiable and can even be conceded, some are highly rhetoric and the rest the state would find it difficult to accept. Three of their demands are related to the US and Afghanistan—that Pakistan should sever its ties with Washington, prevent drone attacks and not support the American efforts in Afghanistan. In principle, the state would agree to such demands, though in practice, it would find it difficult to implement them.

At least rhetorically, the state has been objecting to the American drone attacks and has silently supported the Imran Khan-led attacks and protests against the North Atlantic Treaty Organization (NATO) movement across Pakistan. However, in practice, can Pakistan completely secure itself from the drones and cut off relations with Washington? Pakistan simply cannot afford to do so at this stage, as the recently concluded strategic dialogue between the two countries in Washington would prove. Pakistan is heavily dependent on the economic and military aid at this juncture from the US which it is unlikely to jeopardize. Even on the drone attacks, it would silently agree with the US, though in public would protest under the sovereignty rhetoric. The state is likely to concede the Taliban demands as acceptable, but not practice the same; the US would take the blame, which would suit perfectly the rulers in Islamabad. In fact, they have been playing this double game for the past many years, and fooling the Americans.

The second set of demands of the TTP are related to ceasefire, military operations, release of Taliban prisoners and the removal of security check posts in the FATA. The TTP is well aware that any military operation in the FATA would greatly undermine their network; rhetorically, the TTP would continue to talk about revenge attacks and suitable response, but the reality would certainly hurt them in the FATA and KP. More importantly, the TTP would want the release of some senior Taliban leaders, and numerous other TTP foot soldiers. According to a news report, there are more than 40 senior Taliban leaders and approximately 350 foot soldiers of the Taliban imprisoned. It is also reported that the TTP demand for the release of prisoners includes even the foreign fighters.

As a compromise, the state would release some of the senior Taliban leaders and retain the rest. Rhetorically, the state can claim that it did not release all those who have been released, but would end up letting those who matter for the Taliban to go free. On this issue, perhaps the state would have to be heavily dependent on military's inputs, along with that of the ISI. While the military will agree to a ceasefire, will it agree to remove the check posts? Will the military agree to release all the top leaders of the TTP who have been arrested so far? This is unlikely to be a political question purely.

The third set of demands from the Taliban includes the imposition of Shariah, the Islamic way of governance, reducing the gap between the rich and poor. These demands would be severely problematic from the state's perspective. Can the state afford to even initiate a dialogue relating to the Taliban's version of Shariah and Islamic form of governance?

If what happened in Afghanistan under the Taliban and in Swat under the TTP is to be taken as a yardstick, then the TTP's demand for Shariah and Islamic way of governance would completely blow away the societal harmony within Pakistan. Shias, Ahmedis, Hindus and even Barelvis would be seen outside the purview of the Taliban version of Islam. Even within the Sunni Muslims, women would have to undergo a repressive social regime, as witnessed in Swat a few years earlier. Taliban's version of religion would be difficult to interpret through any Islamic jurisprudence; it would be explained and interpreted narrowly by the TTP leaders, as they see fit; whether it is accepted by the rest of Islamic scholars and the society would be irrelevant to the Taliban leadership.

While the state should totally reject the above demands, the danger of a compromise on this issue cannot be ruled out. This is what the previous government under Zardari did, in terms of the Nizam-e-Adl regulations in the Swat valley. Will Sharif and the rest in Parliament agree to have the TTP run its version of Islam, say within the FATA? There lies the bigger danger, not only for the FATA and Pakistan, but the rest of the entire region in the East and West.

Endgame Taliban: Driven by an Ideology? Or in Search of One?

What is the ideology of TTP? What does the TTP aim to establish? Is there a coherent set of principles for which the TTP is fighting for in Pakistan? In terms of the geographic expanse, is the TTP objective aimed at establishing something within Pakistan or at cutting across the Durand Line in the Af-Pak region? Or, is the TTP looking at a larger geographical canvass beyond the Af-Pak?

Conversely, is there an ideology in the first place, on which the TTP was founded? Or was it established purely as a military strategy by the Afghan Taliban and Al Qaeda—either separately or together? If there is no coherent ideology for the TTP so far under the Mehsud leadership, is it likely to change under the leadership of Mullah Fazlullah, the new leader of Pakistani Taliban, also the erstwhile leader of the Tehreek-e-Nafaz-e-Shariat-e-Mohammadi (TNSM)?

TTP: Is There a Well-explained Ideology?

The simple answer is—no. At least not so far. While there have been numerous statements by the spokespersons of the TTP either justifying their attacks or doings or issuing threats and proclamations, so far, there has not been a clear articulation of what the TTP stands for.

Three reasons could be explained for the lack of a well-articulated ideology by the TTP. First, perhaps the TTP was not born out of an ideological mooring, but a tactical military force for the Al Qaeda–Afghan Taliban network. Second, the TTP's non-monolithic character has failed in creating a unified command, well-defined hierarchy and more importantly a coherent ideology that would bind the organization. The third explanation could be the lack of leadership with adequate ideological skills and more effective articulation of the same.

All the above three explanations need further elucidation.

TTP Was Established by Outsiders Rather than Being Born on an Ideological Mooring

To explain this, one has to analyse the background in which the TTP was established or born. Perhaps, it would be more appropriate to refer to the TTP as being *established* by outsiders (outside the FATA) but in North and South Waziristan, rather than being *born* within the tribal agencies.

This establishment, especially in North and South Waziristan Agencies, did not take place due to internal factors—either religious or political. It is also imperative in this context to explain why the TTP was established and by whom. An explanation leading to the *establishment* of the TTP could be the military needs of the Al Qaeda and the Taliban, especially the former, to provide a cushion to prevent them from being squeezed between the US-led International Security Assistance Force troops across the Durand Line to the west and the Pakistani military to the east of FATA boundaries.

Al Qaeda in particular was in favour of an indigenous group taking on the Pakistani establishment and the reasons for that were easy to deduce. It was clear by that time (2004–2007) that the US was keener to go after the Al Qaeda elements and Pakistan had absolutely no problem in helping Washington in this pursuit. The Pakistani establishment was well aware that the Al Qaeda would become a major threat to its own security and was willing to give them up, as the facts on ground would prove in terms of the Pak–US collusion in going after the Al Qaeda targets within Pakistan.

It was no coincidence then that the Mehsud leadership of the TTP had good relations with the Al Qaeda elements in the FATA, especially the Uzbeks and the Chechens. The Uzbeks backed Baitullah Mehsud and the Al Qaeda, providing the larger funding support to the Pakistani Taliban. Mullah Omar, leader of the Afghan Taliban was made the supreme leader of the TTP, but in reality, the TTP did not have much in connection with the Afghan Taliban. Nor did it want to fight along with the Afghan Taliban on the west of the Durand Line.

TTP Franchisees, Non-monolithic Character and Lack of Ideology

The second explanation for the lack of ideology in the TTP is perhaps because it was not a monolithic organization, nor has it evolved into one, and nor does it have a strict hierarchy. While the core remained in Waziristan led by the Mehsuds, later, numerous groups in other parts of the FATA and the rest of Pakistan started referring to themselves as a part of the Pakistani Taliban.

The TTP could be referred to even as a franchisee organization or a loose network; multiple radical groups fighting for different reasons — from sectarian to anti-state — came together under the rubric of the TTP. In fact, many radical groups — especially the sectarian ones from mainland Punjab, and others such as the TNSM in Swat, which were established much before the 9/11, took the Pakistani Taliban identity, or allowed their identity to be subsumed by the TTP. And in the process, they became identified as the Swat Taliban and Punjabi Taliban.

The TTP is not only a monolithic organization, but also a deeply divided one, where multiple field commanders were known to fight under/for different leaders. This phenomenon could be proved—if one followed the developments immediately after the killing of Baitullah and Abdullah Mehsud. On both occasions, there were wars of succession, with different groups pitching for the TTP leadership. During the latest round, Mullah Omar had to intervene and in fact impose Mullah Fazlullah, as outsider to Waziristan and not from the Mehsud line.

Lack of Leadership Trained in Theological Discourse

The third explanation could be the lack of strong, qualified religious leaders within the TTP, who have been trained in religious discourses. Leaders of the TTP in its formative phase such as Baitullah and Hakimullah Mehsud were neither a *mullah* nor *maulana* in the first place, like some of the other contemporary Taliban leaders on both sides of the Durand Line, for example, Mullah Omar, Mullah Baradar and Mullah Fazlullah. Though educated in seminaries, they were more of fighters and soldiers with tactical acumen in planning and executing violent attacks.

None within the TTP leadership in the formative phase—at the first and second rung—had espoused a religious ideology. Contrary to the TTP leadership based in Waziristan, the erstwhile TNSM leadership in Swat—Sufi Mohammad and Mullah Fazlullah—espoused an ideology based on their own version of religion. The ideological aspects of the TNSM and these two leaders are explained subsequently.

A comparison between the leadership of Pakistani Taliban and Afghan Taliban would clearly reveal the lack of ideological skills of the former, especially under the Mehsuds.

So, What Did the TTP Fight for Until Now?

Under the Mehsuds, the main core within the TTP, with its headquarters in Waziristan, the main target so far has been the state and its leadership—political and military, followed by attacks on the Shias. One could easily make a difference in this as well—in terms of what the TTP's main leadership and core pursued vis-à-vis the multiple franchisees. While the Mehsud-led TTP fighters targeted the state, its franchisee organizations in Punjab, Sindh and FATA had a sectarian agenda.

Suicide attacks were one of the most predominant strategies employed by the TTP in its fight against the state—from the assassination of Benazir Bhutto to the high-profile attacks in Karachi on the PNS Mehran, the TTP unleashed a series of suicide attacks against the state.

Revenge, Retaliatory and Pre-emptive: Political and Military Nature of TTP's Attacks

What were the main objectives of these attacks? To establish an Islamic Ummah or/and to proclaim Shariah? What primary objectives/motivations drove the TTP since it was established?

The high-profile targets would explain that the attacks were more political and military in nature rather than religious. These attacks were carried out by the TTP as retaliation against the drones, or revenge against military operations, or a threat against any impending military operations in the FATA.

Another major political objective of the TTP, in which it used military tactics, is aimed at preventing Pakistan from collaborating with the US. Despite the divide between Islamabad and Washington, there was a substantial collusion of the two, especially in going after the Al Qaeda and its supporters within Pakistan. Numerous Al Qaeda leaders were apprehended by Pakistani security forces and silently handed over to the US since 9/11. In comparison, not many leaders belonging to Mullah Omar's Shura and the Haqqani Network have been apprehended and handed over to the US by Pakistan, or to Afghanistan.

Similarly, on the drone attacks, the TTP was on an offensive against the political and military leadership in Pakistan. Though the latter would condemn the US in public, in private, it would always convey a different message to the American leaders. Despite the acrimony and differences between the two, Islamabad and Rawalpindi did collude with Washington, especially in terms of targeting the Al Qaeda leadership and their supporters in Pakistan. The Wikileaks on the official communication between the American officials in Pakistan and their offices in the US would reveal the Pakistani leadership's duplicity on drone attacks.

Drone attacks have neutralized a substantial section of the Al Qaeda leadership in the FATA and its local supporters, belonging to the TTP. A profile of drone attacks involving the high-value targets belonging to the Al Qaeda and the TTP would confirm the above. As a result, the TTP and its political supporters have been extremely proactive in pressurizing the political and military leadership in Pakistan. While the TTP's supporters and overground sympathizers used the *sovereignty* argument, the Pakistani Taliban used military offensive as a retaliation and revenge.

Thus, the TTP's primary target has remained the state, and reasons are more political and military in nature, rather than religious.

Explaining the Sectarian Attacks under the TTP

If the TTP's targets are primarily political, how would the growing sectarian attacks within Pakistan during the last decade be explained? The *franchisee* phenomenon of the TTP would perhaps explain the sectarian attacks.

Three further questions are relevant to this question: Where did these sectarian attacks take place in terms of geographic expanse? In terms of time expanse, were these sectarian attacks a post-TTP phenomenon, or they existed even before the 9/11? And, who within the TTP carry out these sectarian attacks?

Punjab, especially Southern Punjab, Karachi and two agencies in the FATA—Kurram and Orakzai—have been the primary geographic location of the sectarian attacks. Historically, these three regions have been witnessing sectarian attacks before the TTP was even born. In fact, the sectarian fault lines from Kurram to Karachi predate even the birth of the Taliban in the mid-1990s! These sectarian attacks are being carried out by the erstwhile Sunni militant organizations which are now referred to as the TTP, or more specifically as the Punjabi Taliban. The sectarian divide within Kurram was always there; the TTP's ascendancy has only polarized them further.

To conclude, the TTP, especially led by the Mehsuds, was fighting more for a political and military reason, rather than based on a coherent ideology—especially religious. It was founded as an indigenous group to provide the much-needed space for the Al Qaeda and the Afghan Taliban in the tribal agencies of Pakistan. The primary objective of the TTP was to prevent the Pakistani military from carrying out any military operations against the Taliban–Al Qaeda militants, and to carry out revenge/retaliatory suicide attacks against the state to prevent it from collaborating with the US.

Enter Mullah Fazlullah: Will the TTP Evolve into an Ideological Group?

Mullah Fazlullah is no ordinary militant of the TTP. Unlike the Mehsud leadership before him, Fazlullah would not be satisfied in keeping the TTP a militant force and using violence for political reasons alone.

A flashback on Mullah Fazlullah would be pertinent now. Who was Mullah Fazlullah before the birth of TTP in 2007? Where does he come from and what does he stand for? And, if the media reports are to be believed, why was he chosen personally by Mullah Omar himself to lead the TTP, instead of someone from the Mehsud line?

Mullah Fazlullah has been a part of the TNSM in Swat, the Malakand region to be precise. The TNSM has been fighting for a religious cause in the Malakand region since the 1990s. Sufi Mohammad (though not a *Sufi* either in belief or in practice), who is Fazlullah's father-in-law, was leading a movement for the imposition of Shariah in the Malakand region.

Fazlullah merged into the larger TTP movement when he converted the TNSM into Swat Taliban. Because of his personal influence and that of the TNSM background, not only in Swat, but also in the adjoining (remember Swat is a part of the settled districts of erstwhile Northwest Frontier Province) tribal agencies such as Bajaur and Mohamand, the Taliban movement was much closer to Fazlullah than the TTP leadership in Waziristan. And that would explain the divide within the TTP in these two agencies between the field commanders of the TTP. In fact, Mullah Fazlullah and Baitullah Mehsud have to meet to iron out the differences between the factions in Bajaur and Mohmand agencies.

What would Fazlullah aim at? Will he be satisfied in just providing a space for the Afghan Taliban and Al Qaeda in Pakistan's tribal agencies, or would he become the *veritable arm* of the Quetta Shura and the Haqqani Network? And in the process, will he also become the strategic depth for both the factions of the Afghan Taliban?

An analysis of the past record of Fazlullah and his group would reveal two issues. First, despite the differences with his father-in-law, he was very much a part of the demand for the establishment of Shariah in Malakand. Second, he was no ordinary mullah, but a hardened fighter; in fact, before taking up the mantle of TTP, he was one of the few Pakistani militant leaders who were fighting within Afghanistan.

Though Sufi Mohamand took the credit for establishing the Nizam-e-Adl in Swat, and also the subsequent disaster, Fazlullah was responsible for the numerous radical and violent developments within Swat.

The above are tough questions. Perhaps the security establishment in Pakistan still believes that once the Americans leave Afghanistan and the leadership in Kabul settled favouring Islamabad, militancy led by the TTP would disappear. Perhaps it would, or perhaps the situation would worsen further.

Towards Anarchy

To conclude, what are the talks with the Taliban heading towards? Will the recent round of negotiations during 2013–2014 succeed?

Since the Taliban is talking from a position of strength, it seems to be calling the shots. It is yet to agree to a comprehensive ceasefire, but insists that the state should do so. The TTP has put forward the release of all the prisoners as a precondition, but they keep massacring security personnel. Clearly, despite the talks in progress, the TTP is on an offensive.

What would make the TTP go on a defensive? At this moment (in early January 2014), only two developments would make the TTP become defensive: first, a strong military action within FATA, followed by unanimous political resolve to root out terrorism from Pakistan; second, a deep split within the TTP, with a section openly siding with the state and going against the other faction.

Though there have been talks about a military response against the TTP, it has not taken place so far. Perhaps, the political and military leadership is divided over a military approach, or worse, even within the military and intelligence agencies, there is a divide over whether to pursue a tough approach or not against the TTP. While the divide within the political leadership both at the national level and within the Pashtun leadership on a military approach vis-à-vis the TTP is evident, there is not much in the public domain that would highlight any divide within the military and intelligence. Based on the reluctance of the military, it can only be conjectured that it is not completely convinced about going against the TTP and bringing it down on its knees.

The political leadership is dithering on the endgame. It has not put forward what is acceptable and what is not. The state has failed to ensure that the Taliban ceases violence during the process of talks. Clearly, the state is weak and defensive.

The moderate civil society has less impact on the larger environment, while the Taliban supporters and apologists are proactive and powerful in the streets. While the former's enthusiasm is limited to opinion articles in English newspapers and social media, the latter is enforcing their perspectives through protests and pressure.

Will the TTP implode from within, causing it to disintegrate, and perhaps even fight amongst themselves? As has been explained earlier and observed in the past, the TTP is not a monolithic organization. With Fazlullah being appointed as the leader, for the first time since the formation of the TTP, the leadership has shifted to non-Mehsud hands and to someone who does not have his base in Waziristan. Will the Mehsuds split from the TTP?

Even during the leadership of Baitullah, the Mehsuds did have their own differences and there were reports to hint that all was not well within the Mehsud leadership of the TTP. As could be seen from the factional fights within the Mehsud tribe, not every Mehsud commander is happy and owes complete allegiance to the new TTP leadership. Though nominally they would accept Mullah Omar as their supreme leader, individual Mehsud commanders would not find it easier to go along with a non-Mehsud leadership.

As long as there is a powerful threat of a common enemy (the military in Pakistan), the factional differences within the Mehsuds would be kept aside for the time being. Or as long as the new leadership of the TTP is able to take every Mehsud and Wazir commander in his stride, Waziristan—both North and South—would remain an asset for the TTP. Once the above two issues change in principle, there would be an overarching impact on the larger structure of the TTP.

The military and its intelligence have been trying to win over a few TTP commanders ever since the organization was born. Referred to as pro-state militants, there have been instances of Wazirs and Mehsuds supporting the state and opposing any activities against the state in Pakistan. This section would prefer that the TTP join hands with the Afghan Taliban and fight on the west of Durand Line, rather than in rest of Pakistan.

Besides the above differences, the TTP is also split over the support to foreign militants in the tribal agencies of the FATA. From Uzbek to Chechen, there have been numerous foreign militants who have made Waziristan a base; belonging to the Al Qaeda and loosely knit with multiple other organizations, for example, the IMU (Islamic Movement of Uzbekistan), Waziristan is also home to numerous non-Pashtun and non-Afghan militants from the Muslim world. While a section within Waziristan support them and also benefit financially, another section oppose the same. In the past, there have been deep differences within the Pashtun communities in Waziristan, especially the Mehsuds and Wazirs, and also within the TTP over this issue.

Will there be a split within the TTP? Perhaps there will; but the larger question is whether such a split would bring the TTP down and make it go on a defensive. The state, especially its military and the intelligence agencies may succeed in scoring certain tactical victories in dividing the TTP and creating new groups. But it is unlikely that that would result in the state becoming stronger and bringing peace to the region, which should be the ultimate objective. Given the current situation, it does not seem to be happening.

The present looks imperfect. Unless the state goes on an offensive, the future may well be so.

PART III
Early Warning

14

Communal Divide in Jammu and Kashmir

Kavita Suri

A Short Introduction to Communal History in Jammu and Kashmir

Jammu and Kashmir (J&K) holds a unique place in the annals of Indian union. It is the only Muslim-majority state in the country which also has the history of integrating with the Indian union under *peculiar* circumstances, thrown up in the backdrop of the division of Indian subcontinent and the creation of two free nations—India and Pakistan—out of British India.

Communal divide in the Indian state of J&K is not a new thing. Perhaps the earliest incidents of communal violence in the then princely state of Kashmir took place in 1931 which was followed by an incident of police firing on protestors in Srinagar by Dogra troops. This incident, which resulted in the death of 28 protestors, led to attacks on the homes and property of the Hindus in various parts of the state.[1] The communal divide between the Muslims and the Hindus became prominent in 1947 when thousands of people, mostly Muslims, were killed in the Jammu region in communal riots.[2] Ever since then, communal

---

[1] Praveen Swami, 'Kishtwar Riots: Just Another Chapter in J&K's Politics of Hate', Firstpost.com, 12 August 2013.
[2] Ibid.

divide has surfaced in the state in varying degrees of intensity, and religious polarization has been exploited by the political parties belonging to different shades of public opinion for their own political ends.

In the post-partition era, the initial years of the Sheikh Mohammad Abdullah government in J&K were resented by the people of the Jammu region due to many controversial decisions taken by his new government. A major decision in this direction was the administrative reorganization of J&K in 1948 which resulted in scrapping of Reasi district of Jammu province and merging its major part with Udhampur district, while some areas became part of the then Poonch district (now Rajouri). The enactment of the Big Landed Estates Abolition Act of 1950 was another such step as per which agriculture land from big landlords was seized and distributed among the tillers. However, the same was not applied to orchards and as such, a section of landlords of the Jammu region saw the Act as an attempt to usurp the traditional landholdings of people from the Jammu region while protecting the landowners from the Kashmir region who had big landholdings in the form of orchards.

The simmering unrest in Jammu found its expression in 1952–1953 when Praja Parishad, a political party representing the Jammu region, launched an agitation against Sheikh Abdullah's policies demanding abrogation of Article 370 (a constitutional provision which allowed only state subjects to buy land in J&K), complete integration of J&K with the Union of India, complete jurisdiction of the Supreme Court, full application of the Indian Constitution in J&K, removal of customs barriers between J&K and India, fresh elections to the Kashmir Constituent Assembly, etc.[3]

In the years to come, the tensions between Kashmir and Jammu became increasingly sharp. It is pertinent to mention that the seeds of communal hatred and ill will were sown in 1986 when the first exodus of Kashmiri Pandits took place from Anantnag, the hometown of Mufti Mohammed Sayeed. Mufti Sayeed, the then J&K Congress Committee Chief and an ally of G. M. Shah's party, National Conference (Khalida), ruling the state at that time, in connivance with Dr Farooq Abdullah's National Conference, instigated communal violence aimed at replacing the then Chief Minister G.M. Shah. Eventually, Mufti succeeded in his mission, but it saw the

---

[3] Swami, 'Kishtwar Riots', 2013.

exodus of Kashmiri Pandits from Anantnag. The then All India Congress Committee General Secretary K.N. Singh is on record holding Mufti Sayeed responsible for communal trouble in the state. Sadly, it was not the end of regionalism or religion politics in the state. The decade of 1990s again brought communal divide in the state to the forefront. The breakout of militancy in the state started with the attacks on the symbols of authority of the union government as well as selective killing of members belonging to the Kashmiri Pandit community. This fear psychosis caused by such acts of terror led to near-total ethnic cleansing of minorities from the valley. These were also acts of mass killings of members of the minority community in the valley and other Muslim majority areas of the state. Such events also hardened the sentiment of communalism in some segments of minorities in the state.[4]

The most unprecedented expression of communal divide between the majority and minority community in J&K was witnessed in 2008 when in the month of May that year, the central government and the J&K state government reached an agreement to transfer 99 acres of forest land to the Shri Amarnathji Shrine Board (SASB) in the Kashmir valley to set up temporary shelters and facilities for Hindu pilgrims for the annual pilgrimage. However, this decision was resented by the separatist groups, led by the Hurriyat Conference in the valley who organized huge protests and violent demonstrations in which six people were killed and about 100 injured.[5] Sensing an anti-India sentiment gathering strength in the valley, the Peoples Democratic Party (PDP), a party led by Mufti Sayeed, which was the coalition partner of the ruling Congress party, threatened to withdraw the support to the government unless the decision to transfer the land to the SASB was not revoked. The crisis deepened further when even after revocation of the land transfer to the shrine board the PDP declined to support the Congress-led coalition government, as a result of which the then Chief Minister Gulam Nabi Azad had to step down in July 2008.[6] The decision to revoke the land transfer

[4] Rekha Chowdhary, 'Muslim Identity and Politics of Fundamentalism in Kashmir', Working Paper, Queen Elizabeth House, University of Oxford, Oxford, 1998.

[5] 'Won't Settle for Anything Less than Amarnath Land', *Daily News and Analysis*, 7 August 2008.

[6] 'Jammu Agitation More than Amarnath Land Issue', *Economic Times*, 4 August 2008.

to the shrine board led to the breakout of huge protests in different parts of the Jammu region besides widespread violence in different parts of Jammu division. The national highway to Kashmir was blocked at many places in the region and travel to Kashmir and flow of goods to the valley was severely restricted for many days. Finally, on 31 August 2008, after 61 days, the Amarnath land agitation in the Jammu region ended after an agreement reached between the SASB Sangharsh Samiti and the Governor-appointed panel as per which the shrine board was allowed to make use of 40 hectares of land for providing shelter to Amarnath pilgrims during the relevant period of the pilgrimage.[7]

Yet other example of a massive law and order situation with communal overtones developed in March 2009 which widened the communal divide between the people of two majority and minority communities when Peer Mansoor Hussain, a sitting Member of Legislative Assembly (MLA) of the PDP introduced a bill in the state assembly demanding renaming of district Anantnag to Islamabad and also those of the famous and historical peaks of Kashmir, Hariparbat and Shankaracharya to Koh-e-Maran and Takht-e-Suliaman, respectively.

Meanwhile, separatists in the valley are continuing with their agenda to spread rumours and flare up communal tension in the valley. In 2013, Kashmiri separatist leader Syed Ali Shah Geelani called on his followers not to rent their homes to migrant workers saying it was a conspiracy to stage a partition-style massacre. In the past, Geelani had commented that the migrant workers working in different parts of the valley were responsible for all the crime and alleged immoral practices being followed in the valley.

A Short Note on Recent Developments

Kishtwar town of Kishtwar district in Jammu province situated some 200 km away from Jammu hogged national and international headlines when communal clashes took place between the Hindus and Muslims in August 2013.[8] The communal clashes

---

[7] 'Jammu Agitation More than Amarnath Land Issue', *Economic Times*, 4 August 2008.

[8] 'Kishtwar Mob Runs Riot', *Pioneer*, 10 August 2013.

which began on the morning of Eid and continued almost throughout the day resulted in the killing of three civilians besides leaving dozens of others injured.[9,10] The clashes also saw arson, loot, firing and lawlessness as the antisocial and anti-national elements carrying petrol bottles, guns, sticks and deadly weapons unleashed a reign of terror against the minority community.[11] Over 50 vehicles, petrol tankers, trucks and cars were burnt and over 150 shops and other business establishments including several houses belonging to the minority community were torched. These clashes started when a section of local Hindus objected to the raising of pro-freedom slogans by the members of the majority community who had congregated for the Eid-ul-Fitr prayers.[12] For many hours, it was a free-for-all situation as the violence continued. Surprisingly, the police and civil administration remained mute spectators including the state Home Minister Sajjad Kichloo (who resigned later), who was in Kishtwar only for Eid festivities. This raised questions over the integrity and loyalty of the state authorities. It seemed that the violence was pre-planned as was revealed by the appearance of posters of anti-national figures of the valley, Pakistani flags, etc.

However, it was not the first time that Kishtwar clinched the headlines due to the violent clashes between Hindus and Muslims. Kishtwar has already remained a communal cauldron, and many a time, communal tensions have erupted in the area in the past few years.[13]

Apart from Kashmir valley and the Jammu region which have been hit by communal violence; the once-peaceful Ladakh region has also tasted the communal frenzy in those high altitudes.[14] To begin with the recent, in July 2013, the Buddhist-dominated Zanskar area of Kargil district of Ladakh region witnessed communal tension when a few low-caste, Buddhist families belonging

[9] 'Sectarian Politics Fuelled Kishtwar Riot', *Hindu*, 13 August 2013.

[10] 'Communal Riots Engulf Jammu, Toll Climbs to 3', *Hindustan Times*, 11 August 2013.

[11] Maneesh Chhibber, 'Kishtwar a Tinderbox, Region under Curfew After Clashes', *Indian Express*, Jammu, 11 August 2013.

[12] Asif Iqbal Naik, 'Communal Clashes Mar Eid Celebrations in Kishtwar', *Early Times*, 10 August 2013.

[13] Praveen Swami, 'On an Edge in Kishtwar', *Frontline* 20, no. 17 (2003), available online at http://www.frontline.in/static/html/fl2017/stories/20030829005301700.htm (accessed 18 November 2014).

[14] Balraj Puri, 'Ladakh Sectarianism', *Indian Express*, 15 February 2006.

to the Gara and Beda tribes embraced Islam, thus, provoking attacks on them.[15] They were beaten up, and many restaurants, hotels and shops were damaged.[16] A huge prayer wheel was irreparably damaged by the violent mob. In this incident, the police resorted to lathi-charge and fired on the peaceful demonstrators, injuring a Buddhist youth who was evacuated to Kargil for treatment.[17]

Ladakh, in fact, has been witnessing communal tension since the past two decades. The region is dominated by two communities—Buddhists and Muslims—in Leh and Kargil, respectively. Ladakh has long since been voicing its discrimination at the hands of Kashmiri rulers. In 1989, there were violent riots between Buddhists and Muslims, provoking the Ladakh Buddhist Association to call for a social and economic boycott of Muslims which went on for three years before being lifted in 1992. In Leh district, the Buddhist community boycotted the Muslim community and did not keep any contact or communication with them, even to the extent of boycotting buying things from Muslim shopkeepers or doing business with them. This ended after a few saner voices intervened successfully and temporarily resolved their differences. Again in 2006, the desecration of the Holy Quran at Bodh Kharbu village raked up communal tension.

The tensions between Buddhist and Muslims have continued despite all the efforts to resolve them. Till date, Kargil has not allowed the construction of any Buddhist temple or *Gompa* in their area which has also been a cause of major tension. The settling down of various Muslims from Kargil in Leh district by buying lands and constructing new houses has divided the Buddhist community from within, as a section of Buddhists do not want them to settle down in Leh as it would change the demography of the district, while another section of Buddhists blame other Buddhists only for selling their lands to the Muslims. They say that if the Buddhists would not have sold their lands to Muslims, they would not have been able to buy their lands in Leh and settle down there.

[15] Masood Hussain, 'Zanskar Under Curfew After Rioting over Conversions', *Economic Times*, 25 October 2012.

[16] 'Communal Clashes: Curfew Continues in Zanskar', *Hindustan Times*, 26 October 2012.

[17] 'Troubles on the Roads to Zanskar', *Greater Kashmir*, 13 July 2013.

The communal divide between the two communities is quite wide and can be gauged from the fact that when Leh district got an autonomous hill development council, Kargil alleged discrimination with the Muslims as a result of which the government had to create another autonomous hill council for Kargil district too.[18] The tensions between the two communities have also continued over the conversion of hundreds of Buddhist girls to Islam after their marriage to Muslim boys from Kargil and other areas.

The communal tension has further widened in Ladakh with the formation of the Ladakh Union Territory Front, a political party whose main demand is granting of Union Territory status to Ladakh. The Ladakhis say that the division of Ladakh into two districts of Leh and Kargil in 1974 was itself on communal lines.

The Major Actors

The major actors are all the major political parties in the state of J&K, including the National Conference, the PDP, the Bharatiya Janata Party (BJP), regional parties, separatist parties, etc. Although all these political parties claim that they are ideologically secular, they have always followed quite dubious policies, taken mileage out of it and have never made a serious attempt to check communal violence in the state. For example, in the recent Kishtwar riots, there was a total absence of administration in the area where the rioters continued looting, arson, etc. for hours and hours until the army and police finally arrived and acted. These parties, their heads, leaders and cadres have contributed to the plunging of the state of J&K into an inferno of communal violence. Most of the politicians are, in fact, interested in promoting communal and caste divisions as identity politics benefit them immensely in terms of delivery of votes.[19]

---

[18] Fernanda Pirie, *Peace and Conflict in Ladakh: The Construction of a Fragile Web of Order*, Brills Tibetan Studies Library, vol. 13 (Leiden: Brill, 2007).

[19] See note 4.

There are state actors and non-state actors who are creating a communal divide in the state of J&K.

State Actors

Various political parties such as National Conference, BJP, Rashtriya Swayamsevak Sangh (RSS), Vishva Hindu Parishad (VHP), Congress and regional parties such as Jammu Kashmir Nationalist Front (JKNF), Jammu Mukti Morcha (JMM), Jammu Kashmir Peace Foundation, Ladakh Buddhist Association (LBA), etc., have contributed to further alienate the people. Apart from the continuous neglect of their cultural and political aspirations and economic needs by the Kashmir-based leadership, Jammu's regional discontent, thus, got communal expression. The RSS and the VHP gave a call for a separate Jammu state which could not inspire the local Muslims. As a reaction, organizations emerged for a separate regional status for the Muslim-majority districts of Doda and Rajouri-Poonch.

There are religious parties and religious influences such as that of Wahabi and Deobandi, and Iran's religious influences in districts like Kargil which is dominated by Shia population. The separatists and fundamentalist parties like Jamaat-e-Islami, etc., are also giving rise to communal divide in J&K.

Political parties like the National Conference have also fanned communal divide. In 1999, it issued a draft for partition of provinces on the recommendations of a committee which advocated the creation of six new provinces. (Muslim-majority Rajouri and Poonch districts were to be carved out from the Jammu region as a whole and recast as a new Pir Panjal Province while Udhampur's single Muslim-majority *tehsil* Mahore was to form part of the Chenab province. The rest of the district was to be incorporated into Jammu.[20] Even the Buddhist-majority Leh and Muslim-majority Kargil were to become separate provinces.) There are parties like BJP also which have been raking communal issues in the state while demanding the trifurcation of the state on communal lines — Muslim, Hindu and Buddhist.

[20] Praveen Swami, 'Deepening Divide in Jammu and Kashmir', *Hindu*, 18 July 2008.

Non-state Actors

There are state actors such as Pakistan, its Inter-services Intelligence (ISI) and the various militant and terrorist groups which want to foment trouble in J&K by creating a divide between various communities in the state. The terrorists have already executed scores of massacres of minority communities in all parts of the conflict-hit state with the objective to widen the communal tension between Hindus and Muslims, Kashmiri Pandits and Sikhs. The infamous massacres of Chittisinghpura in South Kashmir in which over 30 Sikhs were massacred, or the Wadhama massacre in which the Kashmiri Pandits were killed or a series of massacres of Hindus in Doda district are a testimony to this fact.

Separatist leaders and individuals have also been furthering communal divide in J&K. The latest is Kashmir's former chief conservator of forests Abdul Qayoom Khan who has filed a petition before the High Court in December 2013 seeking directions to constitutional authorities to use the state flag in all their official cars, offices and office buildings. Similarly, when various leaders of Bajrang Dal, Shiv Sena and VHP claimed that demilitarization and self-rule were existential threats to the state, both All Party Hurriyat Conference and Geelani's Tehreek-i-Hurriyat played an important role in organizing protests with communal overtones.

Major Trends

The issue of communalism in the state of J&K operates at two levels. Firstly, there is the issue of *majority communalism* which has its origin in the sentiment of perceived wrong by a section of majority community in the state who believe that as per the two nations theory, the state, being a Muslim-majority region, should have become the part of Pakistan. Even after the passage of 65 years since becoming the part of the Indian Union, this sentiment still hurts a substantial section of Muslim population, mostly belonging to the Kashmiri ethnic group from the valley. Moreover, the special status granted to the state at the time of its integration with the Indian union has been considerably eroded by the subsequent constitutional provisions, which has further given fillip to the majority communal sentiment in the state.

The second level of communalism witnessed in the state is that of *minority communalism*. The minorities in J&K constitute 33 per cent of the population (as per Census 2011). Among the minorities, the Hindus form the biggest group (29.6 per cent), followed by the Sikhs (2.23 per cent), the Buddhists (1.16 per cent) and the Christians (0.14 per cent). These minorities are mainly concentrated in Jammu province, except for the Buddhists who are largely restricted to the district of Leh and the Zanskar subdivision of district Kargil. The minorities in J&K have held this perception that their interests have largely been ignored by the successive state governments and the focus of development in the state since Independence has only remained valley-centric. People in Jammu and Ladakh region are also dissatisfied about the lack of development projects in the region as well as poor representation of minorities in the state administration. Such feelings have led to the origin of *minority communalism* in the state.

It is the same majority communalism and minority communalism that has been exploited by political dispensation of the two regions of the state for their own political ends. The events of 1947 brought out communal divide in the state in a very profound manner. Loss of a large part of the state, which is now known as Pakistan-occupied Kashmir (POK), mutiny in several units of Muslim-dominated state forces and large-scale violence against the minorities, particularly in the districts of Mirpur and Poonch, led to a severe reaction by minorities, particularly in the Jammu region. Thousands of people were killed during these disturbances, and communal agenda has always retained the centre stage of the political discourse of the state in varying intensity.

The polarization between the majority and minority communities of the state of J&K has remained as it is in the new millennium too. It goes without saying that trust deficit has deepened among the masses.[21] The situation in J&K is volatile and the politicians often play the communal card in an attempt to divert the attention from the maladministration that has plagued the region for several years. In their urge to gain power, some political parties

---

[21] Riyaz Wani, 'Demand for Statehood, UT Status Revive in Two Regions of J&K', www.tehelka.com, 6 August 2013.

might go to any extent to sow seeds of violence and communalism in the fragile state.

Broadly speaking, the situation on the ground remains fragile. In the valley, violence can be sparked by a single actor; in Jammu province, it can be sparked by a single speech, as the Poonch and Rajouri communal tensions indicate. Any stray incidents of spontaneous nature have always led to a communal situation in the region. An incident of normal crime involving members of two communities has the potential to turn into a communal situation. Incidents like the love affair/elopement of the girl of one community with the boy of the other surely assume communal colour in sensitive places like Kishtwar, Bhaderwah, Rajouri and Poonch. In these places, even minor issues have, in the past, resulted in widespread disturbances leading to loss of property and life. One such incident happened in Rajouri in 2000 on a September afternoon when a football arced over the playing field outside the Government Degree College, slamming into a boy standing on the far side.[22] This resulted in a brawl between two groups of students. Apparently, the football was launched by a Muslim player and a Hindu student was hit by it. This incident resulted in the shops and homes being lighted up in flames, serious protests and police opening fire. The net result was loss of four lives and destruction of public and private properties.[23]

Another interesting case on communal situation developed in Poonch in 1988 when a member of the majority community planted a sampling of Chinar in the middle of a ground traditionally being used as a venue for burning the effigy of *Ravana* on Dussehra. He claimed that a local saint, Late 'Sain Mira', came in his dream and told him to plant the sapling there. The Hindus and Sikhs claimed it to be a conspiracy to grab the land used for their religious celebrations. Soon, stone-pelting started between the two communities, followed by arson as the trouble spread to other parts of the district. After a protracted agitation, normalcy returned to the district only after new land was acquired for the construction of a stadium which has since then become the venue

---

[22] Praveen Swami, 'Jammu and Kashmir: A Communal Divide', *Frontline* 16, no. 15(1999), available online at http://www.frontline.in/static/html/fl1615/16150400.htm (accessed 18 November 2014).

[23] Praveen Swami, 'The Two Wars in Jammu', *Frontline*, 17, no. 21(2000), available online at http://www.frontline.in/static/html/fl1721/17210390.htm (accessed 18 November 2014).

for burning the effigy of *Ravana*, and the piece of land on which the dispute had started was converted into a park. In 2007, yet another incident of communal tension triggered off in Rajouri after a few enthusiastic Indian fans, celebrating the victory of India over Pakistan in a one-day cricket match, threw crackers in front of a mosque. Earlier, an anti-encroachment drive by authorities in Poonch had assumed communal colour.[24]

Besides, the national and local media is often instrumental in widening the gulf and fanning tension between the two communities. As was reflected during the Kishtwar riots, people also engaged in a virtual war over social media websites and this too contributed to the spread of violence. With the spread of Internet connections to the remote and far-flung areas of J&K, the people have got exposed to the utility of the Internet and the global media and, thus, communicate with each other through the Internet and their websites or blogs, and even social networking sites such as Facebook or Twitter have become forums for propaganda and information in this border state. The recent examples of the Amarnath agitation and Kishtwar riots throw enough light on how communal disharmony and conflicts are fuelled by fear, suspicion and hatred on the Internet. The different channels of media are the transmission channels through which fear, suspicion and hatred spread.

Major Issues

Major issues regarding communal divide in J&K can be divided into various categories such as political, social, economic, religious, governance, etc.

Political

There has been a feeling of neglect and discrimination among the communities in J&K. While Kashmiris feel that New Delhi has meted out a stepmotherly treatment to them, Jammu and

[24] See note 13.

Ladakh feel that they are given a stepmotherly treatment by the Kashmiri leadership. The feeling of neglect and apathy of successive state governments towards Jammu's political and economic development and the central government's valley-centric thinking has led to the reassertion of Jammu's demand for separate statehood.[25]

Successive valley-dominated state governments were blamed for Jammu's poor share in the state services.[26] In the civil secretariat, Jammu's representation is less. The proportions of employees from the valley and Jammu in the state secretariat and regional services of Kashmir and Jammu are also unbalanced. All 12 corporations of the J&K government had their headquarters in Srinagar with almost 100 per cent of the employees from the valley.

Jammu has also been under-represented in the state assembly and in the Lok Sabha. While it has 37 seats, Kashmir has 47 seats, even though the population is almost the same. There is a clear dominance of the Kashmir region over Jammu in the legislative assembly on the basis of population and area. It is also perceived that the Jammu ministers are always given weaker portfolios in coalition government in the state. Most central funds are spent in Kashmir and not in Jammu, more employment are given to Kashmiris and not Jammuites. Various commissions like the Gajendra Gadkar, Sikri and Wazir commissions were appointed at different times for redressal of grievances of Jammu and Ladakh people, but their recommendations were not implemented.[27]

Good numbers of Kashmiri students are in Jammu institutions while Jammu students are only in a microscopic fraction in Kashmiri institutions. Maximum students of Ladakh study in Jammu, Chandigarh, Delhi, etc. Institutions like Ayurvedic College were closed down in Jammu, whereas Veterinary College, Dental College, Artificial Limb Centre and Physical Training College proposed for Jammu were set up in Kashmir. Share of Jammu students in professional institutions reduced from 45 per cent to 20 per cent during the current regime.

---

[25] Balraj Puri, *Simmering Volcano: Jammu's Relation with Kashmir* (New Delhi: Sterling Publishers, 1983).
[26] Ibid.
[27] Ibid.

Social

There are many social issues which, if addressed, can bridge the communal divide between the communities. Since 1947, the issue of refugees from POK is unsettled. The 1947 refugees from West Pakistan have no voting rights in the assembly elections and do not have any state subjects. The Muzaffarbadi Hindu refugees of 1947 were not allowed to settle in Kashmir but forced to settle in Jammu. Besides, over 3–4 lakh refugees came from across the international border of the Jammu region and settled here, and they are still living in miserable conditions. Such refugees are denied government jobs, education and right to property, etc.

Governance

The issues of governance and development have been raised by the people as corruption, misgovernance and under-development have been dogging the state for the past so many decades. Corruption has become deep-rooted in J&K and an international watchdog Transparency International declared J&K the second most corrupt state in India after Bihar. The far-flung areas still remain underdeveloped with lack of basic amenities like housing, roads or water. Poverty is a big issue in the remote areas. Districts like Kishtwar, which has a literacy rate of seventy per cent, are still counted amongst the most under-developed districts in the region.[28] Jammu and Ladakh have tremendous tourist potential. Tourists do visit these areas, but the development of tourist spots is negligible. Maximum money is spent in the valley. In the jobs also, people allege that there is no balance as Kashmiris have a good number of jobs while Dogras and other minorities have less number of jobs. Buddhists of Ladakh also accuse Kashmiri rulers of discriminating between the Muslims and Buddhists of the area. In the year 1997–1998, 23 Buddhists qualified for Kashmir Administrative Service/Kashmir Police Service but only one was selected, whereas all the Muslims who had passed were selected. Similarly, out of 24 newly appointed Patwaris, 23 were Muslims and one Buddhist. There are several instances like that which widen communal divide in the border state.

---

[28] 'Kishtwar Rocks Parliament, Jaitley Assails J-K Govt for Failure', *State Times*, 13 August 2013.

What Needs to Be Done

In J&K, various political parties have been using communal divide for their own gains as elsewhere in the country.[29] In the days and months to come with the state assembly elections scheduled in J&K in 2014 year end, the extremist religious propaganda may witness acceleration by these politicians for their own political benefits. What is required today is a strong political will to deal with the issue of communal violence and, thus, the change in the political mindset. The real solution lies in providing a responsive government instead of sharpening of communal boundaries for their own benefits. The politicians need to dampen the communal tempers and not stoke the embers of inter-religious conflagration. There needs to be a resolve to not exploit a situation solely to derive political gains. Political leaders and religious representatives have to show resilience and kind-heartedness to accommodate each other's viewpoint in a democratic country like India. They have to shun the political of political opportunism.[30]

Secularization of politics in also quite important for the youth of the state as with secularized politics the political process in J&K could become more cohesive and vibrant. Respecting and embracing each others' communities, cultures and religions have to prevail in J&K, and the people of all the communities should maintain communal harmony.

In any communal situation, police too is a part of the problem rather than the solution. Its failures to deal effectively with communal tension arise mainly from its own inadequacies and also from unabashed politics. Police force can be highly communalized and can show solidarity with any of the community. Besides, it comes under a lot of political influence and political interference. Police also need to work without any political interference and pressure from the political parties or the ruling governments. Many times, police officers have reported such incidents wherein they had been under pressure by the political parties, their hands are tied which makes them helpless to handle communal tensions effectively. Politicians need to stop interfering in such cases immediately and only then

---

[29] 'Successive Governments Have Adopted Imperialistic Policy of Divide and Rule', *Rising Kashmir*, 23 December 2013.

[30] Hari Om, 'Moves Afoot to Divide Jammu on Communal Lines', *Greater Jammu*, 9 January 2014.

can police operate with all necessary freedom ensuring the support and confidence of the public for successfully preventing and containing communal riots. For their effective performance, police need secular orientation from time to time through refresher courses before joining the service and during the service. Such orientations can influence police attitudes in a big way.

Besides, in any communal tension or riots, great onus lies on the police force as they are the ones who directly handle the law and order situations in such challenging times. Their first and foremost responsibility is to prevent any such situation before it arises. For example, in the Kishtwar 2013 communal riots, the police and intelligence had enough reports about communal tension brewing up between the two communities for the past few weeks.[31] Despite this, nothing was done to prevent this or contain such a situation as a result of which major riots took place there. Had the police stepped in at the right time and preventing the riots, valuable lives and huge property would not have been lost.[32]

Police also has a major role to play in containing violence, maintaining the law and order situation, ensuring that no further lives and property are lost and there are no rumours which have the potential to run another riot. Besides, they also need to ensure that immediate relief is provided to the victims of the communal violence. Conducting relief camps and providing security to the camps is one thing, while building confidence among the affected people on the activities of the police forces in containing the disturbances is of equal, if not higher, importance.

In such times of crisis, students and youths should come forward to maintain and sustain the communal harmony, cooperation and mutual understanding, goodwill and tolerance. Student associations, youth wings, religious organizations, members of civil societies, senior citizens, intellectuals, writers and political leaders should come forward to address communalism forever. Youths should come together on a common platform to debate, discuss and argue on various developmental and other issues, so that the doubts could be cleared. There is need to strengthen the bond between the two communities. For example, in October 2013,

---

[31] 'Kishtwar Riots Planned by Separatists: Civil Society Report', *Tribune*, 30 September 2013.
[32] See note 13.

Kishtwar traders under the banner of Anjuman-e-Islamia joined hands with their counterparts in Kashmir in the valley in a bid to strengthen bonds and their trade in Kishtwar. The aim was to rebuild business connections with the valley traders which were snapped despite Kishtwar being more close to the valley.

Inter-regional divides too are emerging J&K, and there is utmost need to remedy the local doubts and grievances. Otherwise, such issues may cause more disturbing stresses and strains than even what militancy had caused. A consultative and advisory council to discuss the unresolved and various outstanding issues for the common interest of the various minorities in the state is the need of the hour. Peace committees can be set up and prior and sustained contact between members of different communities can help in resolution of moderate tensions and pre-empt violence. Less violence is likely to occur if tensions are moderated and community links are fostered.

Corruption, maladministration, regional discrimination, neglect and communal distrust need to be addressed. The development of the neglected or less-developed regions should follow.

National and local media should be instrumental in providing an analytical and unbiased overview of such events in the future, especially the ones with the potency of creating communal rifts. Education, employment, health and other development concerns should be given the topmost priority. These channels have the potential to mitigate conflict. Media is a potent tool to promote communal harmony. To maintain and strengthen communal harmony, the society has to use different channels and mediums. Media is one of the most potent and effective medium given its wide reach, effective delivery mechanism and ability to mobilize public opinion.

There is a need to highlight the composite culture and efforts made by Sufi saints, writers, poets and musicians to build bridges between the two communities, for example, Lal Ded, Nund Rishi, Pirs and Sufis like Pir Budhan Shah of Jammu, etc., besides musicians, architects, poets and others to fuse two cultures together and bring two communities together. Value education should be provided to the youth as it can produce critical thinking and shun prejudiced mindset, prejudices against minorities, etc.

Lastly, after much delay, the controversial Communal Violence Prevention Bill was cleared in December 2013 by the Union Cabinet after the removal of certain provisions, reducing the role of legislation in the handling of riots and making it neutral between communities. The Prevention of Communal and Targeted Violence (Access to Justice and Reparations) Bill, 2013, which is facing stiff opposition from the BJP and some other parties, seeks to make the definition of a group hit by communal violence as community-neutral and leaves the prevention and control of communal violence essentially to the states, with the centre playing a coordinating role. The new bill makes bureaucrats and public servants accountable for any acts of commission and omission while handling communal violence. However, bureaucrats who refuse to obey unlawful orders of their superiors during communal situations cannot be held responsible for dereliction of duty.

Interestingly, the bill 'extends to the whole of India, provided that the Central government may, with the consent of the state of Jammu and Kashmir, extend the act to that state'. The bill, thus, provides Kashmir an easy escape route which in effect reiterates that the bill does not concern itself with the atrocities or violent acts committed on minorities in Kashmir. J&K Chief Minister Omar Abdullah said that any step that will reduce communal violence is a good thing but the implications of the proposed bill on the state has to be discussed before his party, National Conference, takes any decision. 'What effect it will have on Jammu and Kashmir keeping in view the special status of the state, what will be the role of our party and role of the Coalition (partners), it needs to be discussed', he told reporters in Srinagar.

The state of J&K also needs to adopt this bill so that those responsible for communal violence are punished and this acts as a deterrent, thus, reducing the incidents of communal violence in J&K.

Early Warning of Potential Problem in Future Needs to Be Identified

Perhaps the biggest danger lies in poorly managed communal tensions that have the potential to fray this small border state's social fabric. Communal violence in J&K has already resulted in polarization and a rise in extremism. If such violence is allowed to continue and the early warning signs are not recognized and action not taken to curb the same, not only will it give rise to further extremism, but will also portray a bad image of the state and the country as well.

The recent incidents at Kishtwar have thrown enough light over the fact that the tension between the two communities were simmering for the past many weeks and despite the fact that the administration and the government were aware about these tensions, no solid steps were taken to pacify both the sides and resolve the conflict until it took a bigger shape and resulted in mass-scale violence and loss of lives.

The early warnings of potential problems need to be clearly identified and understood in the context of communal tension in J&K. As far as the relations between any two communities—be it the Muslims and Buddhists of Ladakh, Muslims and Sikhs who are a minority community in Kashmir or Hindus and Muslims of Jammu or Kishtwar, or the Muslims and the very small Christian community of Kashmir—are concerned, these have remained fragile for the past many years, especially since the exodus of the minority Kashmiri Pandit community from Kashmir valley in the 1990s.

Small incidents like the conversion of Sikh or Buddhist girls in Kashmir or Ladakh or the burning of the holy Quran have the tendency to vitiate the entire atmosphere; hence, the government needs to be thinking about how to *de-radicalize* the situation. Separatism has not gone away and is also a threat to stability. In the past, incidents such as the attacks on Christian schools in Kashmir have also resulted in communal tension in the valley. Hence, the government needs to be alive to such issues which have the potential to destroy the peace in the area. There is need to realize that once communal tensions are inflamed, they can be exacerbated for local power struggles.

15

Maoists in Northeast India: The Spread of a Rebellion

Wasbir Hussain

Introduction

During April–May 2013, security agencies in Assam were jolted by a startling revelation—the state and the Northeast had been a playing field for Maoists for more than two decades. Until then, it was believed that Maoists have been active in this region only for the last 7–8 years. This revelation came from the interrogation of Maoist leaders who were arrested during those months. On 26 April 2013, police had arrested Aklanta Rabha alias Maheshji and Siraj Rabha alias Bijoy Rabha alias Suraj from the Jorabat area in the outskirts of Guwahati, near the Assam-Meghalaya border.[1] Aklanta Rabha was a central committee member of Communist Party of India (Maoist) (CPI (Maoist)) and Chief of the outfit's Northeast operations, while Siraj Rabha was training instructor of CPI (Maoist) and a landmine expert. Then, on 8 May 2013, veteran Maoist leader Anukul Chandra Naskar, alias Pareshda, was arrested from Cachar district in

---

[1] 'Two Maoist Leaders Nabbed in City', *Assam Tribune*, 27 April 2013, available online at http://www.assamtribune.com/scripts/detailsnew.asp?id=apr2713/at08 (accessed on 14 October 2014).

Barak valley of Assam.[2] He was a member of the Politburo of the CPI (Maoist), the highest decision-making body of the outfit. Security agencies made a few more arrests following these. On 27 April 2013, three women were arrested from Bhalukdubi area of Goalpara district, in western Assam, for helping the duo of Aklanta Rabha and Siraj Rabha.[3] On 15 May 2013, Anukul Chandra Naskar's wife Kabita Rabha was arrested from a rented house in Odalbakra area of Guwahati.[4] She was running a printing press from the rented house and was publishing Maoist literature for distribution across the state.

Interrogations of these arrested Maoists revealed that the groundwork for Maoist activities in the Northeast was laid some 20 years ago. One of the arrested Maoist leaders, Aklanta Rabha, had joined the red brigade during 1991-1992 and has been associated with Maoist activities since then. At the time of his arrest, he was looking after the activities of the Maoists in the Northeast, particularly in Assam and Arunachal Pradesh. His main aim was to establish a sanctuary in the northeastern region so that senior Maoist leaders could hide there when operations by security forces scaled up against them in other parts of the country. According to police sources, Aklanta had accompanied a senior Maoist leader, Sumit *da*, also known as Amitabh Bagchi, to Assam twice, in 2005 and 2007, to strengthen relations with other Northeast-based militant groups and to build up a people's guerrilla army in the region.

On 22 November 2013, the Union Home Ministry extended the Armed Forces (Special Powers) Act, 1958, in Assam for one more year with effect from 4 December 2013 and again gave the state a

[2] 'Top Maoist Leader Picked Up in Cachar', *Telegraph*, 9 May 2013, available online at http://www.telegraphindia.com/1130509/jsp/northeast/story_16876685.jsp#.UpWXHs5acxg (accessed on 14 October 2014).

[3] 'Operation against Red Rebels Intensified in Assam Districts', *Times of India*, 28 April 2013, available online at http://articles.timesofindia.indiatimes.com/2013-04-28/guwahati/38877479_1_ulfa-hardliners-cpi-maoist (accessed 20 October 2014).

[4] 'Woman Maoist Activist Held', *Assam Tribune*, 17 May 2013, available online at http://www.assamtribune.com/scripts/detailsnew.asp?id=may1713/city06 (accessed 20 October 2014).

disturbed area tag under the Act.[5] However, the point to be noted here is that this is the first time that the Home Ministry has cited Maoist activities as one of the reasons for continuing with the *disturbed area* tag.

Thus, while it was thought that Maoist activities in the northeastern region began only some 7–8 years ago, they had actually already been working in this area for long now. It is believed and is likely that during this period they had tried to instil their ideology into sections of the masses and the new recruits/supporters they have been working with. In a region like the Northeast, where problems like poverty, underdevelopment and unemployment are quite visible, the deprived masses are likely to be attracted towards a Maoist ideology. The government and its agencies are aware of the problem and the challenges that lie in containing the Naxal spread and consolidation.

The Genesis of Maoism in Northeast India

The first brush-off that Northeast India had with ultra-Left activities was soon after India's independence. It was spearheaded by the Revolutionary Communist Party of India (RCPI). The RCPI, under the leadership of Pannanlal Dasgupta, had adopted a revolutionary line of armed class struggle.[6] The RCPI in Assam also opted for the line of militant class struggle, and there was armed action by the RCPI cadres in Sibsagar, Lakhimpur, Kamrup and Goalpara districts.[7] This struggle dwindled in the subsequent years with the diminishing influence of the RCPI.

The Naxalbari uprising in neighbouring West Bengal in 1967 also brought some winds of Maoism to the northeastern region. A news report titled 'Special Cell to Deal with Naxalites', published in the

---

[5] 'Another Year of AFSPA', *Sentinel*, 4 December 2013, available online at http://www.sentinelassam.com/editorial/story.php?sec=3&subsec=0&id=176731&dtP=2013-11-30&ppr=1 (accessed 28 October 2014).

[6] 'Revolutionary Communist Party of India', available online at http://www.marxists.org/glossary/orgs/r/e.htm (accessed 20 September 2014).

[7] Assam Police Anti-Maoist Task Force Report, accessed by the author.

Assam Tribune on 24 February 1971, talks of the Assam government setting up a special cell with an Additional Inspector General of Police[8] to, as it said, 'deal with the Naxalite menace which is slowly raising its head in Assam'. The report also talked about 20 arrests having been made, including that of a post-graduate student from Gauhati University. By 1971, the Naxalbari Movement in neighbouring West Bengal might have ceased to be a cohesive force, but Assam had had a brush with Maoism by then.

However, the true genesis of Maoism in the Northeast began during the 1990s, a fact that came to light only in April–May 2013 with the arrest of Maoist leaders Aklanta Rabha and Anukul Chandra Naskar. The interrogation of these leaders has revealed that Maoists have been making inroads into Assam since 1995. It was in 1996 that Aklanta Rabha had first visited Jharkhand (then Bihar). When he arrived at the Jalenga Training Camp of the Maoists in Gumla district, he was surprised to find seven cadres from Assam, six men and a woman, already undergoing training there.[9] These details have brought to light the fact that the Maoists have been actively operating in Assam for at least 17 years contrary to the general belief that they had opened shop only a few years ago.

The Gradual Spread

Maoists have now managed to have a firm hold in the Northeast, and the area which has kind of become a major base for them is the Assam–Arunachal Pradesh border. They have established bases in the Lohit and Lower Dibang Valley districts of Arunachal Pradesh, bordering eastern Assam's Tinsukia district. And this fact has been confirmed by a number of official communications. One such communication from a central agency under the Union

---

[8] The Additional Inspector General of Police referred to was R.C. Dutta.

[9] Wasbir Hussain, 'Can Assam Be Immune to Red Terror?', available online at http://www.sentinelassam.com/mainnews/story.php?sec=1 &subsec=0&id=46484&dtP=2012-01-14&ppr=1 (accessed 21 September 2014).

Ministry of Home Affairs (MHA) says that the CPI (Maoist) is operating in the Assam–Arunachal Pradesh border in the name of the Upper Assam Leading Committee (UALC). It says the UALC is functioning with distinct wings for political and military activities under the command of designated *political commissars* and *military commander*.[10]

Another letter, written by a senior state government official based in eastern Assam to Chief Secretary N.K. Das on 25 October 2011, says that the anti-talk ULFA faction headed by Paresh Baruah was imparting arms training to Maoist cadres on the border with Arunachal Pradesh, across the eastern Assam district of Tinsukia.[11] The letter says that youth in the age group of 20–25 years are lured by the Maoists and the main pull factor for these boys was the lack of economic activity and employment avenues in such far-flung and inaccessible areas such as the Sadiya sub-division of Tinsukia district.[12] The official has sounded an alarm saying that if urgent development initiatives are not undertaken by the government in eastern Assam, particularly in Tinsukia district's Sadiya area, things might go out of hand.

The lid on the organized Maoist activity in the area, mainly in the Lohit and Lower Dibang Valley districts of Arunachal Pradesh, was actually blown in August 2011 when arrested cadres made some startling disclosures. They told interrogators that they used to hold *revolutionary meetings* in their hideouts at regular intervals and that such meetings were attended by anything between 150 and 200 cadres. During one such meeting held in August 2011, the arrested cadres claimed that they had mined a 6-km approach to the venue that was guarded by 60 armed fighters.[13]

Further confirmation of Maoist activity in the otherwise *non-red belt* that was Northeast India can be made from the arrests made

[10] Wasbir Hussain, 'Red Terror on Assam–Arunachal Frontier', 23 November 2011, available online at http://cdpsindia.org/point-of-view67.asp (accessed 1 October 2014)

[11] Wasbir Hussain (ed.), 'Red Terror in Northeast India: Maoists' Link-up with Ethnic Rebels Adds New Dimension to the Region's Security', in *Northeast India: Sustaining Peace Changing Dimensions* (Guwahati: Bhabani Books, 2012).

[12] Ibid.

[13] Interview conducted by the author with a senior police official in Tinsukia district, Assam, in November 2011.

by Tinsukia police of 140–150 militants from the area between May and October 2011, which included around 15–20 Maoist cadres. Again, between November and December 2011, Tinsukia police arrested another 20–30 odd Maoist cadres.[14] Tinsukia police also arrested two Maoist cadres from Namsai area in Lohit district of Arunachal Pradesh, namely Debojit Borgohain and Diganta Thamang.[15] On 9 June 2013, police detained 66 suspected Maoist recruits from Tinsukia railway station as they were about to board the Chennai Express.[16] The drive was carried out after receiving specific information about a large number of youths trying to leave Assam with the intention of joining the Maoists. Most of the 66 detained youths belonged to places like Sadiya, Tangana, Dhola in Tinsukia district, Raajgarh and Tingkhong in Dibrugarh district and Namsai in Lohit district of Arunachal Pradesh.[17] These places are considered Maoist-affected.

The interrogation of arrested Maoist leaders Aklanta Rabha and Anukul Chandra Naskar further revealed the spread of Maoism in Assam and the Northeast. It was revealed that Maoists had managed to increase their influence in the districts of Goalpara, Bongaigaon, Cachar, Karimganj and Kamrup (rural) districts and had created a fresh support base of at least 150 cadres in these districts.[18] Interrogations further revealed that the *char* or riverine areas of Dhubri district bordering West Bengal and forest areas were the new targets of the Maoists.

In 2005–2006, the Maoists set up bases in Goalpara and Sonitpur districts. At least 11 Maoists were killed by security forces in these two districts, although those eliminated passed off as cadres of local militant groups. The Assam Police at that time managed to identify at least two dozen overground sympathizers of the

[14] Tinsukia district authorities revealed during interviews with the writer in January 2012.
[15] See note 10.
[16] 'Maoist Whiff Spurs Cop Act—66 Youths Yanked Off Train in Tinsukia', 11 June 2013, available online at http://www.telegraphindia.com/1130611/jsp/northeast/story_16992659.jsp#.Upg8YM5acxg (accessed 10 October 2014).
[17] Ibid.
[18] Arunav Goswami, 'Maoist Consolidation in Assam: Ominous Portents', 29 May 2013, available online at http://cdpsindia.org/point-of-view87.asp (accessed 10 October 2014).

Maoists, people with Leftist leanings. They were kept under surveillance.[19]

Maoists have also succeeded in making inroads into southern Assam's Barak Valley which comprises of three districts, namely Cachar, Karimganj and Hailakandi. The Valley shares interstate borders with Manipur, Tripura, Meghalaya and Mizoram and an international border with Bangladesh. Aklanta Rabha revealed the names of at least five persons who joined the Maoists 4–5 years ago and are currently working at the village level in Barak Valley to strengthen the base of the Maoists in the region.[20]

Maoists are now looking to establish bases in Meghalaya. Aklanta admitted that he had already established contacts with a number of Khasi youths to bring them into the Maoist fold. Already, 5–6 such meetings have been conducted between the Khasi youths and Maoist leaders. In fact, Aklanta was arrested when he was waiting for the arrival of a few Khasi boys for their periodical meetings. The Khasi boys, however, could not be arrested as they did not turn up at the stipulated time of the meeting. According to police investigations, Maoist leader Amitabh Bagchi alias Sumit da, a politburo member of CPI (Maoist), had asked all local Maoist leaders of Assam to develop a tie-up with Khasis, Rabhas, Garos and people of tea tribes who have been agitating for their political and financial rights for a long time.[21]

The Assam government in May 2013 sent a proposal to the central government to declare nine districts of the state as left-wing-extremism-affected districts.[22] These districts are Tinsukia, Dibrugarh, Dhemaji, Lakhimpur, Golaghat, Sivasagar, Goalpara, Cachar and Karimganj. The proposal said that 35 police station areas of these nine districts are affected by Maoist activities. Those include eight police station areas in Tinsukia, five in Dibrugarh, four in Golaghat, four in Dhemaji, one in Sivasagar, one in Lakhimpur, three in Goalpara, five in Cachar and four in Karimganj district. These nine districts have altogether 103 police stations.[23]

[19] See note 9.
[20] See note 18.
[21] See note 3.
[22] 'Declare 9 Districts as Maoist Affected', *Assam Tribune*, 29 May 2013, available online at http://www.assamtribune.com/scripts/detailsnew.asp?id=may2913/at07 (accessed 14 October 2014).
[23] Ibid.

A report by the Anti-Maoist Task Force of Assam police[24] states that the police have details of 171 Maoist cadres and active linkmen in the state. Out of these 171, particulars of 83 cadres are available in better details. Of the 83 cadres, 21 hail from Sadiya PS area, nine from Tingkhong PS area, seven from Merapani area and six each from Pengeree PS and Kakopathar PS areas. There are also cadres from the bordering districts of Arunachal Pradesh. Also, substantial cadres hail from Dhemaji district. Many districts from middle and lower Assam too have been represented, which indicates the extent of the Maoist tentacles.

The Anti-Maoist Task Force report of Assam Police states three distinct trends in the contemporary Maoist movement in Assam. First, the Maoists are trying to explore ideal conditions for their kind of ideology to grow and strive and to organize Maoist upsurge on the lines witnessed in mainland India. However, progress in this line has been very limited. Second, they are trying to get involved in advocacy campaigns on issues of governance, forest and land rights, mega dams, etc. Here also, according to the Task Force report, they have not been able to make much headway. The third trend is of arming first and then discovering causes. With bases in Arunachal Pradesh, tactical partnerships with local insurgent groups and availability of large number of unemployed youths, this trend may, however, strive for long.

Ideological Line of Maoists

Maoist rebellion in a region passes through four phases. In the CPI (Maoist) parlance, these phases are:

1. Latent phase
2. Early guerilla phase
3. Late guerilla phase
4. Mobile phase.

The Maoist rebellion in the Northeast India is at present in latent phase. The *latent phase* involves mobilization of the masses, political awakening, visiting villages, engaging in small struggles

---

[24] Accessed by the author.

on local issues, picking up students' issues, fighting corruption, short-listing shelters and arms dumps and identification of local militant elements, etc.[25]

Aklanta Rabha, during interrogation, had disclosed CPI (Maoist)'s five-point agenda for the Northeast, which was adopted at a central committee meeting of the CPI (Maoist) in the jungles of Jharkhand towards the end of 2011. The strategy was to: (a) unite all the insurgent groups in the Northeast; (b) to coordinate closely with the anti-talk ULFA faction headed by Paresh Baruah; (c) to raise a people's guerilla army; (d) to set up training camps in the dense jungles of Arunachal Pradesh and (e) procurement of arms and ammunition.[26]

Here let us see the hierarchy of the CPI (Maoist) as revealed by the interrogations of the arrested Maoist leaders.

Central Committee/Politburo
↓
Special Area/Special Zone/State Committee
↓
Regional/Zonal/District/Divisional Committee
↓
Sub-zonal/Subdivisional/Area Committee
↓
Village/*Basti*/Factory/College Committee

The military structure of CPI (Maoist) is as follows:

Central Military Commission + Central Military Command
↓
Regional Military Commission + Regional Military Command
↓
State Military Commission + State Military Command

---

[25] Wasbir Hussain, 'Maoist Strategy Wakes up Assam Government from Slumber', 1 June 2013, available online at http://cdpsindia.org/point-of-view88.asp (accessed 13 October 2014).
[26] Ibid.

According to the MHA, the Maoists profess a violent ideological line to overthrow the democratically elected parliamentary form of government in India.[27] This they plan to do through: (a) armed insurrection; (b) mass mobilization of certain sections of society and (c) tactical partnerships with other insurgent groups operating in different parts of the country.

Now let us discuss how the Maoists are following these three lines in Northeast India.

Armed Insurrection

The militarization process of Maoists in the Northeast has been different from Maoists in mainland India. Neither have they tried to launch major attacks against security forces nor have they attempted to arm the common masses.

However, there is no scope for complacency because the Maoists have already been locked in as many as four encounters with the security forces in which the red rebels had managed to snatch weapons that include AK series rifles.

Details of the four encounters are mentioned below:

- The first encounter between Maoists and security forces took place on 3 November 2010 at Rajgarh area under Tingkhong police station in Dibrugarh district, during which two AK series rifles and one carbine were snatched from the personnel of the 19 India Reserve Battalion.[28]
- The second incident was on 18 September 2011 when Maoists snatched four 0.315 rifles, 63 rounds of ammunition and four mobile handsets from forest guards in Dibru Saikhowa reserve forest in Dibrugarh district.[29]
- On 4 October 2011, one Maoist cadre named Pradeep Gogoi was killed in an encounter with security forces in Ambikapur

[27] 'India Likely to Sensitise EU, Other Countries about Naxals', *Assam Tribune*, 27 November 2013, http://www.assamtribune.com/scripts/epaper.asp?id=nov2713/Page3 (accessed 17 December 2013).

[28] 'Seeing Red in the Northeast', *Hindu*, 25 May 2012, available online at http://www.thehindu.com/todays-paper/tp-opinion/seeing-red-in-the-northeast/article3454090.ece (accessed 29 October 2014).

[29] See note 10.

area of Sadiya subdivision of Tinsukia district. However, during the incident, one 9-mm carbine and 18 rounds of ammunition were snatched by the Maoists from the police.[30]
- On 9 May 2012, four Maoist cadres, including a local commander, were killed in an encounter at Borgora village in Sadiya subdivision of Tinsukia district. Two Maoist cadres managed to escape during the encounter and one policeman was injured. The killed Maoist cadres were Siddhartha Borgohain, Commander, UALC, CPI (Maoist), Rajib Gogoi, Arup Chetia and Kamala Burhagohain. All the killed cadres were local residents of the area. Two AK47, one AK56, six magazines, 150 rounds of ammunition, three grenades, six mobile handsets, 16 SIM cards and several extortion notes were recovered from the slain Maoists. The recovered AK47 rifles were the ones which were snatched from the 19 India Reserve Battalion personnel on 3 November 2010.[31]

The northeastern region has not yet witnessed a full-blown Maoist armed insurrection. But the government and the security agencies should stay alert for such a possibility in the near future. As explained earlier, in this latent phase, Maoists are giving more importance to building shelters and stockpiling arms. But, if proper tabs are not kept on their activities, the region may witness a full-fledged armed Maoist insurrection.

Mass Mobilization of Certain Sections of Society

A region like Northeast India has been an ethnic cauldron and this automatically increases the possibility of the Maoists cutting ice or igniting fire among certain communities and groups harbouring a variety of grievances against the state. The Adivasis in Assam, which comprise the bulk of the tea garden workforce in the state, have a whole lot of grievances. Several Adivasi insurgent

[30] See note 10.
[31] 'Assam Police Kill 4 Maoists in First Anti-Red Encounter', *Times of India*, 9 May 2012, available online at http://articles.timesofindia.indiatimes.com/2012-05-09/guwahati/31640816_1_maoists-assam-police-tinsukia-district (accessed 25 October 2014).

groups have come into being to push these grievances. Some of them, like the Adivasi Cobra Militants, are on a truce. The Maoists are already said to be trying to cash in on these grievances and consolidate their presence in the state.

On 21 December 2011, a delegation of the Assam Chah Mazdoor Sangh, a frontline trade union body affiliated to the ruling Congress in the state, had met Chief Minister Tarun Gogoi and apprised him of attempts by Maoists to recruit youth belonging to the tea community.

> The delegation informed the Chief Minister that many instances of Maoists luring youths belonging to the tea tribes to join them had come to light. If this trend continued, said the delegation, it would spell doom, not just for the tea tribes, but for the entire State.[32]

In fact, the Maoists are said to be paying a salary or stipend of ₹2,500.

The Intelligence Bureau (IB) noted in September 2011 that the CPI (Maoist) has been engaging in activities in Assam and Arunachal Pradesh 'under the garb of local movements, including the Mega Dam Resistance Forum...'. In fact, Assam Governor Janaki Ballav Patnaik also said publicly that Maoists in the state were functioning under various banners including the Mega Dam Resistance Forum.[33] Assam Chief Minister Tarun Gogoi also made statements corroborating what the IB and the Governor had been saying.[34]

On 29 December 2011, Assam Power Minister Pradyut Bordoloi stated that dossiers were being prepared on Maoist elements infiltrating the anti-dam movement in the state. 'We are checking the background of the protestors. We have got information on some, and we are compiling a dossier on them. These elements are basically driven by Maoist ideology and their religion is to

---

[32] 'Tea Body Points to "Dangerous" Maoist Trend', available online at http://www.sentinelassam.com/mainnews/story.php?sec=1&subsec=0&id=101134&dtP=2012-01-14&ppr=1 (accessed 17 December 2013).

[33] See the *Telegraph*, available online at http://www.telegraphindia.com/1111221/jsp/frontpage/story_14908521.jsp (accessed 25 October 2014).

[34] 'CM Hints at China Hand in Anti-dam Movement', *Sentinel*, available online at http://www.sentinelassam.com/mainnews/story.php?sec=1&subsec=0&id=103580&dtP=2012-01-20&ppr=1 (accessed 25 October 2014).

create disorder and unruliness', Bordoloi told a news conference in Guwahati.[35]

Maoists have also formed frontal groups like the Assam Student Youth Organization (ASYO) which was formed by Maoist leader Pallav Borbora, who has already been arrested by the National Investigation Agency (NIA) on 3 June 2012.[36] This group is quite active in the Sadiya subdivision of Tinsukia district. Some other frontal organizations formed by the Maoists are Chah Suraksha Samiti, Mahila Bahini, Biplobi Yuva League, Biplobi Sanskritik League, Biplobi Krishak Committee and Biplobi Kobi Goshthi. Maoists have also published a magazine, *Janagana*, in Kamrup district of Assam.[37]

On 12 February 2011, Odisha police arrested three persons from Assam—Aditya Bora from Tingkhong, and Asik Sabor and Tingraj Orang from Naharkatia in eastern Assam's Dibrugarh district. Of these three, Aditya Bora, who is said to be a central committee member of the CPI (Maoist), was also a member of the ASYO. Sabor and Orang, on the other hand, belong to the tea garden community.[38]

The Odisha capture had, in fact, come within a fortnight of the arrest of six suspected Maoists, including two women, who were picked up from different areas of Assam's northern Dhemaji district. They had been carrying out Maoist activities under the name of Brihat Nadibandh Pratirudh Mancha.[39] The arrested persons were Kishore Das of Maj Kuruwa under Sipajhar police station in Darrang district, Nibash Hajong of Silapathar in Dhemaji district, Dhaniram Das of Lakhipathar Koibartya village under Dhemaji police station, Diganta Gogoi of Borguri in Tinsukia district, Jun Bora of Chowdangpathar under Merapani police station in Golaghat district and Maneka Medhi of Pengeri in Tinsukia district. Kishore Das is said to have

[35] *Seven Sisters Post*, 30 December 2011.

[36] 'Top NE Maoist Ideologue Arrested', *Times of India*, 4 June 2012, available online at http://articles.timesofindia.indiatimes.com/2012-06-04/guwahati/32030479_1_ulfa-aditya-bora-maoists (accessed 25 October 2014).

[37] See note 18.

[38] 'Assam Maoists Held in Orissa', *Telegraph*, 13 February 2011, available online at http://www.telegraphindia.com/1110213/jsp/northeast/story_13575127.jsp (accessed 29 October 2014).

[39] Ibid.

confessed having undergone training at a Maoist camp in Odisha for three months.[40]

In fact, Assam Chief Minister Gogoi has gone to the extent of thinking aloud as to whether there was a Chinese link to the anti-dam protests in the state. On 12 January 2012, Gogoi stated that the anti-dam movement in Assam has been fuelled by people working to further China's interests.[41] Without mentioning any names, Gogoi said,

> Those opposing big dams are actually working for furthering China's interests. China is trying to divert Brahmaputra water but they do not oppose it. China will divert Brahmaputra water if we do not implement our right of use of water resources in the absence of an international treaty on use of water resources [sic].[42]

The fact that the front organizations and the Maoist ideologues are taking forward the Maoist cause can be judged from the affidavit submitted by the MHA to the Supreme Court on 15 November 2013. The affidavit states that, 'The ideologues and supporters of the CPI (Maoist) in cities and towns have undertaken a concerted and systematic propaganda against the State to project the State in a poor light and also malign it through disinformation.'[43] The affidavit further states that it is these ideologues who have kept the Maoist movement alive and are in many ways more dangerous than the Maoist cadres.[44]

Tactical Partnerships with Other Insurgent Groups

On 14 September 2009, the then Union Home Minister P. Chidambaram had admitted that Maoists were tying up with insurgents

[40] 'Assam Maoists Held in Orissa', *Telegraph*, 13 February 2011.
[41] Tarun Gogoi, 'Anti-dam Movement in Assam for China Interest', *Times of Assam*, 13 January 2012, available online at http://www.timesofassam.com/headlines/anti-dam-movement-in-assam-for-china-interest-tarun-gogoi/ (accessed 28 October 2014).
[42] See note 34.
[43] 'Naxal Ideologues More Dangerous; Centre Tells SC', *Assam Tribune*, 16 November 2013, available online at http://www.assamtribune.com/scripts/detailsnew.asp?id=nov1613/at092 (accessed 29 October 2014).
[44] Ibid.

in the Northeast to synergize operations.[45] Now, of course, it is official that Maoists or Naxalites have managed to extend the *red corridor* to Northeast India and have linked up with a number of insurgent groups in the region, adding an entirely new dimension to the area's security situation, besides forcing the authorities to take a re-look at their counter-terror strategies. In fact, the NIA has begun a formal probe to get to the bottom of the linkage between the CPI (Maoist) and the People's Liberation Army (PLA), one of Manipur's, or for that matter the Northeast's, most potent insurgent groups.[46] Besides, official communications originating in Assam state in no uncertain terms that the Maoists in the state are being armed and trained by the anti-talk faction of the United Liberation Front of Asom (ULFA) headed by Paresh Baruah. Maoists have also been trying to forge links with the National Socialist Council of Nagaland-Isaac Muviah (NSCN-IM). Let us go through these *tactical linkages* one by one.

CPI (Maoist)–PLA Nexus

In 2008, the then Military Chief of the CPI (Maoist) Mallojula Koteswara Rao, popularly known as Kishenji, was reported to have visited Thoubal in Manipur. He is said to have held a meeting in October 2008 with the frontline Meitei insurgent group, the PLA, and adopted a resolution to back each other's interests. Reports with security agencies say Kishenji identified himself as Pradip at the meeting that was attended by a team from the ULFA, led apparently by Partha Gogoi. Partha Gogoi was believed to have attended the Manipur meeting under express orders of ULFA Military Chief Paresh Baruah.[47]

In fact, the nexus between the CPI (Maoist) and the PLA has since been corroborated by detained leaders of the Manipuri insurgent group. Disclosures by N. Dilip Singh alias Ningthambam Ranjit alias Wangba, a senior leader of the Revolutionary People's Front (RPF), of which the PLA is a constituent unit, and Arunkumar Singh Salam, his colleague, arrested on 1 October

---

[45] 'Maoists Forging Links with NE Ultras', http://www.assamtribune.com/scripts/details.asp?id=sep1509/at01 (accessed 17 December 2013).

[46] 'NIA to Probe PLA–Left "Nexus"', http://www.sevensisterspost.com/epaper/26.11.11.pdf (accessed 17 December 2013).

[47] Ibid.

2011 in Delhi, not only reconfirm the thickening of the operational relationship between the Maoists and the RPF/PLA, but also unveil their audacious plan to upgrade it to a strategic level.[48] A note prepared by a security agency makes a disturbing reading:

> ...The proposed Strategic United Front, the concept of which is being currently fleshed out by leaders of the two outfits, would eventually incorporate all 'revolutionary groups' including those in Jammu and Kashmir and the Northeast. This development acquires sinister salience when viewed in the backdrop of credible reports about the Chinese security agencies exhorting the Northeast militants to forge a common platform of which Jammu and Kashmir militants and CPI (Maoist) would be crucial constituents to launch synergised campaigns of violence against India....

The arrested PLA leaders are also said to have revealed that their outfit and the Maoists have since built on their intent of mutual cooperation spelt out in their joint declaration in October 2008 during the second congress of the RPF/PLA in Myanmar. Dilip Singh (self-styled Captain, Chief, External Affairs, PLA) in fact was assigned in March 2009 with the job of operationalizing the liaison with the CPI (Maoist) to push their relationship forward. The note by the security agency adds:

> He (Wangba) visited Jharkhand along with his deputy and met senior CPI (Maoist) leaders in April 2009. Based on an agreement during this visit, three PLA traders imparted combat and communication training to CPI (Maoist) cadres of five states (Orissa, Chhattisgarh, Maharashtra, Andhra Pradesh and Karnataka) for two months from August 2010 in Jharkhand....

That this was a nexus that was actually working has now been proved with the security establishment obtaining enough evidence to ask the NIA to launch a full-scale probe. The RPF/PLA, for instance, was said to have provided TH-K-2AT wireless communication sets to the Maoists, more of which were sought by them in 2011. The Maoists had also requested rocket-propelled

---

[48] 'Kishenji's N–E Nexus Exposed', *Tehelka*, 17 December 2011, available online at http://www.tehelka.com/story_main51.asp?filename=Ne171211Kishenji.asp (accessed 29 October 2014).

grenades (RPGs) for carrying out attacks on *enemy camps* with a view to capture an estimated 1,000 weapons or more.[49] The note by the security agency talks of an advance of ₹15 lakh that the Maoists paid to the RPF/PLA for purchase of arms in 2009. The Maoists were said to have purchased a truck to transport such consignments from Imphal.

It was on 8 June 2011 to be precise that the MHA ordered the NIA probe on the basis of which the investigating agency registered a case against the PLA. Before starting its probe against the rebel group, the counter-terrorism agency informed the NIA court in Guwahati that the PLA 'had imparted training to left-wing extremists in the mainland of India', and, therefore, they would start a probe against it.[50] According to NIA, some of the PLA members had visited places like Rourkela, Kolkata, Guwahati and Champai in Mizoram since July 2010 to impart training to Maoist cadres.

Media reports quoting NIA sources said many PLA leaders went to the jungles in Jharkhand and imparted training to Maoist cadres for 39 days between 11 September and 20 November in 2010. The NIA has launched the probe under the provisions of Indian Penal Code (IPC) and the Unlawful Activities (Prevention) (UA(P)) Act. The NIA has registered its first case against PLA under sections 120B and 121A of IPC and sections 17, 18, 18-A and 18-B of the UA(P) Act.[51]

The NIA's mandate in this case is to find out the larger conspiracy behind PLA's alleged plans to *destabilize India* with the help of Maoists and other like-minded militant groups of the Northeast. Apparently, the premier anti-terror agency has also been asked to conduct a probe into PLA's nexus with China.[52] 'A case (number 1/2011) has been registered at the NIA police station in Guwahati under Sections 120 (B), 121 (A) of the IPC and Sections 17, 18, 18-A and 18-B of the Unlawful Activities (Prevention) Act', news reports quoted sources as saying.[53]

---

[49] 'N–E Ultras Train Orissa Maoists – Terror Alliances Set Off Alarm Bells in Delhi', *Telegraph*, 16 october 2011, available online at http://www.telegraphindia.com/1111016/jsp/orissa/story_14628211.jsp (accessed 26 October 2014).
[50] See note 46.
[51] Ibid.
[52] Ibid.
[53] Ibid.

On 21 April 2012, a Maoist leader, Indranil Chanda, alias Ajay Chanda, was arrested in Kolkata by the West Bengal Police.[54] He had connections with senior PLA leaders and was instrumental in trans-shipment of arms from PLA hideouts in Manipur to the Maoist strongholds in Bengal, Jharkhand and Odisha. Chanda was the one who had sent money to the PLA for supplying sophisticated arms and ammunition. According to official sources, the UALC of CPI (Maoist) was also constituted under his initiative.[55]

On 21 May 2012, NIA filed the first charge sheet on links between PLA and CPI (Maoist).[56] The NIA charge-sheeted three PLA leaders for allegedly supplying arms and ammunition and imparting training to Maoists—N. Dilip Singh alias Wangba, Senjam Dhiren Singh alias Raghu and Kh Arnold Singh alias Becon.

On 28 May 2012, NIA's investigating team arrested PLA leader Ibotombi Singh from Gopalpur in Ganjam district of Odisha.[57] He had replaced N. Dilip Singh, alias Wangba (who was arrested in October 2011), in the PLA hierarchy and was given the responsibility of coordinating with Maoists and had gone to Odisha for that job.

NIA filed an additional charge sheet on the CPI (Maoist)–PLA nexus on 18 December 2012.[58] The charge sheet was filed against Maoist leaders Pallab Borborah, Indranil Chanda and Ibotombi Singh, who were all arrested in 2012 from Assam, Kolkata and Odisha, respectively.

[54] Pankaj Sarma, 'Maoist Spills N-E Beans', *Telegraph*, 24 May 2012, available online at http://www.telegraphindia.com/1120524/jsp/frontpage/story_15525277.jsp#.UpgxfM5acxg (accessed 29 October 2014).
[55] Ibid.
[56] 'NIA Charges PLA Rebels with Aiding Maoists', *Telegraph*, 22 May 2012, available online at http://www.telegraphindia.com/1120522/jsp/northeast/story_15515096.jsp#.UpgzL85acxg (accessed 29 October 2014).
[57] 'Top PLA Man Arrested in Odisha', *Times of India*, 30 May 2012, available online at http://articles.timesofindia.indiatimes.com/2012-05-30/india/31899721_1_maoist-cadres-maoist-activities-odisha (accessed 29 October 2014).
[58] 'National Investigation Agency Files Charges against PLA–Maoist Nexus', *Times of India*, 18 December 2012, available online at http://articles.timesofindia.indiatimes.com/2012-12-18/india/35889751_1_pla-external-affairs-dilip-singh-alias-wangba-pla-members (accessed 29 October 2014).

CPI (Maoist)-ULFA Nexus

The first recorded meeting between the CPI (Maoist) and the ULFA was the one in October 2008 when Maoist leader Kishenji visited Manipur for a meeting with the RPF/PLA.[59] The ULFA, as mentioned earlier, was represented by Partha Gogoi, deputed by none other than Paresh Baruah. What transpired at the meeting (if reports shared by security officials are true) was indeed significant. Kishenji apparently wanted groups like the ULFA to stop attacking the *proletariat* or people belonging to the working class (wage earners, etc.). The Maoist leader must have had the serial killing of migrant Bihari workers and settlers by the ULFA in Assam in mind while calling for a halt in attacks on the *proletariat*. The ULFA refused to pay any heed to Kishenji's call. After all, the ULFA is not a pan-India outfit, unlike the CPI-Maoist, and it draws its sustenance from targeting symbols of the Indian state or people from the mainland who are soft targets but identified with the Hindi-speaking ruling class. Later, of course, as events would unfold, the anti-talk faction of the ULFA did take the Maoists under its wings, obviously as a matter of strategy in the wake of the split in the outfit with a large group headed by its chairman Arabinda Rajkhowa entering into a peace dialogue with the Government of India. More than anything else, Paresh Baruah was looking for force multipliers, and the nascent Maoists on the Assam–Arunachal Pradesh border were just the sort of allies he and his group were looking for.

During a media interview published in January 2010, CPI (Maoist) leader Koteshwar Rao had said:

> We unconditionally support ULFA's struggle for self-determination in Assam. We only want them to stop attacking the Indian proletariat. We will continue to engage with ULFA on this issue.... ULFA cannot ignore the revolutionary struggle of Indians and our enormous goodwill for their struggle.... They have to trust us.... I sincerely want ULFA, the PLA and other such groups fighting for separate homelands or for self-determination to fight the exploitative Indian state alongside us....[60]

---

[59] See note 9.
[60] South Asia Intelligence Review, http://www.satp.org/satporgtp/sair/Archives/sair10/10_17.htm (accessed 17 December 2013).

According to reports, Paresh Baruah has been a key supplier of arms and ammunition to the Maoists in India. But now it is charged that the Paresh Baruah-led ULFA faction is supplying sophisticated arms and funds to the Maoists in Assam and elsewhere in the region and this charge has been corroborated by people in authority, including Assam Governor Patnaik.[61]

Also, the fact is that most of the important Maoist leaders of Assam have had links with the ULFA for a very long time.[62] Without a tactical understanding between these Maoists leaders and the ULFA, it would not have been possible for the Maoists to set up bases on the Assam–Arunachal Pradesh border. This is because these areas have been for years dominated by the ULFA and it would not be possible to set up bases there without entering into some kind of understanding with the outfit.

CPI (Maoist)-(NSCN-IM) Nexus

The Maoists are also said to have established links with the NSCN-IM. On 9 May 2010, then Union Home Secretary G.K. Pillai stated that the Union Government was aware that the CPI (Maoist) had been in touch with NSCN-IM. He contended, further, that IM leader Thuingaleng Muivah had confirmed, 'A few years ago, the CPI-Maoist had approached his outfit, apparently to help them with arms.' The meeting had taken place at the NSCN-IM's camp in Hebron near Dimapur (on the Assam–Nagaland border). Reports also indicated that IM leaders attended a Maoist meeting in the Dandakaranya area in Chhattisgarh. It is also suspected that NSCN-IM might be training Maoist cadres.[63]

Government's Anti-Maoist Strategy

The governments at the centre and in the states are trying their best to prevent the spread of Maoism in the country. The centre and the states have their own anti-Maoist strategy. While states

[61] See note 33.
[62] See note 7.
[63] See note 60.

like Andhra Pradesh has been able to come out of the grip of Maoism with its strategy, states like Chhattisgarh and Jharkhand are still facing this menace and it is spreading to new regions like Northeast India. Talking about the Maoist spread to the Northeast, a parliamentary panel has noted that, 'it has potential transborder possibilities of connection, activities and interaction'.[64]

As mentioned earlier, the Assam government, in May 2013, had sent a proposal to the central government to declare nine districts of the state as left-wing-extremism-affected districts. These districts are Tinsukia, Dibrugarh, Dhemaji, Lakhimpur, Golaghat, Sivasagar, Goalpara, Cachar and Karimganj. If these districts are declared as left-wing extremism-affected districts, the Government of India, through the MHA, would provide special infrastructure development fund of ₹10 crore a year for each district.[65] The Union Finance and Home Ministries have since gone through the proposal, and last heard,[66] it was being examined by the IB.

On 1 December 2012, Union Rural Development Minister Jairam Ramesh said that his ministry has asked the centre to declare eastern Assam districts of Tinsukia and Dibrugarh as left-wing-extremism-affected districts.[67]

An Assam Police Task Force, formed to study Maoist activities in the state, has recommended converting the present Commando Battalion into a well-knit offensive unit called Assam Police Commando Organization to counter the growing presence of Maoists in the state.[68] The commando organization will have the following forces under it—the Black Panthers, Assam Police Rangers and Veerangana, the all-women commando force. The task force has also suggested constructing border outposts as per the Andhra model.

[64] 'Maoists Are Moving to Plan, the Aim Is to Capture State Power', *New Indian Express*, 27 October 2013, available online at http://m.newindianexpress.com/voices/60004 (accessed 29 October 2014).

[65] See note 22.

[66] Till December 2013.

[67] 'Declare Tinsukia, Dibrugarh as LWE Affected Districts: Jairam Ramesh', *Hindu*, 1 December 2012, available online at http://www.thehindu.com/news/national/other-states/declare-tinsukia-dibrugarh-as-lwe-affected-districts-jairam-ramesh/article4154054.ece (accessed 29 October 2014).

[68] See note 7.

The Indian government is now likely to sensitize the European Union (EU) and a few other countries about the violence perpetrated by Maoists and ensure that the rebels do not get support from organizations based in those countries.[69] The Union Home Ministry will soon approach the Ministry of External Affairs to sensitize the EU and countries such as Britain, Brazil, Canada and Philippines about the violence being carried out by the CPI (Maoist). The move came after the CPI (Maoist) had recently thanked more than two dozen organizations in Germany, Austria, France, Switzerland, Holland, Sweden, Italy, Norway, Spain, Britain, Brazil, Canada and Philippines who took part in the 24 November 2012 conference in Hamburg for supporting the 'people's war in India'.[70]

Need for Urgent Attention

The Maoists are slowly consolidating their position in the Northeast. The number of unemployed youth in the region is rather high and they can be easily be lured by the Maoists. Besides, there are many remote and under-developed areas in the region with minimum presence of government administration. Therefore, there is a need for paying urgent attention towards this issue. The following steps may be taken by the government authorities in this regard:

- Proper and focused attention should be given to development on the ground, especially those under-developed and inaccessible areas which are likely to come under the influence of Maoists.
- Government officials at all levels, deputy commissioners (DCs), additional deputy commissioners (ADCs), subdivisional officers (SDOs) as well as officers from the departments involved in developmental works, should give proper attention towards implementation of the schemes as well as ensure that these are adequately monitored and supervised.

[69] See note 27.
[70] Ibid.

- Government needs to fill up the vacancies in various development departments, so that development works do not suffer in some areas. For example, in Sadiya Subdivision of eastern Assam's Tinsukia district, there is no child development project officer (CDPO), deputy inspector of schools, subdivisional welfare officer and extra assistant commissioner (EAC). Even the present block development officer (BDO) is just in charge of the post (as of November 2013). As such development works have not been reaching the grassroots. Immediate steps in this regard are required.
- As mentioned earlier, Government of Assam has submitted a proposal with the central government for declaring nine of its districts as Maoist-affected. If declared so, these districts would receive ₹10 crore a year for infrastructural development. The Assam government now needs to carry out a socio-economic survey to assess the existing infrastructure in these districts as well as the livelihood patterns and social demographics of these areas. Based on the findings of the survey, a comprehensive development action plan can be developed by the state government with consultations with the respective district authorities. If this is kept ready, the government can immediately work on implementing the action plan as and when these districts are declared Maoist-affected, leading to the flow of special funds.
- The authorities should ensure engagement of the people of an area in development works in a participative manner.
- Authorities should maintain open channels of communication with the people by collecting feedback from them and promptly redressing their grievances.

Conclusion

Northeast India is now no longer a dot on the Maoist map, but a strategically important region for them. Maoism may sustain in the Northeast due to lack of development caused by various factors, including poor accountability and leakage of development funds, and the area's geography, the porous borders that the region shares with Myanmar, China, Bangladesh and Bhutan.

With frontline ethnic insurgent groups either on a ceasefire or in an advanced stage of peace negotiations with the government, the anti-peace-talk factions of groups like the ULFA could use these Maoists as force multipliers. If an effective security and development strategy is not adopted, the Maoists could well come to fill the void created by ethnic insurgent groups giving up arms and joining the mainstream. The government authorities need to devise a development action plan to give youths in areas like eastern Assam's Tinsukia district or the Lohit and Dibang Valley districts in adjoining Arunachal Pradesh jobs and livelihood options, besides providing connectivity to the far-flung areas. The government also needs to fill up the vacancies in various development departments. Besides, in view of the near-admission by the security establishment in the country that the police and the paramilitary can actually deal with the Maoists and that the Army may not be necessary to combat the *red rebels*, it is important to take a look at policing on the Assam–Arunachal Pradesh frontier. For instance, in the Maoist-infested district of Lower Dibang valley in Arunachal Pradesh, there are only 262 police personnel to look after a 3,900 sq. km area.[71] Without immediate remedial steps, this strategically important northeastern region may once again be intertwined in a vicious cycle of violence.

---

[71] Official Website of Lower Dibang Valley district, http://roing.nic.in/glance.htm (accessed 17 December 2013).

16

Convergence and Divergence of Madhes Politics in Nepal and Its Implications

Sohan Prasad Sha

Introduction

Since the uprising of Madhes in January–February 2007, the prominence of Madhes politics has established in Nepal. Madhes uprising introduced a new kind of political discourse in Nepal. As a result, several new issues emerged into the political discourse of Nepal. One such significant issue was that of ethnic and regional discrimination. Madhes politics raised the issues of 'ethno-nationalism'[1] centrally in Nepali political discourse. The issue of ethno-nationalism became a critical political factor for the people of the southern plain region of Nepal (Tarai).[2] The criticality of the

---

[1] See K. Hachhethu, 'Madheshi Nationalism and Restructuring the Nepali State' (Paper presented in a seminar on Constitutionalism and Diversity in Nepal, Centre for Nepal and Asian Studies, Tribhuvan University, Kathmandu, pp. 1–12, August 2007.

[2] The use of the terms *Tarai* and *Madhes* is interchangeable. However, the political connotation of the words *Tarai* and *Madhes* has been contesting ideas in Nepal. For instance, Tharu inhabitants in Tarai have difference of opinion in terms of their 'identity' assertion as compared to Madhesi. Nevertheless, Tharu/Madhesi shares the experience of being discriminated by caste of high hills elites (CHHE) of Kathmandu establishment. See J.F. Fisher, 'Identity in Nepal: Ethnic, Individual, Political', *Reviews in Anthropology*, 36, no. 2 (2007): 155–174 and B. Gautam, 'Of

ethno-nationalist demand in popular imagination was reflected in the constituent assembly (CA) I election. This popular imagination found its expression with the historical CA I election in 2008, in which regional parties had done fairly well and Madhes politics further re-emerged as the *king-maker* in Nepalese politics—as any government formation cannot be possible without Madhes party's support. However, the failure of CA I to promulgate the constitution of 'Federal Democratic Republic of Nepal'[3] led to serious setbacks for progressive political forces, such as Madhes parties and others, in CA II[4] election held on 19 November 2013 in Nepal. With other things remaining constant to decide on the two most contentious issues of constitution drafting—federalism and the forms of government—how would the new changes, after CA I, play out in Nepalese politics and its implication for peace and stability?

This chapter attempts to forecast the political scenario in Nepal, post CA II. This analysis is based on the observation of various political actors in Nepalese politics. There are several factors of Madhes politics that need to be unpacked in order to develop a comprehensive understanding of the future directions of Nepalese politics. These factors are important for both a critical understanding of Nepalese politics and its future policy directions as well as to a proper understanding of the dynamic nature of Madhes politics itself. These factors are also of significant interest, as they will have significant repercussions on the nature of the coming democracy in the country. First, with the passage of time, while on the one hand, Madhes parties/politics are still in the process of *learning by doing*, on the other hand, they are facing challenges to accommodate themselves with ruling establishment in Nepal wherein democratic political reforms expedited with variety of contending social issues which generated tensions and fierce debates especially on the issue of federalism, on the other hand. Second, the sudden rise of Madhes subnationalist assertions, with demands for the cognition of their identity and its constant radicalization in Nepal. Third, Madhes region

---

Madhes and the Nepali State', *Studies in Nepali History and Society*, 17, no. 1 (2012): 175.

[3] The newly formed first CA I meeting declared the Kingdom of Nepal as 'Federal Democratic and Republic' on 28 May 2008, available online at http://www.nepalnews.com/archive/2008/may/may28/news18.php (accessed 4 January 2014).

[4] Perhaps, Nepal will be the only country to hold twice CA election.

caught in a dichotomized situation between *internal colonialism* and *neocolonialism*, which makes issues more complicated for the future of Madhes politics. Fourth, if the state continues to use the strategy of co-option and coercion in its engagement with Madhes parties to weaken their politics and their political base without addressing the legitimate demands of the people, then the Madhes problem in Nepal may continue to exist in a state of permanent limbo with perpetual impasse. Fifth, the polarization of Nepalese society along the line of *the hill people* (Pahadiya) and *the plain people* (Madhesya) is worrisome and is increasingly becoming a psychological/emotional issue of identity and difference. In these circumstances, how Madhes politics and Nepalese politics will be mutually accommodative in the nation state of Nepal will be a difficult task for diverse political actors to ensure.

In discussing all these factors, this chapter intends to alert the various political actors towards the possible devastating consequences of the political and cultural rifts that have emerged in Nepal. This chapter also tries to suggest ways in which the Madhes problem be addressed within a democratic framework, which can guarantee peace and stability in the region, and to warn against the possible outcomes as well as advance preparedness required to contain and resolve the problem. It is very important that the Madhes problem is democratically resolved through the participation of international actors, civil society groups, public intellectuals and mainstream media. The state of Nepal and other political actors needs to be sensitized towards the legitimate issues of the southern plain region of Nepal, which cannot be possible without the involvement of international community, civil society, public intellectuals and mainstream media. This alone can ensure the *genuine* peace and take the ongoing peace process, which is remarkable, to its logical conclusion.

Background of Madhes Politics

Brief Overview of Tarai/Madhes

Geographically, Nepal is divided into three regions—mountains (Himalayan range), hills (Shiwalik ranges to the northern border) and Tarai/Madhes (the area of Nepal southern plains region of

Shiwalik).[5] The Madhes region is mostly low-lying land consisting of Nepal's 20 districts.[6] This region is also of strategic importance as it shares an international border with India. The administrative set-up of Tarai/Madhesis is likely to create some confusion (inner Madhes and outer Madhes) as 'the district demarcation was not based on ecological or social basis',[7] and it contains the proportion of Shiwalik and mid-mountain areas. This demarcation made holistic planning difficult for Tarai/Madhes region.

The terms *Madhes* and *Madhesi* can be understood through a proper historical perspective and through political assertion of its people. Whereas the word *Tarai* needs to be understood within the framework of a sovereign political territory of Nepal, the term Madhes is derived from the Sanskrit word *Madhyadesh*. The term was used for a geographical region that stretch across a large territory ranging from the foothills of Shiwalik to the Vidhyachal mountain in the south of central India.[8] However, the narrow reference of *Madhes* is a recent phenomenon in Nepal wherein it denotes the southern plain region of eastern and western Tarai. Nevertheless, Madhesis have been defined as the people who inhabit the plain region (non-hills/or non-Pahadis) with distinct language, culture which included various castes of Hindus, Muslims and indigenous Tarai ethnic group (Tharu).[9] However, in terms of political assertion and identity question, it seems that a rift

---

[5] See F.H. Gaige, *Regionalism and National Unity in Nepal* (Berkeley: University of California Press, 1975).

[6] The Tarai/Madhes districts: from east to west; Jhapa, Morang, Sunsari (Far eastern region); Saptari, Siraha, Dhanusha, Mahottari, Sarlahi (eastern region); Rauthat, Bara, Parsa, Chitwan (mid-Tarai); Nawalparasi, Rupandehi, Kapilbastu (western); Dang, Banke, Bardia, Kailali and Kanchanpur (Far western).

[7] S.G. Shah, 'Social Inclusion of Madhesi Community in Nation Building' (paper presented at a conference organized by Social Inclusion Research Fund, pp. 1–2, February 2006, Kathmandu, Nepal).

[8] Ibid.

[9] It is to note that the term Madhesi is not a homogenous entity in Tarai. The Tarai constitute of many linguistic and social/religious diversity. For instance, it is evident from the National report that in Nepal, there are 123 languages spoken as mother tongue and there are 125 castes/ethnicities. In Tarai, Maithili, Bhojpuri, Awadhi, Hindi, Tharu and Urdu are mostly spoken language and castes structure are similar to Bihar and Utter Pradesh of India.

is emerging in the region between Madhesis and indigenous ethnic groups. There are some evidences suggesting that Tharu group, particularly in mid-western Tarai, are counterposed to Madhesi, thus giving signals of *Tharu versus Madhesi* polarization envisaging original inhabitants of Tarai.[10] Even so, after mid-2010, Tharus and Madhesis are asserting their politics and they are united both strategically as well as principally with the issue of federalism.[11]

However, the word *Tarai* connotes the sovereign political territory of Nepal, constituted in the 19th century. Its existence in Nepal is defined through the treaty of 1816 after the defeat with British East India Company while southwestern Tarai, known as *Nayamuluk* (new country), as a reward for Nepalese rulers for assistance to suppress freedom movement (the Sepoy mutiny from 1857 to 1859) in India.[12] Such political arrangements have generated some differences of opinion amongst Madhesi political class. For instance, Madhesi People's Right Forum (MPRF) (2005) argues that 'ever since the treaty was signed between two countries, the Madhesi have been facing national identity crisis' and further argues that ruling elites of Kathmandu have used 'the Tarai people for reserving economic interest of Kathmandu'.[13] In addition, some fringe/armed/criminal groups in Tarai interpret the Madhesi issue in skewed ways. This has further complicated the situation in Tarai region and made any negotiation for the betterment difficult.[14]

The Emergence of Madhes Politics

Since the *jana andolan* of 2006, Nepal has been undergoing a historic transition. Several new factors have emerged in the political discourse shaping and reshaping the popular imagination

[10] See ICG, 'Nepal's Troubled Tarai Region', 2007, available online at http://www.crisisgroup.org/~/media/Files/asia/south-asia/nepal/136_nepal_s_troubled_tarai_region.pdf (accessed 18 November 2014).

[11] B. Gautam, 'Of Madhes and the Nepali State', 187.

[12] See note 10.

[13] Madhesi People's Right Forum, *Conspiracy against Madhes* (Nepal: Madhesi People's Right Forum, 2005), 20–21.

[14] For instance, see C.K. Lal, 'Waiting for Goit', *Nepali Times*, 02–08 May 2008, 395. See G.K. Goit, 'The History of Tarai in Nepal', 2007, available online at http://madhesi.wordpress.com/2007/04/04/history-of-terai-in-nepal/ (accessed 6 January 2014).

for a democratic Nepal. The sudden rise of Madhesi politics has received the overwhelming enthusiasm after the historic Madhes uprising of January–February, 2007. This politics has strongly affirmed the subnationalism of Madhes, which has led to a new national discourse on restructuring of Nepal. The major concerns that Madhes politics asserts in Nepal are the following: the shift from unitary state structure to federal model of governance; right of self-determination; inclusive and representative democracy; distribution of resources; to do away with a monolithic hill-centric nationalism in order to promote inclusive citizenship; respect of culture/language; nationalist ideas to be accommodative of plural values of the country; devolution of power from CHHE which includes Hill Brahmins and Chhetris; from centralized to decentralized system of governance based on identity based federalism.[15]

The history of Madhesi politics/issues goes back to 1951. It was the year when Vedanand Jha formed the Nepal Tarai Congress. Perhaps, this would be the first instance of an identity-based political movement in Nepal, which demanded an autonomous status for the Tarai. This political formation also demanded the recognition of Hindi as a national language and inclusion of Madhesi people in state bureaucracy. The Nepalese regime did not pay any attention to these demands, and on the contrary, the state imposed *one language* policy for the entire nation. The insensitive attitude of the regime led to protest and clashes between Tarai Congress and nationalists. However, in 1959 parliamentary election, Tarai Congress failed to win any single seat while Nepali Congress (NC) got the thumping majority. The charismatic leader Bishweshwar Prasad Koirala, NC, is believed to be politically conscious about Madhesis and known for his respect for social diversity.[16] However, the debates on making of a Nepali nation more inclusive, and respectful of representative democracy, has not seen any considerable progress. Rather it is the institutionalized form of social exclusion that has continued through different constitutions of Nepal, this has made the issue more complicated for the people who are on the margins of ethnicity and other

---

[15] Sohan P. Sha, 'Deconstructing Madhesi Politics', *IPCS* 418, 19 November 2013, available online at http://www.ipcs.org/article/nepal/deconstructing-madhesi-politics-4183.html (accessed 19 October 2013).
[16] ICG, *Nepal's Troubled Tarai Region*, 5.

minority groups.[17] The upsurge of identity assertion post 2006 in Nepal was awareness towards a historical discrimination.

Another account of the Madhesi politics, which shaped the later course of Madhesi politics, was the rise of the prominent leader Raghunath Thakur in 1950s. Interestingly, he has campaigned in Delhi (India) for Madhesi emancipation. He was the first person to write a monograph in 1958 on Madhes politics. In this monograph, he gave voice to and narrated the psychological anxiety that people from the Madhes region faced on an everyday basis. He also wrote extensively about state violence, socioeconomic and political insecurities in the Tarai[18] and demanded the adequate representation to be ensured in every state apparatus. He further demanded, like Vedanand Jha, regional autonomy for Tarai. Since then, many leaders have raised Madhesi issues during 1960s along the similar lines.[19] In addition, the seed of the first republican demand emerged in Nepal from the Madhes. This happened in the backdrop of a bomb attack on King Mahendra in 1962 by Durgananda Jha in Janakpur.[20] This attack was a reflection of and gave voice to growing unease with the monarchy.

During 1980s, under the leadership of Gajendra Narayan Singh, Nepal Sadbhavana Party (NSP) was established. Madhesi politics came up in a consolidated way with the formation of this party. This party tactically avoided the ban and was able to register itself as a political party in 1990. It could do this successfully as it was able to 'evading ban by making their subnational nature

---

[17] The democratic movement started in Nepal in late 1940s. Since then till now, Nepal has many constitutions (1948, 1951, 1959, 1962, 1990, 2007). Again, Nepal is in transition to institutionalize peace and draft constitution through CA. However, Malagodi argues that prior to 2007, the Constitution of Nepal had systemic social exclusion. See, M. Malagodi, *Constitutional Nationalism and Legal Exclusion: Equality, Identity Politics and Democracy in Nepal (1990–2007)* (New Delhi: Oxford University Press, 2013).

[18] See note 5.

[19] B. Gautam, 'Of Madhes and the Nepali State', 175.

[20] See, C. Burkert, 'Defining Maithil Identity: Who is in Charge?' in *Nationalism and Ethnicity in a Hindu Kingdom*, eds David N. Gellner, Joanna Pfaff-Czarnecka and John Whelpton (Amsterdam: Harwood Academic Publishers, 1997), p. 246.

less obvious'.[21] Later on, in 1997, MPRF came into existence, as a non-governmental organization, to promote Madhesi concerns and started to articulate Madhesi voices. MPRF raised the issue of internal colonization, racial and regional discrimination, secular and federal republic, a proportional representation (PR), citizenship to all Madhesi and Hindi as lingua franca, end of religious discrimination against Nepali Muslims, single Madhes province with regional autonomy, etc. MPRF functioned as a social movement and leading force behind the January–February, 2007, Madhes uprising. MPRF registered itself as a political party in April 2007. Thus, the historical experience of Madhesi movement and the trend of Madhes politics has been a fragmented but relentless political struggle for socio-economic political inclusion of Madhesi through the framework of social justice. These struggles were aiming to end the historical discrimination[22] as well as for the establishment of a democratic nation.

Political Actors and Conflict of Interest in Madhes/Tarai

Madhesi political actors have been in all political parties of Nepal. The mainstream national political parties like NC and Communist Party of Nepal-Unified Marxist–Leninist (CPN-UML) — have strong organization base in Madhes. However, the distinction of these parties from Madhesi political parties based on their ideological leanings towards identity questions, that is, Madhesi as a political identity to assert rights of self-determination through federalism is noticeable. The identity question is largely a product of popular Madhesi movement, which has accumulated from last few decades in Nepal. Post 1990, after the establishment of NSP as a recognized mainstream party, Nepal went through or

---

[21] As per the Constitution of Nepal (1990), 'The election commission shall not register any political organization ... on the basis of religion, caste, tribe, language or sex or ...' See M. Malagodi, *Constitutional Nationalism and Legal Exclusion*, 197–198.

[22] The empirical evidence of socio-economic–political discrimination against Madhesis and its economic underdevelopment due to historical/geographical discrimination analysed through data-based research. See note 7.

experienced a very different political culture. The Maoists, CPN-Maoist, launched their people's war in 1996. Maoist party was sympathetic with the Madhesi agenda during the Maoists insurgency period. The Maoists synergized Madhesi's concern while tactically supporting social movements. This helped the cause of Madhes. During this process, the Maoist parties had established Madhesi National Liberation Front in 2000. It was also the period when MPRF was extensively campaigning for the Madhesi and in the process making it a political issue, an issue that was increasingly becoming difficult for anyone to ignore. However, the conflict of interest in the Maoist party concerning the formation of autonomous people's governments of Madhes into two units, Tharuwan (in the west) and Madhes (in the east), on the one hand, while personality clash for leadership, on the other hand, created problems in the path of a united front on the Madhes question. This led to the rise of a splinter group from the Maoist party, Janatantrik Tarai Mukti Morcha (JTMM), as an armed Madhesi militant group under the leadership of Jai Krishna Goit. JTMM later on further splitted into many factions (JTMM under Nagendra Paswan alias Jawala Singh, Visfot Singh, Prithvi Samuha, etc.). These splinter groups further divided into several other groups on several grounds. These political demands were diverge. These demands ranged from independence to unified province within Nepal. In addition, numerous fringe/criminal groups are mushrooming on the name of fighting for Madhes cause. This has made law and order situation fragile in Nepal. On the other hand, parties like Chure Bhawar Ekta Samaj (CBES) also emerged in the process in order to counter/contain Madhesi mobilization. It is interesting to note here that CBES believed to have tactical arrangements with mainstream political parties such as NC and CPN-UML.[23] This makes Madhes movement/activism/politics complex and contradictory.

[23] See ICG, *Nepal's Troubled Tarai Region*, 6–11. See, for the list of armed/fringe groups in Madhes, Bishnu Pathak and Devendra Uprety, *Terai-Madhes: Searching for Identity Based Security*, 2009, Situation Update No. 88. Kathmandu: Peace and Conflict Study Center, 20. For the narratives of Madhes situation on ground through identity politics vis-à-vis armed groups leading to polarization amongst Madhesis themselves vis-à-vis Madhesis and Pahadis (hill people) as already existed fault line in Nepal, which makes situation complicated. See S. Karn, 'Everyday Voilence in Madhes, Identity Politics, Armed Groups and the Parallel Economy', *Studies in Nepali History and Society*, 16, no. 2 (2011): 297–319.

The State Strategy towards Madhes: From Coercive Disruption to Innovative Disruption

The core issue of Madhesi politics (disenchantment of Madhesi people) is the state of apathy in Nepal towards solving the genuine agenda of inclusive/representation in Nepalese state structures. As already mentioned, there has been a steady progress on the boarder political concerns of Madhesi politics, securely in position but not shaky. However, these concerns are far from being institutionally resolved. Madhesi has political grievances that have been longstanding in Nepalese nation-state formation. The existing literature on the formation of nationalist ideas and nationalism in Nepal suggests that the Nepalese nation has been constituted through the category of *others* in order to preserve the political autonomy of the Nepalese state vis-à-vis other nations in the subcontinent, particularly India. This also meant celebrating uniformity (monolithic hills nationalism) which went through, real or imagined, at the cost of social diversity that historically existed in Nepal.[24]

However, post 2006, the sudden rise of ethno-nationalism, established through Madhes movement, changed the atmosphere of Madhesi politics and brought the issues of Madhes in to the mainstream politics of Nepal. However, pre 2006, Madhesi issues had not gained momentum to an extent that would have disrupted the Kathmandu establishment. The existing political establishment, which also included mainstream Nepalese political parties (such as NC and CPN-UML), had not faced much difficulty in galvanizing support in the Madhes region as they had organizational strength. However, pre 2006, the mainstream parties could not address the fundamental regional problems of under-representation of Madhesi, citizenship issues, social/cultural inclusion (rather state-imposed monolingual policies continued), electoral under-representation and state-imposed political

---

[24] See R. Burghart, 'The Formation of the Concept of Nation-state in Nepal', *Journal of Asian Studies*, 44, no. 1 (1984): 101–125. Also see D.N. Gellner, 'Ethnicity and Nationalism in the World's Only Hindu State', in *Nationalism and Ethnicity in a Hindu Kingdom: The Politics of Culture in Contemporary Nepal* (Amsterdam: Harwood Academic Publishers, 1997), 28.

economy of backwardness in Madhes.[25] This process can largely be characterized as *coercive disruption* of Madhesi political issues in the Nepalese monolithic hill-centric nationalism and political process that led to subversion of Madhesi identity.

The post-2007 period in Nepal, considered as Madhesi political awakening for their political assertion brought into the light henceforth the longstanding but ignored issues of the inclusion of the Madhesi discourse in the mainstream political narrative of Nepal. While Nepal went in the process of constitution making through a CA, the debate over assimilation/inclusion of core Madhesi agenda got importance in the national political space. This expedited a democratic political reform process in Nepal. Several of the Madhesi demands/agendas, such as amending the citizenship laws, electoral representation based on population and reservation policy for Madhesi in civil services were institutionally ensured. Howsoever, too little and too late, this process can broadly be categorized as *innovative disruption* marking a rupture in the practices of Nepalese state vis-à-vis a Madhesi question to accommodate Madhes sentiments and towards representative/inclusive democracy.

Recent Development

After the Madhes Movement[26] (January–February 2007), the new political forces emerged, namely MPRF and Tarai Madhes Democratic Party (TMDP). The rise of these political forces and renewed

[25] See ICG, *Nepal's Troubled Tarai Region*, 4–5. There is wide range of literature that argues that Tarai of Nepal is 'internally colonized' from Kathmandu and simultaneously being caught in 'neocolonialism' logic of India as immediate neighbour which led to the underdevelopment of the Tarai region of Nepal. See B. Bhattarai, 'Regional Problem of Tarai: An Analysis', *Red Tarai*, 1, no. 1 (1995) (in Nepali language).

[26] The detail account of Madhes Movement, see B. Gautam, *Details of Madhesh Rebel* (Kathmandu: Martin Choutari, 2008). Also, see K. Hachhethu, 'Madheshi Nationalism and Restructuring the Nepali State' (paper presented in a seminar on Constitutionalism and Diversity in Nepal, Centre for Nepal and Asian Studies, Tribhuvan University, Kathmandu, 1–12, August 2007.

public support to the cause of Madhes led to national discourse on restructuring of Nepalese state. It also called for the right to self-determination through *federalism*. The word *federalism* came into Nepal's mainstream vocabulary after signing of the historic agreement between United Democratic Madhesi Front and Government of Nepal on 28 February 2008. Subsequently, it was included in the interim constitution as a binding principle for the CA.[27]

The historical CA I election was held on 10 April 2008. In this CA election, the major Madhesi political parties—MPRF, TMDP, NSP—contested in which Madhesi parties got a sweeping victory. The victory of Madhesi parties came as a surprise to Nepalese intelligentsia. The final count of election results showed that Madhesi parties in CA I collectively received between 11 and 12 per cent of the nationwide vote (including PR and First-Past-The Post) and 87 out of 601 seats (includes nominated seats).[28] With these results, Madhesi parties were elevated in the national politics. They were eulogized as *king-maker* in Kathmandu politics and subsequently they leveraged their political bargaining to reserve the posts of a president and a vice president from the Madhesi community. The electoral gain of Madhesi parties should be considered as a historic event, especially as never before a Madhesi had been appointed to a post of national political significance. This helped boost the collective conscience and confidence of the Madhesi people in Nepal.[29] Furthermore, Madhesi parties managed to be in every subsequent government formation in Nepal and that cost them with series of splits. For instance, the formation of United Communist Party of Nepal (Maoist), UCPN (M), led by the Maoist Chairman, Pushpa Kamal Dahal in 2008 with the support of MPRF and NSP. In 2009, the

---

[27] See, J. Miklian, 'Nepal's Terai: Constructing an Ethnic Conflict', *International Peace Research Institute* (2009), South Asia Briefing Paper No. 1, 1–16.

[28] See B. Pokharel and S. Rana, *Nepal: Votes for Peace* (New Delhi: Cambridge University Press India Ltd., 2013), pp. 172–173.

[29] However, the election for the first president in Nepal was also seen a major deviation from national consensus among political parties and mistrust added. It is to note that UCPN (M) nominated Ramraja Prasad Singh as a presidential candidate from Madhesi community, which sparked other political parties to nominate their presidential candidate from Madhesi community in lieu to garner support from Madhesi parties.

second government formation under the leadership of Madhav Kumar Nepal, CPN-UML, with the support of MPRF (democratic), a splinter group of MPRF, TMDP and NSP. In 2011, the third government led by Jhalnath Khanal, CPN-UML, with the support of UCPN (M) and MPRF. Lastly, the forth government led by Dr Baburam Bhattarai, UCPN (M), with the support of United Madhesi Democratic Fronts (including MPRF, TMDP and NSP). In May 2012, the CA was dissolved after political parties failed to draft the new constitution—especially on the issues of 'federalism',[30] which is the core demand and premise on which Madhesi politics was/is, based. This caused the overall political disenchantment with their politics. The failure of the CA I was a major setback to the progressive[31] political forces enduring for desperate *change* to make Nepal *new Nepal*.

Nepal's transition for peace and stability prolonged, and nation plunged into the debate for holding another election to the CA II. With this, Nepalese politics hit another roadblock, as there was difficulty in attaining consensus for election and in fixing the constitutional difficulties to hold CA II election.[32] Finally, the sitting Chief Justice of Nepal Supreme Court was appointed to task the Interim Election Government, as political parties could not arrive at any consensus among themselves. In midst of this chaos, CA II election was held successfully on 19 November 2013. In addition, the results of CA II unfolded yet another dynamic of complexity in Nepalese politics. UCPN (M) faced a major setback in CA II election, while Madhesi parties too suffered severely from excessive fragmented political parties. However, Madhesi parties

---

[30] The detail narratives about *federalism* debate among different political actor in Nepal. See ICG. Nepal: Identity Politics and Federalism (2011), Asian Report No.199, International Crisis Group.

[31] In Nepal there is a polarized perception among political parties to characterize progressive political forces (Maoist, Madhesi and indigenous parties) vis-à-vis the status quo political forces (traditional parties such as NC, CPN-UML and right-wing Hindu parties).

[32] The formation of interim election council under the Chief Justice is being criticized as 'a constitutional aberration and a political disgrace' despite the fact that in the political stalemate that ensued it was the only way to strike a consensus to hold CA II election. See C.K. Lal, 'The YES Outbreak', *My Republica*, 6 January 2014, available online at http://myrepublica.com/portal/index.php?action=news_details&news_id=67450 (last accessed on 09 January 2014).

could maintain collectively to get between 11 and 12 per cent of the total vote share and approximately 53 out of 575.[33]

Whatever the election results, one of the remarkable achievements in Nepal during the CA II election was to leapfrog the idea of making Nepal truly a *representative democracy* as well as a *participatory/inclusive democracy*. In this regard, CA I was the most inclusive governing institution of Nepal, ever in the history than in any point of time. While CA II election results unfolded, there is a sense of scepticism and anxiety regarding the issues of the people who continue to live at the margins of the Nepalese society (women, indigenous people, Madhesis and particularly Dalits). The issues concerning these groups need to be incorporated with utmost sincerity in the new constitution of Nepal. In the changed context of CA II, the fear of the reversal of certain issues, such as tweaking the federalism debate, reinstating monolithic hill-centric nationalism while opposing inclusive/progressive nationalism, has emerged. These were the issues that had gained momentum during the period of CA I (2008–2012). Nevertheless, Table 16.1 shows the contrasting evidence that adds further complexity to the recent political development of Nepal. Madhesis have improved their representation in the CA II election outcome. This is likely to improve their representation even if Madhesi parties suffered a setback. This has created a difficult situation for these mainstream parties (NC and CPN-UML) as they have to reconcile to the aspirations of the Madhes community with their traditional hill-centric politics which has been largely hostile towards Madhes community. The political situation should get further complicated as there is a fair chance that the representation of Dalit,[34] indigenous people and women would be less as compared to CA I.[35]

There is no doubt that the people's mandate in CA II election was highly enthusiastic and overwhelming. However, there

---

[33] Out of 601 CA members, 26 seats nominated. For CA II 2013 results, see http://www.election.gov.np/election/np (accessed 21 December 2013).

[34] The Dalits' grievances are longstanding problems in Nepal and if CA will fail to incorporate Dalits issues then the nation will fail at large. See S. Nepali, 'The Nation fails Dalits', *The Kathmandu Post*, available online at http://www.ekantipur.com/2014/01/07/opinion/the-nation-fails-dalits (accessed 8 January 2014).

[35] Madhesi and indigenous people shared strongly the federalism agenda in Nepal.

Table 16.1:
Representation of different groups in constituent assembly of Nepal[36]

Election Results	CA I*		CA II**		Inclusive Representation Scale***	
	No. of Seats	% of Total CA	No. of Seats	% of Total CA	No. of Seat	% of Total CA
1 Women	197	33.77	171	28	198	33
2 Indigenous peoples	219	36.43	173	28	222	37.8
3 Madhesis	117	19.46	161	26	187	31.2
4 Dalits	49	9	42	7	78	13
5 Backward classes	17	2.82	21	3.5	24	4
6 Others (Brahmins, Chhetris, etc.)	206	34.29	221	36	180	30.2

Note: *The data of CA I extracted from O. Gurung.[37]
** The data of CA II proximate estimate extracted from online portal. Available online at http://www.onlinekhabar.com/2014/01/151760/ (accessed 4 January 2014).
*** The data of inclusive representation scale calculated from recently passed ordinance by Government of Nepal on 14 June 2013 (Constituent Assembly Members election ordinance, 2070 BS, in Nepali).

can be a different interpretation of the people's mandate. If one is aware and mindful of the experience of CA I in constitution making/drafting, one must be sceptical about the possible outcomes of CA II. For instance, CA II is merely an extension of CA I to get through constitution drafted in CA II. In this sense, in Nepal, whatever be the CA II result, if the winner is considered as a part of the answer, than the loser is always a part of the problem. Instead of identifying the winner or loser in currently held CA II election, it is desirable to take the holistic views of how Nepal would move forward with her own pathways for peace, prosperity and stability.[38]

[36] It is to note that CA member can stand for different categories at the same time. Therefore, the total calculation of the number of member and percentage vary. For CA II data, the data calculated with 601 member's assumption; but until this date only 575 CA members' results declared while 26 nominated sits in CA is yet to be finalized.
[37] O. Gurung, 'Social Inclusion: Policies and Practices in Nepal', *Occasional Papers in Sociology and Anthropology*, 11 (2009): 1–15.
[38] See Sohan Prasad Sha, '(Un)Making of Madhesi Politics', *IPCS* 4198, 28 November 2013, available online at http://www.ipcs.org/article/nepal/unmaking-of-madhesi-politics-4198.html (accessed 28 November 2013).

Emerging Issues and Trends in Madhesi Politics— An Analysis

Fear of Constant Radicalization due to Prolong Political Transition and Instability

The failure to draft a constitution during CA I was a major setback in Nepal. This led to prolongation of the political transition in Nepal, a transition that was accompanied by some radicalization in regional politics. For instance, the excessive political factionalism in Madhesi parties inevitably led to further radicalization as new political outfits competed for the political space in the region. More importantly, before Nepal drew its federal lines, the new political parties already envisioned federalism if not *Ek Madhes, Ek Pradesh* (one Madhes, one state) then at least two autonomous regions in the southern region of Nepal. Furthermore, if one traces back the history, Madhesi issue is highly sensitive in Nepalese politics. In these conditions, the Madhesi parties who are the political players in mainstream Kathmandu politics will continue to escalate the Madhesi concerns that are highly psychological/emotional[39] in nature. At the same time, there are also some radical outfits/armed/fringe groups outside the political grasp of Kathmandu intending for political transition to prolong in lieu to increase their relevance. There is a fair chance that mainstream Madhesi parties may use and misuse the political vacuum of Nepal, if Kathmandu establishment fails to

---

[39] Madhesis facing discrimination in many forms such as racial, regional and nationalism. See R. Sah, 'Being Madhesi in Kathmandu', *Kathmandu Post*, available online at http://www.ekantipur.com/2013/10/06/oped/being-madhesi-in-kathmandu/379006.html (accessed 18 December 2013). See D. Thapa, 'The Enigma of Identity', *Kathmandu Post*, available online at http://www.ekantipur.com/2011/06/23/oped/the-enigma-of-identity/336149/ (accessed 18 December 2013). See, Prashant Jha, 'The Nationalism Debate', *Kathmandu Post*, available online at http://www.ekantipur.com/the-kathmandu-post/2011/07/26/oped/the-nationalism-debate/224470.html (accessed 10 December 2013). See P. Bhagat, 'New Nepal or Old Nepal', *Kathmandu Post*, available online at http://www.ekantipur.com/the-kathmandu-post/2013/12/14/free-the-words/new-nepal-or-old-nepal/256975.html (accessed 11 October 2013).

accommodate the genuine political concerns of the Tarai region of Nepal. As there is historical wound in Nepal, the 'integration of Tarai into the national framework'[40] needs to be accommodative in its essence for peaceful transition.

Tarai of Nepal: In Middle of Internal Colonialism and Neocolonialism

Geographically, Tarai of Nepal, situated in strategic position, has been a site for political contestation. Moreover, Tarai region's connection in terms of linguistic–cultural affinity with India and the centrality of India to the development of Nepal is of paramount importance. However, especially in recent times. After the Madhes movement of 2007, Madhes became the hot spot for manoeuvring, which brings dissent and discontent of Madhesis with Kathmandu establishment as well as with India. For instance, the Former Prime Minister Girija Prasad Koirala said, 'If India wants, Tarai problems can be solved immediately' while the Madhesi leaders criticized India for 'only using Madhes as a pawn' for larger objectives in Kathmandu politics.[41] However, at the same time, Kathmandu elites had made a political sloganeering using India as a scapegoat to stock *hill-centric nationalism* and garner legitimacy while stereotyping Madhesis as *Indians*. Similarly, Dr Baburam Bhattarai had argued that Tarai is facing dual problems in Nepal and is caught in between *internal colonialism* and *semi-colonialism*.[42] While doing so, Maoists and other politician in Nepal have longstanding demands to scrap differential 1950 Indo–Nepal treaty, which they believe benefits India's neocolonialist design on Nepal.[43] In such a situation, the Madhesi people are facing alienation in twofolds—from both Kathmandu and India—that increased the perplexity of losing their identity

---

[40] See F.H. Gaige, *Regionalism and National Unity in Nepal*, p. 195.

[41] See P. Jha, 'A Nepali Perspective on International Involvement in Nepal', in *Nepal in Transition,* eds Von Einsiedel, Malone and Pradhan (New Delhi: Cambridge University Press, 2012), 332–358.

[42] See note 25.

[43] See J. Miklian, 'Nepal's Terai: Constructing an Ethnic Conflict', *International Peace Research Institute* (2009), South Asia Briefing Paper No. 1, 10.

within a largely Nepali national imagination. The elites[44] of Kathmandu establishment need to do more to change the perception in the realm of constructing *idea of nation* in rightful perspective and integrate Madhesi with utmost respect. Furthermore, there is a fair chance that Madhesi issue will be a foreign policy challenge for India, as Madhesi leaders are looking forward to build stronger ties with bordering region of India (Bihar, Utter Pradesh and West Bengal) as well as federal provinces in Tarai region will have some strategic concerns for India.[45]

Fear of Polarization and Pre-existing Fault Lines in Nepal

The tinderbox of *Madhesi* vis-à-vis *Pahadi* polarization (plain people versus hill people) has long existed in Nepal. It was propagated by Mahendra's cultural nationalism that was based on cultural homogeneity for national unity.[46] The sudden outbreak of Madhes movement in 2007 turned violent to resist such cultural nationalism. The advent of this, even if Madhesi movement premised on perceived political and social inclusion, Madhesi–Pahadi tensions escalated the anti-hills rhetoric. This manifested in terms of sudden migration of hill people from Madhes region. However, the most worrisome part of such tension was that it led to push factors of fear, rising criminality while also challenging traditional power relation.[47] Moreover, there are elements of political binaries in Nepal; one, the ultra-nationalist jingoism that is propagated by hill elites that came from the tradition of Mahendra's nationalist ideas; second, there are radical forces (armed and fringe groups) in Madhes who are trying to legitimize themselves by countering the jingoism to fuel Madhesi nationalism. Therefore, it is necessary to

---

[44] The political commentator, C.K. Lal, usually refer the elites as 'Permanent Establishment of Nepal (PEON)' who imagined themselves as custodian/gatekeepers of Nepali nationalism.

[45] See Dipendra Jha, 'Friends and Neighbours', *Kathmandu Post*, available online at http://www.ekantipur.com/2013/12/25/opinion/friends-and-neighbours (accessed 26 December 2013).

[46] F.H. Gaige, *Regionalism and National Unity in Nepal*, 23.

[47] See U.N. 'Migration Patterns in the Central Tarai: Has an Equilibrium Been Disrupted?' (2012), RCHC Office, 1–8.

be cautious of such fault lines in Nepal in lieu to make Nepal truly diverse and tolerant democracy.

Highly Sensitized Madhes: State strategy to Coerce vis-à-vis Capability to Unite

There is a widely held perception among Madhesis that Madhes movement was a catalyst for their political enlightenment in Nepal. Moreover, Madhesi intellectual and leaders takes 2007 Madhes uprising as a benchmark for their political confidence vis-à-vis Kathmandu establishment. Nevertheless, at times of highly sensitized Madhesi sentiments, the state strategy to co-opt and coerce, perhaps, led to inevitable conflicts. Especially, after CA II election, there is a perception; rather anxiety, with the weakening of Madhesi parties electorally the state could dalliance with the idea of *federalism* as a core issue.[48] Madhesi party has only *federalism* as a core agenda that popularized them in mainstream national discourse and it remains as a source of their political survival. In these conditions, if state strategy to co-opt and coerce continues, then Madhesi parties, as they are highly fragmented and divided, out of compulsion can unite and revert through mass mobilization, which may aggravate the agitation and inevitable clashes. Despite the fact that Madhesi parties are highly fragmented and divided, they may forge tactical alliance for electoral gain/loss and for their political survival.

Not only Madhesi parties but also the dynamic of Madhes movement translated the sense of Madhes based ethnosubnationalism to the leaders from Madhesi community to other political parties too. For instance, on the issues of federalism, Madhesi leaders across the political parties/political lines share the similar ideas. Moreover, Madhesi leaders in non-Madhesi parties started feeling their political significance of being Madhesi due to rise of regional-based nationalism as a federal

---

[48] There is range of opinion editorials in Nepalese media who express such anxiety, after CA II election. For recent editorial see K. Hachhethu, 'CA II Election and Federalism Issues', *Kantipur*, available online at http://www.ekantipur.com/np/2070/9/23/full-story/382038.html (accessed 7 January 2014).

state will inevitably benefit them. In these conditions, the state needs to accommodate Madhesi issues with discretion and open the level playing field for political negotiation that will allow politics of Nepal to move towards stability and peace.

Political Scenario: Early Warning

Nepal is in process of dealing with the rise and decline of the right of self-determination. Certainly, the rise of Madhes in Nepal has unfolded a fierce debate of *federalism* that will not rest merely on tokenism of administrative decentralization but will eventually move towards political decentralization, which ensures devolution of power from Kathmandu establishment to inclusive citizenship. In such a political scenario, as mentioned above, how Nepalese state will accommodate the concerns of Madhes is a herculean task.

First, there is prevailing cultural condition in Nepal, which causes friction on the modalities of *federalism*. For instance, whether Nepal should draw her federal lines based on identity or economic feasibility. Second, the region of Madhes has been suffering with the state-imposed political economy of backwardness that perceives Madhes as being internally colonized and administratively dependent on Kathmandu. Third, the democratic process in Nepal is a very recent phenomenon with lots of social diversity. Fourth, the political institution, judiciary and civil societies—considered as pillar of democracy—have not been well institutionalized and, in fact, at times, seen with sceptical lens. Fifth, post 2006 expedited democratic space in Nepal, the people in marginal lines raised their voice for socio-political assertion from ground.

In such condition, it is commendable that the democratic political reforms in Nepal have leapfrogged many dissents and discontents in Nepalese society but the challenges ahead are to institutionalize these reforms to its logical conclusion for economic prosperity, long-term peace and stability.

While standing on these issues, Madhes movement led to four political scenarios in emerging Nepalese democracy. Ethnonationalism is largely aimed at drawing federal lines, to ensure rights of self-determination, within the administrative set-up of Nepal.

Table 16.2:
The possible trajectory of self-determination movements in Nepal[49]*

		Central Authority	
		Well Institutionalized	Weakly Institutionalized
Leadership strategy	Accommodating	Inverse U curve of identity politics (likely possible scenario towards peace and stability) (Situation 1)	Fragile law and order situation (fringe and criminal groups) (Situation 2)
	Unaccommodating	Demands and coercive strategy(ethnic groups' demands for identity-based federalism and the state carving out federalism demands by delaying strategy) (Situation 3)	Turbulence/breakdown/instability (armed groups) (Situation 4)

Note: *Modified for contextualizing in Nepalese scenario.

Table 16.2 gives a snapshot view of ethnic movement, which has lots of variation among different groups. Particularly, in Madhes, there are active armed groups who resort to rhetoric and extremely radical demands (situation 4). There are fringe elements and criminal groups (identified in situation 2) operating in Madhes that do have radical demands to leverage their bargaining with the state calling themselves political in nature but taking the advantage of fragile law and order situation in the region. The failure of CA I (situation 3) in which the state strategy is to co-opt and coerce simultaneously followed by prolonged process of power negotiation that eventually exhaust the ethnic leaders. However, in Nepal, the unaccommodating nature of leaders' strategy can have detrimental effect because the deepening of

---

[49] Table 16.2 is entirely drawn from Atul Kohli's paper in which he analysed the ethnic movement in India, particularly Tamils in Tamil Nadu during 1950s and 1960s, of Sikhs in Punjab in 1980s and Muslims in Kashmir. However, in Nepal, there is little variation on the magnitude of ethic movement, that is, by and large, struggle to incorporate with recognition of their identity in boarder national framework of Nepal. See A. Kohli, 'Can Democracies Accommodate Ethnic Nationalism? Rise and Decline of Self-determination Movements in India', *Journal of Asian Studies*, 56, no. 2 (1997): 325–344.

democracy in Nepal has opened the level playing field for ethnic leaders. Moreover, the ethnic leaders have political influence to mobilize masses and to impede the constitution drafting process. Constitution is a supreme document of any nation (rather a document of compromise) in which every social institution of nation draws a sense of power as well as responsibility. In addition, a constitutional idea of nation, which is in making, needs to institutionalize, over the period, with active participation of the people. While considering these aspects, Nepali state reduced to only one option to tame the rise of identity assertion, which is to accommodate (situation 1) Madhesi rightful demands and due recognition to their identity. Perhaps, the success of democracy in Nepal can be judged with the parameters that how well Nepalese democracy accommodates her dissents and discontent voices.

Preventive Measures

Frederick Gaige's detailed study of Tarai/Madhes in his book *Regionalism and National Unity in Nepal* in 1975 drew little attention of either Nepalese or foreign scholars. However, after the Madhes movement that perplexed Nepalese intelligentsia to the question that what went wrong in Tarai. To quote Gaige, 'Kathmandu elite, almost all of them hill people, have difficulty thinking of the Tarai as more than a Nepalese-administered but otherwise alien region'.[50] Therefore, the problem of national integration has given many wounds to Nepalese society, and that can be healed only by accommodating a genuine political concern of Madhesis which is, by and large, social inclusion in every state apparatus (institution) of *new Nepal*. Moreover, Kathmandu establishment (CHHE) has to cross over the bridge to generate confidence in Madhes. More so, the change in perspective requires that with the land (gigantic Shiwalik foothills), the people of that region also come in Nepal.

---

[50] See F.H. Gaige, *Regionalism and National Unity in Nepal*, 42.

17

The Political Direction of the Maoist Party in Nepal: Possibilities, Recommendations and Incentives

Sisir Devkota

Introduction

The current Unified Communist Party of Nepal (Maoist) (UCPN-M) was formed in 1994, which was then named as the Communist Party of Nepal, Maoists.[1] After a time span of two years, it launched the Nepalese Peoples War on 13 February 1996.[2] The agenda of the party was to wage an armed struggle against the government to remove the monarch and set up a People's Republic. The civil war which ended with the Comprehensive Peace Agreement in the year 2006 claimed the lives of more than 13,000 Nepali people.[3] The party formed a military outfit named the People's Liberation Army (PLA) to combat the government forces under the Nepalese Monarchy. Initially targeting

---

[1] Communist Party of Nepal—Maoist, *South Asia Terrorism Portal*, 2013, available online at http://www.satp.org/satporgtp/countries/nepal/terroristoutfits/index.html (accessed 31 December 2013).

[2] See note 1.

[3] *BBC News*, 'Peace Deal Ends Nepal's Civil War', *BBC News*, 2006, available online at http://news.bbc.co.uk/2/hi/south_asia/6169746.stm (accessed 31 December 2013).

smaller bases of administrative units in rural parts of the nation, the CPN-M progressively intensified attacks on larger government targets.[4] After the Nepali Royal Massacre in the year 2001, ceasefire meetings were initiated which did not last for a long time. After the breakdown of ceasefire in 2001, the then Royal Nepalese Army was put into action to combat the armed struggle of the Maoists.[5] The year 2003 also saw the Maoist party to be put in the list of terrorist organizations by the US.[6] Intensive fighting continued, especially after the then King of Nepal, Gyanendra, dismissed the government in 2003 and took executive powers into his hand.[7] The 19-day long people's movement in the year 2006 led to a nationwide revolution to force the king to give up executive powers and reinstate people's rule. The same movement also brought the armed Maoist outfit into political mainstream which not only led to the removal of monarchy in Nepal but also to the first constituent assembly (CA) polls in the history of Nepali politics.[8]

The political achievement in 2006 was also the foundation of the Comprehensive Peace Agreement and the reintegration of the Maoist combatants into the Nepal Army. The Peace Agreement was signed on 21 November 2006.[9] The agreement also gave the political space in Nepal to exercise pluralism and democracy and to eventually carryout the first CA elections. The CPN-M won the maximum number of seats in the parliament leaving behind deeply rooted political entities like the Nepali Congress (NC) and

[4] See note 1.

[5] 'Nepal's Maoist Insurgency Reignites', *BBC News*, 25 November 2001, available online at http://news.bbc.co.uk/2/hi/south_asia/1675469.stm (accessed 31 December 2013).

[6] 'After 9 years, US strikes Maoists off Terrorist list', *Ekantipur.com*, available online at http://www.ekantipur.com/the-kathmandu-post/2012/09/06/top-story/after-9-years-us-strikes-maoists-off-terrorist-list/239303.html (accessed on 31 December 2013).

[7] 'Insurgency in Nepal', *GlobalSecurity.org*, 2011, available online at http://www.globalsecurity.org/military/world/war/nepal_insurgency-2004.htm (accessed 30 October 2014).

[8] See note 7.

[9] 'Comprehensive Peace Agreement held between Government of Nepal', Constitution Forum, 2006, available online at http://www.sambidhan.org/peace%20agreements_en.html (accessed 31 December 2013).

the Communist Party of Nepal-Unified Marxist Leninist (CPN-UML).[10] The leader of the Maoist Party Pushpa Kamal Dahal also recognized as Prachanda became the first Prime Minister of the Republic Nepal.[11] The peace process that was initiated in the year 2006 led the nation into a new system of democratic governance. However, political feuds with the Nepali Army regarding the issue of reintegration of the Maoist combatants led to a long political stalemate which also saw the resignation of Prachanda from the post of premiership. The frequent change of Nepali administration and the overarching dispute among not only the political parties in Nepal but also the people on the issue of the nature of federalism led to frequent addition of the CA tenure which ultimately expired in the year 2011.[12]

The dissolution of the CA in 2011 brought the administration under the control of chief justice who was also appointed to hold another round of CA elections that eventually took place on 19 November 2013. The results of the second round of election was disturbing for the Maoist party as it performed below par than its previous election only securing 26 out of 240 seats in the first past the post system (FPTP).[13] Combined the proportional representation (PR) and FPTP seats, the UCPN-M holds the distant third amount of seats in the new CA. The party also alleged of unfair voting and rigging as to the major reason of their loss in elections. Given their current position in Nepali politics as to what they were before, back in the times of their guerrilla struggle to becoming the largest mainstream political party in Nepal in the year 2008, an analysis of their future course is an important question

[10] 'Constitutional Assembly Election 2064', Election Commission, Nepal, 2013, available online at http://www.election.gov.np/reports/CAResults/reportBody.php (accessed 31 December 2013).

[11] 'Maoist Leader Becomes Nepal PM', *BBC News*, 2008, available online at http://news.bbc.co.uk/2/hi/south_asia/7564739.stm (accessed 31 December 2013).

[12] 'Nepal in Constitutional Impasse', *Open Democracy*, 2012, available online at http://www.opendemocracy.net/leena-rikkila-tamang/nepal-constitutional-impasse (accessed 31 December 2013).

[13] 'Constituent Assembly Election 2070', *Election Commission*, Nepal, 2013, available online at http://election.gov.np/CA2070/CAResults/reportBody.php?selectedMenu1=1&rand=1384967216 (accessed 31 December 2013).

to answer in the discourse of contemporary Nepali politics. This chapter will provide the same in three different sections starting with a logical prediction of the future course of Maoists in Nepalese political affair. Secondly, with a recommendation analysis of how they should be moving ahead in the course of future. Thirdly, with an analysis of the civil society incentives for the Maoists to positively develop their political course with the passage of time. Before the triple course of analysis, the chapter will explain why the Maoists in Nepal both of the Baidya and Prachanda faction will not leave mainstream politics.

Political Mainstream: The Need of the Hour

Among any concerns, if there is any for the sceptic in Nepal, the Maoists in Nepal will not leave their earned direction of mainstream politics. The word Maoists is used in general instead of mentioning the two factionalized parties because, in the analysis of their future course and upon questions of whether they would leave the political path, the two cannot be separated as per they being a common entity with a common past. Also because the Baidya's faction only disagrees with the UCPN-M on it making the blunder of signing the Comprehensive Peace Agreement and running for the elections in 2013 under the auspices of the chief justice of Nepal.[14]

To begin with removing any apprehension, the Maoists would not leave its current path mainly because they are already in the mainstream affair which is also because of their achievement from the armed struggle that started nearly two decades back. The country was declared a republic in the year 2008, which was not only the exact aspiration of the People's war but more. The Maoists bargained for the current position of coming out into democratic politics after the Nepali people routed out the monarchy. Leaving the mainstream politics would require an agenda

[14] 'Faced by Party Rift, Prachanda Appeals for Unity', *Zee News*, available online at http://zeenews.india.com/news/south-asia/faced-by-party-rift-prachanda-appeals-for-unity_782058.html (accessed 31 December 2013).

again, this time a stronger one for which the Nepali people would support as they did in the past. The violence of the past will not persuade the majority Nepali population to support any such stance from the party. In fact, the defeat of the UCPN-M in this year's election itself signifies the considerable amount of diminishing support from the people of Nepal. The Gallup South Asia Survey conducted in the year 2011 even explains how the support has not plummeted all of sudden but has been in the process of decline. This also means it has little to do with the theories of how the support is being lost because of the existence of two parties. As per the 2011 survey, 81 per cent of the respondents disagreed that violence like in the past would resolve any political conflicts.[15] Among anything else, this result means if the Maoists leave the current political arrangement, they will have to resort to anything but not violence as in the past, as doing so will further decrease their popularity. In times of Nepal undergoing a great transformation, even for the revolutionaries as they are, leaving the current mainstream which is indeed competitive will be an irrational calculation.

Moreover, from a different perspective to what people think in Nepal, according to the Angus Reid Global Survey, 49.3 per cent of the total respondents wanted the institution of monarchy to remain intact in Nepal whatsoever.[16] It might be arguable that because in paper then, the Maoists did not wage a war directly against the monarchy, it's ideology was and still is in exact opposite poles to that of the system of constitutional monarchy that was prevalent until the year 2008. But if opinion polls suggest such figures, it does indicate, if not correctly representing, how Nepali people feel about different political institutions. The Maoists exiting the political mainstream will only strengthen that unwelcoming thought. Comparing their past two election results will exactly explain how under par they have performed in this year's election. In 2008, the party which was unified gathered around 30 per cent of both the FPTP and PR seats, whereas this

---

[15] 'Nepal Monitor, Nepali Public Opinion 2011: Gallup/SADF South Asia Survey', *Nepal Monitor*, available online at http://www.nepalmonitor.com/2011/10/nepali_public_opinio.html (accessed 31 December 2013).

[16] 'Angus Reid Global, Half in Nepal Want to keep Monarchy', *Angus Reid Global*, available online at http://www.angusreidglobal.com/polls/30506/half_in_nepal_want_to_keep_monarchy/ (accessed 31 December 2013).

time though with the factionalized party, the contesting Maoists, UCPN-M only managed half of what they had achieved previously.[17] Oddly, another reason of why the Maoists would not practice the undemocratic process is also because they are themselves divided into two groups with influential leaders separated in two camps. Not only the general public will question whether and if which faction will first initiate the going back process but the two Maoists will themselves wish the other to forge a lead in such a dangerous move. It is dangerous because it is also not quite sure if one of the parties would support the other in any case. To convince a population of around 30 million,[18] the party has to assert itself and regroup its internal support in the first place.

Coming to practical terms in disseminating the claim of them going back, it is also important to look into what fuelled their political ways of the past. The PLA which played the most vital role in the conflict period has now been successfully reintegrated into the national army. There arises the question of going back, but how? This reality itself plays down all the apprehensions of the Maoists willing and being able to resort to conflict even if they wanted to. Just in case they decide for the unimaginable, it will come out as a confused decision and lack of political integrity of the party in the eyes of the ex-PLA soldiers and supporters. The PLA as it was named was not a national army but was an army for the people unlike regular security forces which are governed by a central authority. Lack of authority will be where the Maoists will struggle if in case it tries to reassemble the dissipated majority of the citizens turned PLA rebels. A huge number of 7000 soldiers opting for cash packages also explain how unpopular the idea would be to go back and start from the scratch.[19] How about international support to their action? The Maoists would not risk losing their recently achieved political legitimacy from various corners of the international community by breaking their democratic promises. It would also be a contradiction on part of the rest

---

[17] See note 10.

[18] '*The World Factbook*', CIA, Nepal, available online at https://www.cia.gov/library/publications/the-world-factbook/geos/np.html (accessed 31 December 2013).

[19] 'Nepal Begins Reintegration of Maoist Fighters,' *Aljazeera*, available online at http://www.aljazeera.com/news/asia/2011/11/20111118171652882539.html (accessed 31 December 2013).

of the international community to support the party which has not been robustly chosen by the citizens themselves. The Maoists would not want that break of ties from both the Nepali people and the international community.

Before the Maoists would weigh the prospects of doing so, they would very much like to follow and replicate a real-world revolutionary examples, where there are none. The problem lies with them being very unique to land upon the parliamentary process after years of guerrilla fighting which also makes them one of a kind. There is a disconnect with other revolutions and even if the Maoists in Nepal make up their mind to alter their political direction altogether, where is the inspiration? Without an inspiration, the prospect might materialize but will certainly not run long and through. Nevertheless, the closest the Maoists could relate to could be the communism in China but again the Maoists in Nepal settled for a bargain unlike the success of Mao's revolution. Competition is an important factor as well and will hugely determine any political prospect in a democratic setting. In the 2013 CA elections, 122 political parties fought for the 601 seats in the parliament.[20] With such wide political choice, will the Maoists in Nepal commit the blunder of not committing after having come so far? The answer is no also because apart from other ideologies, there now exists six different political parties in Nepal which have communist agendas and are a direct competition to the Maoists. If the Maoists in Nepal influenced a large sector of the population to believe in the ideology of communism of classless society by crushing the feudal and bourgeoisie group of the population, the new emerging parties within the same ideology will possibly tide away the support from the people without much effort that has already been put by the Maoists after all these years.

What Next: Possibilities

The losses of seats in the CA II election will mean that the Maoist party both Baidya led and Prachanda's UCPN-M will try to gather public support that has stooped down. The Baidya-led faction

[20] See note 10.

might not have contested the election but the huge turnout of above 75 per cent of the voters casting their choice[21] says how the party's agenda is not well sold among the majority of the population. With the course of time, Baidya's faction will soon realize that before party's unilateral agenda comes people's aspiration and a political party of huge stature as of the Maoists in Nepal will have to accommodate with what the people want. Similarly, given the divide already with Baidya's Maoists, Prachanda's UCPN-M has the major work to do in terms of recollecting the lost support. The election defeat of the UCPN-M is also a loss for the Baidya's party. It is so because, though the party might have continuously clashed against the UCPN-M, in the eyes of the general public, the ideology from which they emanate is the same. That is a disadvantage for Baidya and his leaders but is also something they will have to compromise for some amount of time in the coming years. The first and foremost task of regaining the public support of the Maoists might happen in three different ways.

First, both the Maoist parties will form an understanding coalition if not regroup the party into one again. Though the UCPN-M has finally agreed to the election verdict and to play its role in the parliament as a third comer, they are still dissatisfied and that is where the interests of both meet. For the people of Nepal they fought the people's war together, regaining support in the same fashion will not only be a good move but also a necessary one. Both the parties have significant leaders on their side and because of the same common history they shared, a political disaster of one or a boon will simultaneously affect the other Maoist party. The understanding of this inter-relationship will also be the key to what level the people of Nepal will begin to believe again in the party's promises again. Therefore, both the parties might not mould into a single entity again, there are high possibilities of them echoing the same common sentiments of the Maoist revolution in Nepal without unnecessarily critiquing the other.

Second, the UCPN-M now has the golden opportunity to put them into the equal role of an opposition in the parliament. The CPN-UML has the second highest votes, but it is unlikely to forge neither a political nor an ideological coalition with the UCPN-M. Also, that will further push them away from the Baidya-led

---

[21] See note 10.

CPN-M. UCPN-M having a presence inside the parliament and having a half understanding with the CPN-M will not be the worst scenario in terms of achieving their goals. It will be a challenge for the Maoists to work for the people in Nepal without having the political authority but in another light it also takes away their responsibility to deliver. The Maoists would most likely utilize this chance and cash into their action when the two leading parties, NC and CPN-UML, slip in their own in the coming time. After all the main agenda apart from their dissatisfaction with the structure of politics in Nepal, the CPN-M will also try for the same. The differences among themselves might remain but they might take the same path of their political contribution.

Third, discussion on many of the issues regarding the constitution will emerge out once again as in the past assembly. The Maoists who faced problems acquiring the support of the people in the 2008 parliament will be in the minority's block, hence being in the situation where once their critics used to be. To gather the public will, UCPN-M in the assembly might initiate meaningful debates on various developmental agendas. The parties with the highest seats in the assembly cannot provide an alternative perspective to pressing issues like the kind of Federal states in Nepal, agricultural mechanism for farmers or regarding other social issues. This is a kind of positive critic gap which the Maoists could fill in the near future. The Baidya faction who might or might not join the parliamentary process could just sail on the UCPN-M's back without deteriorating the political situation in hand. People's support will manifold when they visualize the Maoists party as the ones questioning and improving the law bills in the parliament. With less than 90 seats in the 2013 assembly,[22] the Maoists' corner role will be taken seriously as their less than hundred votes will be determinate during the passing of bills and voting on constitutional matters. In a ubiquitous way, the Maoists will be strengthening the core of democratic principles by institutionalizing discussion and making politics difficult for the leading political parties. Above anything, it will make the constitution robust.

One of the important reasons for the losses of parliamentary seats for the Maoists was also due to its incompetent and

---

[22] See note 10.

less dynamic profile of political leaders. The divided party saw many influential leaders opting to join the CPN-M which did not contest the elections. During elections, the losses in this manner could be accounted to two main reasons. First, the people might have settled for other candidates in other parties when they did not find their leaders contesting the election. As mentioned before as well, the people in Nepal will take some time to realize the division within the Maoist party as per their common political history. Second, because of some of the major leaders being the CPN-M faithful and negatively advertising the elections, the people might have lost confidence in the party as a whole. Frequent bomb blasts[23] before the elections and inter-party mishaps are some of the examples of the people's lost confidence. As they share a relationship where one of the parties' actions can severely affect the other, it might be the reason that cost them election victory. As a strategy of the UCPN-M to reinvent its charisma by recollecting influential leadership, the UCPN-M might try and persuade the popular defecting leaders to join into the party that is already into the parliamentary process. That will not only provide a moral boost to the UCPN-M but also send a positive message across the citizens. The party's image and credibility also depends on the type of leaders it consists in the decision-making level. In case where they can persuade the defecting leaders to join the party and the law-making process, the UCPN-M can always accommodate them through nomination. The act of nomination will itself look like a process of reconciliation between the factionalized Maoist party that will send a competitive signal to other parties and a hopeful one for the people in Nepal. This will improve the profile of the leaders inside the party and accumulate the support of the people. The UCPN-M will try to exercise or at least experiment this process as part of their future strategies as harnessing the new leaders that have lost confidence after their comprehensive defeat will be expensive and time-consuming without any surety of success. People's confidence in the leaders of the party

---

[23] Five People Injured in Explosion at Election Rally in Eastern Nepal, *The Times of India*, 10 November 2013, available online at http://timesofindia.indiatimes.com/world/south-asia/Five-people-injured-in-explosion-at-election-rally-in-eastern-Nepal/articleshow/25561763.cms (accessed 31 December 2013).

has decreased so low that the supreme leader of UCPN-M lost his seat in an important constituency in Kathmandu.[24] This reflects the low-level support of the Nepali people. Reinstalling previous leaders into the main party will also lead to the healing process of the dysfunctional leadership. The UCPN-M along with the CPN-M might also encourage civil society intellectuals to be a part of the ideological setup to stretch their reach deep into the people. It might be more important for the UCPN-M than that to of the Baidya's group because of their presence in the parliament. Persuasion will be their key.

The UCPN-M especially needs restructuring and the party leaders have now understood that they require a massive revamping of their policies and direction. The Maoists will most likely restructure their strategies in action as well as in their political statements. Political strategies could be either positive or negative. As much as the amount of seats that they have in the parliament, they have lost the consequential or the defining role in certain decision-making processes. As per their restructuring plan, the party could provide the impression of being more resilient than other political entities. The assembly of Nepal will be engaged once again into various complicated issues regarding the bills in the constitution and not having any major role or responsibility, will automatically provide the party with the tag of being the less fussy one. Major responsibilities will require other parties to deliver in bulk which will also open up cracks of incompetency, irrationality, lack of patience and difficulty of correct judgement. These areas of weak points will be what the UCPN-M or the CPN-M will be looking to tap and turn on its side. The negative restructuring strategy could include consuming bulk of time inside the parliament by defying and creating alliances to block any resolution. Given the reality of no party achieving the absolute majority in the parliament itself, the Maoists could lead the league of the dissatisfied which if not the important one will be very concerning. The Maoists will also see their restructuring process as a chance free from direct responsibility to recapture

---

[24] 'Prachanda Loses Key Election in Kathmandu', *The Hindu*, 22 November 2013, available online at http://www.thehindu.com/todays-paper/tp-in-school/prachanda-loses-key-election-in-kathmandu/article5376912.ece (accessed 31 December 2013).

people's mood and wants. With lesser mistakes in the future and given their wide spread support that once existed along with their immense understanding of people's aspirations apart from any other political group in Nepal will favour them in the long run. The key at the present is to look back at their mistake and improve them which they will carefully execute without crossing the line that is unnecessary for them.

Another possibility of their future direction will be their choice and amount of political coalitions. There could be three different scenarios. The first one would be a coalition with the winner entity of the election to grasp some of the ministerial positions of the government to act and ultimately gather the support of the people. Fighting two is difficult than fighting one is applicable to this scenario. If the Maoists' cannot compete with the top two parties in the parliament, it will try to forge a pact with the NC than with others as it will automatically put the second party CPN-UML in a political dilemma by reducing their political power. NC will also welcome such a coalition to avoid being against the Maoist party and their stubborn stance on specific issues. With such a coalition, the NC will anticipate the success of the second CA in formulating the constitution. The second scenario is a coalition with the parties in the table with low amount of seats. Being a group entity opposition is better and provides more fare than to be a single party without any support. In the proceedings of the second assembly, this kind of coalitions could make or break a law deal. The Maoists will desperately want to lead this role and assert their existence as being significant and strong. The third scenario will be any form of coalition against its ideological ally the CPN-UML. NC will be an opposite ideology any given day but in their future course they will try and sway away the support from their near ideology CPN-UML. Its second position in the preference of the Nepali people also denotes that it is not that people do not support the left ideology at all. It simply means the preference has changed from the Maoists to the CPN-UML. Though the Maoists would want to sway as much support of the people, their first target would be a coalition against the CPN-UML in the first place. The considerably successful run of the CPN-UML in this year's election also gives them hope that though the support has been lost, it can be regained back if they stick to their strategy.

Recommendations: What Should Be their Plausible Course?

Gathering their political support from the people should be their first strategy as part of their future course of action. Mending relations with the Baidya group in an incomplete manner will be insufficient and hazardous. It is so because, in case the UCPN-M cannot carry out the process of locating the common ground between them, it will backfire and will yield as a negative impression among the people as the UCPN-M being unable and incompetent to stick to its own agenda. Therefore, to regain the support from the people using the CPN-M should be comprehensive and total. That means the party has to merge which can be carried out in different possible ways. Merging here would not necessarily mean dissolving one of the parties and creating a single entity, but it means catering for common ground in various prospects. The work could be initiated from the simplest level. The name of the party which uses the beginning as *Unified* of the Prachanda-led faction itself signifies the differences between the two. It shows that not only the party has been divided but they also communicate of how they are better than the other. This mentality in perspective as well as in action has to change if they are to create a plausible relationship especially when one of them is not a part of the constitution making process. The people have expressed their verdict which has been outstanding and highly participative which the Maoists party should retrospect and realize. The UCPN-M is a part of the assembly and should use it as a tool to achieve its goals also making sure to not deteriorate their relations with the divided party. That will be a test for the UCPN-M in the coming days.

Simply being in the opposition and catering to this role will not be enough in the eyes of the Nepali people. Working from the opposition's authority, the UCPN-M will have to do their homework double fold. That is because having been in the jungle for 10 years fighting a guerrilla war and then achieving the maximum number of seats in the parliament thereafter; they do not have the expertise of fulfilling the kind of current role in their entire history. The current situation for the Maoists is also unique because it will be an opportunity to learn and will increase their efficiency as they are put into the seats where they need to deliver without any authority. Also, being in the opposition and working in line with the parliamentary process will be difficult to keep check of their common interests with the CPN-M. The aim of the second round of CA elections is also to deliver the constitution, so wasting any more time will give another wrong impression of the party in whole to the Nepali population. The disadvantage for the Maoists is that they cannot use the same techniques of frequently disrupting the assembly in this year's parliament. Whether the Maoists want it or not they will have to put in genuine effort to formulate the constitution and whether they like it or not, given their minuscule size in the parliamentary body they do not have a choice. The only way to gather the support of the people will also be by the same process.

Persuading the leaders back into the UCPN-M from the CPN-M will not be an easy task or even a good decision if they fail to execute the process carefully. It will not be an easy task because there will always be a question of whether the old leaders who will be persuaded again replace the existing new leaders or not. Replacing the new and inexperienced ones will again create the danger of another party split as persuading the old leaders into other roles will not be a satisfactory argument. Also, before persuading any leader, the UCPN-M will have to have an idea whether the strategy would work in the first place. It might also not be a good idea because defected leaders could defect again which will hamper the UCPN-M in keeping the grip on confidence of its new set of leaders. The party will always face questions of whether to plan the course of future with a new set of majority losing leaders or bring back the lost charm. The problems do not end there. Any inclusion of such nature might also dismantle the central authority of the party as the persuaded old leaders might also question the leadership of Prachanda. This decision might also backfire because once the old leaders find ground inside the UCPN-M, the replaced leaders might opt out for the CPN-M. This scenario will complicate situations and the party will indulge into their ideological battle losing focus in their work at hand that is to make the constitution as per their roles.

The burden of responsibility will not be there but to conceptualize the lost opportunity as a burden will be another mistake for the Maoists which they should try and avoid. The role is small but an important one because of the way they entered into democratic politics. Also, it is not the case that simply being the opposition and initiating the restructuring will improve their public image. The leadership changes in both the parties might be necessary but will again create confusion. UCPN-M willing to co-ordinate with the CPN-M and the latter leadership showing uninterested signs might also put pressure on the leadership of the CPN-M. A functional strategy would be for both the parties to hold if not high level, lower levels inter party discussion to form camaraderie. On the party's development action, both the entities should co-ordinate and most importantly not the let the public misunderstand them on being different on all the issues. The line might well be drawn on the differences of political matters but should not be the case when putting into action of the party's contribution. This strategy will be a mount hill task but not an impossible one especially because of the ways they have come forward in the mainstream politics.

The change in leadership is required albeit in a different way. The Maoists, specifically the UCPN-M has to reconstruct the leadership hierarchy vertically and horizontally over the whole country. The horizontal division of leadership means accounting specific set of people in a particular political area simultaneously so that individual leaders will be held accountable to their respective work. This will also be essential for the Maoists as they prepare for the future state elections in Nepal. This will also increase transparency and increase trust among the supporters. The party leaders will also enjoy decentralization of the power which will automatically boost their confidence and performance. Moreover, the leadership changes should take place in a democratic process that is open and fair to the general public. Inclusion of new members should be encouraged to enhance diversity and new ideas into the party. This is more important because they have a unique opportunity at the present to reshuffle their policies for the many coming elections in the near future. During the past couple of years, the Maoists have had disconnect with the rural Nepal and its agenda, also from where they first started the peoples' revolution. The leaders will have to go back and re-institutionalize their support from the lowest bases of citizen's hierarchy. Leadership will have to grow from rural areas representing people's wants and aspirations. The reason Maoist's lost this year's election is because of their fragmenting support in the rural areas. To make their stay in the oppositions' group successful in all the possible ways, the Maoists will have to regain that support they had in their initial years which will most importantly require them to re-assure their well wishers.

Reassurance will also be required from the Maoists to successfully formulate coalitions with other political parties. Though having lost the elections, with a significant coalition they could play the last and important role in the final constitution making process. Coalitions do not take place without any bargain offered on both the sides. The Maoists will have to carefully select their partners and bargain in such a way to keep their future secure. The major loss in this CA election is not a misery for the Maoists because the current assembly in Nepal acts as a gateway to the future of Nepal which is what they will have to aim in the future. Coalition will also be significantly difficult to achieve for the Maoists because of their differences with the Baidya faction. Improving or even settling issues with the factionalized party along with forming coalitions with the Congress or UML will require smart diplomacy. The Maoist party should opt for the first scenario because of three different reasons. First, an understanding with the top party inside the parliament will provide the near same status as the winners in the workings of the process of law making. It will provide the UCPN-M the political platform to voice its interests in a legitimate and political manner. It will also be a good coalition for the nation because other smaller parties with lesser seats will also get exposure and a considerable role to play in the law-making process.

Second, the coalition should be formed with the NC also because of its stark ideological differences. The Maoists and the NC will be a healthy coalition which will also balance out the issues of monopoly as both the parties have different agendas. It will be important for the UCPN-M because the general public will also view it as a party of the Nepali congress stature. The public support will also be in the UCPN-M's favour when being a part of the coalition with the Maoists. The ideological clash that is prevalent among the lower hierarchy of both the parties and the supporters will also reduce. In many ways, the party's image will be that of compromising and resilient. Third, it will only be the coalition that will be successful because if the UCPN-M forges an alliance with the CPN-UML it will not produce results in the parliament in terms of number of votes for a particular law. In such a case of deadlock where consensus is not met and wastes the constitutional period, the blame will be put on the Maoists for deliberately forging an alliance that would not have produced results. Coalition with other parties which has gathered fewer amounts of seats in the parliament will be disastrous because it will only produce noise and garner nothing substantial. If the party has to put itself in a situation where it can exercise power and play a part nevertheless a small one, the UCPN-M will have to strongly bargain for an alliance with the NC. Will the Congress or the Maoists give up their constitutional agendas in such a case? Especially when it comes to the question of the set-up of the government where the Maoists want a system where the President elect holds all the executive powers and the NC with the notion of the Prime Minister holding the same.[25] The answer is that there will be a compromise regarding what position will hold what kind of powers as the differences are not as huge as other constitutional agendas. Or matters like these when they are already in the coalition can be solved through a simple voting system. The Maoists should also hold to the NC to keep their international support intact as the coalition of such nature by the international community will be seen as a harmony between the right and the left which is one of the indicators of a vibrant democracy. In the same way, a coalition with other political parties or groups would not yield the same results. In these ways, the coalition that the Maoists would prefer if they do should be directly with the winners of the parliament when there are many chances of the NC also looking for the same.

What Would Be the Incentives from the Civil Society?

Post elections and the creation of the new constitution, the civil society in Nepal is well on its course to widen up and assert its importance. There are three major groups working under the banner of *civil society* in Nepal which can play a significant role in

---

[25] 'Political Parties Campaigning Sans Poll Manifesto', *Business Age*, 2013, available online at http://www.newbusinessage.com/Nepal%20Political%20Economic%20News/1979 (accessed 31 December 2013).

persuading the Maoists to develop its democratic path. Also, the interests could be mutual for the civil society groups. The three civil society groups are increasingly growing corporate houses, the private and the public bureaucracy in Nepal and different forms of pressure groups. Growing political stability in Nepal will enhance the political will of the civil society as well which is an increasingly positive development.

The incentives from the corporate sector will be huge. This sector can play an important role of investment provider to the development plan of the party, of which they are very vocal at times. The structuring of the federal units in the country will also require capital investment and depending on the Maoists version of Federal division, it could play the important role of financial support. Development issues like hydropower generation and others will be in the eyes of the investors which will require political execution for which the party can play the most significant role. The Maoists as they argue have their bluebook for the utilization of resources for development which will require investment. In this way, the corporate civil society has the potential for the harnessing of mutual interests. The Maoist party that has recently come into the democratic process have the opportunity of grasping the financial outlet from the corporate sector. One of the specific interest areas would be the funding for their activities. It also includes the opportunities that could come up with the collaboration from business sector for the ex-PLA. A business model that could accommodate employment for the former soldiers would be a give/take relationship for both the party and the investing organizations. The poor infrastructure in Nepal which is grappled without any major business investments will be a perfect market for the pouring of capital enterprises. Given the decreasing popularity of the party in many ways at the present, a comprehensive profit-based business venture encapsulating the Maoists will be the greatest incentive that the Maoists will receive for which they will not miss out for sure.

The second significant civil society group that will play an important role for luring incentive for the Maoists will be the lower and higher hierarchy of bureaucracy of both the public and the private sector inside the country. Administrative policy-making group will be able to offer attractive incentives to the Maoists to deepen their political lobbying and space in all the sectors of society. The private bureaucratic sector will be more important and interested to provide power and influence incentives to the Maoists as they will also require a political direction to enhance their own interests. The incentives that are there for the Maoists to grab could be long gone because of their decreasing support from the people with the losses in the election. The popularity is fading away and to make the most out of the opportunity to penetrate into private interests, the Maoists will have to cash in the chance which will be most certainly on the cards. This private bureaucratic incentive of power and influence will also be important to gain back the lost public support. It will not only create a positive social image but will also equip them with the tools of administering from an oppositions' seat. In regards to the public bureaucratic structure, the Maoists will have the opportunity to gain a huge incentive to carry out their interests that are carried out in the platform of government activities.

The bureaucratic structure of the country will not be affected quite a lot with the change of the government in Nepal. The Maoists, especially being outside of the main players in the parliament will have the opportunity to influence if not exercise their interests in public settings. Instead of leaving the political path of how they are in the democratic process will give them an upper hand in the national administrative discourse which they will lose after going out of the current direction. Bureaucracy affects the political action in a country and in a situation where the Maoists can gain some incentives through it, leaving the political process will not only be dangerous but also destructive for the party's existence in the future. There are three major advantages of bureaucratic incentives for the Maoists. First, it will provide them the only apparatus to exercise and influence government internally. This will be significant because the government which will be made under the auspices of the winners of the parliament will have to compromise on the bureaucratic level to generate political output. This also means they will have the political capital to bargain for their demands. Moreover, it will also strengthen their image of being capable to influence administrative matters. Second, it will be an addition to their political exercising capability in the lawmaking process. Anything that compliments their positive points will not be a bad idea for them. Third, it will provide them with the leverage of acting on the lower hierarchy of the administration of the country that has direct link with the citizens. In this way, they will develop closeness among the citizens unlike other political parties directly handling the administration of the country. It will be a rare opportunity also because of the way they have lost the elections despite being the most talked about political entity in Nepal, if not the most influential one. A bureaucratic incentive will be a boon and the right choice for the Maoists than to leave their political path. If the Maoists are to make a rational calculation, they will not leave their political way giving up the incentives that they could gain in the course of time.

Pressure and different interests groups will be another major civil society group that will provide huge incentive for not only the benefit of the party but also for the future of the political entity. Engaging with political pressure groups that are in the form of non-governmental organizations will improve their accountability and transparency which will also put them in good books of the international community. These pressure groups will provide the party with the incentive to challenge the existing administrative structure inside the nation. The best option for the Maoist party is to gather as much of support from the external spheres as they no longer hold the majority mandate of the Nepali people. It is worthwhile to stay outside the governing responsibilities with all the possible opportunities at hand. Receiving the incentives from pressure groups like such will also allow for the harmonization of the relations with them which had gone sour in their course of political past. Specifically, more than grabbing the incentives of various interest groups, it is important for the Maoists to themselves venture for a partnership with ethnic interest groups to ease out the constitution-making process. Ethnic questions on modelling of the federal structure will emerge again and with a good partnership of the Maoists with those groups will put them in the role of crisis averter as other political parties will be looking for the help of the Maoists in the near future. This will also boost their political impact in Nepali politics for which the general public will also view them in a positive way. Being able to showcase such dominance will also mark their strong return into Nepali politics which will ultimately increase their chances in the upcoming many future elections. For the sustainability of the party, which also faces competition from the Baidya faction will require such connections and there is no better way than receiving it as an incentive. Not continuing the political path could also be decisively harmful as the same pressure groups could go against the party's ambitions which the Maoists would not want in the coming time.

The lesser amount of seats in this year's assembly means that the Maoists will have lesser political space to carry out their political action in the country. The pressure groups will make up for that loss of the party. These groups that penetrate deep into the nations' social issues like development, health, education, agriculture, political legitimacy and human rights will allow the Maoists to ride into the cause of uplifting the interests of the Nepali people. Similarly, this will allow them to insulate the CPN-M into the venture which will portray a positive image of the party in general. With three different civil society groups, namely, the corporate forces, various pressure groups and the bureaucratic setup of the nation luring the lost Maoist party in sticking to the mainstream practice of politics; it is an attractive deal not to make.

Conclusion

The Maoists in Nepal have undergone drastic changes of fate in the recent years. From waging a civil war to joining a democratic process of writing, the constitution within a small span of time is commendable. The future and progress of the political party will also depend on whether it will keep on developing along the same political path. The division of the party into two though highlights the differences between the members who follow the ideology; it also denotes the party's encirclement into democratic values and processes. The existence of two factions within the Maoist ideology itself shows the level of vibrant democracy in Nepal. The Maoists in Nepal have more to lose and less to gain by leaving its current political direction. Moreover, the Maoists both UCPN-M and CPN-M will try to regain peoples' support after the UCPN-M's loss in this years' election. The Maoist party in Nepal will get many positive and profitable incentives from different corners of the civil society. Not opting for such incentive will only lessen the party's lifeblood and its influencing capacity. The party has been commendably following the right political path until now which has to be continued in the near future, that is to avoid rash political decisions and continuously respect peoples' verdict.

18

Sinhala Buddhist Radicalization in Post-war Sri Lanka: 2013 and Ahead

Thiranjala Weerasinghe[1]

Introduction

After three decades of civil war, Sri Lankans expected the post-war period to be characterized by development and reconciliation. As the Government of Sri Lanka (GoSL) since 2009 beefed up its efforts towards reconstruction, resettlement, rehabilitation, reintegration and reconciliation, people witnessed several positive developments. Significant success was achieved in the areas of resettling the internally displaced persons, rehabilitating of the former Liberation Tigers of Tamil Elam (LTTE) carders and launching of infrastructure projects especially in the war-affected areas. Despite the initial progress made by the GoSL and the widespread wish for peaceful coexistence, the island still remains plagued and continues to face several challenges/problems of policy failures hindering the successful transition from post-war to post-conflict state. Indeed this has in effect not only distanced any prospects of peace and long-term resolution of conflict but has created waves of tension and unrest that could take a disastrous turn in the future.

[1] Thiranjala Weerasinghe is a Programme Officer at the Regional Centre for Strategic Studies (RCSS) Colombo, Sri Lanka. The views and opinions expressed in this chapter are solely those of the author. These views and opinions do not necessarily represent those of RCSS.

The callous attitude of the GoSL towards democracy, human rights, freedom and justice has perpetuated the process of strengthening the structural misalignments in the politics and society leading to the marginalization of the minority religious and ethnic groups. From the disregard shown towards the implementation of Lessons Learnt and Reconciliation Commission recommendations that attempted to remedy this sociopolitical and economic anomaly to the emergence of the Buddhist extremist groups such as Bodu Bala Sena (BBS) Ravana Balaya (RB) Sinhala Ravaya (SR) reinforces the process of marginalization.

The increasing violence against minority religious communities — Muslims and Christians — has become a key challenge in the post-war Sri Lanka. There has been a gradual rise of ultra-Buddhist groups who utilize violence, hate-speech and demonstrations against minority religious communities in asserting their Sinhala Buddhist nationalist ideology. Since 2009 there have been a number of incidents reported from all parts of the island accounting mob attacks on places of worship, destruction of religious establishments, protests against religious communities and hate speech on the Internet and media. These widespread attacks on minority religious communities have not only intensified the anxiety, insecurity and vulnerability of these ethnic and religious groups but also have portrayed trends that could escalate in to a protracted conflict in the coming years.

While some of these attacks were not reported in the media, others such as the attacks on the Mosques in Dambulla[2] in April 2012 and Grandpass[3] in August 2013 have been widely reported

---

[2] A mob of around 2,000 Buddhist monks attacked the mosque claiming it be constructed illegally in a sacred Buddhist area. They demanded the demolition of the mosque. Playing to the tune of ethno-religious chauvinism, the prime minister ordered the mosque to be relocated. R. Yehiya, 'Dambulla Mosque Attack: Is There a Hidden Hand?', available online at http://groundviews.org/2012/04/24/dambulla-mosque-attack-is-there-a-hidden-hand/ (accessed 9 January 2014).

[3] The mobs lead by Buddhist monks and their supporters demand the mosque at Kosgas junction, grandpass to be relocated. The Riot police and the Special Task Force had to be called to secure the area and the mosque as mobs had gathered on the streets. Ultra Buddhist organization Ravana Balaya which earlier called for the closing of the mosque denied any involvement in the attack. The BBS has also denied involvement in the

and discussed. At several occasions, the reporting and media coverage itself had been problematic. There were reports inaccurately presenting the details of the incidents and supporting the ultra-Buddhist groups who have championed the attacks. Even among those journalists who took a stand against the attacks, reporting was limited only to the specific attacks, the physical damage caused to places of worship and injuries to the relevant parties. While the basic reporting style is important, such reports continually failed to see the trends of emerging ethno-religious radicalization against the minority groups and the systematic failure of the law and order institutions in protecting the rights and liberties of the minorities. While at one hand this has helped the government to dismiss the attacks as individual events orchestrated by parties with divisive ideologies, on the other it has provided space for these ultra-Buddhist groups to continue the spate of attacks on religious places and persons of other faiths.

Hence, in this regard, year 2013 has been significant in comprehending and evaluating the post-war developments in Sri Lanka in an attempt to assess its conflict proneness as a measure of early warning. The rise of groups such as BBS propagating a Sinhala Buddhist nationalist ideology not only challenges the possibility of a secular country but threatens the existence of minority ethnic and religious communities within the island. Since 2009, the post-war years have witnessed a steady increase in the assertion of Sri Lanka as primarily a Sinhala Buddhist nation and an attempt to assimilate the other minority communities into the ethos of Sinhala Buddhists. There is an ever-increasing intolerance towards the sociocultural and religious differences of the minorities, and most often these differences are viewed as a direct threat towards Buddhism.

---

attack. However, CCTV footage clearly showed mobs led by monks attacking the mosque and some nearby Muslim houses. Muslims retaliated and a few Sinhalese houses were also attacked. After hours of deliberations at the Ministry of Buddha Sasana and Religious Affairs, a solution was reached to relocate the mosque to another old mosque in the area which was planned to be demolished for development purposes. 'Curfew Imposed in Grandpass due to Buddhist Monks Attacking a Mosque', 2013, available online at http://asiantribune.com/node/63914 (accessed 9 January 2014).

The Mahavamsa chronicle, first written in the 6th century ad by a Buddhist monk named Ven Mahanama and then modified subsequently is used to prove the claims of hardliners on the Sinhala Buddhist character of the island. Although it contains a mythical narration of the history of the island, many Sinhala Buddhists believe the chronicle to contain irrefutable facts. Deriving history from the chronicle, there is a widespread claim that Sri Lanka is a Sinhala Buddhist nation and it is the duty and responsibility of the state to protect and propagate Buddhism.

The BBS, RB and SR are the three radical groups who have been successful in launching several campaigns and attacks targeting minority Muslim and Christian population. Particularly, BBS has been successful in attracting a significant suburban support base and organizing several campaigns throughout 2013. Many incidents were reported of damaging mosques, churches and disrupting business places of Muslims. These radical groups formed and headed by Buddhist monks have proclaimed it to be their duty to protect Buddhism in Sri Lanka in the onslaught of challenges. They present themselves as saviours of Buddhism and brand those who fail to accept such an ideology as traitors and destroyers of the 'buddha sasana'.[4]

Many of the arguments put forth by BBS, though logically false and contain no historical basis, cannot be easily pushed under the carpet. Miscalculating the capacity of the fringe groups like BBS to instigate ethno-religious violence leading up to protracted conflicts will be immensely costly. The resurgence of political Buddhism along with Sinhala nationalism, which I singularly term as

---

[4] Watareka Vijitha Thero, a provincial council member of the government from Mahiyanganaya was physically attacked by the members of BBS, after he had criticized the BBS and their ideology and earlier opposed the destruction of a building in the town partly used by Muslim for prayer. He was labelled as a traitor and a person influenced by different agendas. Moreover, the BBS crew was threatened after they had covered one of the BBS rallies held in February 2013 in the suburbs of Colombo, as it was reported that the Sri Lankan members of the crew were 'verbally abused in filthy language, described as "traitors" and accused of having "foreign parents" and working for a "foreign conspirator" who was "against Sri Lanka"'. *BBC*, 'Sri Lanka Hardline Groups Call for Halal Boycott', 2013, available online at http://www.bbc.co.uk/news/world-asia-21494959 (accessed 23 January 2014).

Sinhala Buddhist nationalism have brought forth dark passages in history. For example, the Sinhala–Muslim riots in 1915 lead up to the 1956 general elections, the Sinhala Only Act of 1956, the promulgation of the constitution in 1978, and 1983 programme have all left lasting scars in the psyche of Sri Lankans and specially the minority communities.

The government patronage that these groups have received is quite alarming. With the tacit approval of their agenda and active support of the government through the failure of the law enforcement agencies and justice providers, these radical groups have been affirmed in their militant activism. Moreover, the ultra-Buddhist groups have successfully become the proxies for the government whose interests are not just limited to electoral advantages.

I strongly believe the trends that we witnessed in 2013 not to be new developments altogether but a continuation of a system which is fundamentally skewed in the favour of majority Sinhala Buddhist community. From the constitution to the basic institutions, the country is incapable of providing a rightful place for the minority ethnic and religious communities. The continued frustration on the part of minority communities coupled with other factors such as unemployment, poverty and underdevelopment can trigger situations of tension and conflict. Moreover, economic constraints and difficulties can further accelerate the Sinhala Buddhist antagonism especially towards the Muslims. Such a development could leave a negative impact on the economy as well. While an imminent danger of protracted ethno-religious tension with wider consequences on the polity and economy lingers, a constructive response to avert the situation is still awaited.

Attacks on Places of Religious Worship in Post-war Sri Lanka

As it has been noted earlier, systematic reporting of the attacks on places of religious worship had been a weak link. Although media has covered some of these attacks, there has not been a systematic recording of information in this regard. This has led to many conjectures on the nature and extent of ethno-religious violence since 2009. Especially, the lack of systemic databases on the nature and the extent of violence have been for the advantage of the perpetrators and the actors within the state who tacitly patronize such groups. However, the limited data at hand can still be helpful in revealing the manner in which violence had been unfolding since 2009 and especially in 2013. In this regard, it is profitable to assess the activities and campaigns of BBS as they remain one of the important contenders for Sinhala Buddhist nationalism.

According to a report submitted by National Christian Evangelical Alliance of Sri Lanka 'there were 52 incidents of violence against Christians in 2012, with an increase of 100 per cent compared to 2011. The number of cases has continued to increase: In the period from January to October, 2013, there had already been 65 incidents of anti-Christian violence'.[5] There have been reported incidents of forced closure of churches, acts of vandalism and arson against Christian leaders.

'Attacks on Places of Religious Worship in Post-War Sri Lanka'[6] by the Centre for Policy Alternatives (CPA) lists 65 cases of attacks on religious places of worship between May 2009 and January 2013. As it is noted

> Direct attacks have been reported from all provinces of Sri Lanka, making clear that the threat is not restricted to particular areas. Most of the reported incidents were from the Western province (16), followed by the Eastern province (12), the Southern province (11) and the North-Western province (9).[7]

---

[5] Agenzia Fides, 'Indifference on Behalf of the Government with Regards to the Increasing Number of Attacks Against Christians', 2013, available online at http://www.fides.org/en/news/34851ASIA_SRI_LANKA_Indifference_on_behalf_of_the_government_with_regards_to_the_increasing_number_of_attacks_against_Christians#.UtoIOdK6a00 (accessed 19 January 2014).

[6] Centre for Policy Alternatives, 'Attacks on Places of Religious Worship in Post-war Sri Lanka', 9 March 2013, available online at http://www.cpalanka.org/attacks-on-places-of-religious-worship-in-post-war-sri-lanka/ (accessed 31 October 2014).

[7] Ibid.

Much of the violence directed against Muslims and Christians are linked to BBS. There have been 64 recorded acts of violence from January to September 2013.[8] These include arson attacks, church demolitions, mob attacks and physical assaults. There have been various strategies like tightening administrative regulations for long-established churches to prove their legality for operating. Through such repressive practices an attempt has been made to violate the right of all people to follow a religion of their choice.

Attacks on places of Muslim worship and other institutions between January and July 2013 are recorded as 227. Also, there are 64 cases of attacks on Christian churches and pastors between January and September 2013. In the northern and eastern provinces of Sri Lanka, there have been dozens of Hindu temples destroyed. As reports claims the figures could be much higher as several of these attacks remain unreported.[9]

According to the organization Aid to Church in Need,[10] Sri Lanka is featured under 'high persecution' category and the condition in 2013 is defined as 'situation worsened slightly'. According to the report, organized attacks on churches and ministers have grown from January to May 2013 reporting at least 45 incidences of persecution against Christians.[11]

The figures presented here accounting the number of attacks on Muslims and Christians clearly reveal the gradual increase of the number of attacks during post-war Sri Lanka. As several sources provide the number of attacks (though vary from each other less markedly), the year 2013 has become a significant year

---

[8] Christian Solidarity Worldwide, 'Sri Lanka: Commonwealth Heads of Government Must Press Sri Lanka on Religious Freedom', 2013, available online at http://dynamic.csw.org.uk/article.asp?t=news&id=1902 (accessed 15 January 2014).

[9] S. Deshapriya, 'Attacks on Religious Minorities and Impunity in Sri Lanka', 2013, available online at http://www.srilankabrief.org/2013/11/attacks-on-religious-minorities-and.html (accessed 9 January 2014).

[10] 'Aid to the Church in Need is a Pontifical Foundation of the Catholic Church, Supporting the Catholic Faithful and Other Christians Where They Are Persecuted, Oppressed or in Pastoral Need', available online at http://www.acnuk.org (accessed 9 January 2014).

[11] 'Persecution Mapped Out', 2013, available online at http://www.acnuk.org/persecution-mapped-out (accessed 8 January 2014).

on violent attacks on religious minorities with such incidents as the anti-halal campaigns, rallies and meetings openly employing a anti-Muslim/Christian stance and numerous attacks on churches, mosques and persons of other faiths. The increase in the number of attacks also reveals the gradual rise of ultra-Buddhist groups and their support bases who increasingly become susceptible to ethno-religious indoctrination.

BBS

The BBS was formed in 2011 by monks Kirama Wimalajothi and Galagoda Aththe Gnanasara, the head and general secretary of BBS, respectively. They had broken away from Jathika Hela Urumaya (JHU) a political party consisted of Buddhist monks who first contested for the 2004 parliamentary elections. Galagoda Aththe Gnanasara had been one of the JHU candidates from Colombo District at that time. The headquarters of BBS is located at Sri Sambuddha Jayanthi Mandira in Colombo. It is owned by the Buddhist Cultural Centre, an organization founded by Kirama Wimalajothi. The President Mahinda Rajapaksa declared open the Buddhist Cultural Centre on 15 May 2011.

At the first National Convention held at the Bandaranaike Memorial International Conference Hall in July 2012, BBS passed five resolutions which among other things concentrated on a ban on vasectomy/tubectomy in government health facilities, replacement of the various legal systems used in the country with a single legal system, preferential treatment in university admission for students who attended Buddhism classes, use of monks in government schools to teach history and other classes and no solution for the country's ethnic problems which was based on race/religion.[12]

Over the years, BBS has been involved with several campaigns. One of the earliest campaigns by BBS was in respect of Buddhist Sri Lankans working in the Middle East. According to BBS, these Sri Lankans working in Middle East had been prevented from

[12] 'Buddhist Clergy wants Birth Control Operations Banned', *The Island*, Colombo, 29 July 2013.

practising their religion and had been punished harshly if found to be doing so.¹³

Some of the key initiatives/campaigns BBS has undertaken in 2013 are listed below:

1. BBS stormed Sri Lanka Law College in Hultsdorf, Colombo, on 7 January 2013. Although they accused that the exams results favoured Muslim students, later the allegations were proved to be false. The Law College postponed the new student registration by a week until the investigation was complete.¹⁴
2. Two managers of Cinnamon Bay Hotel in Moragalla, Beruwala were remanded over organizing a theme night with a 'Nirvana style' dinner at what was described as the 'cozy Buddha Bar lounge' meant for a group of French tourists.¹⁵
3. BBS organized a meeting in Maharagama,¹⁶ Colombo, on 17 February 2013 which was attended by around 16,000 people including 1,300 monks. At the rally, the BBS general secretary Galagoda Aththe Gnanasara noted, 'This is a

---

¹³ A Sri Lankan youth employed as a domestic aid had been arrested in Saudi Arabia for worshiping a statue of the Buddha, which is considered an offence according to Shariah law. According to the BBS, the youth bearing passport no. 2353715 identified as Premanath Pereralage Thungasiri had been arrested by Umulmahami Police. 'Arrested for Idol Worship', 2013, available online at http://www.ceylontoday.lk/16-9052-news-detail-arrested-for-idol-worship.html (accessed 10 January 2014).

¹⁴ The Law College postponed registration of the new batch of entrants by a week, acceding to a request by the BBS organization. Hundreds of Buddhist monks gathered opposite the Law College and forced its principal to postpone the registration. D. Edirisinghe, 'Law College Registration Put Off by One Week', *The Island*, Colombo, 8 January 2013.

¹⁵ Colombo Gazette, 'Hotel Managers Arrested over "Nirvana Style" Dinner Event', 2013, available online at http://www.sundaytimes.lk/130127/news/hotel-managers-arrested-over-nirvana-style-dinner-event-30406.html (last accessed on 16 January 2014).

¹⁶ At the same rally, members of the BBC crew had been seriously threatened by the BBS supporters. They had demanded the crew to leave the place adding never to return again. 'Sri Lanka Hardline Groups Calls for Halal Boycott', *BBC*, 2013, available online at http://www.bbc.co.uk/news/world-asia-21494959 (accessed 16 January 2014).

government created by Sinhala Buddhists and it must remain Sinhala Buddhist. This is a Sinhala country, Sinhala government. Democratic and pluralistic values are killing the Sinhala race'.[17] The monk also reiterated the need for them to become an unofficial police force against Muslim extremism. It was in this meeting that they adopted the resolution to end halal certification among other things.

4. After BBS commenced its anti-halal campaign in February 2013, it had initiated widespread anti-Muslim propaganda over the following weeks. While the government refused to confront the BBS over the matter, President Mahinda Rajapaksa by maintaining that halal process should be abolished gave into the demands of this ethno-religious facist group. Although All Ceylon Jamiyyathul Ulama (ACJU) offered the government the responsibility of issuing halal certificates, it refused to take up the task. Under intense pressure ACJU announced that halal logo will not appear on products supplied to the local market. However, the organization on a voluntary basis will continue to issue certificates for export purposes without any charge. In January 2014, ACJU announced that halal compliance certificate for Sri Lanka will be issued by the Halal Accreditation Council (Guarantee) Ltd with effect from 1 January 2014.[18]

5. In February 2013, BBS leader Kirama Wimalajothi declared that the organization will lobby for a ban on burqas and would take up the matter with the government.[19]

---

[17] T. Maeena, 'Neo-fascisms on the Rise in Sri Lanka', 2013, available online at http://gulfnews.com/opinions/columnists/neo-fascism-on-the-rise-in-sri-lanka-1.1150052 (accessed 16 January 2014).

[18] D. Jeyaraj, 'Jamiyathul Ulama Due to Govt Pressure Will Stop Halal Certified Logos Locally as Demanded by the Bodhu Bala Sena', 2013, available online at http://dbsjeyaraj.com/dbsj/archives/18088 (accessed 16 January 2014).

[19] Fathima Sahar, a student at the Faculty of Architecture at the University of Moratuwa wrote an article on the Groundviews, describing her ordeal with the university authority who stopped her in entering the university on 1 August 2013. This is even after she had consented to remove the niqab during lectures and at the security check of the university entrance. Although she had not formally requested permission to wear the niqab at the university, the university falsely claimed so. F. Sahar,

6. A meat inspection facility located in Dematagoda was raided by the BBS on 1 March 2013. This facility functioned under the Colombo Municipal Council. However, BBS levelled allegations of young calves, pregnant cows and water buffaloes being slaughtered at the facility in Dematagoda. All allegations of BBS were proved wrong as it was found that the premises had only been used to inspect meat prior being distributed in the city.[20]
7. Meth Sevana, the BBS' cultural and training centre in Pilana, Wanchawala, Galle District, was officially opened on 9 March 2013 by chief guest Defence Secretary Gotabhaya Rajapaksa, the brother of President Mahinda Rajapaksa.
8. After announcing its success over the anti-halal campaign, the Sinhala Buddhist extremist organization, BBS, revealed its decision to take up the issue of removing a mosque form Kuragala Buddhist monastery complex. The revelation came at a rally held in Kandy on 17 March 2013.[21]
9. Speaking at the BBS rally in Panadura on 24 March 2013, Ven Galaboda Aththe Gnanasara Thero cautioned Sinhalese to protect the nation and rally against Christian and Muslim extremism in the country. Moreover, at the rally he asserted Sri Lanka not to be a multiracial or multireligious country but a Sinhala Buddhist country.[22]
10. At the same rally held in Panadura, BBS Secretary Ven Galagoda Atthe Gnanasara Thero demanded the termination of services of Ms Ferial Ashraff, Sri Lanka's High

---

'The Niqab and the University of Moratuwa', 2013, available online at http://groundviews.org/2013/12/09/the-niqab-and-the-university-of-moratuwa/ (accessed 16 January 2014).

[20] D. Bastians, 'Bodu Bala Sena Storms Dematagoda Slaughterhouse', 2013, available online at http://www.ft.lk/2013/03/02/bodu-bala-sena-storms-dematagoda-slaughterhouse/ (accessed 16 January 2014).

[21] 'Sri Lanka's Buddhist Extremists Vow to Remove Muslim Mosque in Kuragala', *Colombo Page*, 18 March 2013, available online at http://www.colombopage.com/archive_13A/Mar18_1363584917CH.php (accessed 16 January 2014).

[22] 'BBS Insists Lanka not Multiracial', *Colombo Gazette*, 2013, available online at http://colombogazette.com/2013/03/24/bbs-insists-lanka-not-multiracial/ (accessed 16 January 2014).

Commissioner to Singapore. He had accused Ms Ashraff for working against the interest of Sinhala Buddhists and pointing to instances of her anti-Sinhala Buddhist bias.[23]
11. Buddhist monks lead hundreds on 28 March 2013 to vandalize the Muslim-owned Fashion Bug clothes shop in Pepiliyana, Colombo district. The security forces had to be deployed to secure the area. Although there were widespread allegations of BBS' involvement, the monks have denied any of its involvement.[24]

Resurgence of Radicalism: Sinhala Buddhist Nationalism

The end of war in 2009 created a tremendous hope for long-term peace and reconciliation. The defeat of the LTTE and the cessation of the costly war had indeed created an atmosphere conducive for rehabilitation, reconstruction, development and reconciliation. A question that many have raised is whether Sri Lanka was able to seize this unique opportunity in resolving the prolonged conflict and addressing the decades long contested issues.

The end of war was often interpreted by the government to maximize its popularity and appeal towards its voter bases among the majority Sinhala Buddhists. This has convinced a significant number of Sinhalese in supporting the regime. Despite the several shortcomings in policy-making, increasing level of corruption, impunity and lack of transparency, still a considerable number of Sinhalese perceive the regime as the only suitable political party to rule the country.[25] The re-election of President Mahinda

[23] D. Jeyaraj, 'Bodhu Bala Sena Wants Sri Lankan Envoy Ferial Ashraff Recalled From Singapore Immediately', 2013, available online at http://dbsjeyaraj.com/dbsj/archives/19091 (accessed 16 January 2014).

[24] Aljazeera, 'Sri Lanka Violence Prompts Security Measures', 2013, available online at http://www.aljazeera.com/news/asia/2013/03/20133298245623684.html (accessed 16 January 2014).

[25] Over the years, the opposition political parties have been weakened. With several crossovers to the current regime and despicable politics of the opposition parties without a clear agenda has reinforced the popularity of the regime in power. Moreover, the United National Party has always been unable to bank on the larger sections of the Sinhala Buddhists votes.

Rajapaksa to the second term in office and the victories at several provincial council elections subsequently held is an indication on the perception of the majority of Sinhala Buddhist population.[26]

Visual and print media institutions of the government as well as ones privately owned have heavily invested in promoting this image of the regime and the principle actors involved. The regime desperately worked for the recognition of the party leadership in liberating the country from the terrorism of LTTE and initiative towards peace, democracy and development. It also sought to represent the concern, aspirations and anxieties of the majority Sinhala Buddhist community. These efforts of the government in actualizing the maximum political mileage have been most often at the cost of efforts towards reconciliation and conflict resolution. As a result, despite the progress that we have witnessed in the last couple of years (though achieved in limited sectors like infrastructure development), several fundamental issues relating to the conflict (i.e., a political solution, transitional justice, high militarization in north, human rights abuses, denial of language rights and basic living conditions people affected and displaced during war) largely remain unresolved.

One factor that has significantly contributed to this stalemate is the resurgence of radical activism among the ultra-Buddhist groups. The damage that has been caused is enormous. Not only have these groups initiated a fresh outburst of violence, but also many of the conflict-prone issues of the past have been negatively reinforced. For instance, these groups have openly made it clear their opposition towards settling the current conflict on the basis of ethnicity or religion and their readiness to mobilize masses if the government attempts to introduce the 19th amendment to the constitution. Hence, these radical elements have left no space for the resolution of the conflict but initiated fresh impetus for animosity, hatred and suspicion.

There is an increasing trend on the use of these radical elements — as scapegoats — by the current regime. The mutual support

---

[26] President Mahinda Rajapaksa led his party to a landslide victory in parliamentary election with a majority of 1,842,749. UPFA marked a series of sweeping victories in the election of eight provincial councils in 2010. Now the UPFA government enjoys a two-thirds majority in the parliament.

rendered has been beneficial for both the government and groups such as BBS. Even today many have failed to state if the organizations like BBS are only standalone organizations or the portrayal of a symptom of a wider political undercurrent developing in Lanka and especially in the post-war context. If the situation is diagnosed as a symptom of a wider political undercurrent, then Sinhala Buddhist along with sections of the Buddhist clergy have found an 'enemy' that they need to defeat.

The continued spate of attacks on religious minorities and the failure of law and order institutions in 2013 indicate the presence of a strong Sinhala Buddhist regime in power and the diminishing space for minority communities within Sri Lankan society and polity. The public space of minority ethnic and religious groups has been increasingly constrained. This is in no manner giving way to a healthy development. Battered by years of violence, discrimination and afflicted with humiliation and betrayal, the sections that have been at the receiving end could easily become a destabilizing section within the population. The economic troubles, unemployment and lack of opportunities could lead members of these communities to embrace violence. Moreover, the existence of such groups has been used to justify all claims about the alleged aspirations of majority ethno-religious communities of the country.

As it was stated earlier, the radical groups like BBS have received wide support from the current regime. The electoral gains for the government remain a large motivation factor in entertaining and encouraging such radical elements. However, there are other factors that drive an active as well as passive endorsement of the Buddhist radicalism. Several campaigns launched for instance by BBS in 2013 have turned out to be the sources of distraction saving the regime from wider political repercussions. Several important issues that have had a lasting impact on the economy have received less public attention and critical discussion.

First in 2013, a great deal of public discussion was initiated on the significant price revision of electricity for both residential and commercial consumers. Partly, this proposed hike was caused by the failure of Norochcholai power plant which had broken down around 25 times so far. The plant utilization was around 56 per cent up to 30 December 2013. The underutilization and the loss incurred at every breakdown will somehow be borne by the consumers. Despite the glaring failure of Norochcholai power plant, the Chinese company that was responsible for the construction, China Machinery Corporation, has been awarded the contract for the main water supply scheme (one of the biggest supply schemes in the country costing US $230 m) in the Gampaha district. While a handful of politicians have protested against the move, there have been small public debates/discussions over the matter.

Second, the report submitted by the Committee on Public Enterprises reveals the extent of financial mismanagement and gross inefficiency on the part of state-owned enterprises (SOEs). The report clearly asserts that the Ceylon Electricity Board, Ceylon Petrol Corporation, Sri Lankan Airlines and Mihin Lanka Ltd constituted a staggering 98 per cent of the total losses suffered by all SOEs during 2013. They have been claimed to underselling services while concentrating on public-welfare instead of profit-making. This again received less importance compared to the anti-halal campaign of BBS.

Third, the current regime has repeatedly failed to face the challenges posed by the fast-growing health sector. The efficiency and quality of health services provided have gradually declined over the years. The aforementioned challenges are principally emanate from shifting the demographic and socio-economic character of the country, especially associated with the transition to middle-income status. Moreover, the government expenditure (though low middle income countries generally spend 4 per cent of gross domestic product [GDP] on education) on education has witnessed a steep drop to a 10-year low of 1.8 per cent of GDP in 2012. Once again the government has been able to steer away from such criticism.

Especially the post-war era of Sri Lanka is characterized by a renewed debate on the identity of the state. This excessive desire for a monolithic definition of the state in terms of an ethno-religious community has lead to animosity and mistrust. From the time of independence we observe an increasing level of suspicion and mistrust among the different ethno-religious groups that have been principally responsible in widening the ethno-religious divide. Today the ultra-Buddhist groups with their acts of violence and persecution have once more asserted the primary importance that needs to be given for Buddhism over the multicultural and plural identity of Sri Lanka. For instance, the defeat of LTTE and the victory of GoSL forces count as a victory for Buddhism. It is not merely the defeat of the LTTE, a terrorist outfit but the end of Tamil nationalism as well. The triumphalism that was prevalent in the South at the end of war emerges from this fundamental belief of Sinhala/Sinhala Buddhist reign.

The CPA made a press release on 21 August 2013 expressing deep concern over the reports about the new laws to be introduced in relation to the publications that 'defame the original teachings and traditions of the major religions'. As the first step, the draft bill was supposed to establish a 'Buddhist Publication Regulatory Board'.[27] This comes in the background of GoSL's lukewarm response in taking steps to further strengthen laws against hate speech through a new amendment.[28] Such biased laws and regulations provide us an understanding on the influences of Sinhala Buddhist nationalism upon every dimension of state machinery. The construction of Buddhist temples, statues, shrines in North and East, and the escalating number of attacks on the minority communities reinforce the fears and anxieties of minority communities. Many of the religious constructions that are taking place in the North and East are not merely places of religious worship but imposition and assertion of a Sinhala Buddhist ideology that accepts the super-ordination of Sinhala Buddhism at the cost of the rights and freedoms of other minority communities.

Hence, as we witness today, Sinhala Buddhist nationalism is a political ideology which combines focus upon the Sinhalese culture, ethnicity with an emphasis upon the Theravda Buddhism. This basically started as a reactionary movement against colonization—especially the British era—that instituted discriminatory linguistic, educational and economic policies. The wrath of the emerging nationalist groups was initially directed towards

---

[27] Centre for Policy Alternatives, 'Press Release on New Laws over Defamation of Major Religions', 2013, available online at http://www.cpalanka.org/press-release-on-new-laws-over-defamation-of-major-religions/ (accessed 16 January 2014).

[28] Although media has been reporting on Minister Vasudeva Nanayakara's efforts in making necessary preparation to submit a paper to the cabinet proposing to ban hate speech/campaigns against any community or religious group, the progress in this regard has been limited to mere rhetoric.

colonizers and their discriminatory practices. In time the minority ethnic and religious groups with their diverse sociocultural, economic and political affiliations became targets of violence, discrimination and hostility. Today, hatred and violence can be directed against Tamil and Moors as an ethnic minority, Hindus, Christians and Muslims as a religious minority.

However, it is proper to remember today that not all Buddhists are nationalists. The events like the 'Candle Light Vigil' and 'Rally for Unity' attended by large crowds and the presence of the Facebook group 'Buddhists Questioning Bodu Bala Sena'[29] testifies to the presence of moderate groups within Sinhala, Tamil and Muslim communities. Yet the Buddhist nationalist ideology appears to be widely accepted. This is seen in the increased support for the politicians and political parties toeing a pro-Sinhala Buddhist line. Also, it is evident from issues such as favouring a military solution to the ethnic conflict and supporting the maintenance of the unitary state structure, decline of secularism, disregard for minorities' human rights, the culture of impunity surrounding the military, attacks against the media and others critical of the government, and the renewed colonization efforts of the Sinhala Buddhist nationalists in the eastern/ northern province.

Conclusion

The year 2013 has been characterized by a significant rise of religious hatred and violence. While the number of attacks on places of religious worship and persons of other faiths have risen, the nature of violence has significantly altered. Initially, the violence unleashed on minority Christian and Muslim groups were scattered. Also, they were less coordinated and lacked a grand strategy. But the year 2013 witnessed a dramatic shift in the nature of attacks: They appeared to be more organized, principally lead by Buddhist monks, targeting being well calculated, often with

---

[29] A non-partisan community attempts to discuss the BBS's actions, techniques, motives and goals, and question whether they are in line with the Dhamma.

covert state sanction, media coverage, revisionist tendencies and the increasing use of Buddhism as a driving force.

For instance in 2013, the BBS had openly asserted the need for them to become an unofficial police force in fighting what they termed as 'Muslim/Christian Extremism'. The legitimacy of such claims has largely been uncontested. The general public, the religious leaders and the current regime had been too reluctant to denounce such claims and assert the multi-cultural nature of Sri Lankan society. Such a hesitation on the part of many Sri Lankans has lead to an affirmation of the hate campaigns and violence on minorities.

Social media is heavily utilized in reinforcing and spreading across such biases. Throughout the year, Facebook had been increasingly used in making false accusation and an attempt has been made to demonize the minorities. There were references to the birth rates of Muslims and their growth as a direct threat to Sinhala Buddhists as an ethno-religious community and the economic well-being. There is an increasing opinion among certain sections of the Sinhalese community on the need to reject Muslim businesses and products. Although this idea is still getting traction among the majority Sinhala Buddhists, during 2014 there could be wider consensus.

This kind of vilification/demonization of minority ethnic and religious communities will continue. The government will persist to derive maximum political mileage from the activities of radical groups such as BBS. Such manipulative techniques employed by the government will further increase the risk of relapsing to an era of tension and conflict. While the current regime might just be able to maintain the radical elements like BBS within its ambit of power, this could nevertheless lead to the radicalization of the lower middle classes of people living in suburban areas of Sri Lanka. This group has been extremely vulnerable towards ethno-religious radicalization. Poverty, unemployment, underemployment and lack of economic opportunities experienced will further expose these sections of people towards radicalization.

Despite having a significant number of Muslim parliamentarians within the government, the Muslim community has been unable to demand justice and equality from the state. Also, they have refrained from retaliating. The kind of response that the Muslim community will have in 2014 and ahead is yet uncertain.

Since the Sinhala–Muslim riots in 1915, Muslims have attempted to always politically align themselves with the Sinhalese political parties in power. Moreover, it was only in 1980s that a Muslim political party was formed. Still there is a strong hesitation to irk the Sinhala elites. The extent into which the current situation can develop into a protracted conflict or a period of marked tensions and violence will partly depend on the decision on the part of principal interlocutors within the Muslim community in the nature of their response to the increasing level of religious intolerance and persecution.

A continued unrest and a widened ethno-religious divide will temporary serve the current regime. While there is less probability that the government will take any drastic action to combat the kind of militant activism of radical Buddhist groups, under increasing pressure from local and international actors, the government could show indifference to the rising level of radicalism within the country. From President Mahinda Rajapaksa's participation at the inauguration of the Buddhist Cultural Centre in 2011, Defence Secretary Gotabhaya Rajapaksa's presence as the chief guest at the inauguration of the BBS cultural and training centre in 2013 and the to the refusal of the government to resolve the halal issue (later gave into the pressure exerted by the BBS) portrays the kind of government patronage for such groups.

The calculated attacks on minority religious groups in 2013 have been largely spearheaded by Buddhist clergy. The participation of the Buddhist clergy in act of violence had brought forth several challenges for the law enforcement agencies. Many of the video footages of attacks accessed through the web portray the aggressive presence of Buddhist monks who not only were successful in mobilizing the supporters but also prevented the police officers in carrying out their duties. In many instances, the police had become mere onlookers and spectators.

The resurgence of the radical elements within the Sinhala Buddhist community can see the steady demise of moderate elements principally within the majority Sinhala community as well as other minority communities. In the past, LTTE had been successful in eliminating the moderates both within the Sinhala and Tamil communities as they posed a serious threat to their ideology and the use of violence. In the same manner, these radical groups had been targeting the moderate elements within the society accusing them of being 'traitors' and 'children of foreign parents' who would propagate agendas of foreign superpowers. There is a great need of the moderate communities within the country in affirming their due space.

Today, Sri Lankan society and polity stands at an important juncture. While there have been numerous opportunities in achieving a lasting solution for the prolonged conflict in Sri Lanka, they have not been materialized. Increasing trust deficit and widening ethno-religious divide decrease the possibility of long-term peace and increase the chances of Sri Lanka being affected by violence and tension. Although a war is yet a distant possibility, a protracted conflict involving all minority sections within the island will definitely have disastrous consequences.

About the Editors and Contributors

Editors

D. Suba Chandran is Director, Institute of Peace and Conflict Studies (IPCS), New Delhi. His primary area of research includes Pakistan's internal security, Afghanistan, and Jammu and Kashmir. He is currently working on Pakistan in the Next Decade and on Indo-Pak water conflicts, especially, Indus Water Governance. He is also working on 'State Failure in South Asia', exploring what constitutes state failure/fragility in the South Asian context, especially focusing on stability–instability curve and failure in parts, and testing hypotheses of cyclic failure and functional anarchy. He is also Visiting Professor, Pakistan Studies Programme, Jamia Millia Islamia, New Delhi, and an Associate at the Pakistan Study Research Unit (PSRU), University of Bradford. He was the editor of *Armed Conflicts in South Asia*.

P.R. Chari is Visiting Professor, IPCS. He is a former member of the Indian Administrative Service and has served in several senior positions in the central and state governments. He sought voluntary retirement in 1992 after 32 years in the government. During the course of his official career he served two spells (1971–1975 and 1985–1988) in the Ministry of Defence. He retired from the position of Vice Chairman (Chief Executive) of the Narmada Valley Development Authority.

Contributors

Chitra Ahanthem is a journalist based in Imphal, Manipur. She has been Editor of Imphal Free Press, a daily newspaper and her works have been published in the *Times of India, India Today, Sunday Guardian* besides many online websites. Her areas of focus are armed conflict, gender, child rights, and HIV and AIDS. She is also an amateur photographer.

Ashok Bhan is a former Director General of Police who served in various capacities in the state of Jammu and Kashmir during the conflict period. Having joined the Indian Police Service in 1976, he served as Director General of Police (Intelligence), Director General of Police (Prisons), Commissioner of Vigilance, Inspector General of Police of Kashmir Zone, DIG Jammu, SSP Anantnag and SSP Rajouri besides heading the J&K Armed Police, Security Wing and the State Police Academy. He is a recipient of Police Medal for Gallantry, President's Police Medal for Distinguished Service, Police Medal for Meritorious service, Wound Medal, and the Chief Minister's Medal for Honesty and Integrity. Currently he is a Member of Shri Mata Vaishno Devi Shrine Board, Distinguished Fellow of the IPCS New Delhi, Chairman of the J&K Regional Branch of the Indian Institute of Public Administration, and Member of the Executive Council of Indian Institute of Public Administration in New Delhi.

Sisir Devkota was formerly with IPCS.

Wasbir Hussain, a journalist and political commentator, is Executive Director, Centre for Development and Peace Studies, Guwahati, and a Visiting Fellow at the Institute of Peace and Conflict Studies, New Delhi. He is a two-time former Member of the National Security Advisory Board, Government of India.

Ayesha Khanyari is a Research Assistant with the Centre for Internal and Regional Security (IReS) at the IPCS, New Delhi.

Nani Gopal Mahanta is Associate Professor, Department of Political Science and Coordinator of Peace and Conflict Studies at Gauhati University, Assam. A former Rotary World Peace Fellow at the University of California, Berkeley (2002–2004), he has published widely and has been a Visiting Fellow at the Peace Research Institute Oslo (PRIO), Norway. Currently, he is the President of North East India Political Science Association (NEIPSA).

N. Manoharan is Fellow, National Maritime Foundation, New Delhi. He was South Asia Visiting Fellow at the East–West Center Washington (2005) and recipient of Mahbub-ul Haq Award (2006). His areas of interest include internal security, terrorism, Sri Lanka, Maldives, human rights, ethnic conflicts, multiculturalism, security sector reforms and conflict resolution.

Nishchal Nath Pandey is Director of the Centre for South Asian Studies (CSAS), Kathmandu. He was Executive Director (Bisishta Shreni) of the Institute of Foreign Affairs (IFA) under the Ministry of Foreign Affairs where he worked for eight years (1998–2006).

Uddhab Prasad Pyakurel is Assistant Professor in Political Sociology, School of Arts, Kathmandu University, Nepal. He is also associated with various democracy forums, i.e., South Asian Dialogues on Ecological Democracy (SADED), Vasudhaiva Kutumbakam (VK) and Network Institute for Global Democratization (NIGD).

Mirza Zulfiqur Rahman is a PhD candidate in the Department of Humanities and Social Sciences, Indian Institute of Technology Guwahati (IITG), Guwahati, Assam. He works as an independent researcher and writes on various topical issues relating to Northeast India. His areas of interest include research on Northeast India, mainly on issues relating to insurgency, peace-building, development, migration and cross-border exchanges. His current research work is on border studies in Northeast India and transboundary water sharing and management issues between China, India and Bangladesh. He is also working on a project with the Institute of Chinese Studies (ICS), New Delhi, on the Sino-Indian border in Arunachal Pradesh. He is committed to grassroots based alternative community work and development models.

Bibhu Prasad Routray is a Singapore-based security analyst/consultant, and a visiting fellow at the IPCS, New Delhi. He previously served as a Deputy Director in India's National Security Council Secretariat (NSCS), New Delhi. Prior to his official tenure, he served in various think tanks including the Institute for Conflict Management (ICM), Guwahati, Assam, which he headed as

Director. He specializes in decision-making, governance, counter-terrorism, force modernization, intelligence reforms, foreign policy and dissent articulation issues in South and Southeast Asia.

Mariam Safi is Founding Director, Organisation for Policy Research and Development Studies. Her research on topics like the Role of Afghan Women in Peace Process (PEAD), Transitional Justice in Afghanistan: Should Not Repeat Old Issues (AJO), Peoples Perspective on Human Security: Afghanistan (GPPAC) has got her much national and international acclaim. She was formerly Deputy Director of the Centre for Conflict and Peace Studies (2010–2012) based in Kabul, and was the co-founder of the Afghanistan Justice Organization's Strategic Studies Program (2013–2014).

Sohan Prasad Sha is a PhD candidate in interdisciplinary areas of study at Centre for Studies in Science Policy, Social of Social Sciences, Jawaharlal Nehru University. He has previously worked with the IPCS and contributed the articles in range of interests like contemporary political developments, politics in the tarai/ Madhes region and geo-politics of Nepal. His academic research also extended to public policy, sociology of knowledge production, political economy, institutions and development issues of Nepal. His current research work is on comparative study of Nepal with selected economy of South Asia and East Asia to contextualize the development of science and technology for endogenous capacity building, areas of cooperation and alternative policy learning.

Kavita Suri is Associate Professor and Assistant Director, Department of Lifelong Learning, University of Jammu. As the J&K bureau chief of the *Statesman*, one of the oldest national newspapers of India, she wrote and researched extensively on the women of three regions of her state.

Thiranjala Weerasinghe is Programme Officer, Regional Centre for Strategic Studies (RCSS), Colombo. Prior to joining RCSS, he was a lecturer in philosophy at the Ampitiya National Seminary (affiliated to Pontifical Urubaniana University), Kandy. He is currently pursuing his LLB under the international programme of the University of London.

Index

aam admi (common man) civil society movement, 19
Abdulla, Omar, 170
Abdullah, Sheikh Mohammad, 310
Achik Matgrik Liberation Army (AMLA), 106
Afghanistan
  Afghan National Security Forces (ANSF), 37–41
  Bilateral Security Agreement (BSA) with US, 44–47
  conflict, 2013, 31–32
  de jure sovereignty in, 33
  economy, 2013, 27
  education level, 2013, 27
  Human Development Index (HDI) report, 2013, 27–28
  life expectancy ratio of Afghans, 2013, 27
  mortality rates, 2013, 27
  narcotics trade, 43–44
  NATO-led ISAF in, 37–38
  Pakistan's supportive role in peace process, 50–51
  peace and reconciliation process, 47–51
  post-2014, 21–23
  security and transition processes, actors involved in, 28–31
  transition process in terms of security, 37–38
  US counter-insurgency efforts in, 32–34
Afghan National Army (ANA), 23, 40
  absence of 'complex enabling support' and, 40
Afghan National Police (ANP), 23, 40
Afghan Peace and Reintegration Programme (APRP), 48
Akbar Hydari Agreement, 103
All Assam Students Union (AASU), 110
All Bodo Students Union (ABSU), 110
All Parties Conference (APC), 53, 68–69
All Tripura Tiger Force (ATTF), 105
Al Qaeda, 18, 21, 299
American/ISAF forces in Afghanistan, 21–23
Amnesty International, 62
'anti-government elements' (AGEs), 35, 37
anti-Rohingya violence, 11
Arab Spring, 11
armed conflicts
  civil-military relations between India and Pakistan, 15–18
  defined, 4
  in South Asia, 13–24

armed conflicts in Pakistan 2013
  areas of focussed attacks, 53
  attacks on political parties, 60
  in Balochistan, 59
  in FATA, 59–60
  in Karachi, 60
  in KP, 59
  non-state actors, 55–57
  in Peshawar, 59
  sectarian violence, 63–67
  in Sindh, 60
  state actors, 54–55
  suicide attacks, 58–59
  trends, 57–58
  US drone attacks and, 60–62
Armed Forces (Special Powers) Act, 1958, 15, 110, 122, 169, 172, 183, 329
Ashraf, Raja Parvez, 165
Asom Gana Parishad (AGP), 111
Asom Jatiyatabadi Yuva Chatra Parishad (AJYCP), 110
Asom Sahitya Sabha (ASS), 110
Autonomous State Demand Council (ASDC), 111
Awami League, 23
Awami National Party (ANP), 54
Azad, Gulam Nabi, 311
Aziz, Sartaj, 51

Bandaranayake, Shirani, 282
Banerjee, Rana, 167
Bangladesh
  internal dissensions and violence in, 23–24
Baradar, Mullah Abdul Ghani, 50–51
Baruah, Paresh, 103, 342, 347
Bhat, Abdul Ghani, 171–172
Bhattarai, Baburam, 249–250, 253, 264, 268
Bodoland
  Darrang–Udalguri clash, 204–205
  militancy scene in, 205–207
  peace process in, 203–205
Bodoland accord of 2003, 225
Bodoland Liberation Tigerss (BLT), 203
Bodoland People's Front (BPF), 111
Bodoland Territorial Council (BTC), 104, 203–205
Bodo Liberation Tigers (BLT), 104
Bodo Sahitya Sabha (BSS), 111
Borbora, Pallav, 340
Borborah, Pallab, 345
Bordoloi, Pradyut, 339
Borgohain, Debojit, 333
Brahma, Prem Singh, 104
Bru National Liberation Front (BNLF), 105
Bush, George H.W., 7

Central Armed Police Forces (CAPFs), 126, 143–144
Chanda, Indranil, 345
Chin National Front (CNF), 75
Cho, Khine Khine Aye, 73
civil-military relations' problematique, 14–18
civil society organizations (CSOs), 37
Cold Start Doctrine, 17
Commando Battalions for Resolute Action (CoBRAs), 143
communal divide in J&K. *See also* Jammu and Kashmir (J&K), peace process in
  Big Landed Estates Abolition Act of 1950, 310
  communal divide between majority and minority community, 311, 317–320
  early warnings of potential problems, 326–327
  exodus of Kashmiri Pandits, 310–311
  governance issues, 322

Index **421**

history, understanding, 309–312
non-state actors, role of, 317
political factors, 320–321
Poonch incident, 1988, 319–320
present situation, 312–315
social factors, 322
state actors, role of, 316
strategies to solve, 323–326
unrest, 1952-1953, 310
communal-religious links, 9
Communist Party of Burma (CPB), 75
Communist Party of India-Marxist (CPI-M), 111, 127–129, 268, 346–347
  Central Military Commission (CMC), 128
  organizational structure of, 128
  People's Liberation Guerrilla Army (PLGA), 128
conflict management, 126
  anti-Maoist strategy of 'Clear-Hold-Develop', 149
  Left-wing extremism (LWE), 143–148
  Myanmar, 93–98
  Pakistan, 67–70
controversial elections, 4–5
  Afghanistan, 13
  Bangladesh, 5
  Maldives, 13
  Nepal, 5, 13
  nexus between domestic and electoral violence, 13
  in South Asia, 13
Counter-insurgency and Anti-terrorism (CIAT) schools, 143
counter-insurgency (COIN)
in Northeast India, 113–114
US efforts in Afghanistan, 32–34

Dahal, Puspa Kamal, 247, 249, 262, 264–268
Debbarma, Biswamohan, 106

Debbarma, Joshua, 106
Democratic Alliance of Nagaland (DAN), 111
Deuba, Sher Bahadur, 259
Dima Hasao Autonomous Territorial Council (DHATC), 219
Dimasa National Liberation Front (DNLF), 220
Dimasa National Revolutionary Front (DNRF), 220
Dinpuri, Mufti Abdul Majeed, 64
Dobbins, James, 22
drone strikes in Pakistan (2005-2013), 60–62, 70

early warning systems, 10–12
  applications, 11
  of civil unrest, 11
  detection and communication systems, 11
  relevance of, 1
Eastern Nagaland Public Organization (ENPO), 210
Eikenberry, Karl, 33

Failed State Index (FSI), 272
Farooq, Mirwaiz Umar, 171
Fazlullah, Mullah, 70, 303–304
Federally Administered Tribal Areas (FATA), 53
  armed conflicts in, 59–60
flash mobs phenomenon, 12, 14

Garo National Liberation Army (GNLA), 106
Garo Students Union (GSU), 111
Geelani, Syed Ali Shah, 171, 312
Global Peace Index (GPI), 272
Gogoi, Tarun, 339, 341
Gohain, Hiren, 213–214
Goswami, Mamoni Raisom, 213
Guru, Mohammed Afzal, 162–163, 166, 169, 171
Gyanendra, King, 258–260, 375

Haqqani Network, 51, 61, 168, 291
Harkat-ul-Jihad al-Islami (HuJI), 18
Hasina, Sheikh, 5
Hazara killings of Balochistan, 65–66
High Peace Council (HPC), 47
Hill Tiger Force (HTF), 220
Hizb-e-Islami, 51
Hmar People's Convention-Democracy (HPC-D), 105
Human Rights Watch, 62
Hydari, Sir Akbar, 103
Hynniewtrep Achik Liberation Council (HALC), 106
Hynniewtrep National Liberation Council (HNLC), 106

imagined communities, 9
Imam, Syed Manzar, 60
improvised explosive devices (IEDs), 35–36
  remote-controlled IEDs (RC-IEDs), 42
  'victim-activated pressure plate' IEDs (PP-IEDs), 42
India–Myanmar, relation, 85–86
India–Pakistan relations
  Ceasefire Agreement on the LoC, 19
  ceasefire violations and cross-border attacks, 19–21
  Cold Start Doctrine, 17
  dialogue on J&K, 20
  India–Pakistan bilateral dialogue, 164–173
  joint resource development, 20
  Line of Control (LoC) and cross-border attacks, 15–16
  nuclear deterrent relations, 17
  people-to-people relations, 19
  in terms of domestic and electoral politics, 18–21
Indigenous Peoples Forum (IPF), 220
'Indo-Naga conflict', 210
Inter-services Intelligence (ISI), 138
Irabot, Hijam, 188–189
Islamic terror in India, 21

Jaish-e-Mohammed, 18
Jamatiya, Nayanbasi, 106
Jammu and Kashmir (J&K), peace process in
  during 2012, 156–157
  Amarnath land row and, 183
  Article 370 and, 184, 186
  assembly elections in 1996, 2002 and 2008, 178–181
  centre-state relations, 170
  changing nature of violence, 157–164
  Chinese incursions and, 176–178
  communal history of J&K, understanding, 309–312
  communal situation, 183–185
  decline in cross-border terrorism, 164–165
  governance, internal dimension of, 173–175
  hartal calls (2006-2013), 159
  India–Pakistan bilateral dialogue, 164–173
  negotiations with Kashmiri separatists, 171
  political consensus at national level, dealing with, 185–186
  political interventions, 168–173
  preparedness and remedial steps, 181–183
  sectarian violence, issue of, 183–185
  strengthening of democratic institutions, 178–181

terrorist violence (1996–2013), 158
United Nations (UN) Resolutions to solve Kashmir, 165
violence during 2013, 160–162
Jammu Kashmir Liberation Front (JKLF), 20
Jan, Maulana Ahmed, 61
Jha, Durgananda, 358
Jha, Vedanand, 358
Joint Action Karbi Anglong Union (JAKASU), 216

Kachin Independence Organization (KIO), 75
Kachin National Organization (KNO), 75, 78, 80, 84–85, 90–92
Kangleipak Communist Party (KCP), 105
Kanglei Yawol Kanna Lup (KYKL), 105
Karbi Anglona, peace process in, 216–219
pro-talk and anti-talk factions, 218
Karbi National Protection Force (KNPF), 219
Karbi People's Liberation Tiger (KPLT), 218–219
Karbi Riso A-Darbar (KRA-D), 216
Karen National Liberation Army (KNLA), 75
Karen National Union (KNU), 75
Karenni National Progressive Party (KNPP), 75
Karzai, Hamid, 22, 31, 37, 49–50
Kashmir card, 156
Kashmir Valley, 8–9
Kayani, General, 15
Khan, Imran, 292
Khan, Rahimyar, 67
Khaplang, S.S., 103

Khasi Students Union (KSU), 111
Khyber Pakhtunkhwa (KP), 53
armed conflicts in, 59
sectarian violence, 65
Koirala, Girija Prasad, 248, 258

Lahu Democratic Union (LDU), 75
Lashkar-e-Taiba, 18
Left-wing extremism (LWE)
attacking soft targets, 133
conflict management, 143–148
counter-guerrilla operations, 147
countering Naxal threat, 148–15
external linkages of Maoists, 138–143
government efforts in controling, 129–131
government implementation of schemes for security environment, 144–146
Islamic militant groups link of Maoists, 138–139
linkages with militant groups, 134
major actors in, 127–131
method of swarming attacks, 131–133
strategic areas for, 135–136
in urban areas of India, 137
violent incidents and killings due to, 126
Liberation of Achik Elite Force (LAEF), 106
Lintner, Bertil, 95
Lup, Apunba, 111

Madhes politics in Nepal
background, 354–356
core issue of, 361
emergence, 356–359
emerging issues and trends in, 367–371

excessive political factionalism in, 367–368
history of, 357
jana andolan of 2006 and, 356–357
Madhesi People's Right Forum (MPRF), 356, 359, 362–366
polarization, issue of, 369–370
political actors and conflict of interest, 359–360
political insignificance of Madhesi parties, 370–371
state strategy towards, 361–362
Tarai Madhes Democratic Party (TMDP), 362–366
in Tarai of Nepal, 368–369
major armed conflicts, defined, 4
Malik, Rehman, 165
Malik, Yasin, 20
Manipur
designated camp areas, 193
idea of peace in, 190–191
Kuki and Naga groups, 190, 192, 196
Manipur Constitution Act 1947, 188
Meitei insurgency, 188–189, 196
Meitei revolutionary movement, 188
negotiation with insurgents, 197
ongoing peace initiatives, 198–200
SoO and MoUs between government, centre and three militant outfits, 193–194
state of peace talks, 191–196
surrender policy for insurgents, 196–197
Treaty of Accession, 1949, 188
Maoist insurgency in Nepal, 11.
See also Nepal
antagonism between UPFN cadres and NC cadres, issue of, 251–253
devastation of rural economy, 258–259
issue of *jati*, 255–256
jana andolan, 260
main reason for, 254–257
Maoist-related deaths, 256
'March on' programme, 250–251
negative perceptions about government and, 256–257
people perspectives about Maoists, 378–379
'People's War', 249–250, 255
in Rolpa and Rukum, 251–253
Small Farmers Development Programme (SFDP), 250
state of emergency and, 260
Tharus group, 254–255
violent activities, 258
Maoist insurgency in Northeast India, 328–330
arrests in 2013, 329
in Arunachal Pradesh, 329, 331–332
in Assam, 329, 331–335
CPI (Maoist)-PLA nexus, 342–345
CPI (Maoist)-ULFA nexus, 346–347
genesis of Maoism, 330–331
government's anti-maoist strategy, 347–349
Maoist activities, 329
Maoist rebellion, phases of, 335–337
mass mobilization of certain sections of society, 338–341
militarization process of, 337–338
military structure of CPI (Maoist), 336
need for paying urgent attention, 349–350
Revolutionary Communist Party of India (RCPI), 330

spread of, 331–335
tactical partnerships with other insurgent groups, 341–347
Upper Assam Leading Committee (UALC), 332
Maoist party in Nepal
civil society and, 390–394
Communist Party of Nepal-Maoist (CPN-M), 247, 374–375
Communist Party of Nepal-Maoists (Baidya group), 5, 263–269, 377, 380–382, 384, 386, 389, 393
Communist Party of Nepal (Unified Marxist-Leninist) (CPN [UML]), 231, 239, 376
constituent assembly (CA) polls and, 375–376
current position in Nepali politics, 376
People's Liberation Army (PLA), 374
political course of action for future, 386–390
in political mainstream, 377–380
possibilities for restructuring, 380–385
as terrorist organizations, 375
Unified Communist Party of Nepal-Maoist (UCPN-M), 228–229, 239, 247–248, 260–262, 264, 268, 363–364, 374, 376–384, 386–390, 394
United People's Front of Nepal (UPFN), 249
Mautam, 105
Maw, Gwan, 96
Mehsud, Hakimullah, 20, 53, 62, 70, 291
Min, Aung, 94
Mirwaiz-led Hurriyat, 20
Mizo National Famine Front (MNFF), 110

Mizo National Front (MNF), 105, 111
Mizo Zirlai Pawl (MZP), 111
Modernization of State Police Forces (MPF Scheme), 144
Mohilary, Hagrama, 104
Molla, Abdul Qader, 24
Muivah, Thuingaleng, 103
Musharraf, Pervez, 15, 171
Muttahida Quami Movement (MQM), 60, 292
Myanmar
armed conflict in 2013, 86–92
armed groups of, 74–83
Buddhist–Rohingya clashes, 89–90
ceasefire agreement and security reforms, 91–93
China's interests in, 83–84
conflict management, 93–98
creation of a federal army, 94–95
dialogue processes, 93–94
Ethnic Burmans (*Bamars*), 74
explosions as an attempt to alarm public, 90–91
federal army, 94–95
human rights abuses against Rohingyas, 89
India, relation with, 85–86
intermittent clashes between government troops and ethnic armed groups, 88
internally displaced persons' (IDPs) resettlement, 87
issue of trust among ethnic population, 97
KIO agreement with government, 86–87
Nationwide Ceasefire Coordination Team (NCCT), 93
negotiation with rebels, 95–96
NLD, 97–98
opium poppy cultivation in, 92

sentencing of a local reporter, 73
Thailand, relation with, 84–85
UNFC–government ceasefire
  agreement, 93

Nagaland, peace process in,
  207–211
Naga Mothers Association
  (NMA), 111
Naga National Council (NNC),
  102
Naga political insurgent groups
  (NPIGs), 208
Naga Student's Forum (NSF), 111
Nambiar, Vijay, 87, 93
narcotics trade, Afghanistan,
  43–44
Naskar, Anukul Chandra, 328
National Consultative Peace Jirga,
  47
National Democratic Front of
  Bodoland (NDFB), 107, 205–206
Nationalist Socialist Council
  of Nagaland (Isak-Muivah)
  (NSCN-IM), 134, 189, 206–210,
  219–220, 223–224
National Liberation Front of
  Tripura (NLFT), 105–106
National Socialist Council of
  Nagaland (Khaplang) (NSCN-
  K), 189, 208–209, 219, 223
National Socialist Council of
  Nagaland (NSCN), 103, 107
National United Party of Arakan
  (NUPA), 75
Naxalite threat in India, 11
Naxal management by
  government, 129–131
NDFB Anti-talks Factions, 112
Nepal. *See also* Madhes politics
  in Nepal; Maoist insurgency in
  Nepal
  anti-Gyanendra sentiments,
    257–261

  army integration process and
    intra-party conflict of Maoist,
    263–265
  casualties from violent clashes
    between security forces and
    insurgents, 228
  Comprehensive Peace Accord
    (CPA), 261, 374, 377
  Constituent Assembly (CA)
    elections, 228–229, 365–366
  Constituent Assembly
    Committees, 240–241
  cultural condition, 371
  development projects
    implemented, 241–242
  drafting the constitution,
    239–240
  economy, 242
  elections 2013 and peace
    process, 232–238
  energy crisis, 245
  international community, role
    in conducting of elections,
    230–231
  management of Maoist
    combatants, 262
  maternal mortality, 246
  need for political
    decentralization and
    devolution of power, 371–373
  peace process in, 261
  12-point agreement between
    Maoist and Seven Party
    Alliance (SPA), 247, 254, 260
  political formation, post 1990,
    248
  primary education, 245–246
  representation of different
    groups in constituent
    assembly, 366
  royal massacre, 2001, 257–258,
    375
  self-determination movements
    in, 371–373

social hierarchy in, 255
tourism sector, 242–244
New Mon State Party (NMSP), 75
non-state-based conflict, 4
North Atlantic Treaty Organization (NATO), 20
North Cachar Hills Autonomous Council (NCHAC), 219
Northeast India, insurgencies in, 102–103. *See also* Maoist insurgency in Northeast India
adivasi insurgency, 104
in Arunachal Pradesh, 114
in Assam, 104
Bodo insurgency, 104
Border Security Force and, 110
civil society actors and peace processes, 110–111
conflict management efforts, 114–124
counter-insurgency efforts, 113–114
future trends, 124–126
in Garo hills of Meghalaya, 106
insurgent activity in 2013, 112–113
Karbi insurgency, 217
Khongsai's observations, 198
Kuki insurgency, 104–105, 189
in Manipur, 104–105. *See also* Manipur
Meitei insurgency, 104, 188–189, 196
Mizo insurgency, 105
in Mizoram, 105
Naga insurgency, 102–104
principal insurgent groups, 107–109
securitization through development, 123–124
Sengkrak movement, 105
state government, role in tackling, 109–110
state policing system in tackling, 114
surrender policy and protracted peace processes, 117–122
threat of islamist militancy, 115–117
in Tripura, 105
Northeast India, peace in
Bodoland, peace process in, 203–205
Karbi Anglona, peace process in, 216–219
Nagaland, peace process in, 207–211
need for a peace policy, 223–227
and non-implementation of accords, 225–226
North Cachar Hills, peace process in, 219–220
peace talks, notion of moratorium on, 220–223
post-conflict reconstruction (PCR), 225
sustainable peace process, 225
theorizing peace in, 201–203
ULFA, peace process with, 211–216
NSCN-Khole/Kitovi (NSCN-KK) group, 208–209, 223

Omar, Mullah, 50, 291
one-sided violence, 4
Operation All Clear, 104
Operation Bajrang, 104
Operation Rhino, 104
organized violence, 4

Pakistan Muslim League (Nawaz) (PML-N), 53–54
Pakistan People's Party (PPP), 54, 292
Pakistan Tehreek-e-Insaf (PTI), 54
Palaung State Liberation Front (PSLF), 75

Panglong Agreement, 1947, 94
Pa-O National Liberation Organization (PNLO), 75
Patnaik, Janaki Ballav, 339
peace audit, 6–10
  indices, 272
  peace dividend, 7–8
  peace process, 8
  peace reconciliation, 6
  peace with territorial and political integrity, 6
  South Asian context, 6
  undertaking, 9–10
peace dividend, 7–8
peaceful states in Northeast India, 123
peace process, 8
Peiris, Mohan, 282
Peoples' Alliance for Peace Agreement (PAPA), 218
People's Liberation Army (PLA), 105
People's Liberation Front of Meghalaya (PLF-M), 106
People's Revolutionary Party of Kangleipak (PREPAK), 105
People's United Liberation Front (PULF), 105
People's War Group (PWG), 127
Phizo, Angami Zhapu, 102
Pillars of Peace, 272
Positive Peace Index (PPI), 272
'pro-government forces' (PGFs), 36
Provincial Peace Committees, 47

Quetta Shura, 56, 291, 304

Rabha, Aklanta, 334, 336
Rajapaksa, Mahinda, 275, 278, 280, 282–289, 402, 404–405, 407, 413
Rajkhowa, Arabinda, 103
Rao, Mallojula Koteswara, 342, 346
Rao, Muppalla Laxmana, 129
Rasmussen, Anders Fogh, 32
Reang, Dhananjoy, 105
Red Corridor, 134–135
remote-controlled IEDs (RC-IEDs), 42

Saeed, Hafiz Mohammed, 19–20
Saleh, Mufti Muhammad, 64
Sayeed, Mufti, 311
sectarian violence in Pakistan, 63–67, 71, 71–72
  Ahle Sunnat Wal Jamaat (ASWJ) and, 63
  between Barelvi and Deobandi sub-sects, 64
  in FATA area, 65
  Hazara killings of Balochistan, 65–66
  in Karachi, 64
  in KP, 65
  Lashkar-e-Jhangvi (LeJ) and, 63–64
  in Punjab, 66–67
  in Quetta, 66
  between Shias and Sunnis, 64, 71
  in Sindh, 64
  Sipah-e-Muhammad Pakistan (SMP) and, 64
  Tehrik-e-Taliban Pakistan (Pakistani Taliban) and, 64
Sein, Thein, 87
Seng, Gauri Zau, 75
Shah, Ehsan Ali, 64
Shah, Liaquat, 163
Shan State Progress Party/Shan State Army (SSA), 75
Sharif, Nawaz, 15, 19–20, 62, 166–167
Sharif, Raheel, 54
Sharif, Shahbaz, 166
Shillong Accord of 1975, 103
Simla Agreement (1972), 7, 166

Singh, Gajendra Narayan, 358
Singh, Ibotombi, 345
Singh, K.N., 311
Singh, Kh Arnold, 345
Singh, Manmohan, 16, 18, 165–166
Singh, Mohan Bikram, 251
Singh, N. Dilip, 343, 345
Singh, Okram Ibobi, 196
Singh, Senjam Dhiren, 345
Singh, V.P., 14
Soe, Myint, 95
Songbijit faction of the NDFB, 112
South Waziristan Agency (SWA), 61
Sri Lanka
  Bodu Bala Sena (BBS), 396, 402–406
  democratization strategy, 280–283
  development, 278–280
  Divi Neguma Bill, 282
  Eelam War IV, post, 271
  ethnic issue, 283–286
  government attitude towards democracy, human rights, freedom and justice, 395–396
  high-security zones (HSZs), creation of, 274
  'Humanitarian Mission-02', 275
  Janata Vimukti Preamuna (JVP), 280
  Lessons Learnt and Reconciliation Commission (LLRC), 274
  post-war developments in, 397–402
  Ravana Balaya (RB), 396
  recommendations for real and sustainable peace, 286–289
  rehabilitation process of LTTE combatants, 275–277, 287
  security, 273–278
  Sinhala Buddhist Nationalism, 406–411
  Sinhala Ravaya (SR), 396
  13th Amendment arrangement, 284, 287
  violence against minority religious communities, 396
Sri Lankan ethnic conflict, 9
state-based conflict, 4
Swu, Isak Chisi, 103
symbolism, 16

Taliban, 21, 49–51
  attack tactics of, 41–43
Tehrik-e-Taliban Pakistan (TTP), 53, 72
  areas, 291
  civil society perception of, 293
  conflict management and, 67–68
  on drone attacks, 301–302
  factions, 291
  under Fazlullah, 303–304
  as a franchisee organization, 299–300
  functions, 291
  ideology of, 297–298
  imposition of Shariah in Pakistan, 293–295
  leadership issues, 300–301
  negotiating committee of, 291–292
  negotiations between state and, 290
  Pakistan's military vs, 292–293
  perspectives, 304–306
  15-point agenda for state, 295–297
  political and military nature of, 301–302
  relations with the Al Qaeda, 299, 301
  sectarian attacks within Pakistan, 302–303
  sectarian violence, 65
  set of demands, 295–297
Thakur, Raghunath, 358

Thamang, Diganta, 333
Thatcher, Margaret, 7

ULFA Anti-talks Faction, 112
United Liberation Front of Assam (ULFA), 103–104, 107, 134, 332
  peace process with, 211–216
  12-point charter, 215
  pro-talk and anti-talk factions, 216
United Naga Council (UNC), 111
United Nationalities Federal Council (UNFC), 75
United National Liberation Front (UNLF), 104, 189
United Nations Assistance Mission in Afghanistan (UNAMA), 36
United Wa State Army (UWSA), 75
Uppsala Conflict Data Program (UCDP), 4

US counter-insurgency efforts in Afghanistan, 32–34
  civilian casualties, 34–37
  Eikenberry's criticism, 33
  Obama's strategy, 33–34
US-International Security Assistance Force (US-ISAF) forces, 21

'victim-activated pressure plate' IEDs (PP-IEDs), 42

Wa National Organization (WNO), 75
Wazir, Maulvi Nazir, 61

Young Mizo Association (YMA), 111

Zardari, Asif Ali, 66, 165
Zaw, Aung, 97
Zia, Khaleda, 5, 24